Ra

Affirmative Action

rockwell

Race and Representation: Affirmative Action

ZONE BOOKS • NEW YORK • 1998

© 1998 Urzone, Inc.

ZONE BOOKS

611 Broadway, Suite 608

New York, NY 10012

Robert Post, "Introduction: After Bakke"; David A. Hollinger,
"Group Preferences, Cultural Diversity, and Social Democracy:
Notes Toward a Theory of Affirmative Action"; Troy Duster,
"Individual Fairness, Group Preferences, and the California
Strategy"; J. Jorge de Alva, "Is Affirmative Action a Christian
Heresy?"; Judith Butler, "An Affirmative View"; Michel
Feher, "Empowerment Hazards: Affirmative Action, Recovery
Psychology, and Identity Politics"; Marianne Constable,
"The Regents on Race and Diversity: Representations and
Reflections"; Anne M. Wagner, "Warhol Paints History, or Race
in America"; Barbara Christian, "Camouflaging Race and
Gender"; Miranda Oshige McGowan, "Diversity of What";
Rachel F. Moran, "Unrepresented"; Michael Omi and Dana Y.
Takagi, "Situating Asian Americans in the Political Discourse
on Affirmative Action"; Richard Walker, "California's Collision
of Race and Class" © 1996 The Regents of the University
of California. Published by arrangement with the University of
California Press. Michael Rogin, "The Two Declarations of
American Independence" © 1996 Michael Rogin.

Printed in the United States of America.

Distributed by The MIT Press,
Cambridge, Massachusetts, and London, England

Library of Congress Cataloging-in-Publication Data

Race and representation: affirmative action /
edited by Robert Post and Michael Rogin.
    p.   cm.
    Includes reprint of articles originally published in the
journal, Representations.
    Includes bibliographical references.
ISBN 0-942299-48-5-ISBN 0-942299-49-3 (pbk.)
    1. Affirmative action programs – United States.
    2. Discrimination in higher education – United States.
    3. United States – Race relations.
    I. Post, Robert, 1947- II. Rogin, Michael Paul
HF5549.5.A34R33 1998
331.13'3'0973 – dc21
                              97-43038

Contents

APPENDIX

Preface

Race has always surged powerfully through American politics. Sometimes it flows as an ominous undercurrent, implicit and insistent. Sometimes it breaks unmistakably to the surface and convulses the nation.

The growing controversy over affirmative action threatens another such eruption. Paradoxically, the aspiration for color-blind standards reemphasizes long-standing and seemingly irremediable material and social disparities between the races. By seeking to dismantle settlements reached in response to the civil rights movement of the 1960s and 1970s, the current assault on affirmative action has the tragic potential to reignite racial divides.

Although the United States Supreme Court has been chipping away at affirmative action for slightly more than a decade, the first decisive victory for those opposed to affirmative action occurred in 1995, when the Board of Regents of the University of California voted in Resolution SP-1 to prohibit the use of race as a criterion for student admissions. This vote came, to use the phrase coined by Thomas Jefferson to describe the conflict over slavery that led to the Missouri Compromise, "like a firebell in the night." Responding to the alarm, *Representations*, a Berkeley-based interdisciplinary journal of cultural analysis, decided to devote a special issue to the topic of race and affirmative action. Michael Rogin and I accepted the responsibility for editing the special issue.

The present volume expands that special issue. Two major developments in the affirmative action controversy have occurred since the passage of SP-1. The first is the decision of the United States Court of Appeals for the Fifth Circuit in *Hopwood v. Texas*, which declared unconstitutional the efforts of state universities to use race as a criterion for admission. The second is the passage of Proposition 209, an amendment to the California constitution prohibiting all forms of race-based affirmative action by the state. In Part One, articles addressing each of these momentous events have been added to the present volume.

In the period since the publication of the *Representations* issue, the actual consequences of SP–1 and *Hopwood* have begun to become apparent. In both Texas and California the imposition of colorblind standards of admissions has resulted in savage reductions in the racial diversity of incoming students. The crisis of affirmative action has escalated accordingly. Michael Rogin and I decided to expand the original *Representations* issue by canvasing leading intellectuals throughout the country to learn their assessments of this swelling controversy. We have added their comments (in alphabetical order) in Part Two.

Finally, the appendix to the original *Representations* issue contained the text of SP–1. In this volume we have expanded that appendix to include the text of Proposition 209 and the informative report of the American Association of University Professors on the passage of SP–1.

Robert Post

PART ONE

Introduction:

After *Bakke*

Robert Post

There was the sense of violation, of course. At the bidding of a governor anxious to ride the race issue to the White House, the Board of Regents of the University of California, against the opposition of faculty, students, and administration, over the vigorous protests of chancellors and demonstrators, voted to end affirmative action at the premier public institution of the nation's most demographically diverse state.[1] The first major public university to do so. July 20, 1995.

At a stroke, the landscape of higher education had changed. Assumptions about race and ethnicity that had for decades guided policy were suddenly stripped of the armor of institutional inevitability. They were rent open, open to recuperation, revision, repudiation, whatever the newly emerging politics of a dawning era would decree. Stung by this eruption of history, we devote this volume to exploring the new terrain.

Ironically, the University of California had itself helped to create the very legal framework that presently governs affirmative action within higher education. That framework was established in reaction to the University's defense of one of its own affirmative action programs to assist minority groups. The framework provides a clarifying lens for identifying the many questions of policy and principle that presently swirl through the maelstrom of the affirmative action controversy, for the law's tormented and equivocal response to affirmative action closely reflects the national debate.

After World War II, the equal protection clause of the Fourteenth Amendment of the United States Constitution came to be interpreted as strongly disfavoring the use of explicit racial or ethnic criteria by state institutions.[2] This interpretation was part of the national effort to disestablish Southern apartheid. National egalitarian norms were also powerfully articulated by federal legislation. Most relevant to higher education, Title VI of the Civil Rights Act of 1964 prohibited "discrimination" on "the ground of race, color, or national origin" in any "program or activity receiving Federal financial assistance."[3] The reach of Title VI remains quite broad; it applies to "all the operations of" any "college, university, or other postsecondary institution," any part "of which is extended Federal financial assistance,"[4] even to the minimal extent of enrolling "students who receive federal grants that must be used for educational purposes."[5] Affirmative action programs appeared to be in tension with these national norms of nondiscrimination. The first (and only) university affirmative action program to provoke a full-scale Supreme Court constitutional review of these legal constraints was that of the medical school of the University of California at Davis, which was subject to the restrictions of both the equal protection clause and Title VI.

A legal complaint challenging the program was filed on June 20, 1974, and it ultimately resulted in the decisive Supreme Court case of *Regents of University of California v. Bakke.*[6] The Davis medical school had essentially reserved sixteen places out of an entering class of one hundred for persons who were members of one of four "minority groups": "Blacks," "Chicanos," "Asians," and "American Indians."[7] The Court splintered badly in its evaluation of the case. Four justices wrote that the Davis program was a constitutional effort to redress the "effects of past societal discrimination,"[8] and that Title VI "prohibits only those uses of racial criteria that would violate the Fourteenth Amendment if employed by a State or its agencies."[9] Four justices held that the program was illegal because Title VI requires a "colorblind" admission process in which "race" does not provide a "basis of excluding anyone from participation in a federally funded program."[10] These justices did not address the independent restrictions of the equal protection clause.

The fifth and determinative vote was cast by Justice Lewis F. Powell Jr. Although Powell wrote for himself alone, his view carried the balance of power, and it has remained the governing law to this day. Over time, Powell's opinion has come to stand for four propositions: (1) Title VI applies constitutional standards.

(2) The Constitution requires that all explicit state uses of racial criteria, whether or not for benign purposes, be subject to strict judicial scrutiny to determine whether they are narrowly tailored to serve compelling state interests.[11] (3) The state's interest in remedying the generalized and systemic effects of societal discrimination is not compelling and hence cannot justify an affirmative action program.[12] (4) The University of California's objective of attaining "a diverse student body" is constitutionally compelling and can justify the use of racial and ethnic criteria for admissions:

> The atmosphere of "speculation, experiment and creation" — so essential to the quality of higher education — is widely believed to be promoted by a diverse student body.... [I]t is not too much to say that the "nation's future depends upon leaders trained through wide exposure" to the ideas and mores of students as diverse as this Nation of many peoples.
>
> Thus, in arguing that its universities must be accorded the right to select those students who will contribute the most to the "robust exchange of ideas," [the University of California] invokes a countervailing constitutional interest, that of the First Amendment. In this light, [the university] must be viewed as seeking to achieve a goal that is of paramount importance in the fulfillment of its mission.[13]

This last proposition provides the constitutional justification for contemporary university affirmative action programs throughout the country.

In explaining the objective of student "diversity," Powell made very plain that in his view the Constitution could not be read to accept a "diversity" that was defined solely by reference to differences between racial or ethnic groups. The "diversity" that Powell found constitutionally compelling was located instead in the infinitely variable differences among individuals, with respect to which racial or ethnic identity was only a "single although important element."[14]

The legal structure of the Davis medical school program established a fixed quota that automatically set aside sixteen slots for those who were members of four specific groups. The structure of the program thus collapsed the endless possibilities of difference into four discrete and limited categories of group identity.

Powell found the Davis affirmative action program unconstitutional because it rendered race and ethnicity a determinative factor, rather than merely "a 'plus' in a particular applicant's file," a "plus" that would "not insulate the individual from comparison with all other candidates for the available seats."[15] The Davis program was unconstitutional because it recognized only the diversity of racial and ethnic groups, rather than the diversity of individuals.

The crucial fact about *Bakke*, however, is that Powell did not end his judgment with a simple declaration of unconstitutionality. He took the unusual step of appending to his opinion the affirmative action plan of Harvard College, which Powell said he would find constitutional. The Harvard plan celebrated the diversity of individuals, but it also specifically noted that the value of ethnic and racial diversity could be attained only through an admission process that paid "some attention to numbers."[16]

By stretching through dicta to approve the Harvard plan, Powell prospectively sanctioned affirmative action plans that went beyond the recognition of purely individual differences in order to ensure the representation of distinct racial groups. He thereby signified that "diversity" could not in fact be reduced to mere individual variety, but must also be understood to depend on the effective presence of diverse group perspectives.

In dissent, Justices William Brennan, Byron White, Thurgood Marshall, and Harry Blackmun argued that the Davis and Harvard programs were functionally equivalent. "There is no sensible, and certainly no constitutional, distinction between, for example, adding a set number of points to the admissions rating of disadvantaged minority applicants as an expression of the preference with the expectation that this will result in the admission of an approximately determined number of qualified minority applicants and setting a fixed number of places for such applicants."[17] The only difference is that the Harvard program does not "make public the extent of the preference and the precise workings of the system while the Davis program employs a specific, openly stated number."[18] The dissent pressed a formidable functional logic.

Powell's opinion, however, was designed to work as an ideological construct, not merely as a functional one. Powell's ambition was to establish a fragile balance between, on the one hand, allowing academic affirmative action plans to continue as a means of redressing deep social dislocations and, on the other, ideologically destabilizing such plans so as to prevent their slide into a regime of racial and ethnic rights and entitlements.[19] What was "immediately apparent to the public" was thus fundamental to Powell.[20] He was determined both to achieve a pragmatic accommodation to the social necessity of affirmative action and to extract a patent symbolic commitment to the values of individualism.[21] In the process he crafted a remarkable judicial opinion whose "moderation and statesmanship," as Judge Henry Friendly observed, saved the country from "another Dred Scott."[22]

The regents' resolution of July 20 roughly repudiated Powell's delicate and judicious compromise. In truth, however, Powell's opinion had never been free from internal stress and attack. It had never silenced the contention that affirmative action ought to be used to remedy the present effects of past oppression. Such claims for explicit racial and ethnic rights to distributive justice, the implications of which extend beyond the limited context of university admissions and reach into the structure of the labor market, are visible in this volume in the essays of Michael Rogin and Troy Duster; the clear suggestion of their argument is that the joint dissent in *Bakke* of Justices Brennan, White, Marshall, and Blackmun was correct. Moreover, by de facto sanctioning affirmative action programs based on race and ethnicity, the *Bakke* compromise has over the past two decades facilitated the demographic preconditions for the emergence of new claims for racial and ethnic entitlements based on an aggressive identity politics that is both multicultural and separatist. The nature of such claims is traced and analyzed in the essays of Judith Butler and Michel Feher.

As evidenced in the regents' resolution of July 20, the *Bakke* compromise also never fully satisfied those committed to the values of liberal individualism.[23] These values, as illuminated by Jorge Klor de Alva, are deeply embedded within the American liberal and Christian traditions. They are not easily trespassed. In fact it is remarkable in retrospect how pervasive and entrenched affirmative action has become without previously having provoked the kind of frontal challenge represented by the regents' resolution. No doubt this is in part due to the widespread recognition that racial and ethnic categories have throughout the centuries been employed as efficient categories of discrimination and oppression. The rough justice of affirmative action seems from this perspective undeniable. To comprehend the source of Powell's reservations, therefore, it is essential to understand the precise terms of the opposition he establishes in *Bakke*.

There are significant Western traditions — for example, Kantian and Christian traditions — in which the values of individual autonomy are understood as standing outside of history. But, as Marianne Constable illustrates in her article, it is all but impossible to deny either the historical construction or the historical salience of race as a relevant category of social diversity. Race leaches into the regents' resolution despite their best efforts at exclusion. Reva Siegel demonstrates how distinct and even contradictory historical representations of race powerfully affect judicial responses to affirmative action programs. Anne Wagner makes the comprehensive point that historical narratives of race resist suppression even by the most severe and seemingly apolitical efforts of cultural representation to do so.

Powell's opinion in *Bakke*, however, is not such an effort. He does not wish to deny history. The facets of individual diversity that he celebrates, for example, are all historically constructed. When Powell cites Harvard's praise for the diversity that comes from "city dwellers and farm boys; violinists and football players; biologists, historians, and classicists; potential stockbrokers, academics and politicians,"[24] he locates, as he must, individual diversity in historically given and contingent categories.

His opinion, therefore, does not rest on an opposition to the historical construction of difference. It rests instead on the historically grounded, normative, constitutional proposition that race and ethnicity ought not to be used as a ground of state action except in the rarest and most exceptional of circumstances. Powell strongly affirms this proposition in order to condemn the nation's history of official racial discrimination and oppression. So when Justice Blackmun, in his separate opinion in *Bakke*, notes the irony of the fact that universities "have given conceded preferences up to a point to those possessed of athletic skills, to the children of alumni, to the affluent who may bestow their largess on the institutions, and to those having connections with celebrities, the famous, and the powerful,"[25] he fails to engage Powell's central point, which is that when it comes to state action the country's history has made race and ethnicity special and problematic categories.

The question remains, however, how an ideal of racial non-discrimination can be squared with an incontestable history of pervasive official misuse of racial and ethnic categories. The sociologist Niklas Luhmann astutely observes that normative propositions, unlike descriptive ones, are "capable of conformation as form by both conformable and deviant conduct."[26] Whereas we would be merely foolish steadfastly to maintain allegiance to descriptive hypotheses that prove frequently false, the same is not true of our moral commitments. Thus we do not ordinarily understand the commandment against murder to be rendered untenable by a high homicide rate. We are more likely to read the crime statistics as a reason to redouble our efforts to enforce the moral prohibition.

Similarly, a history of discrimination and oppression does not necessarily discredit the constitutional norm that a person's race and ethnicity ought not to matter to the state. It could lead us instead to even greater efforts fully to realize that liberal, individualist ideal. Of course the opposite outcome is also possible. We might come to believe that the ideal is so otherworldly, so pervasively irrelevant and compromised, as to be worthless as a guide to action, and we might demand that a different normative orientation be adopted. Or we might believe that the ideal should be compromised or temporarily suspended in the service of its realistic fulfillment.

The debate over the ideal can have many different possible outcomes. It is clear, however, that the debate will turn on a wide variety of practical, historical, and contingent considerations. It is at this juncture of the argument that the sociological and demographic analyses offered in this volume by Richard Walker become relevant, as do the assessments of political and strategic factors contributed by David Hollinger, as do the personal and experiential reflections recorded by Barbara Christian. In Cass Sunstein's view, the very complexity and difficulty of these issues comprise a strong argument for avoiding dogmatic judicial responses to affirmative action programs.

The crude inconsistency between the ideal of racial nondiscrimination and the fact of racial oppression is most often finessed in liberal thought by confining affirmative action to a discrete and bounded temporal position. Affirmative action, it is said, is necessary as a temporary expedient to overcome past discrimination. In the famous words of Justice Blackmun in *Bakke*, "In order to get beyond racism, we must first take account of race."[27]

Powell's opinion, however, does not take this tack. It instead invokes benefits of diversity that are not represented as temporary. These benefits are figured as structural and atemporal. Of course Powell views these benefits as merely permissive; nothing in his opinion compels universities to seek them, nor does he attempt to define the terms in which they must be embodied. Nevertheless, over time *Bakke* has come to stand for the proposition that race and ethnicity are constitutive of a structural and atemporal value of diversity. This notion of diversity has in turn fostered the paradoxical tendency to view the categories of race and ethnicity as themselves immune from the contingencies of historical construction. Essays in this volume by Miranda Oshige McGowan, Rachel Moran, and Michael Omi and Dana Takagi explore the costs and difficulties of this problematic tendency. At stake are exceedingly important considerations in the practical design of affirmative action programs under *Bakke*.

Whatever the deficiencies of Powell's opinion in *Bakke*, and no doubt they are legion, it has always seemed to me to contain two shining virtues. The first is its effort to justify affirmative action on the basis of the "mission" of higher education. Powell resists characterizing affirmative action as unrelated to educational purposes and hence as externally imposed on universities and colleges. The strength of his approach is now especially apparent, as faculty throughout the University of California system mobilize to resist the regents' resolution on the grounds that it is an improper political imposition on the educational mission of the university.[28] There are signs that defending the institutional autonomy of public universities may become of increasing national importance as "a new group of public-college trustees" appears poised to move "aggressively" to implement far-reaching political "agendas."[29]

Partisans for affirmative action have sometimes, in the heat and intensity of the controversy, failed to appreciate the importance of this point. One can occasionally discern resonances of the highly nihilistic claim that affirmative action ought to be unproblematic because university admissions criteria are arbitrary, so that the refusal to extend preferences based upon racial or ethnic identity is merely discriminatory or unjust. Those concerned to unmask "the myth of merit" and to expose the "subjective nature of university decisions" are particularly attracted to this line of argumentation.[30]

A major problem with this perspective, however, is that it ultimately denies legitimacy to the distinctive educational purposes of institutions of higher learning. If universities and colleges have no particular mission, there can be no principled objection to the regents' subordination of the University of California to the presidential ambitions of the state's governor. But if, on the contrary, there are ends to which higher education ought to aspire, then "merit" in the admission process will be neither mythical nor subjective, but will represent instead the standards of selection best suited for the attainment of those ends.[31]

I do not mean to imply that higher education has any single or simple set of purposes. No doubt the ends of colleges and universities are diverse and various, which is why most colleges and universities employ multifarious measures of merit embodied in complex and seemingly inconsistent standards of admission. Many, if not most, of the goals of higher education are probably best expressed in standards of admission that are neutral with respect to racial and ethnic identity. But this is not the case with respect to all such possible goals.

The institutional autonomy of public universities may best be protected if the issue of affirmative action is addressed in terms of the question of appropriate and inappropriate educational purposes. In *Bakke*, for example, Powell advanced the theory that learning was an appropriate object of higher education and that learning would be improved through a "'wide exposure' to the ideas and mores of students as diverse as this Nation of many peoples." Powell concluded that admission standards could legitimately acknowledge racial and ethnic differences because that acknowledgment was necessary in order to realize the benefits of diversity. While the heuristic premises of Powell's theory are surely subject to debate, it is at least the right kind of debate to be having in the context of affirmative action.

It is important to recognize, however, that the heuristic value of diversity is not the only theory of higher education that would justify standards of admission that acknowledge racial and ethnic differences. In the remainder of this introduction I would like briefly to sketch a different such theory: the creation of a democratic public culture.

Democracy and public education have long been regarded as inseparably complementary. Democracy is the practice of collective self-determination; public education is an investment by the state to disseminate the training and knowledge prerequisite for that practice. The question I wish to analyze concerns the distinctive contribution of public higher education to democratic practice. The question will, I hope, illuminate what I regard as the second great strength of Powell's opinion in *Bakke*, which is its accommodation of affirmative action within a justificatory framework that unsettles the slide toward group rights and entitlements.

"The essence of democracy," writes Jean Piaget, "resides in its attitude towards law as a product of collective will, and not as something emanating from a transcendent will or from the authority established by divine right. It is therefore the essence of democracy to replace the unilateral respect of authority by the mutual respect of autonomous wills."[32] Democracy, we might more precisely say, entails the perpetual process of reconciling the self-determination of autonomous wills with the *collective* self-determination of a polity. This process, which is perennially open-ended, occurs through the medium of a public discourse sustained by a public culture.[33]

Two consequences flow from this formulation. First, there is a strong affiliation between democracy and individualism, because the autonomous wills of individuals are conceptualized as politically prior to and constitutive of the rights of groups. If this were not the case, if the self-determination of individuals were to be subordinated to the identities and norms of particular groups, the possibilities of collective self-determination would to that precise extent be circumscribed.

Second, because of this political individualism, democratic public culture must also be understood as distinct from the cultures of particular groups and communities. Even though we know that in actuality the identities of individuals are formed through socialization into the mores of specific and historical groups and communities, the ideal of self-determination requires that public culture always maintain the possibility of citizens imagining themselves as something other than what they in fact are. Public culture must be large enough to encompass this possibility and therefore to embrace all possible groups and communities. Public culture is, as Thomas Keenan writes, the "realm ... of others, of all that is other to — and in — the subject itself."[34]

Historically and sociologically, public culture typically evolves from "cultural differentiation"; it functions, as the sociologists tell us, as a "universe of discourse" within which distinct communities can nevertheless come together to form a single democratic polity.[35] Public culture appears as a site of difference, in which communication occurs between those who do not share the identity and assumptions that define distinctive communities. Successful participation in public culture therefore requires a special form of cultural capital: the ability to interact in a "critical"[36] manner that establishes distance from local certitudes and thereby creates the possibility of spanning the boundaries between disparate groups.

Institutions of higher education are today a primary source of that cultural capital. They aspire to cultivate the remarkable and difficult capacity to regard oneself from the perspective of the other, which is the foundation of the critical interaction necessary for active and effective citizenship.[37] The cultivation of this capacity is especially important for public universities, for they are in part created to educate generations of future citizens so as to maintain the legitimacy of democratic self-government. Public universities have the educational obligation to dispense the cultural capital at their disposal in a manner that accounts for the health of public culture.

There are many dimensions to this obligation, but certainly one aspect entails facilitating participation in public culture by members of politically salient communities. A political culture without such participation would be neither democratic nor healthy, but merely repressive. In the United States, and especially in California, racial and ethnic identities mark lines of intense political division. If the racial and ethnic rifts that divide us are to be transcended by a democratic state that is legitimate to all sides, there must be articulate participation in public culture that concomitantly spans the lines of these controversies. I would argue, therefore, that the educational mission of the University of California ought to include the obligation to promote this participation.

If "normal" admission standards, by which I mean admission standards formulated to achieve other educational goals of the university, would in effect operate so as to exclude members of politically salient racial and ethnic communities, then the university's obligation to encourage a flourishing public culture may well require standards of admission that explicitly recognize racial and ethnic identity. The justification of these standards would not depend on any theory of group rights or entitlements; it would not reflect the extrinsic goal of compensating for past wrongs or oppression; it would not rely upon any pedagogical theory of the heuristic value of diversity. It would flow instead from the educational goal of fostering the public culture on which rests the success of democratic self-governance. It would follow from the perception that in the United States today democratic legitimacy very much depends on the active participation of an educated and critical citizenry that spans existing racial and ethnic differences.

Because this goal would conceptualize university applicants as potential citizens who are capable of transcending local attachments and identities, it would entail admission standards that, like those proposed by Powell in *Bakke*, ideologically privilege the individuality of applicants. This means that racial and ethnic identity would be relevant, but not determinative. An admissions policy based on the goal of nurturing public culture would thus retain Powell's pragmatic accommodation between a symbolic commitment to individualism and a practically effective response to social dislocation.

It is uncertain whether this justification for affirmative action, if candidly expressed, would pass constitutional muster. But the primary purpose of this volume is to think frankly among ourselves, rather than to speculate about the constitutional interpretation of nine justices. Our fundamental challenge is to decide what we wish to accomplish politically and how we wish to accomplish it, and we may hope that in the end constitutional law will follow the lead of informed judgment.

NOTES

1. The regents resolved that "effective January 1, 1997, the University of California shall not use race, religion, sex, color, ethnicity, or national origin as criteria for admission to the University or to any program of study." The com-

plete text of the regents' resolution appears in an appendix on page 397. The regents' prohibition against the use of the criteria of religion and sex raises important questions that we do not address in this volume.

2. "Nor shall any State...deny to any person within its jurisdiction equal protection of the laws." U.S. Constitution, amend. 14, sec. 1.

3. *Civil Rights Act of 1964*, U.S. Code, vol. 42, sec. 2004 (1994).

4. *Civil Rights Restoration Act of 1987*, U.S. Code, vol. 42, sec. 2000d-4a (1994).

5. *Grove City College v. Bell*, 465 U.S. 555, 558 (1984).

6. *Regents of University of California v. Bakke*, 438 U.S. 265 (1978). For an account of the case, see Bernard Schwartz, *Behind* Bakke: *Affirmative Action and the Supreme Court* (New York, 1988).

7. *Regents v. Bakke*, 274.

8. *Ibid.*, 362 (joint opinion of Justices William Brennan, Byron White, Thurgood Marshall, and Harry Blackmun).

9. *Ibid.*, 328.

10. *Ibid.*, 415–18 (opinion of Justice John Paul Stevens). Stevens's opinion was joined by Justices Warren Burger, Potter Stewart, and William Rehnquist.

11. Lewis F. Powell's actual formulation of the strict scrutiny test was somewhat different. See *ibid.*, 305. For a modern formulation of the strict scrutiny test, see *Adarand Constructors v. Pena*, 115 Sup. Ct. 2097, 2113 (1995). On the influence of Powell's opinion in *Bakke* for modern equal protection doctrine, see *ibid.*, 2108–12.

12. Powell conceded the importance of the state's interest in "ameliorating, or eliminating where feasible, the disabling effects of identified discrimination," but he contended that societal discrimination was by its very nature general and amorphous (*Regents v. Bakke*, 307). Powell was not prepared to accept a rationale for affirmative action that he believed would cede to "all institutions throughout the Nation" the power to use racial criteria "at their pleasure" to establish affirmative action programs to assist "whatever groups are perceived as victims of societal discrimination" (*ibid.*, 310). The modern Court has explicitly adopted this position. See *Richmond v. J. A. Croson Co.*, 488 U.S. 469 (1989); *Wygant v. Jackson Board of Ed.*, 476 U.S. 267 (1986).

13. *Regents v. Bakke*, 311–13.

14. *Ibid.*, 315–19. For a discussion of the two different kinds of diversity, see Robert Post, "Cultural Heterogeneity and Law: Pornography, Blasphemy, and the First Amendment," in *Constitutional Domains: Democracy, Community, Management* (Cambridge, MA, 1995).

15. *Regents v. Bakke*, 317.

16. *Ibid.*, 323.

17. *Ibid.*, 378.

18. *Ibid.*, 379.

19. For a good discussion of Powell's intentions, see John C. Jeffries Jr., *Justice Lewis F. Powell, Jr.* (New York, 1994), 455–501.

20. "There is no basis for preferring a particular preference program simply because in achieving the same goals that the Davis Medical School is pursuing, it proceeds in a manner that is not immediately apparent to the public"(*Regents v. Bakke*, 379 [joint opinion of Brennan, White, Marshall, and Blackmun]).

21. The present Court is now also engaged in extracting a symbolic commitment to individualist values, in the context of a pragmatic adjustment to racial realities, in the area of reapportionment plans designed to maximize minority representation. Compare *Miller v. Johnson*, 115 Sup. Ct. 2475 (1995), with *De Witt v. Wilson*, 115 Sup. Ct. 2637 (1995). As the Court stated in *Shaw v. Reno*, 113 Sup. Ct. 2816, 2827 (1993), the first of these cases, "reapportionment is one area in which appearances do matter." By contrast, the Court's enforcement of individualist values in the area of employment has not at all been merely symbolic. See *Richmond v. J. A. Croson Co.*, 488 U.S. 469 (1989).

22. Quoted in Jeffries, *Justice Lewis F. Powell, Jr.*, 498.

23. Indeed, as I write this introduction, a panel of the United States Court of Appeals for the Fifth Circuit has just struck down an affirmative action plan based on the rationale of *Bakke* at the Law School of the University of Texas at Austin. The Court held that Powell's "lonely opinion in *Bakke*" should no longer be regarded as controlling precedent because intervening Supreme Court cases stand for the proposition "that any consideration of race or ethnicity by the law school for the purpose of achieving a diverse student body is not a compelling interest under the Fourteenth Amendment." *Hopwood v. Texas*, 78 F. 3d 932, 944–45 (5th Cir. 1996). The Court observed that "diversity fosters, rather than minimizes, the use of race. It treats minorities as a group, rather than as individuals." *Ibid.*, 945.

24. *Regents v. Bakke*, 322.

25. *Ibid.*, 404.

26. Niklas Luhmann, *Risk: A Sociological Theory*, trans. Rhodes Barrett (New York, 1993), 55. For a full elaboration of the point, see Niklas Luhmann, *A Sociological Theory of Law*, trans. Elizabeth King and Martin Albrow (Boston, 1972), 31–35.

27. *Regents v. Bakke*, 407.

28. See, e.g., "Depoliticizing UC," *Sacramento Bee*, 15 January 1996, B6.

29. Patrick Healy, "The Republican Contract with Higher Education: Activist Trustees Raise Questions on Finances, Curriculum, Racial Preferences," *Chronicle of Higher Education*, 26 January 1996, A26.

30. Martha S. West, "Gender Bias in Academic Roles: The Law's Failure to Protect Women Faculty," *Temple Law Review* 67 (1994): 134–43.

31. See Kenneth L. Karst and Harold W. Horowitz, "Affirmative Action and Equal Protection," *Virginia Law Review* 60 (1974): 961–63; Richard H. Fallon Jr., "To Each According to His Ability, from None According to His Race: The Concept of Merit in the Law of Antidiscrimination,"*Boston University Law Review* 60 (1980): 864–76. If in fact the ends of higher education cannot be advanced by *any* selection criteria, a most unlikely hypothesis, then a lottery may perhaps be the fairest process of admission.

32. Jean Piaget, *The Moral Judgment of the Child*, trans. Marjorie Gabain (New York, 1948), 366.

33. The argument of this and the subsequent two paragraphs is fully developed in Post, *Constitutional Domains*, 134–96.

34. Thomas Keenan, "Windows: of Vulnerability," in Bruce Robbins, ed., *The Phantom Public Sphere* (Minneapolis, MN, 1993), 133.

35. Carroll D. Clark, "The Concept of the Public," *Southwestern Science Quarterly* 13 (1933): 311–15. See Robert E. Park and Ernest W. Burgess, *Introduction to the Science of Sociology* (Chicago, 1924), 254; Kenneth Ewart Boulding, *The Image: Knowledge in Life and Society* (Ann Arbor, 1956), 137–47.

36. Alvin W. Gouldner, *The Dialectic of Ideology and Technology: The Origins, Grammar, and Future of Ideology* (New York, 1976), 98.

37. For a classic and eloquent statement of this position, see *Wieman v. Updegraff*, 344 U.S. 183, 194 (1952) (Felix Frankfurter, concurring).

The Racial Rhetorics of

Colorblind Constitutionalism:

The Case of *Hopwood v. Texas*

Reva B. Siegel

Since the founding of our nation, the project of constitutional democracy in the United States has been haunted by conflicts between the nation's ideals of egalitarianism and its practices of racial subordination. The original Constitution referred to chattel slaves obliquely as "*other* persons," counting them for purposes of representational apportionment as "three fifths" of "free persons," and barring any constitutional amendment that might forbid their importation prior to 1808.[1] The Constitution's rhetorical indirection, as much as the temporary restriction it imposed on the procedures for amendment set forth in Article V, testify to the unstable compromise the framers forged at the founding. We inherit today the legacy of this compromise, born of a charter for nationhood which William Lloyd Garrison once called "a covenant with death, and an agreement with hell."[2] A civil war and several constitutional amendments later, the Supreme Court continues to negotiate contradictions between the nation's democratic ideals and its racial practices through rhetorical indirection, albeit of a different character.

Over the centuries, strategies for reconciling conflicts between the nation's ideals and practices have evolved, producing changes in the rule structure and justificatory rhetoric of racial status law.[3] The language of federalism, citizenship, property, privacy, freedom, and equality have all played important roles here. For, as conflicts precipitate changes in the rules by which Americans regulate race relations, the discourses in which Americans represent race relations change as well. During the era of chattel slavery, the Court unapologetically defined citizenship as the property of white persons;[4] today, with the demise of slavery and de jure segregation, the Court embraces the "ultimate goal" of "eliminating entirely from governmental decision making such irrelevant factors as a human being's race."[5] The rhetoric of colorblind constitutionalism is but another mode of talking about race, invoking the social fact of racial stratification in the course of denying its normative significance. As the nation's experience over the last several decades illustrates, the discourse of colorblindness can be invoked in support of distributive principles that alleviate or preserve racial stratification. This essay will demonstrate how some current usages of the discourse presuppose and protect the racial stratification of American society.

In this essay, I examine the rhetoric of colorblind constitutionalism in the case of *Hopwood v. Texas*,[6] in which the Fifth Circuit held that the University of Texas "may not use race as a factor in law school admissions."[7] The *Hopwood* case has attracted national attention because the court's reasoning calls into question the constitutionality of race-conscious admissions policies at public educational institutions and, possibly, private schools as well.[8] In *Hopwood*, the Fifth Circuit repudiated Justice Powell's opinion in *University of California v. Bakke*,[9] and held that the University of Texas Law School could not take race into account for purposes of admitting a diverse student body. The court also imposed quite strict constraints on the use of race-conscious admissions for purposes of remedying discrimination, past or present, in the Texas public education system. The court understood that its articulation of constitutional constraints on diversity and remedial uses of race in educational admissions would imperil conventional affirmative action programs. It viewed this result as warranted by Supreme Court cases that have recently imposed "strict scrutiny" on "benign" forms of race-conscious regulation.

As I will show, the diversity and remedial holdings of the *Hopwood* opinion are premised on two conflicting and irreconcilable conceptions of race, and so expose contradictions in the larger body of equal protection jurisprudence on which the case draws. Quoting liberally from the Supreme Court's recent opinions, the Fifth Circuit invokes both "thin" and "thick" conceptions of race. Sometimes the *Hopwood* opinion insists that race is but a morphological accident, a matter of skin color, no more. At other times, *Hopwood* discusses race as a substantive social phenomenon, marking off real cultural differences amongst groups. These conceptual inconsistencies are not incidental to the opinion, but instead arise out of the conflicting justifications the Supreme Court has offered for imposing constitutional restrictions on race-conscious regulation. Invoking these contradictory conceptions of race, *Hopwood* construes the Constitution to restrict government from regulating on the basis of race *and* construes the Constitution to protect the existing racial order. In a concluding, genealogical section of the essay, I show that, since Reconstruction, white Americans have frequently coupled talk of colorblindness with racial privacy rhetoric that seeks to protect relations of racial status from government interference. As this historical analysis reveals, current affirmative action law does not rest solely on values of colorblindness or racial "nonrecognition"; it also draws on a normative discourse about the racial private sphere, a domain of racial differences that the state may not disturb. If we read the contradictory racial rhetorics structuring affirmative action jurisprudence in light of this historical tradition, it is easier to understand their underlying preoccupations and considerable persuasive power.

In my view, debates over racial equality are impoverished if they focus on affirmative action alone. As I have elsewhere argued, more pressing questions of constitutional law and public policy are presented by the many forms of facially neutral state action that currently perpetuate the racial stratification of American society.[10] Yet, for this very reason, I believe it is important to examine the rhetorical grounds on which the Supreme Court has authorized, and progressively undermined, affirmative action programs. In applying strict scrutiny to benign forms of race-conscious regulation, the Court encourages the belief that affirmative action programs present one of the gravest threats to racial justice in America today. In my judgment, there are many facially neutral state practices — in the areas of criminal law, education, housing, employment, and political participation — that present far more significant threats to racial justice than do race-conscious remedies. These forms of facially neutral state action help perpetuate the forms of racial stratification that affirmative action redresses. Yet, the Court reviews equal protection challenges to such facially neutral practices deferentially, on the assumption that they are adopted in good faith.[11] Meanwhile, the Court applies strict scrutiny to race-conscious measures, intervening in the political process to protect the interests of whites as it does not when plaintiffs challenge facially neutral state action that has a disparate impact on minorities and women. In short, the prevailing equal protection framework identifies race-conscious remedies as pernicious discrimination, while characterizing other modes of state action that sustain the racial stratification of American society as presumptively race neutral. By analyzing the racial rhetoric of the *Hopwood* opinion, we are in a better position to understand the rhetorical strategies through which the Court has defined questions of racial equality in America today.

The Roots of the *Hopwood* Case

The admissions policy challenged in the *Hopwood* case was adopted by the University of Texas Law School in an effort to overcome decades of racially exclusionary admissions practices in the state's schools. Fact finding conducted by the district court established that racial segregation in the Texas public education system was mandated by the state's constitution and reached well into the modern period. Texas adopted a policy of official resistance to the Supreme Court's decision in *Brown v. Board of Education*,[12] a policy that resulted in numerous lawsuits and court-imposed desegregation plans over the ensuing decades. As of May 1994, the district court found, desegregation lawsuits remained pending against more than forty Texas school districts.[13] Officially mandated segregation prevailed in the state's system of higher education as well. Until 1947, there was only one state-supported institution of higher learning open to black students in Texas, which offered no form of professional training.[14] It was during this period that a black student first challenged the white-only admissions policy at the University of Texas Law School. A state court directed the legislature to create a separate law school for blacks;[15] but in 1950, the United States Supreme Court held in *Sweatt v. Painter*[16] that the state would have to admit the black student into the all-white University of Texas Law School. Sweatt left the law school in 1951 without graduating, after being subjected to racial slurs from students and professors, cross burnings, and tire slashings.[17]

As late as 1980, an investigation by the Department of Health, Education, and Welfare's Office for Civil Rights concluded that Texas still had "failed to eliminate vestiges of its former de jure racially dual system of public higher education, a system which segregated blacks and whites";[18] this same investigation also found that Hispanics were significantly underrepresented in state institutions.[19] In this period, Texas submitted a plan to achieve compliance with federal civil rights laws, in an effort to protect its share of federal education funding. As the district court rather dryly pointed out, it was Clarence Thomas, in his capacity as Assistant Secretary of Education, who ruled in 1982 that the Texas plan "was deficient because the numeric goals of black and Hispanic enrollment in graduate and professional programs were insufficient to meet Texas's commitment to enroll those minority students in proportion to the[ir] representation among graduates of the state's undergraduate institutions."[20] Under federal pressure, Texas revised its plan to include goals for increasing black and Hispanic student enrollment in professional and graduate programs at traditionally white institutions.[21] In 1987, Texas officials determined that the state still had not met the goals and objectives of the plan and developed a successor plan to avoid federal action.[22] At the time that the *Hopwood* plaintiffs filed suit challenging the admissions policy at the University of Texas Law School, the Office of Civil Rights had not yet determined that the state had desegregated its schools sufficiently to comply with federal civil rights laws.[23]

In the early 1990s, the admissions procedure in place at the law school relied heavily, but not exclusively, on a numerical index that was the product of a student's LSAT score and grade point average (GPA), with the latter adjusted to reflect the assumed strength of the student's undergraduate institution and major. Numerical ranges identified applicant scores that would presumptively result in admission or denial, with applications in the middle range reviewed more extensively by committee to determine whether the student would be admitted to the school. A somewhat higher numerical index was established to determine admissions of nonresident students, and a somewhat lower range was established to determine admissions of black and Mexican-American students, whose applications were reviewed by a separate subcommittee.[24] By state law, the law school was required to admit an entering class of at least five hundred students a year, comprised of no more than 15 percent nonresidents. (The nonresident cap was recently increased to 20 percent.[25]) In addition, the law school sought to meet the targets established by the Office of Civil Rights through the Texas plan of 10 percent Mexican-American students and 5 percent black students in an entering class.[26] (The enrollment targets, described as "aspirations only, subject to the quality of the pool of applicants," reflected an effort to achieve an entering class with levels of minority enrollment generally consistent with the percentages of black and Mexican-American college graduates in the state.[27])

The *Hopwood* litigation started when four students — three men, one woman, all white — who were denied admission to the law school, filed suit, claiming that the law school's admission procedures were racially discriminatory. The gravamen of their complaint was that they presented GPA and LSAT scores that might have gained them admission to the law school had they been of a different race.[28] The district court ruled that there were constitutional defects in the law school's admissions procedures, but also determined that "legitimate, nondiscriminatory grounds exist[ed] for the law school's denial of admission to each of the four plaintiffs and that, in all likelihood, the plaintiffs would not have been offered admission even under a constitutionally permissible process."[29] According to the district court, the law school could take the race of applicants into account, both for purposes of ensuring a diverse student body and for purposes of remedying present effects of past discrimination in the state's system of public education. The court ruled, however, that under the Supreme Court's decision in *Bakke*, the law school could not isolate minority and nonminority applicants and concluded that the law school would have to revise its admissions procedures to "afford each individual applicant a comparison with the entire pool of applicants, not just those of the applicant's own race."[30]

The Fifth Circuit's Ruling in *Hopwood*

On appeal, the United States Court of Appeals for the Fifth Circuit ruled that, under applicable Fourteenth Amendment precedents, the University of Texas "may not use race as a factor in law school admissions" "even for the wholesome purpose of correcting perceived racial imbalance in the student body."[31] As the court construed recent Supreme Court cases requiring strict scrutiny of race-based governmental action, neither achieving a diverse student body nor remedying past discrimination provided a sufficient justification for the affirmative action plan at the University of Texas Law School. In so holding, the Fifth Circuit applied the reasoning of some of the Court's more recent equal protection cases to educational affirmative action in more aggressive terms than other appellate courts to date. Examining the Fifth Circuit's justifications for striking down the law school's admission policy illuminates the conflicting currents of racial reasoning informing the law of affirmative action.

The court opens its opinion by quoting Justice Scalia: "'Racial preferences appear to "even the score"... only if one embraces the proposition that our society is appropriately viewed as divided into races, making it right that an injustice rendered in the past to a black man should be compensated for by discriminating against a white.'"[32] With this opening salvo, the court makes clear its judgment that it is wrong to view American society as "divided into races" and so to compensate for past injustices against blacks "by discriminating against a white." The way to expiate past acts of racial discrimination is not to put African Americans as a group in the position in which they might have been but for discrimination, but instead to adopt a firm stance against acts of racial discrimination — including the "discrimination" whites suffer when their opportunities are constrained by policies of racial rectification. The court frames the question of affirmative action in terms that place discrimination against *white* Americans at the forefront of constitutional analysis, echoing popular objections to affirmative action policies advanced by "angry white males." Thus, an objection to affirmative action that begins by renouncing a group-based conception of the American polity simultaneously advances a legal argument premised on a group-based conception of the American polity. On this reading, the Fourteenth Amendment protects the interests of white Americans against the claims for racial rectification advanced by black Americans.

The *Hopwood* opinion begins in this vein, describing the mechanics of the law school's admissions process in terms that emphasize the injustices that affirmative action policies inflict on white Americans. As is conventional in these matters, the narrative emphasizes numbers over all other factors relevant in admissions, without devoting any consideration to the social factors that shape numerical measures of educational attainment.[33] The *Hopwood* opinion offers a detailed account of the numerical ranges employed to evaluate the candidacy of minority and nonminority applicants, pointing out that "these disparate standards greatly affected a candidate's chance of admission."[34] The court's account calls attention to *racial* variances in admissions ranges, dropping into a footnote the observation that "residency also had a strong, if not often determinant, effect" on admissions,[35] and barely remarking on the varying weight given grade point averages earned at different undergraduate institutions.[36] In short, the narrative throws racial discrepancies in admissions ranges into stark relief, while treating as equitably inconsequential the variance in admissions opportunities produced by the school's policy of favoring residents and its practice of weighting grades in accordance with the reputation of the undergraduate institution, despite its predictably class salient impact on admissions. In this narrative, achievement is defined by numbers, and the only noteworthy departure from a strictly numerical ranking system is defined by race.

In attending to the forms of racial displacement that an affirmative action policy might effect, the *Hopwood* opinion reflects concerns expressed by various justices in the splintered Supreme Court opinions of the 1970s and 1980s, which cautioned that race-conscious remedies must be carefully circumscribed so as not unduly to burden the interests of "innocent" third parties. Justice Powell took the lead in articulating such views. For example, in *Bakke*, Justice Powell expressed concern about "forcing innocent persons . . . to bear the burdens of redressing grievances not of their making"[37] and warned

> *All state-imposed classifications that rearrange burdens and benefits on the basis of race are likely to be viewed with deep resentment by the individuals burdened.* The denial to *innocent persons* of equal rights and opportunities may outrage those so deprived and therefore may be perceived as invidious. *These individuals are likely to find little comfort in the notion that the deprivation they are asked to endure is merely the price of membership in the dominant majority and that its imposition is inspired by the supposedly benign purpose of aiding others.* One should

not lightly dismiss the inherent unfairness of, and the perception of mistreatment that accompanies, a system of allocating benefits and privileges on the basis of skin color and ethnic origin.[38]

Because of his concern about harm to "innocent" members of the "dominant majority," Justice Powell sought strictly to limit the circumstances in which race-based remedies were allowed:

> No one doubts that there has been serious racial discrimination in this country. But as the basis for imposing discriminatory legal remedies that work against innocent people, societal discrimination is insufficient and over-expansive. In the absence of particularized findings [of discrimination], a court could uphold remedies that are ageless in their reach into the past, and timeless in their ability to affect the future.[39]

For similar reasons, Justice Powell advocated constraints on race-based remedies, even in cases involving the rectification of identified discrimination.[40]

Throughout the 1970s and 1980s, Supreme Court justices reasoned about the equities of racial remedies in terms that openly worried about the interests of white people — except that white people were generally referred to, collectively, as "innocent people."[41] Thus, when the Court evaluated the kinds of relief courts or legislatures could provide African Americans and other minorities who suffered race discrimination, it imposed constitutional restrictions on racial remedies for the express purpose of protecting the interests of "innocent" third parties.[42] Perhaps even more significantly, when white plaintiffs complained that racial remedies entrenched on an educational or employment opportunity to which they believed they were rightfully entitled, the Court treated the complainants as stating a claim of race discrimination, often seeming to equate such claims with the race discrimination African Americans and other minorities suffered.

In this period, the Court was in fact divided about whether to treat the race discrimination claims of whites and blacks in symmetrical or asymmetrical terms. To the extent that policies of racial rectification constrained the opportunities of whites, whites could indeed claim to be injured by race-based state action; but if this injury amounted to "race discrimination," it was a form of "race discrimination" not wholly commensurable with the race discrimination that African Americans have suffered, whether analyzed from the standpoint of history or social meaning. Is every act of racial differentiation an act of race discrimination or does race discrimination involve a systematic practice of group subordination? The Court struggled with this question during the 1970s and 1980s as it attempted to decide whether policies of racial rectification should be reviewed under the "strict scrutiny" framework it had developed to review, and invalidate, traditional forms of Jim Crow legislation. When a majority of the Court finally declared in the 1989 *Croson*[43] decision that state-sponsored affirmative action policies would be reviewed under a strict scrutiny framework, and then in the 1995 *Adarand*[44] case that federal affirmative action policies would be similarly scrutinized, the justices seemed definitively to embrace the view that race discrimination directed at whites and blacks was commensurable from a constitutional standpoint (even as they hedged the question by indicating that under highly circumscribed circumstances, affirmative action policies might be constitutionally permissible).[45] Yet, at the same time as the Court accorded special constitutional solicitude to the race discrimination claims of whites, it subtly shifted its rationale for according strict scrutiny to race-conscious remedies.

In its more recent pronouncements on affirmative action, the Court no longer talks so openly about protecting the interests of "innocent" third parties. Instead of focusing on the harm racial remedies inflict on white Americans, the Court's opinions now focus on the harm that racial remedies inflict on *black* Americans. The Court has now clearly decided that white plaintiffs who challenge an affirmative action plan have stated a claim of race discrimination sufficient to trigger strict scrutiny. ("To whatever racial group . . . citizens belong, their 'personal rights' to be treated with equal dignity and respect are implicated by a rigid rule erecting race as the sole criterion in an aspect of public decision-making".[46]) Yet, when explaining why affirmative action policies should be evaluated as presumptively unconstitutional under a strict scrutiny framework, the Court currently emphasizes the ways that racial remedies can injure racial minorities. In *City of Richmond v. J.A. Croson*,[47] Justice O'Connor explained that an affirmative action plan must be evaluated under a strict scrutiny framework because (1) it is often quite difficult to determine "what classifications are 'benign' or 'remedial' and what classifications are in fact motivated by illegitimate notions of racial inferiority or simple racial politics"; (2) "classifications based on race carry a danger of stigmatic harm" and so may "promote notions of racial inferiority and lead to a politics of racial hostility";[48] and (3) a more permissive standard of review "effectively assures that race will always be relevant in American life, and that the 'ultimate goal' of 'eliminat[ing] entirely from governmental decision-making such irrelevant factors as a human being's race' ... will never be achieved."[49] It is only in this brief reference to "racial hostility" that *Croson*'s justification for applying strict scrutiny to the race discrimination claims of white plaintiffs adverts to the racial interests and attitudes of white people, and it does so in terse and unelaborated terms. With the justifications for strict scrutiny of affirmative action focusing on harm to minorities, the Court can invoke the Fourteenth Amendment to constrain legislative action in terms that are more congruent with the amendment's historic purposes.

Given these recent developments in the Court's equal protection jurisprudence, it is therefore not surprising that the bulk of the Fifth Circuit's analysis in *Hopwood* explores the constitutional equities of affirmative action without ever expressly invoking the interests of white Americans. Drawing on recent Supreme Court cases, the Fifth Circuit reasons that the University of Texas Law School lacked constitutionally sufficient grounds to employ an affirmative action component in its admissions process — either for purposes of enhancing the diversity of its student body or for purposes of remedying racial discrimination. It is worth examining the justifications the Fifth Circuit offers for striking down the law school's admission policy on each of these grounds, for the diversity and remedial sections of the *Hopwood* opinion rest on two utterly incompatible conceptions of race, and so expose deep conflicts in the Supreme Court's most recent pronouncements about race-conscious remedies. At the very least, these conceptual conflicts call into question the concerns underlying the Court's decision to apply strict scrutiny to "benign" forms of race-conscious regulation. More deeply, the competing conceptions of race invoked in *Hopwood* and the Court's recent equal protection cases raise questions about the forms of racial consciousness animating current usages of colorblindness discourse.

Rejecting Diversity Justifications for Affirmative Action

Ever since the Supreme Court's decision in *University of California v. Bakke*,[50] educational institutions have justified affirmative action programs by emphasizing the goal of attaining a diverse student body. The defendant medical school in the *Bakke* case in fact advanced multiple justifications for its use of affirmative action in admissions, but the justices only judged two purposes of constitutional magnitude. Of the five justices who sanctioned educational affirmative action in *Bakke*, four justices thought that remedying the effects of societal discrimination supplied the school a compelling reason for adopting an affirmative action plan;[51] Justice Powell, however, did not. Powell instead adopted an approach to race-conscious admissions that incorporated significant criticisms of affirmative action policies, while upholding them on nonremedial grounds.

In *Bakke*, Justice Powell criticized remedial justifications for affirmative action as resting on an untenable "two-class theory" of the Fourteenth Amendment.[52] Paraphrasing Nathan Glazer, Powell announced that, in the years since the Civil War, "the United States had become a Nation of minorities"[53]: "[T]he white 'majority' itself is composed of various minority groups, most of which can lay claim to a history of prior discrimination at the hands of the State and private individuals."[54] For this reason, Powell argued, the Court could not allow state actors to rectify race discrimination as they saw fit. Members of many groups could lay claim to such an entitlement and would deeply resent state policies "that rearrange burdens and benefits on the basis of race," even if "the deprivation they [were] asked to endure" were justified as "the price of membership in the dominant majority ... inspired by the supposedly benign purpose of aiding others."[55] Thus, Powell reasoned that "the purpose of helping certain groups whom the faculty of the Davis Medical School perceived as victims of 'societal discrimination' does not justify a classification that imposes disadvantages upon persons like [the plaintiff], who bear no responsibility for whatever harm the beneficiaries of the special admissions program are thought to have suffered."[56] Only where there were findings of race discrimination made by a competent governmental body would Powell sanction affirmative action for remedial purposes.[57] Yet Powell did go on to suggest that school administrators might take race and ethnicity into account in making admissions decisions for purposes of achieving an diverse student body — so long as race and ethnicity were not the sole criteria of diversity, and so long as all applicants had an opportunity to compete for every seat in the class.[58] Justice Powell's opinion in *Bakke* seemingly rejected and obliquely accepted the case for race-conscious admissions, burying questions about rectifying America's racial caste system in a celebration of America's ethnic pluralism. Although joined by no other justices, the opinion had sufficient pragmatic appeal that achieving student diversity has since become the conventional rationale for affirmative action in education.

In *Hopwood*, the Fifth Circuit drew national attention by rejecting Justice Powell's reasoning, and ruling that the pursuit of student diversity did not supply a constitutionally sufficient basis for adopting a race-conscious admissions policy. To support its judgment, the Fifth Circuit emphasized that Justice Powell's opinion in *Bakke* was joined by no other justices, and that, since *Bakke*, a majority of the sitting justices had authored or joined opinions that severely criticized diversity justifications for race-conscious regulatory policies. While it remains an open question whether the Court is ready to repudiate Justice Powell's *Bakke* opinion,[59] several recent decisions of the Court have challenged viewpoint-based justifications for race-conscious regulation in cases involving voting rights and broadcast licensing.[60] The Fifth Circuit succinctly summarized the Court's recent criticism of viewpoint-based justifications for race-conscious regulation: "To believe that a person's race controls his point of view is to stereotype him."[61] Quoting one of Justice O'Connor's dissenting opinions which Justices Rehnquist, Scalia, and Kennedy joined, the Fifth Circuit stated: "'Social scientists may debate how people's thoughts and behavior reflect their background, but the Constitution provides that the government may not allocate benefits or burdens among individuals based on the assumption that race or ethnicity determines how they act or think.'"[62] Reasoning from this standpoint, the Fifth Circuit concluded:

> [T]he use of race in admissions for diversity in higher education contradicts, rather than furthers, the aims of equal protection. Diversity fosters, rather than minimizes, the use of race. It treats minorities as a group, rather than as individuals. It may further

remedial purposes but, just as likely, may promote improper racial stereotypes, thus fueling racial hostility.

The use of race, in and of itself, to choose students simply achieves a student body that looks different. Such a criterion is no more rational on its own terms than would be choices based upon the physical size or blood type of applicants.[63]

Hopwood's repudiation of the diversity rationale for affirmative action in educational admissions rests on an amalgam of positive and normative claims. At the simplest level, the Fifth Circuit invokes the norm that group-based generalizations offend the Constitution: Under strict-scrutiny analysis, the state may not impute a particular point of view to an individual because of her group membership. (In fact, nothing in the record supports the court's claim that the admissions policy imputes particular points of view to individuals who belong to different social groups; as described, the policy would seem to allow group members to bring to the institution whatever distinctive experience or outlook they happen to have — thus facilitating dialogue in which students can discover the ways in which perspectives may cohere or diverge within and across groups.)

But the Fifth Circuit's objection to the diversity rationale rests on positive, as well as normative, claims. As the court sees it, the problem is not merely that the Constitution is intolerant of group-based generalizations, but that the generalizations supporting the admissions policy are themselves empirically unfounded. As the court puts it, "[t]he use of race, in and of itself, to choose students simply achieves a student body that looks different." On this account, race is nothing but morphological accident, a matter of skin color, physical size, or blood type, no more. The diversity justification for race-conscious admissions is therefore irrational because race has no identifiable social content, and any assumption that it does amounts to invidious racial stereotyping.

The stereotyping objection to diversity rationales for race-conscious remedies is a "second-generation" objection to affirmative action programs, one that emphasizes injury to the minority beneficiaries of such programs. Consistent with this approach, the Fifth Circuit goes on to enumerate additional objections to diversity-based affirmative action, invoking the *Croson* opinion for the proposition that "'[c]lassifications based on race carry the danger of stigmatic harm. Unless . . . reserved for remedial settings, they may in fact promote notions of racial inferiority and lead to the politics of racial hostility.' "[64] Thus race-conscious admissions policies that seek to diversify a student body stereotype and stigmatize their beneficiaries, and, more generally, "undercut the ultimate goal of the Fourteenth Amendment: the end of racially motivated state action."[65]

In rejecting the diversity rationale for affirmative action, the Fifth Circuit squarely embraces the view that race is devoid of socially relevant content, a "criterion [that] is no more rational on its own terms than would be choices based on the physical size or blood type of applicants."[66] Quoting Richard Posner, the court insists that " 'the use of a racial characteristic to establish a presumption that the individual also possesses other, and socially relevant, characteristics, exemplifies, encourages, and legitimizes the mode of thought and behavior that underlies most prejudice and bigotry in modern America.' "[67] Yet, at the same time that the court insists that race may not be used as a proxy for social characteristics that might have relevance in admissions — "such as [the] economic or educational background of one's parents"[68] — the court also acknowledges that these "factors may, in fact, turn out to be substantially correlated with race,"[69] and emphasizes that they may be constitutionally considered in admissions so long as they are "not adopted for the purpose of discriminating on the basis of race":[70] "the key is that race itself not be taken into account."[71] Lurking beneath the court's assertion that race is but a morphological accident with no significant social content is a very different conception of race: one that plays a pivotal role in the court's analysis of affirmative action as a remedy for racial discrimination.

Restricting the Remedial Applications of Affirmative Action
The *Hopwood* opinion makes quite clear that, under prevailing Supreme Court opinions, remedying identifiable racial discrimination is a constitutionally compelling reason for adopting an affirmative action plan. At the same time it emphasizes that the Constitution only allows the use of affirmative action for remedial purposes in narrowly circumscribed circumstances. As the Fifth Circuit reads Supreme Court case law, affirmative action can be employed for the purpose of remedying the "present

effects of past discrimination," but not for the purpose of "reme-dying the present effects of past *societal* discrimination."[72] Draw-ing on plurality opinions of the 1980s, the Fifth Circuit construes statements prohibiting the use of affirmative action to remedy societal discrimination to mean that "the state's use of remedial racial classifications is limited to [rectifying] the harm caused by a specific state actor."[73] Moreover, before a state actor can imple-ment an affirmative action plan, "it 'must ensure that ... it has strong evidence that remedial action is warranted.' "[74]

The Fifth Circuit selectively discusses the justifications that various justices have advanced for restricting the remedial use of affirmative action to those circumstances where a state actor can show convincing evidence of prior acts of discrimination. The *Wygant* case from which the Fifth Circuit liberally quotes explains that affirmative action policies should be so limited to ensure that the policies do not unduly burden innocent people.[75] The Fifth Circuit's opinion does not mention this concern about bur-dening innocent parties, but it justifies the constitutional restric-tions imposed on the remedial use of affirmative action by quoting a passage from the *Croson* case that explains why the government must supply evidence of prior discrimination before adopting an affirmative action plan:

> [A] generalized assertion that there had been past discrimination in an entire industry provides no guidance for a legislative body to determine the precise scope of the injury it seeks to remedy. It "has no logical stopping point." "Relief" for such an ill-defined wrong could extend until the percentage of public contracts awarded to [minority businesses] in Richmond mirrored the percentage of minorities in the population as a whole.[76]

Quoting *Croson*, the Fifth Circuit observes that "'an amorphous claim that there has been past discrimination in a particular indus-try cannot justify the use of an unyielding quota.' Such claims were based upon 'sheer speculation' about how many minorities would be in the ... business absent past discrimination."[77]

Reasoning from these passages, the Fifth Circuit concludes that the district court erred in allowing the University of Texas Law School to employ an affirmative action policy to remedy dis-crimination in the state's educational system: "[A] remedy reaching all education within a state addresses a putative injury that is vague and amorphous. It has no logical stopping point.' "[78] As the Fifth Circuit acknowledges, in *Croson*, the Court did indicate that in appropriate circumstances, state or local government could rectify the effects of private discrimination within its own legislative jurisdiction, in order to avoid becoming a passive participant in private discrimination;[79] but, the Fifth Circuit discounts this more expansive account of government's remedial authority,[80] insisting that a governmental unit can only rectify effects of discrimination which that particular governmental unit has caused. "[W]hen one state actor begins to justify racial preferences based upon the actions of other state agencies, the remedial actor's competence to determine the existence and scope of the harm and the appropriate reach of the remedy is called into question."[81] "Such boundless 'remedies' raise a constitutional concern beyond mere competence. *In this situation, an inference is raised that the program was the result of racial social engineering rather [than] a desire to implement a remedy.*"[82] The court then concludes that, despite the long history of overt discrimination in University of Texas Law School admissions,[83] such discrimination ended in the 1960s when the school implemented its first program designed to recruit minorities,[84] and further concludes that there are no present effects of the school's past discrimination of sufficient magnitude to warrant the school's use of affirmative action in admissions.[85]

What is the basis of the Fifth Circuit's "inference" that an affirmative action program at the University of Texas Law School designed to remedy the effects of discrimination in the state's educational system would be "the result of racial social engineering rather than a desire to implement a remedy"? As the Fifth Circuit analyzes it, the law school lacks information about the extent of such discrimination and would therefore have to proceed on the basis of assumptions about the degree to which the underrepresentation of minorities in the competitive applicant pool was attributable to discrimination. But the *Hopwood* court insists that no legitimately remedial affirmative action program can rest on such assumptions. Following the *Croson* opinion, the *Hopwood* opinion insists that there is no way of knowing how many racial minorities would participate in any given social endeavor in the absence of discrimination; making assumptions about such matters without proof is "'sheer speculation.'" In short, it is constitutionally impermissible to assume that in a world without discrimination minorities would participate in various social endeavors at the same rate as other social groups.[86] For the *Hopwood* court, affirmative action goals premised on assumptions about proportional participation raise "the inference that the program was the result of racial social engineering rather [than] a desire to implement a remedy." (The pejorative reference to social engineering derives from a famous article attacking affirmative action authored by Morris Abram, who objected to a new generation of "social engineers" in the leadership of the civil rights movement who believe that "the government's role [is] to bring about proportional representation."[87])

In the early days of the civil rights movement, the federal judiciary was confident that significant racial disparities had their roots in discrimination, but over the decades critics of civil rights law have energetically contested that assumption and courts have gradually retreated from it, requiring ever more detailed proof that social stratification is the product of discrimination perpetrated by the particular agent whose practices are contested.[88] The Supreme Court's opinion in *Croson* employed this body of anti-discrimination law to restrict constitutionally permissible uses of voluntary affirmative action,[89] and *Hopwood* in turn applied *Croson*'s reasoning with zeal. As the Fifth Circuit construes the Fourteenth Amendment, it is a violation of equal protection for a state actor to adopt a race-conscious remedy premised on the assumption that in a world without discrimination, African Americans and other minorities would participate in various social endeavors at the same rate as whites.

Hopwood's Internal Contradictions and Underlying Preoccupations

By this point it should be clear that the diversity and remedial sections of the *Hopwood* opinion are premised on two deeply conflicting conceptions of race. The diversity sections of the opinion assert that race is but a morphological accident, a matter of skin color, no more: "The use of race, in and of itself, to choose students simply achieves a student body that looks different. Such a criterion is no more rational on its own terms than would be choices based upon the physical size or blood type of applicants."[90] On this view, race has no socially relevant content, and provides no basis for choosing among white and black applicants for admission to the law school. The Constitution forbids the University of Texas Law School from assuming that applicants of different racial backgrounds differ. But the remedial sections of the opinion make precisely the opposite assumption about race. Here the *Hopwood* opinion asserts that there *are* socially relevant differences among racial groups. It is "'sheer speculation'...how many minorities would be in [a] business absent past discrimination," and the Constitution forbids the University of Texas Law School from assuming that, in a world without discrimination, members of minority groups would participate and achieve in various social endeavors at the same rate as members of other groups. In short, the two sections of the opinion make diametrically opposing positive and normative claims about race. Indeed, if we distill the normative argument of the *Hopwood* opinion, we discover that the law school's affirmative action plan is unconstitutional because the Constitution forbids the law school from assuming that applicants of different racial backgrounds are different and because the Constitution forbids the law school from assuming that applicants of different racial backgrounds are the same. Thus, as the *Hopwood* opinion draws on the Supreme Court's recent equal protection cases, it reveals that these equal protection cases employ quite contradictory modes of reasoning about race.

It is clear enough that the racial rhetoric in the diversity sections of the *Hopwood* opinion is drawn from the civil rights tradition. This portion of the opinion turns concepts of racial "stereotyping" (and stigma) on the diversity rationale for affirmative action, drawing perhaps as well on academic criticisms of race and gender "essentialism."[91] But the racial rhetoric in the remedial sections of the *Hopwood* opinion seems to come from a very different source. Here the court reasons about race as a cultural phenomenon, drawing perhaps on commentators such as Nathan Glazer, Morris Abram, or Dinesh D'Souza, who analyze race as a form of ethnicity and explain racial status as a product of the cultural resources various groups bring to the task of assimilating to the norms of the dominant culture.[92] If we take seriously the justifications for restricting racial remedies spelled out in *Croson* and *Hopwood*, we confront a view of race-as-culture that seems in deep tension with the professed aims of colorblind constitutionalism.

The analysis of race-conscious remedies contained in the *Croson* and *Hopwood* opinions seems to distinguish between licit and illicit forms of racial stratification. The analysis begins from the premise that we can in fact distinguish between racial formations that are the product of discrimination and those that would exist in the world "absent discrimination." That racial stratification which state actors can prove is traceable to institutional acts of racial discrimination may be rectified by race-conscious remedies. But racial stratification that cannot be shown to be the product of such discrimination is licit — and protected by the Fourteenth Amendment of the United States Constitution. *Hopwood*'s injunction against "racial social engineering" bars the state from pursuing policies of race-conscious remediation that risk disturbing "natural" forms of racial stratification, that is, those racial distributions that arise from differences in tastes or talents among racial groups. (Note how equal protection doctrine restricting the remedial use of affirmative action is concerned about the risk that racial remedies might alter real differences among racial groups — *not* the risk that race discrimination might go unrectified.) If one follows the logic of concerns about proportional representation and racial social engineering expressed in *Croson* and *Hopwood*, it appears that strict scrutiny doctrines under the Fourteenth Amendment radically restrict the use of race-conscious remedies in order to protect and preserve real differences among racial groups. To say the least, this is a counterintuitive ambition for a body of law that embraces as its "ultimate goal" the purpose " 'of eliminating entirely from governmental decisionmaking such irrelevant factors as a human being's race.' "[93]

Colorblind Constitutionalism: Some Genealogical Reflections

At least, the goal of preserving differences among racial groups *seems* like a counterintuitive ambition for a body of law that embraces values of colorblindness. It seems more plausible as an account of colorblind constitutionalism if one revisits the origins of the discourse, in early Fourteenth Amendment jurisprudence of the Reconstruction era. In this period, it remained an open and hotly contested question whether, and to what extent, racial status distinctions would survive under the body of civil rights law that would be required to disestablish chattel slavery. This was the sociolegal universe in which talk of colorblindness was born.

The white Americans who drafted and ratified the Fourteenth Amendment debated the meaning of emancipating African Americans in a discursive framework that is unfamiliar to many Americans today. In this period, some white Americans defined freedom from slavery as equality in civil rights; others insisted that emancipating African Americans from slavery entailed equality in civil and political rights; but most white Americans who opposed slavery did not think its abolition required giving African Americans equality in "social rights."[94] Social rights were those forms of association that, white Americans feared, would obliterate status distinctions and result in the "amalgamation" of the races.[95] Objections to granting freedmen "social equality" appear throughout the debate on emancipation, before and after the Civil War. Both those who supported and those who opposed civil rights reform asserted that equality in social status could not be legislated ("the social status of men is determined by original capacity, and cannot be fixed or safely tampered with by legislation"[96]), but opponents of reform transformed this descriptive claim into a normative argument — objecting to various civil rights measures on the grounds that the legislation would impermissibly *promote* social equality between the races.[97]

The Court's opinion in *Plessy v. Ferguson*[98] unfolds within this discursive framework. In *Plessy*, the Court drew on social rights discourse to explain why laws mandating racial segregation of public transportation were consistent with the Fourteenth Amendment's guarantee of equal protection of the laws: "The object of the amendment was undoubtedly to enforce the absolute equality of the two races before the law, but in the nature of things it could not have been intended to abolish distinctions based upon color, or to enforce social, as distinguished from political equality, or a commingling of the two races upon terms unsatisfactory to either."[99] The majority in *Plessy* believed that government could not draw racial distinctions in matters concerning civil and political rights (e.g., rights of contract or jury service), but contended that access to public transportation involved an associational or "social" right, and so implicated questions of "social, as distinguished from political equality," beyond the reach of the

Fourteenth Amendment's guarantee of equal protection of the laws. As the majority explained: "If the civil and political rights of both races be equal one cannot be inferior to the other civilly or politically. If one race be inferior to the other socially, the Constitution of the United States cannot put them upon the same plane."[100]

As is well known, Justice Harlan dissented from the *Plessy* decision, arguing that segregation of public transportation violated the Fourteenth Amendment. In Justice Harlan's view, access to public transportation involved a civil right, hence could not be the subject of racially discriminatory regulation.[101] But Justice Harlan's dissenting opinion did *not* assert that "colored citizens" were the social equals of white citizens, or that the law should make them so; indeed, passages of his dissent — including the famous colorblindness argument — continue to emphasize distinctions between legal and social equality:

> *The white race deems itself to be the dominant race in this country. And so it is, in prestige, in achievements, in education, in wealth and in power. So, I doubt not, it will continue to be for all time, if it remains true to its great heritage and holds fast to the principles of constitutional liberty.* But in view of the Constitution, in the eye of the law, there is in this country no superior, dominant, ruling class of citizens. There is no caste here. Our Constitution is color-blind, and neither knows nor tolerates classes among citizens. In respect of civil rights, all citizens are equal before the law.[102]

As the narrative progression of the colorblindness passage illustrates, the legal equality of which Justice Harlan spoke *presupposed* continuing social *in*equality. His opinion subsequently reiterated this distinction between legal and social equality: "[S]ocial equality no more exists between two races when traveling in a passenger coach or a public highway than when members of the same races sit by each other in a street car or in the jury box, or stand or sit with each other in a political assembly."[103] When Justice Harlan asserted that "in the eye of the law, there is in this country no superior, dominant, ruling class of citizens. There is no caste here. Our Constitution is color-blind," he was arguing that the legal system should not distribute certain entitlements ("civil rights") in accordance with the prevailing order of racial status relations. It is the social condition of racial stratification that makes the concept of *colorblindness* intelligible as a distributive principle.

The discourse of colorblindness involves what Neil Gotanda has called a practice of racial "nonrecognition."[104] The discourse presupposes a series of intelligible status distinctions ("color," "class," "caste") which it refuses to take account of in certain legal situations. The majority and the dissent in *Plessy* were in disagreement about the kinds of legal situations in which the Fourteenth Amendment required the government to adopt a stance of racial nonrecognition. But they were in agreement that law neither would nor should eliminate racial stratification — or, as they put it, bring about "social equality." In short, in this era, the practice of colorblindness, or racial nonrecognition, did *not* aspire to bring about the social equality of the races. In the nineteenth century, racial nonrecognition did not hold itself out as form of public pedagogy intended to inspire private emulation; indeed, its proponents repeatedly and emphatically disclaimed any intention of meddling with the private discriminations all Americans were at liberty to cultivate.

Thus, in the Reconstruction era, colorblindness discourse expressed a commitment to distribute legal entitlements in ways that defied the prevailing order of racial status relations; but the practice of racial nonrecognition was not intended wholly to disestablish racial stratification. Those joined in debate over the meaning of the constitutional and statutory provisions adopted in the wake of the Civil War understood such laws to guarantee the emancipated slaves *legal* equality, but they agreed that the law neither would nor should enforce the *social* equality of the races. In short, in the Reconstruction era, discourses of racial nonrecognition were commonly coupled with, and bounded by, privacy discourses that posited a domain of racial recognition beyond the proper reach of civil rights regulation. There is a logic to this rhetorical coupling. Once the federal government adopted civil rights laws conferring equality on the emancipated slaves, those seeking to defend relations of racial inequality had to justify limitations on the reach of such status-disestablishing laws. The defense of racial inequality could, and most certainly did, assume the form of assertions about the natural inferiority of blacks. But, in contests over the meaning of civil rights laws embodying principles of equality, the defense of racial inequality increasingly assumed new rhetorical form, articulated as a set of counterprinciples constraining the reach of civil rights law itself. And so, during the Reconstruction era, overtly hierarchical discourses of racial status were gradually translated into a rhetoric of privacy and associational liberty concerned with protecting racial status relations from governmental interference.

It is, of course, possible to invoke the discourse of colorblindness unconstrained by concepts of a racial private sphere beyond the state's power to regulate; many in the modern civil rights movement have invoked concepts of colorblindness in this fashion. But the public/private distinction that undergirds the majority and dissenting opinions in *Plessy* has proven remarkably robust. As we will see, there are many proponents of colorblindness who currently embrace some form of this racial public/private distinction, still expressed in civil rights idiom as the distinction between legal and social equality. Now, as then, the concept of legal equality presupposes an ongoing condition of social inequality that law neither can nor should attempt to eradicate.

But if racial discourses of the private have persisted into the modern era, they have also assumed new rhetorical forms. In the Reconstruction era, white Americans discussed their prerogative to maintain racial status distinctions in the idiom of associational liberty or "social rights."[105] (Their continuing insistence that law neither could nor should mandate social equality testified to the clear understanding that maintaining a system of racial caste was at stake.) While opponents of civil rights legislation employed this same rhetoric of associational liberty in the 1950s and 1960s[106] — and some, including Charles Murray, continue to employ it today[107] — racial discourses of the private are now more commonly couched in a related, but distinct, market idiom that emphasizes individual and group competition.

For example, in his recent book, *What It Means to Be a Libertarian*,[108] Charles Murray first attacks the Civil Rights Act of 1964 on the grounds that it abridges "freedom of association,"[109] but then goes on to assert that the antidiscrimination statute interferes with natural and legitimate forms of social stratification: "At any moment in history a completely fair system for treating individuals will produce different outcomes for different groups, because groups are hardly ever equally represented in the qualities that go into decisions about whom to hire, admit to law school, put in jail, or live next door to."[110] According to Murray, federal antidiscrimination laws erroneously presume that gross discrepancies in racial or gender representation are attributable to discrimination, when instead such discrepancies are the product of meritocratic competition among groups.[111] Since Nathan Glazer elaborated this ethno-cultural account of social stratification to challenge the evidentiary assumptions of antidiscrimination law in the 1970s,[112] narratives of intergroup competition have played a central role in critiques of civil rights law. Dinesh D'Souza is currently their most prominent exponent. D'Souza rejects bias or bigotry as the reason why "America is developing something resembling a racial hierarchy — Asians and whites at the top, Hispanics in the middle, African-Americans at the bottom"; he contends this hierarchy exists because "African-Americans are not competitive with other groups in our society."[113] "Merit produces inequality not only between individuals, but also between groups."[114]

Narratives of group competition now play a central role in critiques of affirmative action. For example, in his influential article attacking affirmative action as "social engineering," Morris Abram embraces "the American system" as a "free market system," which in his view "guarantees civil and political rights," but not "social and economic rights."[115] In such a system, he argues, there will naturally be social stratification:

> Because groups — black, white, Hispanic, male, and female — do not necessarily have the same distribution of, among other characteristics, skills, interest, motivation, and age, a fair shake system may not produce proportional representation across occupations and professions, and certainly not at any given time. This uneven distribution, however, is not necessarily the result of discrimination. Thomas Sowell has shown through comparative studies of ethnic group performance that discrimination alone cannot explain these ethnic groups' varying levels of achievement. Groups such as the Japanese, Chinese, and West Indian blacks have fared very well in American society despite racial bias against these groups.[116]

Abram attacks proponents of affirmative action as "today's social engineers," who do not view justice as "an individual's claim to equality before the law" but instead seek "a particular distribution of social, economic, and political power among groups." "This new conception of justice," he argues, "necessarily repudiates the ideal of the rule of law — a law that 'would treat people equally, but...not seek to make them equal.'"[117] A story about competition among groups with different genetic and cultural endowments explains, and justifies, relations of racial status; a story about maintaining appropriate distinctions between the public and private spheres explains, and justifies, legal rules that preserve relations of racial status. As Dinesh D'Souza concludes his attack on affirmative action and the Civil Rights Act of 1964: "What we need is a long-term strategy that holds the government to a rigorous standard of race neutrality, while allowing private actors to be free to discriminate as they wish."[118] He distills this prescription into a call for the "separation of race and state."[119]

One can discern different rhetorical strains of racial privacy discourse as one examines the justifications the *Croson* and *Hopwood* courts offer for the restrictions they impose on remedial affirmative action. When the Supreme Court struck down the minority business set-aside at issue in the *Croson* case, it condemned the Richmond City Council for engaging in constitutionally offensive "racial balancing" rather than racial remediation because the program was premised "upon the 'completely unrealistic' assumption that minorities will choose a particular trade in lockstep proportion to their representation in the local population."[120] Echoes of *Plessy*'s claim that the Fourteenth Amendment could not have been intended "to enforce social, as distinguished from political equality" inform the insistence that affirmative action policies cannot rectify "societal discrimination" or promote proportional representation or otherwise engage in what the *Hopwood* court calls "racial social engineering." These are modern expressions of racial privacy rhetoric, positing a domain of racial inequality that civil rights law cannot reach or appropriately aspire to rectify. From the first that Justice Powell argued that it was unconstitutional for state actors to employ affirmative action policies to rectify societal discrimination, his purpose was to protect "innocent" parties whose interests might be entrenched on by racial remedies.[121] Though no longer justified so bluntly, the claims that affirmative action policies cannot rectify "societal discrimination" or promote proportional representation or otherwise engage in "racial social engineering" variously express this same, and continuing, concern that race-conscious remedies may entrench on the relative social position of whites. This underlying concern often finds more overt expression in popular debate and in the reasoning of some of the lower federal courts. A federal district court recently summarized the law of affirmative action by quoting the colorblindness passage in Justice Harlan's dissent and then observing:

> In a perfect world, neither reverse discrimination nor affirmative action would constitute legal issues. Indeed, *these social engineering programs serve primarily to aggravate racial tensions, not to heal past wounds.* However, taking our long and sad history of racial discord into account, *the United States Supreme Court permits conscious discrimination against white males to compensate for past injuries inflicted upon minority groups.*[122]

What is striking is that, in ambivalently authorizing and then progressively undermining affirmative action, the United States Supreme Court has rarely presented itself as concerned about protecting the social position of "white males." Justice Powell initially offered an unusually frank account of his reasons for prohibiting the use of affirmative action to rectify societal discrimination — one that emphasized the "deep resentment" and "outrage" that "innocent persons" might experience at being deni[ed]... equal rights and opportunities" as "the price of membership in the dominant majority"[123] — but such discussion is no longer commonplace, adverted to only in oblique references to affirmative action stimulating "racial hostility."[124] Now the rationales for restricting affirmative action emphasize the injuries race-conscious remedies inflict on racial minorities, or depict such constitutional restrictions as the product of colorblind "consistency." As the Court explained its commitment to "consistency" in *Adarand*: "'the standard of review under the Equal Protection Clause is not dependent on the race of those burdened or benefited by a particular classification.'"[125] Like many recent colorblindness arguments for restricting affirmative action, *Adarand* applies the practice of racial nonrecognition in ways that protect the social position of whites, but in terms that disclaim any interest in preserving the existing racial order, and, if anything, claim a fervent interest in hastening the day of its final disestablishment.[126]

In short, the discourse of colorblindness is remarkably flexible; its sociopolitical salience is dependent on the context in which it is invoked. When Justice Harlan or the modern civil rights movement invoked the discourse of colorblindness to challenge the rule structure of de jure segregation, the discourse supported a demand for disestablishment of race-based distributive rules supporting the existing racial order. Today, the state no longer employs openly race-based distributive rules to maintain racial stratification. With the regime of de jure segregation discredited, status-enforcing state action has evolved in rule structure and justificatory rhetoric. Now state action that perpetuates racial stratification is couched in facially neutral distributive rules and justified as advancing legitimate, nondiscriminatory ends. Now, it is those seeking to disestablish racial stratification who are using the tools of race-conscious regulation, and opponents of such initiatives have seized on the rhetorical materials of the civil rights movement to advance principled justifications for prohibiting, or radically restricting, the ambit of such status-disestablishing initiatives. In the nineteenth century, at the inception of America's experiment with disestablishing slavery, it was still feasible to advance an interest in preserving the existing racial order (or the right to discriminate in one's associations) as a basis for opposing or restricting civil rights regulation. Today, of course, claims about preserving the existing racial order do not carry the same authority, while expressing a commitment to principles of racial equality is understood to state a "legitimate, nondiscriminatory" reason for restricting civil rights initiatives that seek to alleviate the racial stratification of American society.[127] Under these circumstances, discourses of racial nonrecognition can now be employed in ways that preserve the existing racial order.

The justificatory rhetoric of racial status law is always evolving, mutating as conflicts precipitate shifts in the rule structure of racial status law.[128] In the nineteenth century, when race-based regulation of African Americans was commonplace, the *Plessy* Court drew on racialized discourses of the private to justify restricting the ambit of civil rights laws embodying rules of racial nonrecognition. Now, with the demise of de jure segregation, the

Court employs the rules and rhetoric of racial nonrecognition to restrict new, race-conscious forms of civil rights legislation, but it also justifies restrictions on such legislation by invoking a private sphere of racial differentiation that civil rights law may not aspire to disestablish. The contradictory representations of race that *Hopwood* draws from the Court's recent equal protection cases reflect this synthetic rhetorical strategy. The claims about race-as-morphological-accident that justify repudiating diversity rationales for affirmative action are expressions of what Neil Gotanda calls "formal" race,[129] part of the rhetoric of racial non-recognition, while the claims about race-as-culture that justify restricting remedial uses of affirmative action have deep roots in racial discourses of the private, referring to a domain of racial recognition "beyond" the proper reach of civil rights regulation. There is ample precedent for this synthetic rhetorical strategy. As we have seen, rhetorics of racial nonrecognition have been employed in conjunction with rhetorics of racial recognition since the days of Reconstruction, as Americans have debated the proper reach of civil rights regulation.

The Racial Commitments of Colorblind Constitutionalism

While some who argue that the state may only act in a rigorously colorblind fashion are rather forthright in their desire to protect the right of private citizens to discriminate without state interference (e.g., Murray, Epstein, D'Souza), the Court has continued, albeit at times weakly, to enforce civil rights legislation governing market place transactions,[130] and has ambivalently allowed race-conscious remedies, undermining but not quite prohibiting them. Moreover, the Court — unlike some of its more conservative critics — intermittently justifies the restrictions it imposes on affirmative action as promoting a world where we can finally get "beyond" race. For example, in *Adarand* the Court emphasized that race-based preferences give rise to the perception that their beneficiaries "are less qualified in some respect that is identified purely by their race," a perception that "can only exacerbate rather than reduce racial prejudice, [hence] delay the time when race will become a truly irrelevant, or at least insignificant, factor."[131] In restricting race-conscious remedies, the Court now presents itself as seeking to liberate the nation from racial consciousness.[132] What weight should we give this claim?

As we have seen, in *Croson* and *Adarand*, the Court adopted a strict scrutiny framework that elevates the standing of white plaintiffs to contest race-conscious remedies and suggests that their claims of race discrimination have much in common with the race discrimination that minorities suffer; the Court has thus given constitutional protection to the injuries whites suffer as members of a racial group, even as it refuses to construe the equal protection clause to redress the grievances they suffer as members of income or occupational groups adversely affected by government policies. In short, the Court has applied strict scrutiny in ways that would seem to reflect and reinforce the racial-group consciousness of white Americans. But the Court also insists that in applying strict scrutiny to affirmative action, it is protecting the minority beneficiaries of such programs from the racial hostility, stereotyping, and stigma that resentful whites may direct at them. Of course, the Court itself has played a role in encouraging the resentment of affirmative action which it then claims it must accommodate. Still, if we suppose that the Court is ultimately a majoritarian institution, perhaps it has taken the only leadership role it can in permitting race-conscious remedies as "suspect" social undertakings. As a majoritarian institution, the Court may well be persuaded that restricting race-conscious state action is the best way to ameliorate racial consciousness in the polity at large. The Court might well hold this view in good faith — even if the strategy it has adopted focuses on the symbolism of governmental action, while ignoring the ways that persisting racial stratification will itself perpetuate racial consciousness.

Given all this, one might conclude that the Court is indeed struggling to bring about the day "when race will become a truly irrelevant, or at least insignificant, factor"[133] — even if it has chosen contestable means for achieving this goal. But it becomes harder to credit the Court's claim that it is attempting to move the nation "beyond" race as one considers the racial privacy discourse the Court invokes to justify restrictions on affirmative action. Consider, for example, the race-conscious views and commitments that the Court has expressed when it differentiates legitimate forms of affirmative action from constitutionally illegitimate forms of "racial balancing." As the Court has defined it, a race-conscious remedy is illegitimate "racial balancing" whenever such a remedy alleviates racial stratification that is the product of "societal discrimination" or disturbs racial formations that would naturally exist "absent unlawful discrimination."[134] In so reasoning, the Court has embraced a "thick" conception of race, expressing its view that, even in a world where there was no discrimination, there would *still* be occupational differences (and, presumably, income differences) among racial groups. More importantly, it has harnessed this view of race-as-culture to a normative discourse about the proper uses of state power, interpreting the Constitution to prohibit government from altering such natural racial differences. Whatever one thinks about the claim that there would be important racial differences in a world without race discrimination — and such claims must remain speculative because we have never inhabited such a world — they assume very different meaning as a foundation for a privacy discourse concerned with protecting such "natural" differences from governmental interference. When the Court, which generally espouses judicial deference, intervenes in the political process to prevent legislatures from disturbing racial stratification that is "merely" the product of societal discrimination and to prevent legislatures from altering cultural differences among racial groups that would naturally exist in a hypothetical world that has never existed, it seems safe to say that the Court is more involved in preserving the racial status quo than its claims about getting beyond race would seem to suggest.

But still, it can be objected, the Court has only intervened in the political process to inhibit *race-conscious* efforts to alleviate racial stratification; it has always allowed legislatures to use facially neutral means to attack the same problem.[135] Bearing this in mind, we could read the Court's use of racial privacy discourse as an ill-considered and ultimately incidental ground of objection to race-based state action. Whatever view of racial stratification the Court's embrace of racial privacy discourse would seem to express, the Court has, after all, voiced other objections to race-conscious remedies. As the Court and numerous critics of affirmative action have pointed out, such regulatory measures involve practices of racial group assignment that at this juncture of American history have become the site of heightened social conflict.

Given the unstable social meaning of race-conscious remedies, the Court could reasonably conclude that the quest to ameliorate racial stratification would be better pursued by formally race-neutral means.

Suppose, then, that the Court were committed to eliminating racial stratification, but, for reasons of principle or pragmatism, believed that it was wrong for government to pursue this goal by race-conscious means. Having taken the unusual measure of intervening in the political process to invalidate race-conscious efforts to ameliorate racial stratification, the Court might then use its institutional authority to encourage legislatures to adopt facially neutral means of achieving the same end. If legislatures reformed educational, zoning, and criminal laws or any number of social welfare policies that affect the life prospects of minority communities, such facially neutral measures might promote integration of basic social institutions just as surely as affirmative action programs do — and without the kind of conflict that race-specific regulation now engenders.

But if the Court *permits* legislatures to ameliorate racial stratification by facially neutral means, it certainly does not employ its institutional authority to encourage them to do so. In the years since the demise of de jure segregation, minority plaintiffs have repeatedly brought law suits challenging facially neutral forms of state action that contribute to the racial stratification affirmative action redresses. The Court might have construed the equal protection clause to require heightened scrutiny of facially neutral polices that have a disparate impact on minority communities — an interpretation of the Fourteenth Amendment that would commit the moral authority of the equal protection clause to the alleviation of racial stratification, without requiring government to act by race-based means.[136] On this view, the constitutional guarantee of equal protection of the laws would require the state to govern impartially, constraining the state from enacting policies that significantly disadvantaged subordinate social groups, unless the state could articulate a weighty justification for adopting policies that aggravated the racial stratification of American society. But the Court does not treat facially neutral state action that aggravates racial stratification as raising significant equal protection concerns. Since the days of *Bakke*, the federal judiciary has reviewed challenges to drug-sentencing guidelines, residential zoning rules, and educational funding and districting policies that disparately burden minority communities on the presumption that such regulation is constitutional unless animated by discriminatory purpose; this is a quite restrictive standard, often defined as tantamount to malice or an intent to harm, which plaintiffs have great difficulty in proving and which the Court justifies as warranted by the deference courts owe to coordinate branches of government.[137] In short, the Court's willingness to intervene in the political process to restrict race-conscious initiatives intended to alleviate racial stratification utterly dissolves when it reviews facially neutral state action having a disparate impact on minorities; in these cases, concerns about the Court's position as a "counter-majoritarian" institution suddenly assume preeminence. Thus, today doctrines of strict scrutiny function primarily, if not exclusively, to restrict race-conscious initiatives intended to alleviate racial stratification, while the Court treats the forms of facially neutral state action that continue to perpetuate racial stratification as presumptively race-neutral, and warranting only the most deferential review. This is the larger constitutional context in which colorblindness objections to race-conscious remedies deserve to be evaluated.

For several decades now the Court has ambivalently sanctioned affirmative action, while subjecting the policies to increasing restrictions. In deciding *Hopwood*, the Fifth Circuit ignored these signs of begrudging tolerance and imposed more severe restrictions on educational affirmative action than the Court has yet embraced; but, as we have seen, the Fifth Circuit derived the core, and conflicting, rationales for its decision from the Supreme Court's recent rulings on race-conscious remedies. In this sense, *Hopwood* is the fruit of the Court's recent rulings on race-conscious remedies.

Since the *Hopwood* decision, minority applications and admissions at the University of Texas Law School have fallen precipitously. The University of Texas Law School has now offered positions in the fall 1997 class to 11 African American students, down from 65 last year, and to 33 Hispanic students, down from 70 last year.[138] Early in the summer, there were no black students willing to attend, although at present, 4 African-American and 21 Hispanic students are planning to enroll in the first-year class of 494 students.[139] In short, it seems that the University of Texas Law School will have an entering class that is less than one percent black — no small achievement for an institution that was (once?) white by law.

If we consider the racial privacy rhetorics that accompany *Hopwood*'s use of colorblindness discourse — in particular, its condemnation of the law school's admission policy as "racial social engineering" — it is hard to view this result as an unintended by-product of the court's decision. As we have seen, *Hopwood* finds its roots in *Plessy v. Ferguson* — *both* the majority and dissenting opinions.

NOTES

1. U.S. Constitution, Article I, Section 2 (emphasis added).

2. At the annual meeting of the Massachusetts Anti-Slavery Society, William Garrison offered the following resolution, which was adopted on January 27, 1843: "Resolved, That the compact which exists between the North and the South is a covenant with death, and an agreement with hell — involving both parties in atrocious criminality, and should be immediately annulled" (Massachusetts Anti-Slavery Society, Eleventh Annual Report [Boston: Oliver Johnson, 1843], appendix, p. 94).

3. For an account of this historical dynamic, see Reva B. Siegel, "Why Equal Protection No Longer Protects: The Evolving Forms of Status-Enforcing State Action," *Stanford Law Review* 49 (1997): 1111.

4. See *Scott v. Sandford*, 60 U.S. 393, 407–26 (1856).

5. *City of Richmond v. J.A. Croson Co.*, 488 U.S. 469, 495 (1989) (O'Connor, J., plurality opinion) (quoting *Wygant v. Jackson Bd. of Educ.*, 476 U.S. 267, 320 [1986] [Stevens, J., dissenting]).

6. 78 F. 3d 932 (5th Cir. 1996).

7. *Ibid.* at 935.

8. The *Hopwood* opinion addresses the constitutionality of race-conscious admissions policies under the equal protection clause of the Fourteenth Amendment, which constrains state actors. However, recipients of federal education funds may be held to similar standards under Title VI of the Civil Rights Act of 1964. For discussion of this question, see Robert Post's introduction to this volume. The plaintiffs in the *Hopwood* case brought a Title VI claim in addition to their constitutional claims, but the Fifth Circuit did not squarely address the question of whether its holding bound private recipients of federal funds. Most private schools in Texas now construe the court's ruling as controlling their

admissions decisions through Title VI. See Sylvia Moreno, "Private Colleges Expect Changes in Policy," *Dallas Morning News*, 3 July 1996, 5B.

9. 438 U.S. 265 (1978).

10. See Siegel, "Why Equal Protection No Longer Protects."

11. *Ibid.* at 1133–44.

12. 349 U.S. 294 (1955).

13. *Hopwood v. Texas*, 861 F. Supp. 551, 554 (W.D. Tex. 1994), *rev'd*, 78 F. 3d 932 (5th Cir. 1996).

14. *Ibid.* at 554–55 and n. 4.

15. See *Sweatt v. Painter*, 210 S.W. 2d 442 (Tex. Civ. App. 1948).

16. 339 U.S. 629 (1950).

17. *Hopwood*, 861 F. Supp. at 555.

18. *Ibid.* at 556.

19. *Ibid.*

20. *Ibid.*

21. *Ibid.*

22. *Ibid.* at 557.

23. *Ibid.*

24. *Ibid.* at 560–63.

25. *Ibid.* at 563 and n.33.

26. *Ibid.* at 563.

27. *Ibid.*

28. The class admitted for the fall of 1992 had an overall median GPA of 3.52, and an overall median LSAT of 162 (89th percentile). The median figures for non–minorities were a GPA of 3.56 and an LSAT of 164 (93rd percentile); for blacks, a GPA of 3.30 and an LSAT of 158 (78th percentile); and for Mexican–Americans, a GPA of 3.24 and an LSAT of 157 (75th percentile) (*Ibid.* at 563 n.32). The district court supplied no precise figures for the variance in GPA and LSAT scores between resident and nonresident admittees, but did indicate that because many nonresident applicants had credentials "well above those of the presumptively admitted residents … the presumptive admission and denial scores were set at a higher level for nonresident applicants" (*Ibid.* at 561 n.22).

29. *Ibid.* at 581.

30. *Ibid.* at 578–79.

31. *Hopwood v. Texas*, 78 F.3d 932, 934–35 (5th Cir. 1996).

32. *Ibid.* (quoting *Croson,* 488 U.S. 469, 528 [1989] [Scalia, J., concurring]).

33. See generally Susan Sturm and Lani Guinier, "The Future of Affirmative Action: Reclaiming the Innovative Ideal," *California Law Review* 84 (1996): 953, 968–97 (discussing literature on income, race, and gender bias in standardized tests).

34. *Hopwood*, 78 F.3d at 937.

35. *Ibid.* at 935, n.2.

36. *Ibid.* at 935 ("Of course, the law school did not rely upon numbers alone. The admissions office necessarily exercised judgment in interpreting the individual scores of the applicants, taking into consideration factors such as the strength of a student's undergraduate education..."). The Fifth Circuit notes that the plaintiff, Cheryl Hopwood, "was dropped into the discretionary zone for resident whites..., however, because [the admissions officer] decided her educational background overstated the strength of her GPA" (*Ibid.* at 938). The court omits reference to the fact that Hopwood's grades were earned at a community college and a state university. See *Hopwood v. University of Texas*, 861 F. Supp. 551, 564 (W.D. Tex. 1994).

37. *University of California v. Bakke*, 438 U.S. 265, 298 (1978).

38. *Ibid.* at 294 n.34 (emphasis added).

39. *Wygant v. Jackson Bd. of Educ.*, 476 U.S. 267, 276 (1986) (Powell, J., plurality opinion) (emphasis added).

40. See *Bakke*, 438 U.S. at 308 ("remedial action usually remains subject to continuing oversight to assure that it will work the least harm possible to other innocent persons competing for the benefit").

41. Intermittently, the justices distinguished white people according to degrees of innocence, as when Justice Stewart observed, "Except to make whole the identified victims of racial discrimination, the guarantee of equal protection prohibits the government from taking detrimental action against innocent people on the basis of the sins of others of their own race." *Fullilove v. Klutznik*, 448 U.S. 448, 530 n.12 (1980) (Stewart, J., dissenting). More commonly, "sinning" white Americans were obliquely depicted as deceased, as when the justices discussed affirmative action as a remedy for the present effects of *past* discrimination.

42. There is now a substantial body of commentary on the discourse of white innocence in the Court's affirmative action cases. See, e.g., Thomas Ross, "Innocence and Affirmative Action," *Vanderbilt Law Review* 43 (1990): 297; Thomas Ross, "The Rhetorical Tapestry of Race: White Innocence and Black Abstraction," *William and Mary Law Review* 32 (1990): 1; Kathleeen M. Sullivan, "Sins of Discrimination: Last Term's Affirmative Action Cases," *Harvard Law Review* 100 (1986): 1; see also Cheryl Harris, "Whiteness As Property," *Harvard Law Review* 106 (1993): 1707, 1781–84.

43. 488 U.S. 469 (1989).

44. 515 U.S. 200 (1995).

45. See *ibid.* at 224 ("'the standard of review under the Equal Protection Clause is not dependent on the race of those burdened or benefitted by a par-

ticular classification'") (quoting Croson, 488 U.S. 469, 494 [1989] [O'Connor, J., plurality opinion]). But cf. *ibid.* at 2114 (arguing that even if all forms of race-based state action are analyzed under the same standard of review, it will still be possible for courts to differentiate between benign and invidious forms of race-based state action).

46. *Croson*, 488 U.S. 469, 493 (1989) (O'Connor, J., plurality opinion) ("'rights created by the first section of the Fourteenth Amendment are . . . guaranteed to the individual'") (quoting *Shelley v. Kraemer*, 334 U.S. 1, 22 [1948]).

47. 488 U.S. 469 (1989).

48. *Ibid.* at 493 (O'Connor, J., plurality opinion).

49. *Ibid.* at 495 (O'Connor, J., plurality opinion) (quoting *Wygant v. Board of Education*, 476 U.S. 267, 320 [1986] [Stevens, J., dissenting]).

50. 438 U.S. 265 (1978).

51. *Ibid.* at 362 (Brennan, J., concurring in the judgment in part and dissenting).

52. *Ibid.* at 295 (Powell, J., concurring).

53. *Ibid.* at 292. See Nathan Glazer, *Affirmative Discrimination: Ethnic Inequality and Public Policy* (New York, 1975), 201 ("We are indeed a nation of minorities; to enshrine some minorities as deserving of special benefits means not to defend minority rights against a discriminating majority but to favor some of these minorities over others"). A lengthy quotation from this passage of Glazer's book appeared in one of the amicus briefs submitted in the case. See "Brief Amici Curiae of Anti-Defamation League of B'nai Brith" at 18, *University of California v. Bakke*, 438 U.S. 265 (1978) (No. 76–811). See also Charles R. Lawrence III & Mari J. Matsuda, *We Won't Go Back: Making the Case for Affirmative Action* (Boston, 1997), 48 (discussing influence of Glazer's book on Justice Powell's *Bakke* opinion).

54. *Bakke*, 438 U.S. at 295 (Powell, J., concurring). Even as Justice Powell undertook to deconstruct the concept of "whites" as a group, he nonetheless referred to the minorities composing the majority as "white," as the language quoted in the text illustrates. At the outset of his opinion, Powell characterized the groups in question as "European." To substantiate his claim that "the United States had become a Nation of minorities," Powell quoted a federal regulation (also quoted by Glazer) that stated: "Members of various religious and ethnic groups, primarily but not exclusively of Eastern, Middle, and Southern European ancestry, such as Jews, Catholics, Italians, Greeks, and Slavic groups, continue to be excluded from executive, middle-management, and other job levels because of discrimination based upon their religion and/or national origin." *Ibid.* at 292, n.32. (quoting 41 C.F.R. § 60–50.1(b) [1977]). Cf. Glazer, 75 (quoting same provision).

55. *Bakke*, 438 U.S. at 294, n.34 (Powell, J., concurring).

56. *Ibid.* at 310 (Powell, J., concurring).

57. *Ibid.* at 307–9.

58. *Ibid.* at 316–19.

59. For a sophisticated analysis of the various justices' views on this question, see Akhil Reed Amar & Neal Kumar Katyal, "*Bakke*'s Fate," *U.C.L.A. Law Review* 43 (1996): 1745.

60. *See* note 91 below (citing Supreme Court cases).

61. *Hopwood v. Texas*, 78 F. 3d 932, 946 (5th Cir. 1996).

62. *Ibid.* at 946 (quoting *Metro Broadcasting v. FCC*, 497 U.S. 547, 602 [1990] [O'Connor, J., dissenting]).

63. *Ibid.* at 945.

64. *Ibid.* at 947 (quoting *Croson*, 488 U.S. 469, 493 [1989] [O'Connor, J., plurality opinion]).

65. *Ibid.* at 947–48.

66. *Ibid.* at 945.

67. *Ibid.* at 946 (quoting Richard Posner, "The DeFunis Case and the Constitutionality of Preferential Treatment of Racial Minorities," *Supreme Court Review* [1974]: 12).

68. *Ibid.* at 947, n.31.

69. *Ibid.* at 948.

70. *Ibid.* at 947, n.31.

71. *Ibid.* at 948.

72. *Ibid.* at 949 (emphasis added).

73. *Ibid.* at 950.

74. *Ibid.* at 950 (quoting *Wygant v. Board. of Education*, 476 U.S. 267, 277 [1986] [Powell, J., plurality opinion]).

75. The Fifth Circuit relies heavily on the Supreme Court's splintered opinion in *Wygant v. Jackson Board of Education*, 476 U.S. 267 (1985), where a plurality opinion by Justice Powell and a concurring opinion by Justice O'Connor repeatedly expressed these concerns. See *ibid.* at 276 (Powell, J., plurality opinion) : "No one doubts that there has been serious racial discrimination in this country. But as the basis for imposing discriminatory legal remedies that work against innocent people, societal discrimination is insufficient and over expansive. In the absence of particularized findings, a court could uphold remedies that are ageless in their reach into the past, and timeless in their ability to affect the future." See also *ibid.* at 287 (O'Connor, J., concurring in part and concurring in the judgment) (public employer may undertake an affirmative action program which furthers a "legitimate remedial purpose . . . by means that do not impose disproportionate harm on the interests, or unnecessarily tram-

mel the rights, of innocent individuals directly and adversely affected by a plan's racial preference"); *ibid.* at 288 (endorsing the plurality's view that "a governmental agency's interest in remedying 'societal discrimination,' that is, discrimination not traceable to its own actions, cannot be deemed sufficiently compelling to pass constitutional muster under strict scrutiny" and citing Justice Powell's *Bakke* opinion for support).

76. *Hopwood*, 78 F. 3d at 950 (quoting *Croson*, 488 U.S. 469, 498 [1989]).

77. *Ibid.* (quoting *Croson*, 488 U.S. at 499).

78. *Ibid.* at 950 (quoting *Wygant v. Board of Education*, 476 U.S. 267, 275 [1986] [Powell, J., plurality opinion]). For the same reasons, the court determines "that the University of Texas System is itself too expansive an entity to scrutinize for past discrimination." *Ibid.* at 951.

79. For the Supreme Court's discussion of this question, see *Croson*, 488 U.S. 469, 503–4 (1989); see also *ibid.* at 491–92, 509 (O'Connor, J., plurality opinion).

80. *See Hopwood*, 78 F.3d at 955 n.49.

81. *Ibid.* at 951.

82. *Ibid.* (emphasis added).

83. See text accompanying notes 12–23 above.

84. *Hopwood*, 78 F.3d at 953.

85. *Ibid.* at 952–56.

86. Objecting to the affirmative action plan challenged in the *Croson* case, the Supreme Court observed that "[i]t rests upon the 'completely unrealistic' assumption that minorities will choose a particular trade in lockstep proportion to their representation in the local population," and quoted one of Justice O'Connor's opinions to the effect that "'it is completely unrealistic to assume that individuals of one race will gravitate with mathematical exactitude to each employer or union absent unlawful discrimination.'" *Croson*, 488 U.S. at 507–8 (quoting *Sheet Metal Workers v. EEOC*, 478 U.S. 421, 494 [1986] [O'Connor, J., concurring in part and dissenting in part]).

87. See Morris B. Abram, "Affirmative Action: Fair Shakers and Social Engineers," *Harvard Law Review* 99 (1986): 1312, 1313.

88. For a discussion of the early race cases, see Vicki Schultz, "Telling Stories About Women and Work: Judicial Interpretations of Sex Segregation in the Workplace in Title VII Cases Raising the Lack of Interest Argument," *Harvard Law Review* 103 (1990): 1750, 1771–75. For an early and influential critique of the evidentiary presumptions of antidiscrimination law, see Glazer, 33–76 (arguing that judicial enforcement of the Civil Rights Act of 1964 had transformed its goal from "equal opportunity" to "statistical parity"). For a leading case in which the Supreme Court signaled that it was adopting a more cautious

approach to the question of proving discrimination, see *Hazelwood School District v. United States*, 433 U.S. 299, 307–8 and n.13 (1977) ("Where gross statistical disparities can be shown, they alone in a proper case may constitute prima facie proof of a pattern or practice of discrimination" but "[w]hen special qualifications are required to fill particular jobs, comparisons to the general population [rather than to the smaller group of individuals who possess the necessary qualifications] may have little probative value").

89. In *Croson*, the Supreme Court invalidated Richmond's minority business set-aside program for city contracting, despite the fact that African Americans comprised half the city's population but minority businesses received only 0.67 percent of the city's prime construction contracts. See *Croson*, 488 U.S. at 479–80. According to the Court, the city's program was constitutionally defective, among other reasons, because the city had failed to gather evidence that would demonstrate that low minority participation in city-generated construction work was attributable to discrimination in the award of prime or subcontracts. When the city pointed to the fact that minority membership in the local contractors' associations was very low, the Court refused to infer that the absence of minority participation was attributable to discrimination: "There are numerous explanations for this dearth of minority participation, including past societal discrimination in education and economic opportunities as well as both black and white career and entrepreneurial choices. Blacks may be disproportionately attracted to industries other than construction." *Ibid.* at 503. The Court held that before Richmond could adopt a remedial affirmative action plan, it would have to establish at least a prima facie case that there was discrimination in the bidding process, by demonstrating a discrepancy between the percentage of minority firms that received prime or subcontracts and the percentage of minority firms in the relevant market that were qualified to undertake prime or subcontracting work in public construction projects. *Ibid.* at 501–2.

In so ruling, the Court applied law governing proof of a prima facie case of employment discrimination to the voluntary affirmative action context. As the Court itself acknowledged, this inquiry is designed to identify whether discrimination occurred in a transaction in which a particular agent was involved (relevant where the imposition of liability is concerned); it will not identify structural barriers to participation in the transaction in question — factors the Court referred to as "past societal discrimination in education and economic opportunities."

90. *Hopwood*, 78 F.3d at 945.

91. Feminist and antiracist arguments about "essentialism" are now being appropriated and transformed by opponents of race-conscious remedies, much as the colorblindness argument was. Initially, scholars analyzing gender and

race stratification described how an observer's social status or position could influence her perception of social relationships, arguing that this kind of positional bias often results in "essentialist" claims — generalizations about group experience that reflect the experience of certain, socially privileged group members rather than the experience of all group members. By the late 1980s, the critique of essentialism was appropriated by critics who were not interested in problems of positional bias, but instead objected to the possibility of making *any* general claims about the distinctive situation, experience, or "voice" of groups that have suffered discrimination. Cf. Angela P. Harris, "Foreword: The Jurisprudence of Reconstruction," *California Law Review* 82 (1994): 741, 754–55 (describing the "essentialism" debate).

With this new focus, the critique made its way into Supreme Court jurisprudence, supplying a new basis for objecting to "benign," race-conscious civil rights measures (e.g. race-based preferences in the award of radio broadcast licenses; race-conscious design of voting districts). Not only did such race-based programs discriminate against white people; now they were also said to discriminate against people of color by making "stereotypical" assumptions about the perspectives or opinions of people of color. See, e.g., *Miller v. Johnson*, 515 U.S. 900, 911–12 (1995) ("When the State assigns voters on the basis of race, it engages in the offensive and demeaning assumption that voters of a particular race, because of their race, 'think alike, share the same political interests, and will prefer the same candidates at the polls.'") (quoting *Shaw v. Reno*, 509 U.S. 630, 646 [1993]); *Metro Broadcasting v. FCC*, 497 U.S. 547, 604 (1990) (O'Connor, J., dissenting) ("Such [race-based] policies may embody stereotypes that treat individuals as the product of their race, evaluating their thoughts and efforts — their very worth as citizens — according to a criterion barred to the Government by history and the Constitution.").

92. See, e.g., Michael Omi and Howard Winant, *Racial Formation in the United States From the 1960s to the 1990s* (2d ed. New York, 1994), 16–23 (discussing group of scholars who analyze race as ethnicity in order to explain the relative ability of African-Americans and immigrant ethnic groups to assimilate into American society); Dinesh D'Souza, *The End of Racism: Principles for a Multiracial Society* (New York, 1995) (arguing that the subordinate status of African Americans is better explained by cultural "pathologies" of the group than by theories that trace group status to genetic endowment or racial discrimination). For some examples of this mode of reasoning, see notes 108–19 below and accompanying text.

93. *Hopwood*, 78 F. 3d at 948 (quoting *Croson*, 488 U.S. 469, 495 [1989] [O'Connor, J., plurality opinion] [quoting *Wygant v. Jackson Board. of Education*, 476 U.S. 267, 320 (1986) (Stevens, J., dissenting)]).

94. See Siegel, "Why Equal Protection No Longer Protects," 1119–20.

95. As a Republican congressman observed in the early days of Recon-struction: "The greatest source of strife in this matter seems to be a fear of social equality and a personal mixing up and commingling of the races; but...it is folly to assume...that because a citizen is your equal before the law and at the ballot-box he is therefore your equal and must needs be your associate in the social circle." *Congressional Globe*, 40th Cong., 3d Sess., app. 241 (1869) (remarks of Rep. William J. Blackburn), quoted in Alfred Avins, "Social Equal-ity and the Fourteenth Amendment: The Original Understanding," *Houston Law Review* 4 (1967): 640, 644, n.27.

96. *Congressional Globe*, 40th Cong., 2d Sess., 1409 (1868) (remarks of Sen. James W. Patterson, a Republican who voted for the Fourteenth Amendment), quoted in Avins, at 643.

97. See, e.g., *Charge to Grand Jury — The Civil Rights Act*, 30 F. Cas. 999, 1001 (C.C.W.D.N.C. 1875) (No. 18,258) ("Any law which would impose upon the white race the imperative obligation of mingling with the colored race on terms of social equality would be repulsive to natural feeling and long estab-lished prejudices, and would be justly odious.... The civil rights bill neither imposes nor was intended to impose any such social obligation. It only proposes to provide for the enforcement of legal rights guaranteed to all citizens by the law of the land, and leaves social rights and privileges to be regulated, as they ever have been, by the customs and usages of society"). For other examples of "social equality" discourse, see Siegel, "Why Equal Protection No Longer Pro-tects," 1121–27.

98. *Plessy v. Ferguson*, 163 U.S. 537 (1896).

99. *Ibid*. at 544.

100. *Ibid*. at 551–52.

101. See *ibid*. at 554, 562 (Harlan, J., dissenting).

102. *Ibid*. at 559 (Harlan J., dissenting) (emphasis added).

103. *Ibid*. at 561.

104. See Neil Gotanda, "A Critique of 'Our Constitution is Color-Blind'," *Stanford Law Review* 44, (1991): 1, 5–6.

105. See Siegel, "Why Equal Protection No Longer Protects," 1124, 1126.

106. *Ibid*. at 1128 and n.75.

107. See, e.g., Charles Murray, *What It Means to Be a Libertarian: A Personal Interpretation* (New York, 1997), 81–89 (attacking the Civil Rights Act of 1964 on the grounds that "[i]n a free society freedom of association cannot be abridged"); see also D'Souza, *The End of Racism*, 544–45 (arguing for repeal of the Civil Rights Act of 1964 on the grounds that it is a "universal," "defensible and in some cases even admirable trait" to "prefer [hiring] members of one's

own group over strangers"); Richard A. Epstein, *Forbidden Grounds: The Case Against Employment Discrimination Laws* (Cambridge, 1992) (arguing that in a free society people have a right to enter into voluntary transactions that other parties should be at liberty to accept or refuse).

108. Murray, *What It Means to Be a Libertarian*, 81–89.

109. *Ibid.* at 81.

110. *Ibid.* at 85.

111. *Ibid.* at 85–86 ("[A] system that...judg[ed] each case perfectly on its merits[] would produce drastically different proportions of men and women hired by police forces, blacks and whites put in jail, or Jews and gentiles admitted to elite law schools").

112. See, e.g., Glazer, *Affirmative Discrimination*, 62–63 (arguing that antidiscrimination law erroneously assumes that, absent discrimination, there would be random distribution of women and minorities in all jobs, when the distribution of jobs among minority groups is best explained by differences in educational qualifications, regional variables, and difficult to quantify factors "such as taste or, if you will, culture").

113. Dinesh D'Souza, "Improving Culture to End Racism," *Harvard Journal of Law and Public Policy* 19 (1996): 785, 789.

114. *Ibid.* at 788.

115. Abram, 1325.

116. *Ibid.* at 1315–16 (footnotes omitted).

117. *Ibid.* at 1317.

118. D'Souza, *The End of Racism,* 544. Charles Murray concludes his attack on the Civil Rights Act of 1964 along similar lines. He contends that government must act in colorblind fashion, but that citizens have a right to freedom of association; consequently, "[t]he good kinds of discrimination must be applauded. The bad kinds of discrimination must once again be made wrong, not illegal." Murray, *What It Means to Be a Libertarian*, 89.

119. D'Souza, *The End of Racism,* 545 (attributing the phrase to Jennifer Roback).

120. *Croson*, 488 U.S. 469, 507 (1989).

121. See text accompanying notes 37–40 above.

122. *Peightal v. Metropolitan Dade County*, 815 F. Supp., 1454, 1461 (S.D. Fla. 1993) (footnote omitted) (emphasis added).

123. See text accompanying note 38 above.

124. See text accompanying note 48 above.

125. *Adarand Constructors v. Pena*, 515 U.S. 200, 224 (1995) (*Croson*, 488 U.S. 469, 494 [1989] [plurality opinion]).

126. See text accompanying note 131 below.

127. There are some historical ironies here. Those, such as Robert Bork, who in the 1950s and 1960s professed fidelity to principles of associative liberty as a reason for opposing civil rights laws that sought to alleviate racial stratification by enlarging the sphere of racial nonrecognition now profess their fidelity to principles of racial nonrecognition as a reason for opposing civil rights laws that seek to alleviate racial stratification by race-conscious means.

128. See generally, Siegel, "Why Equal Protection No Longer Protects"; Reva B. Siegel, "The Rule of Love: Wife Beating as Prerogative and Privacy," *Yale Law Journal* 105 (1996): 2117, 2175–87.

129. Gotanda, "A Critique of 'Our Constitution is Color-Blind'," 6–7.

130. See *Wards Cove Packing Co. v. Antonio*, 490 U.S. 642 (1989) (revising burdens of proof for disparate impact claims in employment discrimination cases to ensure that the Civil Rights Act of 1964 would not create incentives for employers to adopt "racial quotas" or otherwise attempt to hire a racially balanced workforce in order to avoid civil rights law suits).

131. *Adarand Constructors v. Pena*, 515 U.S. 200, 229 (1995).

132. In *Croson*, the Court argued that it was necessary to restrict policies of racial rectification in order to inhibit various social groups from pressing similar demands, the effect of which cumulatively would be to destroy "[t]he dream of a Nation of equal citizens in a society where race is irrelevant to personal opportunity and achievement." *Croson*, 488 U.S. at 505–6.

133. *Adarand*, 515 U.S. at 229.

134. See, e.g., *Croson,* 488 U.S. 469, 507–8 (1989).

135. See, e.g., *ibid.* at 507–9.

136. During the 1970s, some federal courts were interpreting the Fourteenth Amendment in this fashion, but the Court decisively rejected this approach in *Washington v. Davis*, 426 U.S. 229 (1976). See Siegel, "Why Equal Protection No Longer Protects," 1133–34, 1144–45.

137. See *ibid.* at 1133–44.

138. See Jayne N. Suhler, "Texas Professional Schools See Few Minorities Decline in Fall Numbers Linked to Court Decision," *Dallas Morning News*, 5 June 1997, 1A.

139. See Karen Brandon, "In California, Minority Enrollments Falling at Leading Law Schools," *Chicago Tribune*, 6 July 1997; Suhler, 1A.

The Two Declarations
of American Independence

Michael Rogin

Begin with the facts. The founding Hollywood movie, *The Birth of a Nation*, celebrates the Ku Klux Klan. The first talking picture, *The Jazz Singer*, was a blackface film. The all-time top film box office success is *Gone with the Wind*. Blackface minstrelsy was the first and, before movies, the most popular form of mass culture in the United States. Burnt cork and the frontier myth together produced a self-conscious, distinctive, American national culture, the culture that gave birth to Hollywood. Blackface minstrelsy and the myth of the West declared nationalist independence from the Old World. Whereas the political Declaration of Independence made an anticolonial revolution in the name of the equality of all men, the declaration of cultural independence emerged not to free oppressed folk but to constitute national identity out of their subjugation. White supremacy, white over black and red, was the content of this national culture; its form was black and red over white, blacking up and Indianization: "The wilderness ... strips off the garments of civilization and arrays [the colonist] in the hunting shirt and moccasin," wrote Frederick Jackson Turner. "The outcome is ... a new product that is American."[1]

So much is indisputable in spite of political agendas that would wish American history away. How to understand the conflicted relations that the history of the United States ought to force on our attention? Relations between equality and white supremacy, politics and culture, racial domination and racial desire, the two Declarations of Independence — so much is legitimately contested ground. It is the ground on which must rest any discussion of affirmative action.

Both the political and cultural Declarations of Independence crossed racial lines, the latter displaying the racialized bodies whited out beneath the former's universalist claims. "That old Declaration of Independence" extended what Abraham Lincoln called "the father of all moral principle" to those not "descended by blood from our ancestors."[2] Speaking for equality, the Declaration promised that immigrants could become Americans and black could turn white. Minstrelsy, showing that for some Americans blackness was only skin deep, allowed whites to turn black and back again. Whether one understands blackface as the alternative to the Declaration or the return of its repressed, the two forms together provided Americans with an imagined community, a national home. But the forms that transported settlers and immigrants beyond their Old World identities rested on the fixed statuses of those who did not choose to make the journey, Native and African Americans. And the differentiation of white immigrant workers from colored chattel, organic to the creation of race-based slavery at the origins of the United States, repeated itself — under burnt cork and Jim Crow — for the waves of European immigrants that came to these shores after legal slavery had come to an end. The people held in bondage and denied all citizenship rights fronted for the making of Americans. What is the bearing of our racialized national culture on the color-blind invocation of individual rights?[3]

The First Declaration of Independence
John Patrick Diggins, Distinguished Professor of History at the City University of New York, has also recently discovered two Declarations of Independence. His first Declaration derives "equal and inalienable" rights from the "state of nature." "The second part of the Declaration, which no one remembers," charges Diggins, introduced a "spurious...list of grievances" against George III. Affirmative action inherits this "shameless politics of whining," according to Diggins, only now "white racists and male chauvinists have replaced George III as the specter of complaint." Defending the "hereditary privilege" that the first Declaration attacked, affirmative action on Diggins's account rejects the first Declaration's "individualistic spirit" in favor of "group opportunity."[4]

Diggins's list of grievances reaches its "ultimate hypocrisy" when Thomas Jefferson blames the king of England for slavery.

Jefferson's hypocrisy extends to his critic, however, for by invoking slavery to oppose affirmative action, the historian who claims to be repudiating the second Declaration of Independence is actually speaking from inside it. The climax of Diggins's second Declaration exposes the Orwellian logic — slavery is freedom — by which the Jefferson who evades responsibility for the peculiar institution becomes the father of affirmative action, and those who recognize the historical burden of slavery and white supremacy are made to endorse the hereditary privilege they are actually fighting against.

Splitting the first Declaration from the second, the Distinguished Professor of History is making American history disappear. For the original American state of nature on which Diggins and Jefferson stand spawned not only individual rights but also Indian dispossession and chattel slavery. The slave owner who fathered the Declaration of Independence bequeathed to Americans a doubled national birth in hereditary group privilege and individualism, as Diggins recognizes, but he did so by conjoining slavery to natural right. The Declaration of Independence, demanding freedom from enslavement to England for a new nation built on slavery, is the core product of that mésalliance in political theory, just as blackface is its central cultural progeny. Instead of dividing the Declaration of Independence in two to save us from affirmative action, better to understand the symbiosis to which affirmative action is one response.

The racialized foundations of the United States erupt on the surface of the document declaring our national birth. The Declaration is now a visibly hysterical text, since the editors of Jefferson's autobiography (in which Jefferson included the Declaration) use three typefaces to distinguish between three drafts: the passages of Jefferson's original that remain in the final version, those excised by the convention, and those added to Jefferson's language. Although the entire Declaration shows the marks of multiple authorship, only the section on slavery is rendered incoherent by their omnipresence. Jefferson himself, as Diggins recognizes, sought to blame the king of England for inflicting slavery and the slave trade on the colonies, although the crown's effort to regulate the trade in slaves, sugar, rum, and molasses was actually a cause of the Revolution. But Jefferson's displacement of the crime was too antislavery for other southern delegates, and the document signed at Independence Hall retains only the accusation against George III of inciting slave insurrection.[5]

The Declaration of Independence, as its multiple drafts expose, bequeathed a Janus-faced legacy to the new nation — the logic on the one hand that the equality to which white men were naturally born could be extended to women and slaves, and the foundation on the other of white freedom on black servitude. Slavery's deep embeddedness in the United States produced the Declaration's slide from condemning slavery for inflicting bondage to blaming slaves for demanding freedom (a displacement about which Diggins, concerned instead to defend George III, is silent). As that reversal infected Jefferson himself, moreover, it took a sexualized turn. Faced with southern resistance, including his own, to ending hereditary servitude, Jefferson grounded slavery in an irredeemable defect in black bodies that neither conversion to Christianity nor emancipation could cure. Jefferson's *Notes on Virginia* appended to his proposal to emancipate slaves the speculations of "science" on the inferiority of Africans in "nature." Because black men desired white women, wrote Jefferson, they could not be freed without "staining the blood" of their former masters. Although the father of the Declaration favored returning freed slaves to Africa, his twin policies of segregation — slave and Indian removal — worked only in Indian policy. Jefferson's wish to "remove [blacks] beyond the reach of mixture," conflicting as it did with actual white dependence on African Americans, issued forth in a quadruple fantasy — that interracial sex was a barrier to emancipation, that it stained blood, that it was driven by black and not white practice, and that colonization could solve the problem.[6]

Slave owners like Jefferson — his father-in-law, his nephew, and likely the father of the Declaration himself — produced children "descended by blood from our ancestors" whose condition, Lincoln notwithstanding, followed that of their slave mothers. Claiming that it was the black desire for white that required the separation of the races, Jefferson inverted a white desire for black. That desire took the forms of labor and sex, chattel slavery and miscegenation, in Jefferson's time. As expressive performance — blackface minstrelsy — white possession of black would help produce a second, cultural, Declaration of Independence during the age of Andrew Jackson.

The Second Declaration of Independence

Indian land and black labor generated the Euro-Afro-Americas trade that laid the foundation for commodity agriculture, industrial production, and state power in the United States. Slavery not only financed and undergirded the American Revolution; by keeping the propertyless proletariat racially stigmatized and in chains, as Edmund Morgan showed, it permitted the assertion of natural rights for the white population without threatening social revolution at home.[7] Chattel slavery, the expropriation of Indian and Mexican land, and the repressive use and exclusion of Chinese and Mexican American labor were the conditions of American freedom rather than exceptions to it.

Racial subordination formed the American nation, giving racist stereotypes an intractable material base resistant to the wish for equality. Thus white predation was inverted and assigned to colored nature, most famously in the attributions to Indians of violence and lack of respect for the property of others, and in the assignment to black men of laziness and the sexual desire for white women. The fantasy of racial contamination names, against itself, the contaminated origins of the United States in white supremacy. But a paradox lies at the heart of the racial basis of the formation of the United States. For the development of a distinctive national identity, the emancipation of the United States from colonial dependence on England, derived not only from expropriated Indian land and black labor but also from a proclaimed intimacy between whites and peoples of color. The society that developed materially from establishing rigid boundaries between the white and dark races developed culturally from transgressing those boundaries. Hysteria over the mixing of bodily fluids issued forth in racial cross-dressing. The supremacist elevation of the white above the inferior races constituted red and black as points of attraction. White men entered, in sexual and theatrical invasion, the black bodies they had consigned to physicalized inferiority. Minstrelsy practiced what James Snead calls " 'exclusionary emulation,' the principle whereby the power and trappings of black culture are imitated while at the same time their black originators are segregated away and kept at a distance."[8] Racial aversion alone cannot account for the American history of race-based inequality. American identity was formed as well out of destructive racial desire.

Westward expansion, market revolution, and political democratization produced a national culture in the antebellum United States. Ralph Waldo Emerson's demand that intellectual "emancipation" follow political freedom and Herman Melville's insistence that "the Declaration of Independence makes a difference" both found fulfillment in Jefferson's dual legacy of natural rights and natural, race-based, inequality — on the one hand in the literature of the American Renaissance, and on the other in the "American School" of anthropology, which derived racial hierarchy from scientific measurements of the skull. As artists and scientists were striving for international renown, moreover, the mass public was devouring sensation novels, reform tracts, domestic melodramas, gothic stories, captivity narratives, and frontier tall tales. The canonized writers themselves drew on "a raw and vibrant Americanism" in popular literature, writes David Reynolds, to combat staid, genteel European imports. The Age of Jackson produced the frontier hero — Daniel Boone, Davy Crockett, Leatherstocking. But when James Gordon Bennett decided in the 1830s to "blacken his face," to attract an audience for the *New York Herald* with scandal and sensation, his turn of phrase pointed to the most popular and nationalist form of all. For the Jacksonian period was marked by urban as well as westward expansion. And it also gave birth — in the cities, not the countryside, among the new working class and not the pioneers, in relation to African not Native Americans — to the first form of American mass culture: blackface minstrelsy. Like Leslie Fiedler's classic American literature, minstrelsy was an all-male entertainment form, combining racial and gender cross-dressing, male bonding and racial exclusion, misogyny and drag.[9]

The Age of Jackson, which began a decade before Old Hickory first ran for president with the slave-owning general's nationalist military campaigns against English and Native Americans, combined political and cultural democratization. American blackface is a product of that moment. Yankee, backwoodsman, and blackface minstrel, emerging simultaneously in assertions of American nationalism, were the first voices of the American vernacular against aristocratic Europe. Each proclaiming a regional identity — Northeast, West, and South — each also came to signify the new nation as a whole. The Yankee became Uncle Sam. The backwoodsman metamorphosed into the western hero of the frontier myth. But both these figures were surpassed in national appeal by the minstrel. Edwin Forrest was, in 1820, the first actor on the American stage to impersonate a plantation slave. Three years later, T. D. Rice, claiming to imitate a crippled black hostler, began to "jump Jim Crow." Coming out of the commercial bustle on the Ohio River, associating Jim Crow with crossdressing racial performance by blacked up white before it acquired the later meaning of the legal segregation of the races, the enormously popular "Daddy" Rice combined Yankee, frontiersman, and minstrel into a single national icon. Dan Emmett introduced the blackface minstrel troupe in New York in 1842, and minstrels performed at the White House two years later. For the next half century "our only original American institution," as one minstrel called it, remained the most popular mass spectacle in the United States.[10]

Minstrelsy's successors, vaudeville, Tin Pan Alley, motion pictures, and radio, did not so much displace as incorporate blackface. It also spread to the urban nightlife that, at the turn of the twentieth century, drew the respectable working and middle classes out of their homes and into places of public entertainment. Only in "the world of commercial amusements . . . that straddled the social divisions of class and ethnicity," writes David Nasaw, "could [urban dwellers] submerge themselves in a corporate body, an 'American' public." The blacked up white body unified the body politic and purified it of black physical contamination. Public sites signified their respectability by barring or segregating African Americans in the audience as they presented "darkey shows" and "coon songs" on stage.[11]

Ethnic stereotypes performed in blackface were a vaudeville staple. Freeman Gosden and Charles Correll, white men with black voices, invented the serial form that established a distinctive niche for radio. Their *Amos 'n' Andy* became the most popular radio show at the end of the jazz age and the beginning of the New Deal. *Show Boat*, the first Broadway musical play (where the story was more than a pro forma excuse for the songs), premiered the same year as *The Jazz Singer*, 1927. *Show Boat*'s subplot featured one major trope in racial mixing, the tragic mulatta who tries to pass; the play utilized the other, blacking up (*The Jazz Singer*'s subject), since Tess Gardella, billed as "Aunt Jemima," played Queenie in blackface. As *Show Boat* also testifies, white

Americans created a national popular music by capitalizing on black roots, from Stephen Foster's "Oh! Susanna" and "Old Folks at Home," performed by minstrels in the age of Jackson, to Irving Berlin's "Alexander's Ragtime Band," George Gershwin's "Swanee," and Jerome Kern's "Old Man River" during the blackface revitalization of the early twentieth century, to Elvis Presley and his successors, who took off from black music and performance styles after literal blackface had lost national legitimacy. Most important of all in the first half of the twentieth century were motion pictures.[12]

The Old Hollywood

Hollywood's importance in making Americans, in giving those from diverse points of class, ethnic, and geographic origin a common imagined community, is by now a commonplace. What is not often noticed is that four race movies — *Uncle Tom's Cabin* (1902), *Birth of a Nation* (1915), *The Jazz Singer* (1927), and *Gone with the Wind* (1939) — provide the scaffolding for American film history. They instantiate the transformative moments in American film — combining box office success, critical recognition of revolutionary significance, formal innovations, and shifts in the cinematic mode of production.[13]

Whereas the racialized character of mass entertainment appeared on the blackface surface in the decades surrounding the Civil War, motion pictures in classic Hollywood normally buried their racial foundations in white over black. Romances, melodramas, social problem pictures, westerns and other adventure stories, historical epics, gangster and detective films, comedies — it is rare to find black and white (in the racial sense) at the center of these genre films. But the transformative moments in American cinema go beneath the marginal, everyday, African American presence on screen — as servants, entertainers, and buffoons. When film took its great leaps forward, it returned to its buried origins. Then it exposed the cinematic foundations of American freedom in American slavery.

With Edwin S. Porter's trilogy of 1902–3, the history of American movies begins. It begins with race. Porter filmed, successively, *The Life of an American Fireman*, a semidocumentary about the modern city, *Uncle Tom's Cabin*, an entirely familiar drama set (as his subtitle announced) "in slavery days," and *The Great Train*

Robbery, the first important movie western and the first block-buster film. The overwhelming majority of early motion pictures, whether real or staged documentaries or filmed vaudeville routines, did not tell stories; each segment of Porter's trilogy did, for Porter was initiating the shift to the cinematic narratives that would shortly dominate the industry. Porter was not just telling any stories, moreover, but those that composed national mythography. He was bringing into the new century and the new medium the three figures who had long defined American regional identity: Yankee (modernized as urban-dweller), frontiersman, and minstrel.[14]

Porter chose techniques that matched the already-existing regional symbolisms. Although the most lavish and expensive film to date, and the first to use intertitles, *Uncle Tom's Cabin* was formally the least innovative of Porter's three breakthrough films. Set in the past and in the South, *Uncle Tom's Cabin* is static; set in the metropolitan present and on the moving frontier, the other two films are dynamic. *Fireman* displays the heterogeneity of modern urban life and the absence of a singular bourgeois subjectivity.[15] *Uncle Tom's Cabin* has, by contrast, a single point of view, and it is not an abolitionist one. The conflict in the film occurs not between antislavery heroes and proslavery villains, but rather between the plantation and the outsiders who threaten it. Those menacing the slaves intrude into the happy, interracial, plantation home. The plantation features emotional, physical contact among Tom, Little Eva ("Tom and Eva in the Garden"), and St. Clair, and (in several scenes) happy, dancing slaves. (The combination of the two modes would reach the screen again in the enormously popular 1930s Shirley Temple/Bojangles Robinson southerns.) Whether as entertainers or protagonists, all the blacks are whites in blackface; the prefilmic form of popular entertainment most organically incorporated into *Uncle Tom's Cabin* is minstrelsy.[16]

Uncle Tom's Cabin imagines American community in the historical and personal past — the lost child, Little Eva, and the maternal, sacrificed, Uncle Tom. These figures had such a hold on the American imagination — coming as they did from the most popular novel and set of touring theatricals of the nineteenth century — that seven more silent film versions would follow Porter's in the next quarter-century.[17]

Sergei Eisenstein distinguished in D.W. Griffith between modern form and traditional, patriarchal, provincial content. That contrast separates not form from content in Porter, but *Fireman* from *Uncle Tom's Cabin* — with the crucial difference that Porter does not depict the traditional as patriarchal but shows it through a maternal blackface lens. Eisenstein's distinction entirely fails to capture *Birth of a Nation*, however. Porter filmed three separate regional identities; Griffith combined them into a single national epic. *Birth of a Nation* (1915) originated Hollywood cinema in the ride of the Ku Klux Klan against black political and sexual revolution. "The longest, costliest, most ambitious, most spectacular American movie to date," its technique, expense, length, mass audience, critical reception, and influential historical vision all identify *Birth* as the single most important movie ever made. *Uncle Tom's Cabin*, with Porter at the camera, derived from the artisanal mode of film production; *Birth* confirmed the period of directorial control.[18]

Griffith's antebellum plantation may have a more patriarchal inflection than Porter's, but both filmmakers line up the plantation with loss and defeat. Griffith's new nation is not born from northern victory in the Civil War, however, but from the ride (derived from *The Battle of Elderbush Gulch*, his own western movie) of the Ku Klux Klan. The Klan rides to rescue not a mother and child threatened by fire but a white woman menaced by a black rapist. As if to underline the status of the black menace as white fantasy, *Birth*'s two rapists and mulatto seductress are whites in blackface. White sheets smash blacked-up faces in the climax of *Birth of a Nation*. Griffith's fundamental contribution to full-length motion pictures was to join "the intimate and the epic";[19] he linked the personal and the historical through racial fantasy. Transcendentalizing the material birth pangs of immigrant, industrial America, Griffith supplied the postbellum United States with its national myth of origins.

Just as Griffith emancipated cinema from its dependence on prefilmic entertainment, so he rose above the film audience of which Porter was a participant part. Film historians argue over whether films before Griffith actually spoke for their immigrant working-class audiences and not just to them. What is certain is that the period in film history that followed Griffith brought immigrants to Hollywood power. By the 1920s men like Porter and Griffith had lost out to immigrant Jews, whose rise to the top of the motion picture business coincided with the development of the Hollywood studio system.[20]

The men creating mass production studios were rising from their working-class and petty entrepreneurial roots to positions as captains of industry. They were transforming local scenes of maker/distributor/audience interaction into centralized hierarchies that revolved around producer power, mass markets, and star fame. As was not the case with the artisanal mode of film production (and with the exception of certain directors and stars), a clear line now separated owners and executives from workers. Given the importance of the immigrant working class as an audience for early cinema, that immigrant Jews should come to dominate Hollywood only once they left the ghetto behind is from one point of view a paradox. From another — that exemplified by Louis B. Mayer when he changed his birthday from the day of his first birth to July 4 — it exemplifies the American dream.

That dream of ethnic Americanization, the moguls' own story, is the subject of the first talking picture, the founding movie of Hollywood sound, *The Jazz Singer* (1927). *The Jazz Singer* was a pure product of the studio system, a production assembly line that turned out film after film. Alan Crosland directed *The Jazz Singer*, but Warner Brothers was in charge. But if the genius of the system, in Tom Schatz's phrase,[21] produced *The Jazz Singer*, the film celebrated an individual genius, Al Jolson. The blackface performer Jolson was the most popular entertainer of his day, and *The Jazz Singer* turned his success story into a generic family melodrama of immigrant generational revolt. Whereas *Uncle Tom's Cabin* and *Birth of a Nation* used burnt cork unselfconsciously, innocently exposing the white stake in possessing imaginary blackness, *The Jazz Singer* makes the blackface method its subject. Burnt cork is the magical substance and transitional object that catalyzes the jazz singer's American family romance, his wish to replace his natural parents, give birth to himself, and — singing "My Mammy" to his gentile girlfriend and his immigrant Jewish mother — emotionally to negotiate the resulting breach. Reborn in blackface, the jazz singer makes melting-pot music for his new American home. Burnt cork initiates him into intense expressive states — the melancholy of loss, the agony of conflict, and the ecstasy of paradise regained. To make himself over into "a new product that is American" (in the urban version of Turner's frontier) the jazz singer puts on the mask of the black American who, as the condition for ethnic mobility, must remain fixed in place.[22]

Birth of a Nation was the most widely seen movie of the silent period, The Jazz Singer broke all existing box office records, and Jolson's blackface sequel, The Singing Fool (1928), became the leading money-maker between Birth of a Nation and Gone with the Wind (1939). That David O. Selznick production was the first example of the producer unit system, the method of making films that would come to dominate the new Hollywood, where an entrepreneur assembled the team for a single blockbuster. Gone with the Wind remains, in constant dollars, Hollywood's all-time top box office success.[23]

By the time Selznick made Gone with the Wind, the racial formula for cinematic breakthrough was fully in place. Gone with the Wind established the future of the technicolor spectacular by returning to American film origins in the plantation myth. Jolson sang "My Mammy" in blackface to his immigrant Jewish mother. Selznick hired Hattie McDaniel because he could "smell the magnolias" when the actress came dressed for her screen test "as a typical Old Southern Mammy." Although the producer compared the political objections to Gone with the Wind to the campaign against Birth of a Nation, Selznick also insisted he had "cleaned up" Margaret Mitchell's Pulitzer Prize–winning novel. Turning the book's black rapist into a poor white, having a black man run to rescue Scarlett instead of to rape her, Selznick portrayed his black characters as "loveable, faithful, high-minded people" who, as he put it, "would leave no impression but a very nice one." Black sexual aggression menaces white freedom in Birth; black loyalty supports white freedom in The Jazz Singer and Gone with the Wind; it perhaps even allows, Diane Roberts has suggested, a safe sexual darkening of Scarlett and Rhett. Mammy is Scarlett's foundation; she is the ground for the jazz singer's mourning, for his losing and finding a home. Although Selznick replaced Jolson's blackface mammy with the putative real thing, far from playing themselves in Gone with the Wind, black actors and actresses were assigned roles minstrelsy had already defined.[24]

In the foundational movies of classic Hollywood as in the routine studio product, black Americans swing between positive and negative poles, from "benevolence, harmless and servile guardianship, and endless love," in Toni Morrison's words, to "insanity, illicit sexuality, and chaos."[25] The first movies to attack race prejudice, made in the wake of World War II, challenged Hollywood's imaginary white Negroes in literal or figurative blackface. But those films, in spite of their intentions, bore an unacknowledged indebtedness to the tradition they wanted to repudiate.[26] The civil rights political victories of the 1960s, far more revolutionary than those films, took the most important strides toward racial equality since the end of Reconstruction. The civil rights movement fell short of its goals, however, producing in reaction not the multicultural regime that many commentators imagine with horror but rather a politics of binary racial polarization.

The New Hollywood

The two Declarations of American Independence always enjoyed relations of mutual support — racism justifying the exclusion of peoples of color from Jefferson's apparent universalism, popular culture supplying the low bodies dematerialized in high-principled abstraction. The universalist judgment against those trapped in their own particularities placed "race under representation," in David Lloyd's pun, by preserving an ideal realm uncontaminated by lower selves and lower orders. Blackface represented in culture those denied self-representation in politics.[27]

Discrediting literal burnt cork left unshattered the deep structure of American history, in which the black role must serve whites. The defeat of legalized white supremacy did make a difference, however. Whereas Jim Crow made radical the extension of the first Declaration of Independence to African Americans, current invocations of "civil rights" avoid responsibility for the open racial secret by clothing their demonology in color-blind wrappings. As long as pervasive material inequality between whites and peoples of color coexists with formal legal equality, racialized representations will shadow the language of individual rights to dominate American politics and culture.

Whereas the exclusion of blacks from American politics had permitted cleavages among whites, the entrance of African Americans onto the political stage in the 1960s introduced a race-based regime into national two-party competition. A majority among whites has voted against a majority among peoples of color in every presidential election since 1964, and racial codes dominate public discourse. If, as a *New York Times* reporter has recently written, "cultural issues like abortion, pornography, and homosexuality" lack the "political heft" of the "social issues" — "racial preferences, ... capital punishment and prisons and knocking people off welfare" — that is because the (euphemistically labeled) "social issues" target racialized minorities.[28] Moreover, just as blackface Americanized European immigrants by underlining the demarcation between white and black, so the new immigration (that also dates from the civil rights era, from immigration law changes of the 1960s) has widened the divide between model minority members on the one side and "illegal aliens," "welfare queens," and violent black men on the other.

The racialized political discourse that took on new life in the 1960s has intensified in recent years — as is evident simply by listing the names (in chronological order) of Willie Horton, Clarence Thomas, Rodney King, Rickie Ray Rector, Lani Guinier, Jocelyn Elders, and O. J. Simpson.[29] It climaxed in Simpson's year, 1994. Gaining control of both houses of Congress in 1994 for the first time in forty years, Republicans initiated the Contract with America to which the attack on affirmative action belongs.

1994 political science: California governor Pete Wilson, who favors denying citizenship to children born in the United States of "illegal aliens," successfully promotes a state initiative depriving undocumented immigrants of health, education, and welfare benefits and requiring nurses, doctors, teachers, and social workers to turn suspects (identifiable by their color and accent) in. He also sponsors an initiative requiring life sentences for all those convicted of three violent crimes, a law supported at the national level by President Bill Clinton. Clinton's 1994 crime bill extends the death penalty, fatal evidence of American exceptionalism from other Western democracies, to increasing numbers of convicts and categories of crimes. California's Three Strikes Initiative, along with the extended prison sentences mandated in other state and federal laws, will require shifting billions of dollars in scarce state resources from higher education to the prison system. The main cause of the expansion of the prison population so far lies in drug policy, where enormous racial disparities in conviction and sentencing for comparable offenses have helped produce a disproportionately black and Latino prison population. "The negro" is no longer the "model prisoner" of early social science, celebrated for his "cheerful" adjustment to slavery; all the more reason to confine him to jail.[30]

In California, as in other states, a prison industrial complex is replacing both the military industrial complex and the public education system. California blacks and Latinos, heavily overrepresented in the prison industrial complex (people of color are incarcerated at six times the rate of whites), are greatly underrepresented in higher education, a disproportion that will increase with the Wilson-initiated end of affirmative action in the state university system and passage of the Wilson-supported "California Civil Rights Initiative" prohibiting consideration of race in hiring and educational admissions. Whites, who will soon be a minority in California, still comprise a large majority of the voting population. Although Governor Wilson is racializing California politics to regain lost popularity at home (successfully winning reelection as governor but failing in his campaign for the White House), the *New Republic*'s editor praises the state's "diverse multiracial population" for supporting the governor against racial divisiveness and in favor of "equality before the law." Also acting in the name of constitutional color blindness, the Supreme Court anticipates the 1994 election returns by ruling out race as a predominant consideration in drawing congressional district lines (now that racial gerrymandering is, for the first time, being used to elect representatives of color).[31]

Newt Gingrich, the new Speaker of the House of Representatives after the 1994 elections, proposes another carceral institution besides the prison, the orphanage, to house the offspring of unwed mothers whom the Contract with America would deprive of state aid to dependent children. The parental tie may be severed for Gingrich, as in the original peculiar institution, because the condition of these children would follow that of their mothers. (The Speaker of the House did not reference slavery, of course, but the 1938 Mickey Rooney movie, *Boys' Town*.) The sins of the mothers for which the children are to be punished — ending Jefferson's restriction of desire to black men — are sexual. Jefferson had suspected that the evidence of science would find that blacks were "by nature" separate and unequal. Daniel Patrick Moynihan, author of the report on "The Negro Family" that first blamed racial inequality on black "matriarchy," is one of only eleven senators to oppose ending welfare entitlements for the children of unwed mothers. Moynihan nonetheless offers the opinion in 1994 that the rise in out-of-wedlock births "mark[s] such a change in the human condition that biologists would talk of a 'speciation' — the creation of a new species." *Speciation* is the Darwinian word for the evolution of a population that (the Jefferson/Moynihan wish?) cannot interbreed with the species from which it developed.[32]

Speciation is merely Moynihan's free association. Richard Herrnstein and Charles Murray's 1994 best-seller, *The Bell Curve*, providing full scientific apparatus, claims to have discovered racially based, genetic differences in intelligence. *The Bell Curve* received, in the fall of 1994, the *New York Times Book Review* seal of approval, along with J. Philip Rushton's revival of nineteenth-century scientific racism's theoretical core (in the enterprise that provided elaborate scaffolding for Jefferson's original musings and for the science of the "American School"), the fantasy that evolution had created three separate races, the Mongoloid, the Negroid, and the Caucasoid.[33]

1994 Hollywood: The year's major motion pictures pay homage to *The Jazz Singer* and *Birth of a Nation*. *The Jazz Singer* returns twice, once in Woody Allen's *Bullets over Broadway*, set in the 1920s, which opens with *The Jazz Singer*'s "Toot, Toot, Tootsie" and features a grotesque mammy; and once in Whoopi Goldberg's *Corrina Corrina*, set in the 1950s, in which Corrina Washington cares for Manny Singer's silent motherless daughter and restores her voice, saves his advertising agency job by jazzing up his singing jingles (here the specific source is Louise Beavers's mammy role in *Mr. Blandings Builds His Dream House*), and, in the film's climax, finally overcomes Manny's emotional rigidity as he buries his head in her arms.

Corrina is a black culture donor, in Cecil Brown's phrase; her relationship to Manny offers the now ubiquitous Hollywood promise that personal bonds (usually between men) can overcome historically rooted racial inequality.[34] African Americans are also culture donors in the two movies that achieve the greatest combined critical and popular success of 1994, the films that bring *Birth of a Nation* up to date. *Pulp Fiction* is energized, following *Birth*, by an imaginary black underworld (to recall Toni

Morrison's words) of violence, "insanity, illicit sexuality, and chaos." Linguistically, libidinally, and politically, blacks govern this Reconstruction world turned upside down; *Pulp Fiction*'s interracial buddies live in terror of the black crime boss and stud for whom they work. In one of the major stories that comprise the film, the two hit men must dispose of the spattered remains of the "nigger in the car" whom they have inadvertently blown away. Another episode, the central one, climaxes when the intimidating black boss is cut down to size in a graphically depicted anal rape.

Pulp Fiction was one of two films to monopolize the 1994 Academy Award nominations. It lost out to another interracial buddy movie (best picture, director, actor, editing, screenplay adaptation, visual effects), *Forrest Gump*. Senate majority leader Bob Dole, running for president against the "nightmares of depravity" in Hollywood and rap music, offers the "family fare" of *Forrest Gump* as his alternative.[35] And one traditional mode of family entertainment on which that movie draws is blackface, for a repeated joke makes harmless good fun (or so the filmmakers and senate majority leader seem to think) of a black soldier's protruding lower lip — the classic grotesque black mouth of minstrelsy. The film's idea of fellowship is to bond its feebleminded hero with this slow-speaking, bewildered-looking, Stepin Fetchit and, after he dies, with a double amputee.

Creating a community of the afflicted, *Forrest Gump* imagines itself speaking for equality, the first Declaration of Independence. In the film's myth of origins, however, the second Declaration of Independence gives birth to *Forrest Gump*. A few months before *Forrest Gump*'s release, the Library of Congress repressed what J. Hoberman calls our national "birth rite" by excluding *Birth of a Nation* from its collection of "Cinema's First Century."[36] Not to worry. Just as *Bullets over Broadway* opens with the sound of *The Jazz Singer*, so *Forrest Gump* offers at its beginning the image of *Birth of a Nation*. As Forrest tells the story of his own birth, what appears on screen is a Ku Klux Klan scene lifted (or simulated) from Griffith's film. Cutting from *Birth*'s hero masking his face to the massed, white-sheeted men on horseback ("they dressed up as ghosts, or something"), the interpolated footage illustrates the work of the founder of the Klan, "the great Civil War hero" Nathan Bedford Forrest, for whom the 1994 Forrest was named.

(The visual quotation stops before *Birth*'s Klan goes to work, lynching a blackface rapist.) *Birth of a Nation* thus takes its place at the head of the other newsreels from American history — the John Kennedy, Robert Kennedy, and John Lennon assassinations; the George Wallace, Ronald Reagan, and Gerald Ford attempts; the Richard Nixon resignation; and the Lyndon Johnson speech — through which Forrest will move (in the award-winning visual effects) and that will fail to touch him. *Forrest Gump* passed *Star Wars* in 1995 to move into third place among the top grossing movies of all time.[37]

"You can't defend practices that are based on group preferences as opposed to individual opportunities," says Connecticut Senator Joseph Lieberman in the spring of that same year. Affirmative action "is un-American ... because ... America is about individuals, not about averages or groups."[38] One need not endorse the remedy of affirmative action to see that Lieberman is calling on the first Declaration of Independence to make the second one disappear. His falsification of American history, however, speaks the truth it is intended to bury, for the accusation of un-American activities (once the stock in trade of the House Un-American Activities Committee) turns opponents of white supremacy into aliens in their own land. Innocent of the history that has named him, Forrest Gump is not alone.

NOTES

1. Portions of the present essay are adapted from my *Blackface, White Noise: Jewish Immigrants in the Hollywood Melting Pot* (Berkeley, 1996). The Turner quotation is in Frederick Jackson Turner, *The Frontier in American History* (New York, 1920), 4.

2. Abraham Lincoln, speech at Chicago, 10 June 1858, in *Abraham Lincoln: Selected Speeches, Messages, and Letters*, ed. T. Harry Williams (New York, 1957), 91–92.

3. Also a metaphorical cross-dressing, and in no way merely second in importance to minstrelsy, the frontier myth made out of Indian dispossession a politics and culture that both overlaps with and departs from the race relations visible under burnt cork. The frontier myth is chronicled elsewhere, most authoritatively now in Richard Slotkin's trilogy, *Regeneration Through Violence: The Mythology of the American Frontier, 1600–1860* (Middletown, CT, 1973), *The Fatal Environment: The Myth of the Frontier in the Age of Industrialization, 1800–*

1890 (New York, 1985), and *Gunfighter Nation: The Myth of the Frontier in Twentieth-Century America* (New York, 1992).

4. John Patrick Diggins, "The Pursuit of Whining," *New York Times*, 25 September 1995, A11.

5. Thomas Jefferson, "Autobiography," in *The Life and Selected Writings of Thomas Jefferson*, ed. Adrienne Koch and William Peden (New York, 1944), 25–26; James A. Rawley, *The Transatlantic Slave Trade: A History* (New York, 1981), 311–19, 342–46; Stephen Hopkins, "The Rights of Colonies Examined [1763]," in *Tracts of the American Revolution, 1763–1776*, ed. Merrill Jenson (Indianapolis, 1967), 41–62.

6. Thomas Jefferson, *Notes on Virginia*, in *Life and Selected Writings*, 256, 262. See also Winthrop Jordan, *White over Black: American Attitudes Toward the Negro, 1550–1812* (Chapel Hill, NC, 1968), 429–81; James Campbell and James Oakes, "The Invention of Race; Rereading *White over Black*," *Reviews in American History* 21 (1993): 172–83.

7. Edmund Morgan, *American Slavery, American Freedom: The Ordeal of Colonial Virginia* (New York, 1975).

8. James Snead, *White Screens/Black Images* (New York, 1994), 60.

9. F. O. Matthiesen, *The American Renaissance: Art and Expression in the Age of Emerson and Whitman* (New York, 1941); Stephen Jay Gould, *The Mismeasure of Man* (New York, 1981), 42; Michael Rogin, *Subversive Genealogy: The Politics and Art of Herman Melville* (New York, 1983), 15–23, 70–76; David S. Reynolds, *Beneath the American Renaissance* (New York, 1988), quoted 170, 174, 205; Lawrence Buell, "American Literary Emergence as a Postcolonial Phenomenon," *American Literary History* 4 (Fall 1992): 411–42; Leslie Fiedler, *Love and Death in the American Novel* (New York, 1960). The indispensable studies of nineteenth-century minstrelsy are Robert Toll, *Blacking Up: The Minstrel Show in Nineteenth-Century America* (New York, 1974); William W. Austin, *"Susanna," "Jeannie," and "The Old Folks at Home": The Songs of Stephen C. Foster from His Time to Ours*, 2d ed. (Urbana, IL, 1989); Alexander Saxton, *The Rise and Fall of the White Republic: Class Politics and Mass Culture in Nineteenth-Century America* (New York, 1990), 119–80; David R. Roediger, *The Wages of Whiteness: Race and the Making of the American Working Class* (London, 1991); Eric Lott, *Love and Theft: Blackface Minstrelsy and the American Working Class* (New York, 1993). A full discussion of minstrelsy would have to address what Lott and Roediger (from different perspectives) make central, the origins of blackface in the northern white working class.

10. Michael Rogin, *Fathers and Children: Andrew Jackson and the Subjugation of the American Indian* (New York, 1975); Joseph Boskin, *Sambo: The Rise and Fall of an American Jester* (New York, 1986), 70; W. T. Lhamon Jr., "Constance

Rourke's Secret Reserve," introduction to Constance Rourke, *American Humor: A Study of the National Character* (1931; reprint, Gainesville, 1986), xxiii, xxiv; Rourke, *American Humor*, 95–104; Lott, *Love and Theft*, 56; Toll, *Blacking Up*, 1–30 (quoted 1); Saxton, *Rise and Fall of the White Republic*, 118–23.

11. Lewis Ehrenberg, *Steppin' Out: New York Night Life and the Transformation of American Culture* (Chicago, 1981); Michael Rogin, "The Great Mother Domesticated: Sexual Difference and Sexual Indifference in D.W. Griffith's *Intolerance*," *Critical Inquiry* 15 (Spring 1989): 525–30; David Nasaw, *Going Out: The Rise and Fall of Public Amusements* (New York, 1994), 1–2, 45–61, 91–94, 115–16 (quoted 45).

12. Melvin Patrick Ely, *The Adventures of Amos 'n' Andy: A Social History of an American Phenomenon* (New York, 1991); Ethan Mordden, "'Show Boat' Crosses Over," *New Yorker*, 3 July 1989, 94; Austin, *"Susanna," "Jeannie,"* and *"The Old Folks at Home"*; Gary Giddins, *Riding on a Blue Note: Jazz and American Pop* (New York, 1981), 5–17.

13. I first made this claim in "Blackface, White Noise: The Jewish Jazz Singer Finds His Voice," *Critical Inquiry* 18 (Spring 1992): 417–20. The following pages expand on and modify that argument.

14. The definitive treatment of Porter is Charles Musser, *Before the Nickelodeon: Edwin S. Porter and the Edison Manufacturing Company* (Berkeley, 1991). On early cinema see also (among many other sources, some cited here) Nasaw, *Going Out*, 134–53, 166; John Fell, ed., *Film Before Griffith* (Berkeley, 1983); Miriam Hansen, *Babel and Babylon: Spectatorship in American Silent Film* (Cambridge, MA, 1991), 23–125; David Bordwell, Janet Staiger, and Kristin Thompson, *The Classical Hollywood Cinema: Film Style and Mode of Production to 1960* (New York, 1965), 183.

15. Compare Musser, *Before the Nickelodeon*, 212–30; Tom Gunning, "Weaving a Narrative: Style and Economic Background in Griffith's Biograph Films," *Quarterly Review of Film Studies* 6 (Winter 1981): 12–25; Tom Gunning, "The Cinema of Attractions: Early Film, Its Spectator, and the Avant-Garde," in Thomas Elsaesser, ed., *Early Cinema* (London, 1990), 56–62; Noel Burch, "Narrative/Diegesis: Threshold, Limits," *Screen* (July–August 1982): 16–33; Janet Staiger, *Interpreting Films: Studies in the Reception of American Cinema* (Princeton, 1992), 101–23; Hansen, *Babel and Babylon*, 90–125.

16. William L. Slout, *"Uncle Tom's Cabin* in American Film History," *Journal of Popular Film* 2 (Spring 1973): 137–52; Donald Bogle, *Toms, Coons, Mulattoes, Mammies, and Bucks* (New York, 1973), 3; Thomas R. Cripps, *Slow Fade to Black: The Negro in American Film, 1900–1942* (New York, 1977), 12–14; Edward D. C. Campbell Jr., *The Celluloid South: Hollywood and the Southern Myth* (Knoxville, TN, 1981), 12–14, 37–39; Staiger, *Interpreting Films*, 101–23.

17. Richard Koszarski, *An Evening's Entertainment, 1915–1928* (Berkeley, 1990), 184.

18. Sergei Eisenstein, *Film Form* (New York, 1949), 197; J. Hoberman, "Our Troubling Birth Rite," *Village Voice*, 3 November 1993, 2–4 (quoted 3); Bordwell, Staiger, and Thompson, *Classical Hollywood Cinema*, 90–142, 183. The discussion of *Birth of a Nation* here is derived from my " 'The Sword Became a Flashing Vision': D.W. Griffith's *Birth of a Nation*," in *"Ronald Reagan," the Movie and Other Episodes in Political Demonology* (Berkeley, 1987).

19. Koszarski, *An Evening's Entertainment*, 214.

20. Bordwell, Staiger, and Thompson, *Classical Hollywood Cinema*, 87–112; Robert Sklar, "Oh! Althusser!: Historiography and the Rise of Cinema Studies," in Robert Sklar and Edwin Musser, eds., *Resisting Images: Essays on Cinema and History* (Philadelphia, 1990), 19–32; Neal Gabler, *An Empire of Their Own: How the Jews Invented Hollywood* (New York, 1988).

21. See Tom Schatz, *The Genius of the System: Hollywood Filmmaking in the Studio Era* (New York, 1988).

22. I discuss *The Jazz Singer* in "Blackface, White Noise."

23. William K. Everson, *American Silent Film* (New York, 1978), 373–74; " 'Gone with the Wind' Champ Again," *Variety*, 4 May 1983, 5; Bordwell, Staiger, and Thompson, *Classical Hollywood Cinema*, 320–29.

24. Carleton Jackson, *Hattie: The Life of Hattie McDaniel* (New York, 1990), 35, 46–51 (quoting Selznick); Patrice Storace, "Look Away, Dixie Land," *New York Review of Books*, 19 December 1991, 24–27; John D. Stevens, "The Black Reaction to *Gone with the Wind*," *Journal of Popular Film* 2 (Fall 1973): 367; Diane Roberts, *The Myth of Aunt Jemima: Representations of Race and Region* (New York, 1994), 171–81.

25. Toni Morrison, "Introduction: Friday on the Potomac," in Toni Morrison, ed., *Race-ing Justice, En-gendering Power: Essays on Anita Hill, Clarence Thomas, and the Construction of Social Reality* (New York, 1992), xv.

26. See my " 'Democracy and Burnt Cork': The End of Blackface, the Beginning of Civil Rights," *Representations* 46 (Spring 1994): 1–34.

27. Compare David Lloyd, "Race Under Representation," *Oxford Literary Review* 13 (Summer 1991): 81; Catherine Gallagher, "The Politics of Culture and the Debate over Representation," *Representations* 5 (Winter 1984): 115–47; Daniel Boyarin and Jonathan Boyarin, "Diaspora: Generation and the Ground of Jewish Identity," *Critical Inquiry* 19 (Summer 1993): 706–7; Gould, *Mismeasure of Man*, 49; Toni Morrison, "Unspeakable Things Unspoken: The Afro-American Presence in American Literature," *Michigan Quarterly Review* 28 (Winter 1989): 14–18.

28. Adam Clymer, "The Presidents' Analysts," *New York Times Book Review*,

10 December 1995, 12. Like the author of the book he is reviewing (Ben Wattenberg, *Values Matter Most* [New York, 1995]), Clymer uses the "social" label to avoid facing up to race.

29. Dramatis personae for the visitor from Mars: George Bush won the presidential election of 1988 by teaming his opponent, Massachusetts governor Michael Dukakis, with *Willie Horton*, the black man who had raped a white woman while on furlough from a Massachusetts prison. *Clarence Thomas*, whose only qualifications were his far-right Christian political associations and the color of his skin, won confirmation to the Supreme Court by accusing those who believed Anita Hill's accusations of sexual harassment of engaging in a "high-tech lynching." After the white policemen whose beating of a black man, *Rodney King*, was recorded on video and played repeatedly on national television, were acquitted by an all-white suburban jury, South Central Los Angeles erupted in flames. Governor Bill Clinton revived his 1992 presidential campaign by flying back to Arkansas to witness the execution of *Rickie Ray Rector*, a brain-damaged convicted black murderer. Clinton withdrew his nomination of *Lani Guinier* as assistant attorney general for civil rights after the *Wall Street Journal* called her a "quota queen" for proposing alternatives to the effective disenfranchisement of black voters who, in a racially polarized electorate, occupy permanent minority statuses. Clinton fired *Jocelyn Elders*, the first black woman surgeon general, for refusing to condemn masturbation as a form of safe sex. *O. J. Simpson* — complete the sentence yourself.

30. Alexander Cockburn, "Beat the Devil," *Nation*, 27 November 1995, 656; Alfred Holt Stone, "Is Race Friction Between Blacks and Whites in the United States Growing and Inevitable?" *American Journal of Sociology* (1908): 692, quoted in Stephen Steinberg, *Turning Back: The Retreat from Racial Justice in American Thought and Policy* (Boston, 1995), 160.

31. Mike Davis, "Hell Factories in the Fields," *Nation*, 20 February 1995, 229–33; Richard Walker, "California Rages Against the Dying of the Light," *New Left Review* 209 (1995): 60–61; Fox Butterfield, "Political Gains by Prison Guards," *New York Times*, 7 November 1995, A1, A15; Andrew Sullivan, "Affirmative Action Is Dead, Even If Clinton Doesn't Know It," *International Herald Tribune*, 25 July 1995, 6. The Supreme Court decision (1993) is *Shaw v. Reno*. For Bob Dole's version of "civil rights," co-authored with the freshman black congressman from Oklahoma elected in 1994, see Bob Dole and J. C. Watts Jr., "A New Civil Rights Agenda," *Wall Street Journal*, 27 July 1995, 6.

32. "The Fight over Orphanages," *Newsweek*, 16 January 1995, 22. Lee Rainwater and William Yancey, *The Moynihan Report and the Politics of Controversy* (Cambridge, MA, 1967), reprints Daniel Patrick Moynihan, "The Negro Family: The Case for National Action," by the then assistant secretary of labor

in the Lyndon Johnson administration, now the senior senator from New York. See also Todd S. Purdom, "The Newest Moynihan," *New York Times Magazine*, 7 August 1994, 36; Robert Pear, "Moynihan Promises Something Different on Welfare," *New York Times*, 14 May 1995, A13; Robin Toner, "Senate Approves Welfare Plan That Would End Aid Guarantee," *New York Times*, 20 September 1995, A1, A17.

33. Richard J. Herrnstein and Charles Murray, *The Bell Curve: Intelligence and Class Structure in American Life* (New York, 1994); J. Philip Rushton, *Race, Evolution, and Behavior: A Life History Perspective* (New Brunswick, NJ, 1994); Malcolm W. Browne, "What Is Intelligence and Who Has It?" *New York Times Book Review*, 16 October 1994, 3, 41, 45–46.

34. On the role of black culture donors in the major 1994 movies, see Cecil Brown, "Doing That Ol' Oscar Soft Shoe," *San Francisco Examiner, Image Magazine*, 26 March 1995, 25–27, 38–41. Aware of the irony, I am borrowing from his discussion. On interracial friendship as Hollywood's solution to the race problem, see Benjamin DeMott, "Put on a Happy Face: Masking the Differences Between Black and White," *Harper's*, September 1995, 31–38.

35. Bernard Weinraub, "Senator Moves to Control Party's Moral Agenda," *New York Times*, 1 June 1995, A1, B10; Bob Dole, "To Shame an Industry," *New York Times*, "Letters," 8 June 1995, A15.

36. Hoberman, "Our Troubling Birth Rite," 2–4.

37. "The Top Money Makers, for Now," *New York Times*, 14 May 1995, H22.

38. Todd S. Purdom, "Senator Deals Blow to Affirmative Action," *New York Times*, 10 March 1995, A10.

Group Preferences, Cultural Diversity, and Social Democracy: Notes Toward a Theory of Affirmative Action

David A. Hollinger

Affirmative action needs a coherent theory. The fair evaluation and survival of programs justified in the name of affirmative action require it. But such a theory has proved elusive, largely because the people who support affirmative action disagree among themselves about what it is and why we need it. While the press is filled with pro and con argumentation, little scrutiny has been given to the structure of the remarkable conversation now under way within the ranks of the people who hope that at least some affirmative action programs can be saved. The disagreements that animate this conversation are visible in public discourse only in muted form. In private, they are expressed more candidly.

Some acquaintances tell me that affirmative action is good because it promotes cultural diversity within the student body and the faculty. Others ridicule this argument as an example of ethno-racial essentialism, carrying the expectation that culture follows blood. My most adamantly antiessentialist friends make the case for campus affirmative action on a wholly different basis: a need to expand the middle class within certain demographic blocs whose members, because of a prejudice triggered by the physical characteristics that serve to identify these blocs, have been historically prevented from achieving upward social mobility. But this is far from the only point at issue. One colleague will tell me that affirmative action is necessary for police departments but not for universities. What relevance affirmative action may have to higher education, another will interject, applies to student admissions but not to faculty hiring. Yet another colleague, learning that this opinion is held by a mutual friend, will condemn the absent apostate for his outrageous moral conceit ("*We* don't need it but businesses and cops do? Ha!") and will proclaim faculty hiring to be the symbolic center of the entire affirmative action enterprise. Meanwhile, one voice will support affirmative action in hiring in all labor markets but not in promotions, while another will speak with passion and cite statistics about "glass ceilings." Critics who preach "merit" against affirmative action are being disingenuous, one person will insist, because the merit system in the university amounts to a complex of subjective preferences created by power and privilege. Yet another equally committed advocate of affirmative action will argue that standardized merit criteria should control the bulk of the admissions and hiring processes, but that a preference for minorities is, like athletic admissions, a valid exception.

In these conversations on my own campus, one colleague will declare that affirmative action in a university must be related directly to an educational function, while another, hearing this quoted, will roll her eyes at such quaint idealism and explain earnestly that the university is an institution like any other and should be used as a manifold instrument of social change. Some people hold affirmative action to be necessary for several ethnoracial groups but no longer for women, while others argue that women need affirmative action in certain contexts, including fire departments and such academic disciplines as engineering and physics. It is said that affirmative action is never appropriate for immigrants but is fully justified for African Americans on account of slavery and its legacy. Someone else will complain that anti-Asian discrimination is worse than most people realize, and yet another voice will suggest that Latinos of all varieties — even recent immigrants from Argentina — should be the beneficiaries of affirmative action on account of the conquest of Mexico in 1848 and the history of American exploitation in the context of the Monroe Doctrine. It may be said that affirmative action is a form of reparations; or, on the contrary, that the concept of reparations is "a hopeless can of worms" except in the case of specific Japanese American families interned during World War II. What really counts, one practical soul will observe, is representation: groups that are underrepresented need affirmative action and we should not divert ourselves with hairsplitting histories of the comparative victimization that lies behind this or that specific case of underrepresentation. "Buying into the representation model," another colleague will sputter, is the fatal mistake that is "bringing affirmative action down."

Affirmative action has much to fear from its enemies, but its future is cast into even greater doubt by the honest divisions within the ranks of its friends. And the honesty of these divergent vindications of affirmative action make them all the more worthy of scrutiny.

The friends of affirmative action have long gotten along without a theory of the sort now demanded in the face of potentially successful opposition. "Affirmative action was never formulated as a coherent policy," notes Stephen Steinberg in a recent, vehement defense of affirmative action, "but evolved through a series of presidential executive orders, administrative policies, and court decisions."[1] Moreover, affirmative action lost an element of clarity it once had when it became entangled with multiculturalism. Indeed, the first step toward a viable theory of affirmative action is to sharply distinguish it from the defense and appreciation of cultural diversity. The effort to protect Americans from the effects of past and continuing ethno-racial discrimination is centered primarily on the physical, not the cultural, properties of human beings. At issue is the significance of the "ethno-racial pentagon," a remarkable artifact virtually unique to the contemporary United States.[2]

Residents of the United States have become accustomed to being classified as African American, Latino, indigenous peoples, European American, or Asian American. Every individual is assigned space in the unequally sized and unequally empowered blocs of this five-part demographic structure. And for good reason. These currently popular labels are based, of course, on the classic color codes — black, brown, red, white, and yellow — that mark the lines of traditional prejudice. They serve well as predictors of the dynamics of mistreatment, and thus as a foundation for initiatives designed to protect people against such mistreatment or to compensate them for it.

Multiculturalism has too often used the ethno-racial pentagon as a convenient basis for organizing the defense of cultural diversity. An example is the widely publicized action taken in 1989 by the faculty of the University of California at Berkeley to require undergraduates to complete a course involving the comparative study of at least three of five designated cultures. The three were to be selected from the ethno-racial pentagon. To be sure, there is plenty of culture in all five blocs of the pentagon. And much of it was created under racist conditions. Racist understandings of what color and shape mean have limited the kinds of cultural choices and creativity people can attain. The pentagon is obviously relevant to cultural studies. Multiculturalism's campaign to win wider public recognition for the cultural creativity of African Americans, Latinos, indigenous peoples, and Asian Americans has been altogether admirable. But culture also transcends these barriers, and multiculturalism has been slow to act on this elementary insight. The ethno-racial pentagon gets its architecture from neither culture nor biology, but from the dynamics of prejudice and oppression in American history and from the need for political tools to overcome the legacy of that victimization. By failing to resist the use of these gross categories for identifying cultures, multiculturalism has saddled us with a program for cultural diversity grounded not in an analysis of actual cultural difference but in a history of victimization justified by what we now recognize to be biologically superficial indicators of human groups. Multiculturalism has not struggled hard enough against the authority that society has traditionally allowed such physical characteristics as skin color and the shape of the face to exert over culture.

What the ethno-racial pentagon is really good for is identifying people according to the physical characteristics that render them most vulnerable to mistreatment and designing antidiscrimination remedies, including affirmative action programs. An individual who has every right to protection from discrimination on the basis of his or her involuntary classification as a member of a historically disadvantaged ethno-racial group may have no interest whatsoever in the culture popularly associated with that group. In some situations, the Anglophilic Chicano writer Richard Rodriguez is no less subject to abuse as a Latino than would be a member of the National Council of La Raza. Even so adamant a proponent of color blindness as Justice Clarence Thomas, were he incautious enough to run a red light in some neighborhoods, deserves protection against the likes of Mark Fuhrman.

Once all antidiscrimination remedies, including affirmative action, are disentangled from multiculturalism, one can more easily address another point of frequent uncertainty. To what extent is the very term *affirmative action* a euphemism for "group preferences"? Steinberg, in an effort to introduce some coherence in the discussion, argues that we should no longer shy away from talking about group preferences. This is the matter of deepest concern to most of the people who argue about affirmative action. Steinberg reminds us that when affirmative action is construed as "outreach," as the going out of one's way to admit, hire, or promote someone who might otherwise be overlooked as a result of their perceived membership in a historically disadvantaged group, even Clarence Thomas claims to be for it.[3]

I believe Steinberg is correct to insist that advocates of affirmative action from now on ought to make their case, as Steinberg himself does, by unambiguously defending preferences for some groups at the expense of others. To do otherwise is not only to invite confusion but also to obscure, as Steinberg claims, the fact that most of what is regarded as progress under affirmative action — especially the increased numbers of black people in certain occupational positions within the workforce and the professions — can be attributed not to outreach, but to the "goals and timetables" that push employers and institutions toward the actual preferring of some individuals over others on the basis of their sex or ethno-racial status.[4]

Persons comfortable with outreach, including those who believe group preferences were once justified but are no longer, would do well to stop calling themselves advocates of affirmative action. Let the old term die. Events have deprived it of what power it once had to denote a single cluster of initiatives. It is group preferences that need clear justification. Outreach can go forward with very little additional theoretical discussion. Once *affirmative action* is retired from our working vocabulary and replaced with *outreach* and *group preferences*, the challenge of developing a coherent theory for the latter can be more easily recognized.

The basic terms of that challenge are contained in two questions raised by Randall Kennedy. "Do we ultimately want to create a plural society in which racial groups such as African Americans have an official status (like Native American tribes) as collectivities to which individuals belong, or do we want an integrated society in which an individual's race is of no legal significance?" Following this query, Kennedy offers another: do we want group preference as "a transitional institution that will at some point wither away," or as "a permanent feature of our society that will accommodate competition between contending ...groups?"[5]

Until fairly recently, contrasting answers to Kennedy's two questions mattered little. Very different justifications of group preferences and sharply conflicting understandings of the place of such preferences in the long-term development of the society could yield the same policy result when avowed group preferences were relatively new and were not seriously threatened. But today, the answers to Kennedy's questions matter. If one envisions a highly articulated plural society in which each individual is understood to have his or her place within one or another of a set of enduring and legally empowered identity groups, one can more easily accept group preferences as a permanent feature of American public life. One wastes little time deciding how much political energy to devote to their defense; obviously, they must be defended. And one need not be disturbed if one function of these preferences is to reinforce and perpetuate the standardized identity groups. In this view, such reinforcement and perpetuation can be a good thing, as it constitutes a realistic response to the realities of power and prejudice ignored by the folks who continue to indulge the discredited liberal fantasy of a color-blind America.

But deciding how hard to resist the diminution of group preferences demands more reflection if one instead holds to the old ideal of a society in which the physical traits that mark ethno-racial identity would be allowed to exercise less and less ordinance over the lives of individuals. Group preference then makes the most sense as a temporary expedient that compromises anti-racialist principles, but that was made necessary by the formidable barriers put in place by the historic failure of the United States to live up to what Gunnar Myrdal called "the American Creed."[6] Dramatic and truly extraordinary steps were needed, and in 1965 President Johnson was right, in this view, to take such a step when he issued the executive order that began affirmative action.

If all along you have been regarding group preferences as an unfortunate, if necessary, *exception* to the principle that ethno-racial distinctions should not inspire different treatment, you are surely obliged to take notice when this principle is finally voiced across the widest political spectrum ever. This is so even if the doctrine's advocates now include political interests that have shown relatively little concern with the evil effects of ethno-racial distinctions, whose motives for joining up now are highly suspect, and whose will to act effectively on sound doctrine remains in doubt. Pure hearts are rare in politics, and alliances based on them are narrow.

Similarly, if all along you have been regarding group prefer-ences as a *temporary* measure and now, after they have been in place for a while, you are confronted with a formidable move-ment to end them, you are surely obliged to pause for at least a moment to consider how long you think they should last. Orlando Patterson has done exactly this. Patterson has proposed giving affirmative action, as he persists in calling it, a time limit: ten more years.[7]

In the remainder of this essay I want to identify and address briefly several issues of potential concern to those who assume, as I do, that group preferences can be justified in the United States in our time only as a temporary expedient, and who accept, as I do, the long-term goal of equal treatment of individuals regard-less of ascribed or asserted ethno-racial identities.

One issue quickly resolved is whether the problems to which group preferences were originally aimed remain real. They do. People who deny the reality of racism seem to me not worth the time and energy it takes to argue with them. A second issue I take to be easily answered is whether group preferences have accomplished anything of value. The greater number of non-whites and women in many professional, occupational, and edu-cational spaces in which they had been discriminated against is surely attributable, in part, to the success of group preferences as an antidiscrimination remedy. The growth of the middle class among African Americans, in particular, is a vital, historic conse-quence of group preferences that is in no way gainsaid by the fact that the bulk of the black beneficiaries of group preferences have been already removed from the most degrading and limiting of social circumstances below the poverty line.

Exactly how much progress has been made during the last thirty years is yet another question, and one much harder to answer. Survey research concerning white attitudes and empirical studies of the economic position and occupational status of the several ethno-racial blocs relative to what they had been twenty or thirty years ago are important. But the relevance of such studies is easily exaggerated. Even if we accept the conclusions of many social scientists that white racism has declined somewhat, and even if we accept studies summarized by Abigail Thernstrom, Henry Louis Gates Jr., and others to the effect that we now have fourteen times more black engineers than we did thirty years ago, and eleven times as many black lawyers and judges and so on,[8] one can still insist that there remain significant, ethno-racially specific barriers to the progress individuals can make in this society. Contending over how much or little progress has been made can become a dangerous diversion. It yields the impression that one can decide the future of group preferences simply by measuring a bit more precisely the intensity of, first, the prejudice harbored by empowered whites and, second, the wealth and income of a given nonwhite group. Such measurements constitute too narrow a context for deciding the fate of group preferences.

We need to look also at the economic and social settings in which racism now resides. When we do that, we are overwhelmed — or at least I think we should be — by the drastically escalating scale of problems broader than those to which group preferences are addressed. I refer to economic and social problems that have gotten worse during the years since group preferences were accepted as a political priority of the liberal Left. Poverty is worse now than when war was temporarily declared on it. The standard of living for many so-called middle-class Americans has been in sharp decline for some years now. We have a greater percentage of our citizens in prison than does any other industrialized nation in the world. Life in the inner cities is worse by most indicators than it was when the Kerner Commission presented its gloomy report in 1968. More individuals are more likely to be the victims of crime in more locations than used to be the case. The public schools are successfully meeting the needs of a smaller and smaller percentage of the nation's young. More of America's children go without basic social services than at any time since the 1930s.

This prodigious economic and social hemorrhage is not unrelated to racism, but the problems that constitute this hemorrhage are broader than racism and demand political responses beyond ethno-racially defined programs. These problems are more deserving of our attention than ever before, and they provide a potential basis for the construction of political alliances across ethno-racial lines. The point is not that racism has diminished and therefore group preferences are now less needed than they used to be. Whatever truth there is in that point — and I think there is some truth in it — is dwarfed by the truth contained in another point: *so many other problems have gotten so much worse.*

But not because of group preference. White workers have probably paid a greater price for the gains of nonwhite workers than is usually admitted by enthusiasts for group preferences, but whatever this price may be, it surely remains a drop in the bucket of social blood that constitutes the hemorrhage to which I refer. The exaggeration of the impact of group preferences is a widely and properly condemned instance of demagoguery on the part of rightist politicians.

When group preferences are scrutinized in relation to the actual scale and scope of injustice in the United States today, however, the standard leftist critique of group preferences as developed by Theda Skocpol, Jim Miller, Jim Sleeper, and others invites a sympathetic hearing.[9] Perhaps group preferences amount to a quick fix, a relatively inexpensive set of programs that obscure broader and deeper impediments to the achieving of a just society, that divide the liberal Left, and that allow the Right to appropriate the high moral ground of antidiscrimination originally contributed by the liberal Left? What better way to keep the liberal Left isolated, and to prevent it from mobilizing around economic and social issues, than to maneuver it into a loudly proclaimed "no retreat" position on group preferences?

This speculation raises a closely related issue. Is there sufficient economic space in which group preferences can be reasonably expected to obtain the political support they must possess in order to survive? It is unlikely that group preferences would have been put into effect and expanded under the economic conditions that now prevail. It is not simply that working- and lower-middle-class whites are racist — although many are — nor is it simply that they are insensitive to historic injustices suffered by nonwhites, although many are that, too. Rather, working- and lower-middle-class whites are now subject to economic circumstances that make it more difficult for them to respond with even a modicum of generosity to the needs of persons even more disadvantaged than they are. These circumstances also make it more difficult for these people to resist the unscrupulous scapegoating by the politicians who tell them that their own immiseration is a consequence of preferences for other groups. The ritualistic blaming of popular racism for opposition to group preferences — indicated by Paul Sniderman and Thomas Piazza's *The Scar of Race* to be terrible inaccuracy[10] — threatens to obscure how diminished the economic space is that once enabled elected officials, agency administrators, and courts to develop group preferences in the first place.

Alongside the transformed economic context in which racism and antiracist programs operate we need to consider the changed demographic context. Massive immigration from Asia and Latin America and an extraordinary increase in self-identification of indigenous peoples has taken place during exactly the years that entitlement programs have been expanded. When President Johnson first used the term *affirmative action* in 1965, there was no doubt about on whose behalf the action was to be taken in a society divided significantly between "white" and "black." During the 1970s and 1980s, however, the United States accepted the ethno-racial pentagon. The granting of entitlements to Asian Americans, indigenous peoples, and Latinos rendered more complex the task of theoretical justification that would eventually become inescapable.

The Immigration Reform Act of 1965 was not expected to produce any significant increase in immigration but has in fact brought into the United States more than twenty million legal immigrants. More than three-fourths of these legal immigrants, Peter Schrag reminds us, qualified instantly for group preferences of the sort designed to deal with historic injustices suffered by longtime American citizens of African descent.[11] American Indians have historically obvious claims on American resources more comparable to the claims of African Americans than to those of immigrants, but the Indian, or Native American, case offers unique challenges to theory. Many of the benefits available to Indians derive not from ethno-racial status, but from membership in tribes that are, technically, political entities with sovereignty. Should persons who self-identify as Indians without specific tribal authorization be the recipients of group preferences even if they are physically undistinguishable from whites whose features do not trigger acts of discrimination? Today's defenders of group preferences cannot dodge the responsibility of clarifying the basis for the preference to be afforded to each of the different, potentially relevant groups.[12]

That group preferences should be reserved for blacks alone is a striking implication of Steinberg's *Turning Back: The Retreat from Racial Justice in American Thought and Policy*. Although Steinberg refers to programs that have targeted women as a group, none of the arguments he makes for group preferences are women-related. Steinberg mentions Latinos and Asian Americans only in relation to immigration patterns, not in relation to group preferences. He makes no mention whatsoever of indigenous peoples. Steinberg joins the growing host of writers arguing that immigration from Latin America, especially, has severely undercut the economic opportunities of African Americans. The immigration policies currently in effect constitute part of what Steinberg sees as a liberal betrayal of a historic commitment to the welfare of the descendants of slaves. Indeed, Steinberg's entire case for group preferences is made on the basis of the historically unique experience of black people within the United States. He writes in an overheated "no retreat" idiom, complete with invective against such voices of "retreat" as Paul Starr, William Julius Wilson, Shelby Steele, and Stephen Carter, but Steinberg's book can easily be read as a charter for retreat from some programs: those that benefit nonblacks. Although Steinberg himself does not draw out these implications as directly as I have, his basic instinct has been sound: a coherent theory of group preferences is easiest to generate if one has in mind the African American group.

A coherent theory of group preferences needs to contain a program for dealing with the vast, impecunious white population of the United States in terms that go well beyond the criticism of this population for being racist. A broad social democratic program in the United States might appeal to the interests of many white as well as minority citizens.[13] Social democracy is a very elusive goal, given the current direction of American politics. Valuable programs now in place might well be dismantled while some of us are thinking how marvelous it would be to have a more comprehensive social democracy. But when it comes to identifying pipe dreams, the preservation of group preferences is also a strong candidate. Whatever specific programs for group preference survive, the prize on which I hope American eyes can be kept is a larger one. A coherent theory of affirmative action should be part of a coherent vision for the United States.

NOTES

This essay has been developed from a workshop presentation at the Center for the Study of American Cultures, University of California at Berkeley, 8 September 1995. For helpful comments I am indebted to Carol J. Clover, Joan Heifetz Hollinger, J. Jorge Klor de Alva, Michael Omi, and Robert Post.

1. Stephen Steinberg, *Turning Back: The Retreat from Racial Justice in American Thought and Policy* (Boston, 1995), 165.

2. The concept of the "ethno-racial pentagon" is developed in David A. Hollinger, *Postethnic America: Beyond Multiculturalism* (New York, 1995), from which the next two paragraphs are adapted.

3. Steinberg, *Turning Back*, 165.

4. *Ibid.*

5. Randall Kennedy, "Yes and No," *The American Prospect* (Spring 1992): 116.

6. Gunnar Myrdal, *An American Dilemma: The Negro Problem and Modern Democracy* (New York, 1944), 3–25.

7. Orlando Patterson, "Affirmative Action on the Merit System," *New York Times*, 7 August 1995, A13.

8. See, e.g., Abigail Thernstrom, "The Futility of Black Rage," *Times Literary Supplement*, 10 June 1994, 14.

9. For representative comments of Jim Sleeper and Jim Miller, see the symposium "Race & Racism: American Dilemmas Revisited," *Salmagundi* nos. 104–5 (Fall 1994–Winter 1995), esp. 37–38, 51, 110; for Theda Skocpol, see her "The Choice," *The American Prospect* (Summer 1992): 86–90. See also the contributions by Nicholas Mills and Michael Lind to the symposium "Affirmative Action Under Fire," *Dissent* (Fall 1995): 470–73.

10. Paul Sniderman and Thomas Piazza, *The Scar of Race* (Cambridge, MA, 1993).

11. Peter Schrag, "So You Want to Be Color-Blind: Alternative Principles for Affirmative Action," *American Prospect* (Summer 1995): 41. Schrag's discussion of the Immigration Reform Act draws upon the work of Hugh Davis Gra-

ham. Schrag's article is one of the most sensible discussions of group preference I have seen. It came to my attention only after this essay was in draft.

12. For a refreshingly open discussion of this question with the specific case of law school admissions in mind, see Paul Brest and Miranda Oshige, "Affirmative Action for Whom?" *Stanford Law Review* 47 (May 1995): 855–900, esp. 900, where the authors conclude that "no other group compares to African Americans in the confluence of the characteristics that argue for inclusion in affirmative action programs."

13. For an example of the kind of society-wide economic analysis in which I believe the debate over group preferences should be more firmly nested, see Edward Luttwak, "Turbo-Charged Capitalism and Its Consequences," *London Review of Books* (2 November 1995): 6–7.

Individual Fairness,

Group Preferences,

and the California Strategy

Troy Duster

Prologue

Even the fiercest antagonists are unaware of how the ghost of
Richard Nixon hovers above the nation as we go through our
current struggle over the fate of affirmative action. Nixon did
more than any other president to promote and institutionalize
affirmative action. While John Kennedy issued the initially limited executive orders in 1963, and while Lyndon Johnson had
maneuvered through Congress the 1964 civil rights legislation
that mandated selected forms in the workplace, it was Nixon
who demanded and required that corporate America institute
programs of affirmative action from inside the corporate walls.

Why? Was Nixon really such a partisan of the use of law to
help those excluded by both law and custom from full participation in the society? Hardly. Nixon's support for affirmative action
was based on the shrewd, if cynical, calculation that this beautiful
wedge issue would fracture the Democratic Party's old coalition
of labor, Jews, and blacks. In their accounts of the Nixon strategy, his senior aide for domestic affairs, John Ehrlichman, his
chief of staff, H.R. Haldeman, and most recently historian Kenneth O'Reilly each reveal a piece of the story of Nixon's scheme
to use race policies and affirmative action to plant and nurture
the seeds of dissent.[1] By insinuating affirmative action into the
fabric of the workforce, Nixon was certain that it would someday
come home to benefit the Republican Party. While he saw clearly
that *group interests* were central to the fate of affirmative action,
not even Nixon could foresee that those group interests would

reincarnate themselves in the disguise of claims to individual fairness. Surely Nixon is wearing, even now, that familiar taut smile, for the Republican Party has seized on what it regards as a propitious moment to pick the Nixon-ripened plum called California. To understand this return of the Ghost of Sixties Past, we need to describe first the ideological terrain on which it is staged.

The Gratifying and Effective Appeal to Individual Fairness

In the current attack on affirmative action, there is a full arsenal and wide-ranging artillery. There are conservatives (George Bush chief among them) who vigorously opposed the 1960s civil rights legislation that opened up public accommodations and voting — self-styled conservatives who now with heartfelt sympathy and notable poignancy wring their hands and express their deep and humane concerns for the stigmatizing effects on those selected through affirmative action. Then there are the newly emerging closet *class* analysts of social stratification in America who pronounce that racial discrimination against blacks and browns is a thing of the past, that America is no longer a racist society. Their claim does not end here. They argue that, when it comes to university admissions, the sons and daughters of the well-heeled black and Latino middle class are pushing out the deserving poor among Asians and whites.[2] Affirmative action would be palatable, they say, but only if it were class-based,[3] since, they claim, the truly needy, the most impoverished in the nation, are untouched by affirmative action.[4]

But the trump card in the deck, the perfect squelch, and the most effective and the most frequently cited attack revolves around the idea of *fairness* — and most particularly, around a specific rendition of fairness to the individual. Here the rhetoric is seamlessly simple and the surface representation flawless: we are presented with two individuals, one white male and one Latina from the same school. The white male has a high school grade point average (GPA) of 4.0, while the Latina has a 3.5 GPA. They apply to the same university, yet she gets in and he does not. How can that be fair? Since he did not personally discriminate against anyone, at least one-on-one, how can he be blamed for acts of racial discrimination committed long before he was born? So long as the question of fairness to two individuals is thus framed, so long as the dialogue is thus set so that there is no other context to these two individuals save their disembodied existence as high school GPAs, the argument against affirmative action on the issue of fairness seems compelling and is certainly politically effective.[5]

Take the same image to the workplace. A white male has been a good cop for a few years longer than his black coworker, has performed better on written tests, and yet is passed over in favor of that black for promotion. Is it true that only the morally bankrupt could see anything here but unfairness?

But are two individuals and their test scores ever the whole story of fairness in *any* society? At the extreme, let us take the current situation in South Africa. Imagine that whites had spent the last half century creating and implementing laws that permitted them, as whites, to accumulate wealth and land and power, to have access to universities and corporate boardrooms, to have wages five to ten times that of black workers doing the same labor. Imagine that blacks had to carry identification cards in order to move out of legally enforced residences in squalid all-black townships and villages, where there was no running water, no sewage drainage, and underfunded and poor schools. Such a thing might have happened. Then imagine that one day, in 1993, after forty-five years of official apartheid, white monopoly on access to good jobs and good education suddenly came to a *legal* end — but not before whites had accumulated more than ten times the wealth of blacks.

Imagine then that the new president, a black man imprisoned for twenty-seven of those years because of his opposition to those policies, should issue guidelines trying to redress some of those past grievances; that he and his cabinet call for a plan of "affirmative action" to redress the following situation: in 1992, when the writing was on the wall and apartheid's days were numbered, the corporate managers at Telkom, South Africa's national telephone company, an organization with more than fifty-eight thousand employees, did a quick review of the racial composition of its corporate structure. In late 1993, they found one more black manager than many expected — that is, they found one. By the second half of 1995, Telkom employed eighty-three black managers and has since embarked on an aggressive affirmative action program to recruit and hire more.

Would it then be imaginable that some group of whites would

step forward and cry foul? They already have. More than five thousand white workers have threatened to strike to protest the new policy.[6] As for the rhetoric as to why affirmative action is morally wrong: "It's reverse discrimination," complained A.C. van Wyk, spokesman for the Mine Workers Union of South Africa, a union that still bars blacks from joining! The extraordinary manipulation of power through language goes further: critics of those affirmative action programs in South Africa that would place blacks in positions held exclusively by whites for the last half century are now dubbing affirmative action "neoapartheid." *The banner under which this all flies is fairness to the individual!*

Now let us imagine an even more unlikely circumstance, in which a group with two thousand years of historic privilege, which has accumulated wealth and power as a consequence, then suddenly turns around and says, "From now on, we are only individuals" — the caste system of India, for example. For more than two thousand years, certain groups had access to literacy — indeed, were required by the caste system to be literate. And, in contrast, other groups were channeled into occupations that required differing skills, training, and education. Finally, some in this system were "outcastes" — literally outside the system and therefore "untouchable": if one inside the system touched one outside the system, ritual cleansing was required in order to dispel the pollution created by this contact.

Ironically, the apartheid system in South Africa officially began (1948) just one year after the caste system officially, formally, legally ended. But just because the laws ended the caste system, two thousand years of habit, pattern, ideology, *and privilege* were not erased. The caste system had prohibited the lowest castes from drawing water from the same wells, from walking down the same paths, and, most relevant to today's debates about individual fairness, had forbidden the children to go to schools — any schools.[7]

And so the government embarked on a program to redress these past exclusionary policies; much later that policy would be renamed affirmative action. Scheduled castes were provided with at least 12.5 percent of vacancies in government positions subject to open, nationwide recruitment. Not only were places in the workforce set aside for occupancy by members of the scheduled castes, but places in universities and in law schools were also allotted for formerly disenfranchised groups.[8] In 1961, after a review of the situation, the figure was raised from 12.5 to 15 percent set-asides. By 1990, the government actually set aside more than 20 percent of jobs that it controlled for the scheduled castes and scheduled tribes. And can one guess what the Brahmans argued?

They called the plan "reverse discrimination" and said that it would hurt their chances of finding work after graduation.[9] They argued that to use any group criterion would not be fair to those individual Brahmans who had studied hard and got better grades than lower-caste applicants. No matter that the Brahmans were the group required to be literate so that they could avail themselves of the sacred books. No matter. After centuries of accumulating cultural capital by their membership in a group category, many Brahmans took to the streets to demonstrate and riot, arguing that the caste system was dead and gone; that from now on, they were only individuals; that, in short, only individuals without any significant remnants of caste privilege remained in India. Suddenly, after more than two thousand years of the caste system during which familial access routes to privilege were afforded to individuals because of their membership in a group, now nothing remained but *objective* grade point averages.

Both the Brahmans and the white South Africans who oppose policies to partially redress gross injustices that favored their group can retreat to a comfortable position of personal nonculpability: "Since I didn't personally discriminate against anybody, I can't be blamed for apartheid (or caste stratification), and so I should not be penalized for something I didn't do." And with that marvelously simple sleight of hand, Brahmans in India and white South Africans can wash their hands of the privilege that they experience, born to positions of enormous social and economic advantage. Indeed, since there are only individuals, and individual responsibility and individual entitlement are the only currency in the contemporary discourse about race policies and affirmative action policies, not having had a personal hand in the oppression of others makes one innocent. The mere fact that one's group has accumulated wealth ten times that of another group is rendered irrelevant by the legerdemain of invoking individual fairness. We are all individuals, but we are also simultaneously members of families, nation-states, racial and/or ethnically designated groups, and sometimes religious groups. "Fairness to the individual" must always have a social and historical context — ignoring that context is a cheap political trick in the service of the ideology of those in power.

The Irrelevance of Apartheid and Caste, or Parallels Found?

But, you may be feeling by now, what has this to do with affirmative action in the United States? What could be more irrelevant to the American situation than apartheid in South Africa and caste in India? We are not a caste system, but an open class society. Asians, for example, have come to these shores in the last two decades and achieved remarkable comparative success.

And although there was slavery, Bob Dole felt the need to take the Senate floor in July 1995 to tell the nation: "That was a long time ago." Be that as it may, there are some disturbing parallels between the American system of social stratification and those of South Africa and India. Significant wage and salary differences between the races persist, with blacks earning anywhere from about two-thirds to three-quarters the wages and salaries of whites. Since this gap has narrowed somewhat over the last three decades, analysts who wish to portray the situation as one of a slow improvement inevitably focus on these figures. However, focusing merely on wage and salary differences obscures a critical measure of wealth — net worth. Wages and salaries depend on employment, and in the current economic situation of the United States, there is far less job security than previously. A combination of massive downsizing and layoffs, and seasonal and part-time employment, characterizes much of the contemporary work setting. Different spheres of work are more likely to employ whites than blacks. Blacks, for example, are more likely to be employed in the public sector, the target of systematic and often effective attacks by conservatives for the last decade and a half. All of this means that wages and salaries are not the most secure measures by which to assess the likelihood of sustained socioeconomic status and long-term wealth. When one attempts to get a loan, for example, net worth (43 percent of which is based on housing equity) is a far better predictor of success.

Financially, the biggest difference between whites and African Americans today is in their median net worth, which is overwhelmingly attributable to the value of equity in housing stock. In 1991, the median net worth of white households ($43,279) was more than ten times that of the median net worth of African American households ($4,169).[10] Where did this shocking ratio of 10 to 1 come from? How did it happen? Slavery may have been "a long time ago" but three things happened in this country in 1935, when Bob Dole was twelve years old, that set the stage for why affirmative action would be placed on the national agenda in the 1960s. Far more than has previously been recognized, the United States government, in trying to legislate its way out of the Great Depression, created a heavily racialized state that, with the passage of three crucial laws in 1934–35, systematically advantaged whites. While there is some truth to the claim that the New Deal of Franklin Delano Roosevelt was designed to provide a "floor of protection for the industrial working class," it was in fact the brokered compromises over the New Deal that simultaneously "reinforced racial segregation through social welfare programs, labor policy, and housing policy."[11] How, and why?

In 1935, Roosevelt had put together a fragile coalition of northern industrial workers and southern whites still engaged primarily in an agrarian economic order. During this period, more than three-quarters of the black population still lived in the South, but since they could not vote there, FDR did not need even to try to court the black southern electorate. Most of them sharecropped and were tied to the plantation economy at poverty-level wages.[12] Those who were not sharecroppers were engaged in day labor — with most of these employed at two dollars per hundred pounds of cotton, which translates into two dollars per day for a strong worker.

Black women worked as maids, making two dollars per week on average. White southerners in control of key positions in Congress explicitly voiced fears that any federal programs that would put money directly into the pockets of blacks would undermine the very infrastructure of this plantation economy. As chairs of the powerful committees of the House and Senate, they blocked any attempt to change the agrarian system that indentured black sharecroppers. Because of this opposition, which is documented in memoranda between the Congress and the White House, FDR compromised, and agricultural workers and servants were excluded from the Social Security Act of 1935. The exclusion of agricultural workers and house servants appears race-neutral in retrospect. At the time, however, the key actors said they would block all Social Security legislation if it included blacks.

Similarly, the Wagner Act of 1935, labeled in some circles the Magna Carta of labor, was on closer inspection the Magna Carta of white labor. The original version, which permitted the organization of industrial labor and legalized collective bargaining, prohibited racial discrimination. But the American Federation of Labor[13] and the same constellation of white Southerners who controlled the key committees of the Congress fought it, and the final version permitted racial exclusion.[14] By allowing the racial exclusion language for closed shops, blacks were blocked by law from challenging the barriers excluding them from the newly protected right to collective bargaining.

Finally, in 1934, Congress passed the National Housing Act, which sealed the fate of America's cities, creating the social policy and economic basis for sustained and exacerbated racial segregation. While many commentators have blamed "white flight" for the creation of ghettos and barrios, it was actually this heavily coded racial policy of the U.S. federal government that created white enclaves in the suburbs. In 1939, the Federal Housing Authority's *Underwriting Manual* guidelines for granting housing loans explicitly used race as the single most important criterion: "If a neighborhood is to retain stability, it is necessary that properties shall be continued to be occupied by the same social and *racial* classes."[15]

On this basis, for the next thirty years whites were able to get housing loans at 3 to 5 percent, while blacks were routinely denied such loans. For example, of 350,000 new homes built in northern California between 1946 and 1960 with FHA support, fewer than 100 went to blacks. That same pattern holds for the whole state, and for the nation as well. Between 1935 and 1950, eleven million homes were built in the United States with federal assistance, and, as Abrams documented, "discrimination against Negroes was a condition of federal assistance."[16] The official Code of Ethics (*sic*) of the National Association of Real Estate Boards not only barred its members from selling houses across the racial divide, but also put teeth in its prohibition. In a 1943 brochure entitled "Fundamentals of Real Estate Practice," the association outlined grounds for expulsion of realtors who violated race-based sales, and then stated explicitly what constituted problematic behavior:

> The prospective buyer might be a bootlegger who would cause considerable annoyance to his neighbors, a madame who had a number of Call Girls on her string, a gangster, who wants a screen for his activities by living in a better neighborhood, a colored man of means who was giving his children a college education and thought they were entitled to live among whites.... No matter what the motive or character of the would-be purchaser, if the deal would instigate a form of blight, then certainly the well-meaning broker must work against its consummation.[17]

The urban redevelopment programs sponsored by the federal government under the National Housing Act of 1949 also served to undermine the financial solidity of the black community. Freeways in major cities were aligned so that they almost universally cut through core areas of black settlements, while connecting the white suburbs to the central business districts. As a direct result of these programs, many urban black areas lost their neighborhood shopping districts and successful small businesses. Redevelopment was soon followed by race-conscious systematic mortgage redlining,[18] which had a spiral effect on the economic vitality of scores of black communities.[19]

Does this perhaps sound a bit more like caste and apartheid than a mobile open class society of individuals deeply concerned with fairness? And, I should add, Bob Dole was by now twenty-six years of age.

Boom for Whites, 1947–62:
The Impetus Behind Affirmative Action
After World War II ended, the United States economy experienced a remarkable surge, an economic boom fueled by a combination of production and consumption in durable goods unequaled in the nation's history. Cars, refrigerators, tractors, new housing constructions, steel production, and a host of ancillary industries and businesses "took off" and generated an extraordinary growth period throughout the 1950s. However, blacks in the South were still disenfranchised and without Social Security, and in the North,

unable to penetrate labor unions — and unable to obtain housing loans.

Thus, while one part of America was routinely and systematically experiencing an economic boom and resurgence, another part was locked by law and custom out of that surge. During the 1950s, the Dwight D. Eisenhower administration had seen the problem, but pursued a strategy of trying to convince white employers to open up access to black workers. Several states had Fair Employment Practice Commissions, but these commissions had no enforcement powers unless or until an employer was *caught in the act* of discriminating. Even when discrimination was proven, redress was on an individual, case-by-case basis. Not only was the burden on the individual to prove discrimination, but even if this could be decisively proven by catching the culprits in the act, damages were awarded only to that single person.

This burden of proof borne by individual plaintiffs gave employers remarkably little incentive to change their racially exclusionary hiring practices. An employer of seven thousand white workers could easily afford to pay a few thousand dollars in fines or damages to the unlikely black plaintiff. Employers routinely justified their racially exclusionary policies by arguing that, if they hired blacks, their white workers would not work alongside them, and certainly not below them, whether in the trucking industry or at major retail sales outlets. This argument extended even into sports, prohibiting blacks from jobs as quarterbacks, managers, and coaches. There were few cries of "we are all individuals" from the 99 percent white worksite of the 1950s. Moreover, while in an all-white workforce, in a racially segregated society, some racially exclusive practices were inadvertent, unconscious, and the "normal" outcome of reliance on friendship circles of those already employed, active strategies for racial exclusion were always present. These included: refusing to keep records of employee racial makeup; when records were available, stonewalling the Fair Employment Practice Commissions; and using screening and testing devices designed to maintain the all-white worksite.

Because of the prevalence of these tactics, in 1960 the federal government, under the newly elected president John F. Kennedy, decided to step in and, at the very least, put some teeth into areas it controlled. The government's most effective strategy was to monitor and calibrate federal contracts to big companies doing business with the federal government. Initially, affirmative action was therefore a specific and limited response of the government to long-term systemic racial exclusion — but only at the worksite.

But not just employers doing business with the government were racially exclusive. The all-white unions of the United States, following the Wagner Act's permission of racial exclusion, also were very slow to open up to blacks. Even though the legal language for racial exclusion had been dropped by the late 1950s, it was quite common for unions, whose members were well paid, to remain all white well into the 1970s. For example, Los Angeles Steam Fitters Local #250 did not have a single nonwhite among its more than three thousand members in 1972.[20] Only after the Nixon administration issued Executive Order 11246 in 1971, "requiring [that] dated numerical targets for hiring, training, and promoting minorities be set by firms that hold government contracts," did the Steam Fitters finally introduce a black apprenticeship program in 1972. It is important to note that it was exactly at the midpoint between the 1935 racialized exclusionary legislation and the 1995 full-scale attack on affirmative action that the laws and practices initiating affirmative action were put in place. By now, Bob Dole was nearly fifty years of age.

Screening, "Individual" Competence, and Intent to Discriminate

Controversy over the use of tests to screen prospective employees has been a significant part of the debate over affirmative action from the beginning. In *Griggs v. Duke Power* (1971), the Supreme Court ruled unanimously that the Equal Employment Opportunity Commission guidelines for testing potential employees were valid. Here is the key language:

> The Civil Rights Act proscribes not only overt discrimination, but practices that are fair in form, but discriminatory in operation. The touchstone is business necessity. If an employment practice which operates to exclude Negroes cannot be shown to be related to job performance, the practice is prohibited.

And on the use of tests, the Court went on to say:

On the record before us neither the high school completion requirement nor the general intelligence test is shown to bear a demonstrable relation to successful performance on the jobs for which it is
used. Both were adopted, as the Court of Appeals noted, without
meaningful study of their relationship to job performance ability.[21]

In this ruling, the Court clearly articulated a position that acknowledged the effect of the "routine practices of institutions,"
without regard to individual intent to discriminate. Since the
Court changed, however, with Ronald Reagan's and George Bush's
appointments after 1980, there has been a reversion to the older,
pre-1963 conception of *individual* racial discrimination.

Although the Court has continued to rule that Title VII of the
1964 Civil Rights Act allows affirmative action programs in employment without a showing of individual intent to discriminate,
it has narrowed the grounds on which a discriminatory pattern
can be determined.[22] With respect to the constitutional requirement of equal protection, the Supreme Court has ruled for the
last decade that there must be individual motivation, intention-
ality, and personal culpability in order to justify race-based programs to redress past inequalities. The Court's injunction is much
like saying that unless we can find some memo indicating that
the Brahmans intended to discriminate against members of the
scheduled castes, there can be no redress. But individual Brahmans need not intend to do anything if the very fabric of Hindu
society is saturated with practices — institutional, systematic, and
organized — that effectively discriminate against those of other
castes. Ironically, we have come almost full circle back to where
we began in the early and mid-1960s, when affirmative action
was deemed necessary because employers could always claim
that *individuals* were being excluded not as members of a group
but because of personal disqualifying factors.

With these developments, "the individual" has returned as the
centerpiece of a new rhetorical strategy by conservatives, both
white and black, to maintain the historic advantage of racial privilege. Carefully invoking an early speech of Martin Luther King
Jr., they try to seize the mantle of the civil rights movement. It
was King, after all, who said that we should all be "judged by the
content of our character, not the color of our skin." This is the
famous phrase Shelby Steele picked for the title of his book *The*

Content of Our Character,[23] and he and others (including the governor of Louisiana, Mike Foster)[24] have used it to mount an attack on affirmative action. They ignore what King said just a year later, even before his venture north to Chicago: "Whenever the issue of compensatory or preferential treatment for the Negro is raised, some of our friends recoil in horror. The Negro should be granted equality, they agree: but he should ask nothing more. On the surface, this appears reasonable, but it is not realistic."[25]

In his famous 1963 "I Have a Dream" speech, King referred to breaking down more than two centuries of legally sanctioned exclusionary racial preferences and practices that had disenfranchised blacks in the South. By 1966, King faced fierce *collective resistance* from the all-white unions of Chicago after trying to open up employment there in the mid-1960s. By 1968, the year of his death, he had become one of the strongest voices in America supporting race-specific initiatives to help break down the employment barriers.

From Boom Period to Job Loss and Job Insecurities

Just as the period from 1947 to 1962 was a time of economic boom for the great majority of the white population (while the great majority of the black population was experiencing systematic exclusion from employment, housing, and even voting), the last two decades (1976–96) have witnessed a level of job loss and job insecurity that the country has not seen since the Great Depression.

Job Loss, Red Herrings, and Red Flags

Between 1990 and 1992, California lost 1.5 million jobs.[26] While cutbacks in the defense industry accounted for 300,000 of those jobs, and the continual hemorrhaging in the manufacturing sector cost an additional 200,000, the biggest hit of all came in wholesale and retail trades, accounting for 900,000 of the jobs lost in the state.[27]

Unemployment reached 9 percent in California in 1992 — and that includes only those who are still looking, of course. Competition for new jobs has been fierce, and after one has lost a job (and cannot get rehired at an attractive or equivalent new job), one of the first questions is: who is to blame? As the lines of the unemployed got longer and longer in California, affirmative action provided a ready-made scapegoat. As we have seen, blacks constitute only about 7 percent of California's population. Thus, they were a much smaller force in electoral politics than in many other states. Moreover, and most critically, because California is the plum of plums in the electoral college, Republicans saw a remarkable opportunity to wave a red flag. Just as Nixon's support for affirmative action was strategically calculated to drive a wedge between the Democratic coalition of blacks, Jews, and labor, now, a quarter century later, a parallel political calculation plays a parallel role.

The Nike Story, AT&T Downsizing, and Megabank Mergers

By waving the red flag of affirmative action, the Republicans engage in a strategy of diversion: for if Californians really understood the implications of the Nike story fully, they would realize that the massive job loss the state experienced from 1990 to 1992 had little to do with affirmative action. Nike, based in Beaverton, Oregon, began as a wonderfully simple American business story. For its first three years of operation, from 1969 to 1972, Nike was a fledgling company with little to distinguish it from other shoemakers. Then, in 1972, a running coach at the University of Oregon, William Bowerman, placed a piece of malleable rubber on a waffle iron and demonstrated to Nike owner Phillip Knight an idea that would "take off, running." With this cushioning piece of rubber attached to the soles, shoes would become both lighter in weight and more durable. In twelve years, sales rose from $2 million in 1972 to $919 million by 1984.[28]

Nike discovered the profits that could be turned by closing its U.S.-based factories and replacing them with much cheaper labor in Asia. In 1988, Nike was paying an average of $6.94 per hour to American workers. However, in Korea workers were earning less than one-third that amount. So in 1989, Nike closed its last American factory, in Saco, Maine. They turned at first to South Korea in the early 1980s and contracted with the Sung Hwa corporation.[29] Things went well-enough until the end of the decade, when the South Koreans earned the right to unionize and to strike. In 1988, Nike bought 68 percent of its shoes from South Korea — but when the labor trouble hit, Nike moved quickly, and with

Sung Hwa as intermediary, opened factories in Tangerang, Indonesia, a squalid industrial boomtown on the outskirts of Jakarta. There, a worker in the shoe factory is paid 14 cents per hour, or approximately $1.08 per day. Contrast this with the $55 per day average wage of the U. S. footwear factory worker, and we glimpse why Nike's sales exceeded $3 billion in 1991, why profits surged to $287 million that year (the highest ever), and why less than one percent of its more than eighty-eight million pairs of shoes sold annually are made outside of Asia. To repeat, not a single pair of Nikes is now manufactured in the United States. And while South Korea was making nearly 70 percent of Nike shoes in 1988, cheaper and unorganized labor in China,[30] Indonesia, and Thailand forced Korean production down to only 42 percent.[31]

As Ballinger points out, the Indonesian worker in that Tangerang factory, working six days a week, for ten and a half hours per day, takes home a paycheck at the end of a month equivalent to $38.[32] A single pair of Nikes routinely sells for double that price.

But job loss through the export of labor to other parts of the world is only one part of the story. In late 1995, AT&T (American Telephone and Telegraph) announced the elimination of forty-four thousand jobs. This move was less a function of export, more a feature of downsizing to accommodate the replacement of American workers, not with a labor force outside the country, but with sophisticated computer circuitry. The same thing goes for the recent trend of bank mergers. While the lead paragraphs in these stories emphasize the increased size, volume, and wealth that will result from creating megabanks, buried in some later paragraphs is always the account of the loss of six thousand to fourteen thousand jobs.

If the 1950s and early 1960s were economic boom periods for whites in the U. S. labor force, then the 1980s and 1990s were contrasting decades of economic downsizing/busts, with a corresponding decline of purchasing power — and of course, a declining sense of job security. In this context, politicians have a very important choice. They can elect to take the issue of job loss head on, and confront the political and economic policies generating that job loss; or they can purposefully try to deflect from the real issue of a shrinking labor force by focusing attention on "racial preferences" and "racial quotas."

The displacement is purposeful and inflammatory since pollsters know that if the question of affirmative action is posed as a matter of social justice, of reducing discrimination against disenfranchised and excluded groups, even American white males are inclined to support it. But by naming the same practices as "race preferences," the bull is guaranteed not only to charge, but to charge at the wrong target.

Why California Was Chosen as the Proving Ground for the Attack on Affirmative Action

In 1935, concentrated in the rural south and disenfranchised, blacks were not a political force to be reckoned with in voting for the presidency. Thus, FDR could, and did, side with the white southerners to continue that disenfranchisement. But when blacks migrated to the North from 1940 to 1960, they began voting in those northern states, becoming a significant political force. Eighty-seven percent of blacks migrated to seven northern industrial states during this period: New York, New Jersey, Pennsylvania, Ohio, California, Illinois, and Michigan. In 1960, black voters gave John Kennedy the winning margin in New Jersey, Michigan, Illinois, Texas, and South Carolina.[33] Nixon would have won the election if he had won these states. From the ashes of Nixon's defeat emerged the southern strategy to fracture the Democratic coalition.[34] The Republican analysts saw clearly the contradictions of the coalition. White racists in the South, they reasoned, could be shown to share more with white laboring groups in the North who wished to keep their historic racial privilege (seniority, Wagner Act racial exclusion), and perhaps even with Jews, if they could just insinuate this race card: that the redress of past discrimination and its current legacy were not in the interests of whites.

A number of observers from across the country have wondered why California became the testing ground for the Republican's assault on affirmative action. The answers lie in a fourfold tier of forces that appear complex at first glance, but when examined closely and in combination, provide a remarkably simple answer. First, California is far and away the largest state. With a population of 31.3 million, it far outsizes the runner-up, New York State, which has only 18.2 million.[35] California's fifty-four electoral votes in a winner-take-all election are a fat plum.

Second, California's population has, over the last two decades, become less and less white — or, conversely, more and more racially heterogeneous and multiethnic. While the national figure for whites is approximately 80 percent, in California, whites make up only 57 percent of the population. Moreover, while blacks are about 12 percent of the national population, they constitute only about 7 percent of the California population. Americans of Asian descent are now the third largest racial group in the state, at nearly 10 percent of the population. Finally, the number of Latinos, principally of Mexican descent, exceeds 25 percent of the total state population. The critical feature of this multiethnic terrain is the combined demographic and political fact that blacks are the fourth largest racial/ethnic group in the state, something that is true nowhere else in the country.

Third, these first two factors combine with an assessment of who is voting. California may be only 57 percent white, but the electorate for the state is approximately 80 percent white. While Latinos and Asian Americans constitute more than one-third of the population of the state, they are notoriously absent from the voting booths. In the 1992 election for mayor in Los Angeles, for example, whites, who are only 37 percent of the population of the city, constituted 70 percent of the electorate. At the other extreme, Latinos — 41 percent of the L.A. population — constituted a mere 8 percent of the electorate. And while whites (mainly con) and blacks (mainly pro) are sharply divided in their views on affirmative action, Latinos and Asians are both more evenly divided and ambivalent. Thus, Latinos and Asians tend to be self-canceling in the larger picture of the affirmative action debate in California — returning this situation to a black versus white dynamic. While the growing "minority" presence that will make California the first majority-minority state feeds white anxiety, there is less of an electoral counterbalance provided by people of color.

Looking again at the L.A. mayoral race, the white population voted as a generally solid racial bloc for the white candidate. Blacks actually voted more disproportionally for Michael Woo (an Asian American and the more progressive candidate) than did Asian Americans, who were more likely to split their votes between Republicans and Democrats or stay at home. Just as Rudolf Giuliani, the Republican mayoral candidate in New York, got whites to cross over and vote as a racial bloc in that otherwise heavily Democratic city, Republican Richard Riordan accomplished the same feat in Los Angeles. White bloc voting for white candidates and "white group interests" has become one of the untold stories of American politics.

The Republican Party analysts saw this clearly. Kevin Phillips forecast in 1969 the fracture of the Democrats that would give the Republicans a stranglehold on the white South.[36] Now we have a California strategy: under the disguise of individual fairness, the Republicans blame affirmative action for shrinking workforce opportunities, hoping that enough whites, especially those who have experienced the massive job losses discussed earlier, will read the message subliminally.

And not only are jobs at issue. Fourth, and finally, Governor Pete Wilson has targeted the admissions policy of the University of California, for decades the most highly ranked public university in the nation by any measure.[37] Because of both the urban setting and the high prestige of the two major urban undergraduate campuses (Berkeley and Los Angeles), a far greater number of students apply for admission to them than there are spots available. In the fall of 1995, for example, 22,811 people applied to Berkeley for approximately 3,405 spots. Of those 22,811, over 9,550 had 4.0, or straight A, grade point averages.[38] Moreover, an additional 4,000 had grade point averages above 3.8. Governor Wilson smelled blood. On 20 July 1995, he attended his first Board of Regents meeting in three years to engineer a close vote (fourteen to ten including Wilson) to roll back affirmative action.

Why have conservatives, including Pete Wilson, Dinesh D'Souza, and George Will, become so passionately articulate about individual fairness only in these times? A substantial part of the answer, and the conclusion to this paper, comes in the form of a parable from a true story about college admissions at midcentury.

Conclusion: Brandeis, Fairness, and White Male Affirmative Action

In the two years before Brandeis University first opened its doors in 1948, the brand new team of admissions officers deliberated at length on what kind of freshman class they wanted to admit. Not much of a problem: they wanted "the best and the brightest."

Unsurprisingly, they decided to use high school grade point averages and the small battery of aptitude test scores then available. But some were mightily surprised with the results, namely, that women would constitute nearly 70 percent of the freshman class if these were the only criteria. Desiring more gender balance, they decided to employ other criteria, namely sex, and achieved a freshman class that was remarkably balanced. The graduating class of 1952 was 52 percent male, 48 percent female. Yet, at no time did we hear the anguished cries from Nathan Glazer and Irving Kristol that less qualified Jewish males were getting in to Brandeis unfairly, bumping more qualified females. Isn't it interesting which battles ideologues choose to fight, and when they see "fairness" as it applies to selective group interests?

I am not attacking the Brandeis decision. Quite the contrary, I take the position that institutions should have explicit mandates, and these can, and sometimes should, transcend the interests of any particular individual. Such mandates can be defended or attacked. If having an all-female college (Mills, in Oakland, California) is the mandate, then even if a male has a 4.25, he cannot get in. If having an all-male college (Citadel, in South Carolina) is the mandate, let it be out in the open, defended and debated, sustained or overturned. If the mandate withstands rigorous scrutiny about its "fairness" (and "fairness" is not a reliance on individual grade point averages), then it should be honored. The difficult territory of racially exclusive institutions demands still further an articulated and defended rationale for a mandate. Defending an all-Brahman school on the grounds that Brahmans are "polluted" by the presence of members of the scheduled castes or that Brahmans just happen to score, as individuals, higher on aptitude tests, is quite different from excluding a member of a "lower" caste even though she or he has the requisite qualifications, *as an individual*, or including members of the scheduled castes because of the historic accumulation of privilege monopolized by Brahmans. During the civil rights movement, the White Citizens Councils of the South formed to exclude blacks from participation in key institutions and from matriculation at the major research universities. To equate affirmative action with "race preferences" is to purposefully confuse patterns of exclusion by the privileged with efforts to include the previously (and currently) excluded.

Just as ending affirmative action will not reverse the massive loss of California jobs, neither will it build a new university campus to accommodate the massive influx of students into the California system since 1980. But the campaign against "racial preferences" and for individual fairness aims to lull students and their parents into the false belief that if affirmative action ended, there would be places at Berkeley and UCLA for all those both qualified and interested.

So long as Pete Wilson waves this red flag, whether or not his Republican political appointees on the Board of Regents acknowledge it, they are engaged in a partisan political struggle and the ghost of Richard Nixon's southern strategy will have come home to his native state.

Notes

1. See John D. Ehrlichman, *Witness to Power: The Nixon Years* (New York, 1982); H.R. Haldeman, *The Haldeman Diaries: Inside the Nixon White House* (New York, 1994); H.R. Haldeman with Joseph DiMona, *The Ends of Power* (New York, 1978); Kenneth O'Reilly, *Nixon's Piano: Presidents and Racial Politics from Washington to Clinton* (New York, 1995).

2. California Governor Pete Wilson has played this theme continually — most recently in an op-ed piece; "Why Racial Preferences Must End," *San Francisco Chronicle*, 18 January 1996, A20.

3. Jerome Karabel, " 'Affirmative Action' and UC's Political Theater of the Absurd," *San Francisco Examiner*, 19 July 1995.

4. One of the most frequently cited objections to affirmative action is that it benefits only the better off among minorities and women. This assertion is glib, facile, and inattentive to a body of literature that contradicts it with substantial data. In the period before the civil rights movement and the attendant affirmative action legislation, black women in the South faced barriers in their pursuit of a wide range of occupations, save that of domestic servant. To call this group of women either privileged or bourgeois is a cruel hoax, yet that is exactly what the current rhetoric asserts. Here are the facts: The textile mills of the South, which had completely excluded these women as possible employees, suddenly opened up and provided them thousands of jobs as laborers, operatives, and craft and service workers. Throughout much of the nation, affirmative action provided blacks, for the first time, with access to employment in police and fire departments, public service jobs in parks, and private sector employment in the building trades. Even though this wedging open of formerly

closed employment opportunities certainly did not prevent massive poverty for a large portion of the black population, it is empirically demonstrable that affirmative action provided a way out of poverty for hundreds of thousands, even millions of *poor* blacks, not just those from the middle class. See Jill Quadagno, *The Color of Welfare* (New York, 1994); Gertrude Ezorsky, *Racism and Justice: The Case for Affirmative Action* (Ithaca, NY, 1991); Jonathan S. Leonard, "Splitting Blacks? Affirmative Action and Earnings Inequality with and Across Races," in Barbara D. Dennis, ed., *Papers in the Proceedings of the Thirty-Ninth Annual Meeting of the Industrial Relations Research Association* (Madison, 1986); Richard L. Rowan, "The Negro in the Textile Industry," in Herbert R. Northrup et al., *Negro Employment in Southern Industry: A Study of Racial Policies in Five Industries* (Philadelphia, 1970).

5. In a recent poll of 240,082 college students in a national survey conducted by UCLA's Higher Education Research Institute and reported on the front page of *USA Today* on 8 January 1996, 70 percent agreed that race should be given "some special consideration by admissions officers" — but in the same survey, 50 percent said that affirmative action should be abolished. The analysts of the survey noted that it is the negative political imagery around the term "affirmative action" that explains this finding.

6. Bob Drogin, "South Africa's Hot Issue — Affirmative Action," *San Francisco Chronicle*, 22 August 1995, A8.

7. See Frederick G. Bailey, *Tribe, Caste, and Nation: A Study of Political Activity and Political Change in Highland Orissa* (Manchester, UK, 1960).

8. The term *scheduled caste* was first used by the Simon Commission and then embodied in the Government of India Act of 1935. Up until this time, the term *untouchables* was used. Mohandas Gandhi renamed these groups *Harijans* but many resented and rejected the name. After 1938, the word *Harijan* was officially replaced by the government with the term *scheduled caste*, which has been in place as the formal term ever since. Of course, in the population at large, the terms *Harijan* and *untouchables* are still used in various locations. See B.D. Purohit and S.D. Purohit, *Handbook of Reservation for Scheduled Castes and Scheduled Tribes: On the Matters Concerning Employment, Education, and Election* (New Delhi, 1990); Government of Karnataka, Dept. of Personnel and Administrative Reforms, *Brochure on Reservation for Scheduled Castes, Scheduled Tribes, and other Categories of Backward Classes in Services and Posts* (Bangalore, 1987).

9. "Students in India Riot over Favored-Job Plan for Backward Castes," *Oakland Tribune*, 25 August 1990, A7.

10. Bureau of the Census, Statistical Brief (Washington, D.C., 1991).

11. Quadagno, *Color of Welfare*, 3–32. Quadagno is part of an emerging scholarship that reexamines the role of race in explaining United States domes-

tic policy for the last half century. See also Douglas Massey and Nancy Denton, *American Apartheid* (Cambridge, MA, 1993), and Kenneth O'Reilly, *Nixon's Piano*. There were, of course, earlier analysts who described parts of the picture. For example, Charles Abrams, writing in the 1950s and 60s, had documented how the Federal Housing Authority's policies were explicitly racist. See Charles Abram's "The Housing Problem and the Negro," in Talcott Parsons and Kenneth Clark, eds., *The Negro American* (Boston, 1966), 512–24.

12. Quadagno, *Color of Welfare*, 21.

13. The CIO was far more receptive to blacks than the AFL, but complete racial exclusionary practices in many CIO locals continued well into the 1970s.

14. Quadagno, *Color of Welfare*, 23.

15. Abrams, "The Housing Problem," 524.

16. *Ibid.*

17. *Ibid.*

18. Literally, those authorized to make loans at banks would draw a red line around a black community, and no one inside that red line could get a loan. Until 1949 the FHA also encouraged the use of restrictive covenants banning African Americans from given neighborhoods and refused to insure mortgages in integrated neighborhoods. Thanks to the FHA, no bank would insure loans in the ghetto, and few African Americans could live outside it. See Quadagno, *Color of Welfare*, 24–25.

19. Massey and Denton, *American Apartheid*, 20–53.

20. Ezorsky, *Racism and Justice,* 36.

21. *Griggs v. Duke Power*, 401 U. S. 424 (1971).

22. See *Richmond v. J. A. Croson Co.*, 488 U. S. 469 (1989).

23. Shelby Steele, *The Content of Our Character: A New Vision of Race in America* (New York, 1990).

24. "A New Governor Acts to Halt Affirmative Action," *New York Times*, 12 January 1996, A21; Governor Foster is reported to have said that Martin Luther King Jr. "sort of believed like I do" about affirmative action, namely, that he, Foster, could not find any evidence that King wanted racial preferences in hiring.

25. Martin Luther King Jr., *Why We Can't Wait* (New York, 1964).

26. Richard Walker, "California Rages Against the Dying of the Light," *New Left Review* 209 (January–February 1995): 45.

27. Figures are from the California Employment Development Department.

28. "Winged Victory," *The Economist*, 2 December 1989, 84.

29. Jeffrey Ballinger, "The New Free-Trade Heel," *Harper's*, August 1992, 46.

30. Mark Clifford, "The China Connection: Nike Is Making the Most of All That Cheap Labor," *Far Eastern Economic Review* 155 (5 November 1992): 60.

31. Mark Clifford, "Spring in Their Step," *Far Eastern Economic Review* 155 (5 November 1992): 56–57.

32. Ballinger, "Free-Trade Heel," 46.

33. Quadagno, *Color of Welfare*, 26–27.

34. O'Reilly, *Nixon's Piano*; Kevin P. Phillips, *The Emerging Republican Majority* (New Rochelle, NY, 1969).

35. The most recent official data available are from the Statistical Abstracts of 1993.

36. O'Reilly, *Nixon's Piano*; Phillips, *Republican Majority*.

37. In the recent rankings by the National Research Council, seventy-eight departments in the nine-campus system ranked among the top ten, far and away the highest percentage of top-ranking departments at any institution of higher learning.

38. The high number of 4.0 grade point averages is a function of both grade inflation in the high schools and of "advanced placement" courses. In the wealthier areas of the state, students can take these special courses and increase their grade point averages well over the 4.0 level. Thus, on closer inspection, a 4.0 GPA may simply indicate that the student had access to these advanced placement courses. In poorer areas and, indeed, among the more than twelve hundred California high schools. the great majority do not offer any advanced placement courses.

Is Affirmative Action

a Christian Heresy?

J. Jorge Klor de Alva

for Albert J. Raboteau, who blazed the way

The Christian Soul of Liberalism

In 1965 president Lyndon Johnson, speaking of the unprecedented affirmative action policies he was championing and cog-
nizant of the dissension they would precipitate, stated: "We have
to press for them as a matter of right, but we also have to recognize that by doing so, we will destroy the Democratic Party."[1]
Thirty years later, his remarks appear prophetic. While the social
and political divisions resulting from affirmative action are not the
only reason for the party's end-of-century decline, media evidence
during the election year of 1996 continues to suggest that few
other causes match affirmative action in its capacity to unsettle
the nation's perennially contested political and moral balance.[2]

What is it about the arguments for and against policies of
selective restitution and collective assistance based on immutable
physical characteristics that give them the power to affect American politics so deeply? Given the myriad answers offered so far,
the near silence on the role theological beliefs and Christian
ideologies have played in the struggle over affirmative action is
surprising, especially as religious commitment continues to be a
major, if not dominant, motivating force in American life.[3] With
this in mind, this essay attempts an exploration — however in-
choate — of some salient ways in which religious ideas may have
come to influence the ongoing debate. The question posed in the
title is therefore not meant to be facetious. Indeed, I want to argue
that, *if affirmative action policies are truly illiberal, as most of their*

opponents assert, they may also have to be considered non-Christian.

My line of reasoning rests in part on the close connections that exist between liberalism and Christianity. I nevertheless take note from the start that the links are not evident to those who believe that religion no longer plays (or should play) a critical intellectual or moral role in the public and civic spheres.[4] More important, I recognize that these ties are difficult to accept for Americans, most of whom grew up believing that liberalism — with its emphasis on civil equality and freedom of speech and, therefore, its concern with religious freedom and the separation of church and state — is a worldly political and moral philosophy that, though Western in origin, transcends temporal and cultural boundaries. After all, since the eighteenth century much intellectual and political energy has been successfully spent in the effort to conceal liberalism's culture-specific foundations. By taking as their model the seemingly objective paradigms of Western science and the ostensibly neutral language of mathematics, many thinkers in the West have interpreted liberalism's culturally embedded practices, and political and moral philosophies, as universal phenomena resulting from the equally objective and neutral demands of both universal logic, apperceived through "natural reason," and metaphysical realism, inexorably restrained by the dictates of "natural law." It follows that in the reckoning of moderns who hold these positions, illiberal formulations would not necessarily have to be construed as non-Christian.

In his masterful essay on the politics of recognition, however, Charles Taylor persuasively argues that "liberalism is not so much an expression of the secular, postreligious outlook...as a more organic outgrowth of Christianity," which "is to say that liberalism can't and shouldn't claim cultural neutrality." In fact, he adds, "the very term *secular* was originally part of the Christian vocabulary."[5] To be sure, liberalism owes its origin and its conditions of continued possibility to the West's abiding commitment to modern (and not so modern) translations of a number of critical Christian beliefs and valuations, in whose absence neither a politically liberal nor a morally Christian society could exist.

Foremost among these theological premises is the belief that each person has a separate and autonomous soul, equal to any other soul in the eyes of God, which is capable of salvation only on an individual, personal basis — whether through the performance of good works, through faith, or through a personal "conversion" experience. Of course, the shift from the religious recognition of persons as independent bearers of an individual, egalitarian moral status before God to the contractual idea of persons being right-bearing with a civil status equal to all other fellow citizens took centuries of warfare and debate, much of it focused on removing the church from affairs of state. Still, what made the language of natural rights, citizenship, freedom, tolerance, and pluralism possible was the painstaking construction of grammars of canon law, natural law, and common and civil law, all of which gained their legitimacy — then as today — from their congruence with the basic premises and valuations of Christianity.

Liberal civil and political society similarly evolved in the eighteenth century out of, and justified itself through, Christian principles translated by intellectual and political elites into the language of natural law and human rights. The guiding principle of such a society included civic equality — as a this-worldly reflection of the otherworldly mystical body of Christ composed of the fellowship of the baptized — and the separation of church and state, popularly captured in the biblical command to "render unto Caesar the things that are Caesar's and unto God the things that are God's." In effect, as Larry Siedentop has argued, liberal theories of the person and society have their origin in, and maintain their legitimacy through, the conceptual and normative matrix that Christianity has continued to provide for the West.[6]

Antinomianism as Process and Heresy

This matrix, however, has always been a much contested framework. Since its dawn during the apostolic age, Christianity has never been of one mind in its social thought, its theology has never been monological, and its doctrines have had to struggle continually to maintain their status as dogma. At all times Christianity has had to deal with a series of irresolvable tensions, as Christian theology and social policy are permanently riddled with oppositional principles and contradictory commands that might logically be derived from equally accepted dogmas or rules. Christian truth, then, is in part understood as the consequence of the productive tensions between real or apparent opposing positions.

From the beginning, heresy — as a denial of a defined doctrine — usually resulted from overemphasizing or excluding either one side or another of the church's many antinomies. This antinomic dialectic, which has contributed greatly both to Christianity's theological growth and its denominational proliferation, always had to be contained within socially integrative bounds if it was to do its spiritual and pastoral work of salvation and unified guidance. Consequently, when a heretical belief was popular but not a threat to the foundational doctrines of the church, initial condemnations were often followed by accommodation and the meaning of what counted as Christian was thereby enriched. But when the defenders of orthodoxy declared a belief or practice to have surpassed the limits of productive tension — because the disclaimed doctrine threatened to undermine the raison d'être of the faith — and the willfully defiant failed to prevail, the outcome was emphatic condemnation, generally followed not only by a formal rejection but also by active persecutions, excommunications, or executions. Thus Gnosticism's belief that Christ neither fully assumed a human body nor died; Pelagianism's denial of the transmission of original sin to Adam's descendants; or the Albigenses' assertion that Christ was only an angel with a phantom body, and therefore neither suffered nor rose again — all precipitated devastating persecutions that brought the heresies to an end.

The early traditional church, of course, was not always successful in crushing grave heresies, even some that threatened its very existence. Protestantism, the first modern Christian heresy, is the obvious example; antinomianism, hiding in the folds of the Reformation, was another. Like the more popular Waldenses, the antinomians survived persecution by ultimately joining the Reformation movement in the sixteenth century, but, unlike the Waldenses, antinomians never comprised a specific community of believers that could be persecuted as a single deviant group. Instead, the ideas of antinomianism have been present in numerous heretical or sectarian movements since the dawn of the early church and have survived as doctrines to the present within a number of sects.

As a heretical concern, the doctrine of antinomianism, as its name suggests,[7] focused on the belief that, because of the redemptive power of God's grace, Christians do not have to obey the Mosaic Law or any moral law at all to be saved. Among some antinomian Gnostic sects, whose Manichaeanism articulated a sharp, opposing division between matter and spirit, a consequent indifference to bodily actions made licentiousness totally acceptable. This rejection of obedience as legalistic rather than spiritually necessary rested, at first, on the antinomians' interpretations of the convictions of Augustine and Paul, and, later, on Martin Luther's doctrine of justification by faith alone. Antinomianism's fate was linked, therefore, to that of the Protestant controversies and grew as Protestantism gained ground.

In its most extreme form it existed within the left wing of the Protestant Reformation spearheaded by the Anabaptists. They were accused of antinomianism — and later persecuted and executed by the thousands by established Protestants and Catholics — for opposing any cooperation between church and state, daring to rebaptize themselves (a crime then punishable by death), disclaiming infant baptism as a blasphemous formality, refusing to swear civil oaths or bear arms for the state, and, in some places, promoting polygamy and a communistic form of theocracy.

After this militant phase, however, antinomian Protestants settled into less extreme practices and dogmas so that by the end of the eighteenth century they had assimilated for the most part into recognized denominations. Consequently, the brand of antinomians given birth to by the evangelical movement — then greatly expanding in the course of its European and American revival — were more invested in "conversion" as a totally inner experience of rebirth into a new life and as the authentic and only source of good works, than in communalism, antisacramentalism, or a belligerent separation of church and state. Thus, although troublesome to their neighbors and local governments for their separatist ways, in the United States the pacifist wing of the antinomian Anabaptists, surviving as Mennonites and Hutterites, came to be considered more exotic than threatening; meanwhile the roots of another kind of antinomianism, that of the evangelicals and Quakers, sunk deep into the American soil once tilled by enslaved Africans.

The Second Modern Christian Heresy

As suggested earlier in this essay, Christianity has unfolded through the workings of what I have pompously called its antinomic dialectic. At the center of this process has been the tension between Christian universalism and particularism. Universalism was commanded in the Old Testament by later Hebrew prophets who assumed their God had an interest even in some non-Jews. But the New Testament was less hesitant. Christ commanded his apostles to be fishers of all men and women. Later the Christian Fathers translated this into the church's commitment to bring everyone under the fold of its pastoral authority and, by making baptism available to all, within the mystical body of the church where Christ reigned as head. Jesus, after all, was believed to have died for all humankind and therefore no one was to be excluded from His saving grace. The Christian ideal of community and fellowship has consequently always been strong. But so has its commitment to the particularism implied by its orthodox assertion that salvation through Christ's suffering is a solitary matter negotiated individually between each person and God.

Christian theology thus maintains that society is composed of autonomous individuals, each and everyone of whom, in the eyes of God, has a soul equal to the soul of any other. "In the eyes of God": but what about in each other's eyes? Although Christianity never claimed a nonhierarchical society as an ideal nor condemned differences in wealth, status, or power, the long tradition of Christian corporatism was founded on the ideal of reciprocity based on spiritual equality and concerned fellowship among all. Leviticus 19.18 is the locus classicus: "Thou shalt love thy neighbor as thyself." This theme is developed by a number of prophets including Isaiah (for example, 42.1, 3), Jeremiah (7.5–7), and Ezekiel (34.16). And this prophetic legacy is likewise continued throughout the New Testament: for instance, with Paul warning the Christians in Rome that they can never discharge the debt of love they owe each other (13.8–10); Luke's recounting the tale of the Good Samaritan who cared for his neighbor as he would have cared for himself (10.30–37); and John's parable concerning the healing at the pool of Bethesda, which underlines that the paralyzed man could be saved only with the help of the other members of the community (5.7).

Throughout the two millennia of Christianity this balance between individualism and collectivism has been difficult to negotiate. The pendulum has swung continually between the celebration and denunciation of the autonomous individual, as it has oscillated between the promotion and censure of the privileging of the common good over individual needs. Not surprisingly, in our days both the Catholic and Protestant denominations have seen fit to criticize the excesses of capitalism's selfish, consumerist-oriented individualism and socially irresponsible greed, while condemning communism's disregard for the dignity and autonomy of the individual.

As has been noted, liberalism's assumption that society is constituted of free and equal (under the law) individuals in part grew out of the natural law and (later) common law translations of Christian metaphysical and axiological doctrines concerning the existence of souls and their equality in God's eyes. In Larry Siedentop's brief but brilliant essay on the common Christian foundations of individualism and liberalism, he reminds us of the evolution, through the natural law tradition, of the important distinction between the person as a moral agent and the social roles that such a person happens to, or is made to, occupy. "Thus," he argues, "a primary role shared by all equally was distinguished from secondary roles [such] as those of father, servant, or woman." As the meaning of *individual* changed from moral agent to the agent's social role, a "role which organizes any society founded on civic equality," medieval feudal caste differentiations were undermined, and this civic egalitarian role — as opponents of affirmative action argue today — "remains a threat to ascriptions of permanent inequality of status anywhere." "Thus," he concludes, "Christian ontology is the foundation for what are usually described as liberal values in the West — for the commitment to equality and reciprocity, as well as the postulate of individual freedom."[8] But a collapse of the distinction between moral agent and social role remained a constant possibility. And this potential fusion can logically be identified as both illiberal, for rejecting civil equality on the basis of free individuals, and non-Christian, for heretically denying the equality, singularity, and independent fate of each individual soul.

By the middle of the fifteenth century a series of economic transformations and technological advances in Western Europe set the stage for just such a catastrophic collapse, for millions of human beings, of the spiritual distinction between the New Testament's equal-in-the-eyes-of-God *individual*, as "moral criterion,"[9] and the not-necessarily-equal-in-the-eyes-of-one's-peers social *role*, as, in this case, economic category. The vectors of this heretical collapse would lead away from spiritual and ontological singularity to profane sociological collectivity, the latter composed of the hapless men and women whose metaphysical substance and subject position would be transformed, by those with the power to do so, into a fixed economic being-*cum*-role determined solely on the basis of membership in a rigid and debased social category outwardly marked by specific, denigrated physical traits.

This non-Christian displacement of the individual by his or her social role, which made it unnecessary to believe that each mortal had a personal soul that would stand in solitude before a judging God, developed a tragic logic. I suggest that this tragic logic resulted primarily from the impressment needs and exchange practices elaborated in the course of the rise of a modern, Western system of mass slavery, which focused overwhelmingly on only one (though large) geographic area containing a variety of humans who generally shared common physical features distinct from their ultimate owners. With this metaphysical collapse of supernatural singularity into, at best, some form of spiritual generality, a new heresy came into being. As with nearly all Christian heresies, this one depended in part on the Bible, particularly the well known story of Noah's curse on Ham (Genesis 9.22–27). But its theological underpinnings rested on more subtle grounds. While an African's physical features were understood by some as mere "accidents" (in the scholastic sense of nonessential qualities), biblical tradition emphasized that the outward characteristics of a people could be a spiritual sign of an internal state. In the seventeenth-century words of the Jesuit Alonso de Sandoval, "the black complexion of the Ethiopians did not derive only from the curse layed by Noah on his son Ham . . . but also from an innate and intrinsic quality, with which God created him"; that is, Africans are black as a consequence "of the will of God or of the particular qualities that these people intrinsically have."[10]

The heresy rests, therefore, not on the fact that a people is considered cursed with slavery and denigrated features as a result of being descended from an ignoble son of Noah — this position was considered orthodox, since the slaves' worldly afflictions did not imply the existence of souls different from those of their masters. It rests, rather, on the identification of a particular set of physical characteristics (mere "accidents") with the ontologically fixed category of bondspersonhood. That is, in the Aristotelian (pagan, nominalist) sense, the accidents, including bondsperson-hood, constitute all there is to the enslaved person. In the heretical Christian sense, physical features and social and spiritual status as part of a collectivity become the totality of the constituents of a being who, as a consequence of this nonrealist construction, is deprived of an essential, ontological singularity and, therefore, of a personal, eternal soul.

How could this heresy come into being? I propose that what today might be described as the "racialization of souls" resulted in part from the novel legal and moral justificatory practices needed to maintain a semblance of religious and civil order in the context of an unprecedented scale of enslavement, which even in the seventeenth and eighteenth centuries, when slavery was both legal and morally sanctioned, was widely recognized as mired in a menacing ooze of potential sins, illegalities, and rebellions. Seeking morally and legally to simplify their participation in the large-scale version of the biblically and globally sanctioned institution of servitude (at a time when its far more limited counterpart had nearly run its course in most parts of Europe), many Christians committed themselves to a new and ominous heresy as they sought to collapse the two poles of the central antinomy of Christian eschatology and social thought rather than to pursue a balance between them.[11]

This heresy put into theological question, in many quarters, the soundness of the ideal of an inclusive community, based on love for one's neighbor as for one's self, as the basis of a universal Christian society. Among charitable Christians, part of the reason for this failure of spiritual and social reciprocity was the impossibility of following Christian precepts while attempting to negotiate the fundamental contradiction slavery presented between the legal status of a bondsperson as object and his or her natural status as a human being. To resolve the contradiction, the less scrupulous sellers, buyers, and impoverished competitors of slaves often resorted to a callous bureaucratic regard for them as existentially constituting no more than a "piece" of a set; that is, as being ontologically incomplete, never constituting anything more than a part of a "cargo" of chattel goods. As the numbers of enslaved Africans grew geometrically, the effect of this impersonalization, coupled with other issues raised below, was to facilitate the belief among many that these hapless people were unblessed with whatever it was that made one an individual. In effect, the idea crystallized for many that slaves must be devoid of a personal soul.

Therefore, quite apart from the traditionally sanctioned justifications for removing individuals from civil society through enslavement — such as servitude for debt, imprisonment following a just war, criminal behavior punishable by bondage, or birth to a slave — the previously necessary requirement of personal fault, or unfortunate individual circumstance, was set aside. In its place came an unprecedented concern with an irrevocable status of exclusion from civic and religious life resting primarily on involuntary inclusion in a social category, whose essential mark of membership was a set of physical differences not shared with the privileged Christians. While the deplorable state of "race" relations today tempts many to search, as did both the slavers and the slaves in the past, for some intrinsic, inevitable, or timeless reason for the devastating phenomenon just described, we are better served by an exploration, however brief, of one of the mechanisms by which this heretical category (of personal soullessness) was built into specific socioeconomic practices, whose mode of subjectification made attractive to many the establishment of a set of unprecedented "racial" limits to Christian fellowship.

Considerable anachronistic speculation aside, we still have much to learn about why this fusion of person and category took place, although today we know a great deal about how it happened. I will not summarize here the now canonized emplotments of the horrifying narrative of terror for Africans and self-degradation for Europeans that slavery entailed.[12] What I want to emphasize, instead, is that this fusion, particularly in what became the United States, led many to a monstrous modern heresy centered on the construction of a novel category of humanity distinguished by physical features that were made to signify either an absence of soul or the existence of an irredeemable one — a group whose spiritual life, if any, must necessarily exist outside the Christian community of fellowship and reciprocity. Not even in the case of the much-abused American natives was a "pagan" category, a "savage" condition, or a radical cultural alterity ever translated by Westerners into such a powerful configuration of incommensurability, which even the imperative of Christian universalism could not overcome.[13] But this powerful new heresy, which I suggest sits at the spiritual and ideological center of the debate around affirmative action, did not evolve overnight. And as could be expected, it was moved by different causes at different times.

One of these provocations, especially during the period when most slaves were African-born, may very well be linked to the voluntary and involuntary ignorance among stateside traders and buyers of slaves concerning the practices by which Africans came to be ensnared in the local traps set out by African and European slavers. My argument can be summarized as follows: although the various relevant jurisdictions each had distinct laws that changed over time, by the seventeenth century in British North America, the theological, legal, and moral legitimacy of the enslavement of any one individual rested primarily on his or her having been made a prisoner of a just war, having been found guilty of perpetrating some serious offense punishable by slavery under the laws applicable to the offender, or being the child of a slave. Yet, as is well known, most Africans enslaved in Africa were probably victims of contrived wars, local legal and religious ruses, and forceful random apprehensions. I say "probably" because it is precisely the constant and ubiquitous incertitude on this point, whether feigned or genuine, that I believe contributed to setting the context for the novel heresy.

To begin with, we know from the many extant documentary sources that New World consumers of slave labor knew very little about Africa, African polities, or the processes by which Africans were involuntarily impressed. And they obviously knew next to nothing about the individual circumstances by which any one of the slaves they were selling or purchasing, with the exception of those born in the Americas, had come to his or her tragic state. Even the Europeans stationed in Africa were ordinarily ignorant of the unfortunate circumstances that led any one African to be caught by a slaver. This ignorance became even more typical as the actual processes of enslavement moved farther away from the coast and became so institutionalized that Europeans rarely participated in them personally. Indeed, by the eighteenth century most seizures took place far enough from the coastal forts to be beyond European surveillance, with the effect that it became "easier to dissociate Negro servitude from the violent act of enslavement." Together these circumstances contributed greatly to making an ontological connection between Africans and slave status appear "natural," especially to those who had something to gain by this identity.[14]

This grim situation logically compelled stateside traders and holders of African-born slaves to create generic fictions about the cultural, legal, and personal pasts of the bondspersons they knew in order to undermine the moral demands made by the singularity of both the captive's humanity and his or her experience of subjugation; demands that together represented a constant threat to every master's claim to a just title or a clear conscience.[15] The brutality of the effects of slavery's central contradiction — the requirement that human subjects be dealt with as personal possessions — and the rampant illegality and abuses intrinsic to mass slavery engendered the need for deindividualization, generalization, and stereotypification. Through these techniques the recognition of an equality of souls between enslaved Africans and non-Africans became nearly impossible for the majority of the privileged, many of whom, to resolve the tension of the contradiction, denied Africans a soul altogether.

The net effect of the personal, social, and legal need to avoid the pangs of conscience, the scandal of corruption, or the semblance of illegality, coupled with the physical, cultural, and institutionalized distance between the scene of apprehension and the site of sale, was to further the erasure of the individuality of any one African and to promote the transformation of his or her singularity into an undifferentiatable reflection of a collective social, legal, and spiritual category. This last point, of course, is not altogether novel.[16] But what deserves emphasis is the extent to which the very process of feigned or real ignorance concerning any one individual's loss of freedom was central to the construction, particularly in British America, of a new category of human organization that collapsed the individuality of each constituent into a social whole. This generalized legal and spiritual disregard for the specific life circumstances of each enslaved African helped to make possible at the local level the impersonal interactions and negative ideologies that would permit the extensive scope, transnational fluidity, economic order, and social organization required at the intercontinental level by modern mass slavery. In order to permit the slaving system to work at the rate of productivity required by large-scale, globalized plantation agriculture, the modern mechanisms of generalizability — the focus on category and grid over particularity and cell — were deployed with a vengeance. The physically distinct characteristics of the enslaved Africans obviously not only facilitated the process of their bondage; but, as many believe, also may have made this form of industrialized slavery possible altogether.

In sum, if his or her belonging to the category of the physically distinct (dark-skinned, and so on) was socially and legally considered grounds enough to presume that the person in question was a licit slave, once had been a licit slave, or could be a licit slave, then the knowledge, nearly impossible to obtain but juridically and morally required, concerning the specific circumstances of his or her enslavement and sale was obviated. Although much more needs to be understood about the effects of this horrendous contrivance, it is clear that enslaved Africans paid dearly for it, especially as this stratagem ultimately helped to transform them in the eyes of the privileged into a mere category rather than a collection of aggrieved souls worthy of compassion and restitution. Perhaps only with another major heresy would the deplorable consequences of the second modern Christian heresy be reversed.

The Last Christian Heresy?
The radically un-Christian heresy that denied to millions of men and women Christianity's spiritual egalitarianism and universality was at heart ontological, but its illiberal consequences were obviously more than metaphysical. After all, this heretical erasure of the singularity of the individual was the critical religious gesture at the center of the origin of the idea of "race" as a spiritual, cosmological, and ultimately social organizing principle. Through the widespread determination that Africans were essentially a different species of people because they lacked spiritual individuality, they were for the most part excluded as a group not only from the possibility of personal salvation (by those who denied them an individual soul) but also from Christianity's universal community of fellowship and reciprocity.

Besides the practical solutions this homogenization offered concerning the determination of a legal title, by making the need to investigate or know the details of any specific slave's apprehension or past seem unnecessary, the heresy that made *race* a fundamental category likewise resolved the system's most troubling contradiction — the need to treat humans as things — by denying a unique individuality to Africans and instead permitting their treatment as morally indistinct members of a necessary socioeconomic category. Resolved also was the pragmatic civil and religious problem of what to do with these indispensable but demeaned laborers because, as primarily role players in an economic system rather than persons in a moral world, they could be treated in an illiberal manner that would be immediately recognized as morally reprehensible if attempted on any other group. The implications of this homogenization for the lives of African Americans, of course, were devastating at the time, and continued to be so after slavery and the corporate category of *slave* were replaced, following the Civil War, with segregation and the collective category of *race*.

For these and many other historical reasons, Christianity came only slowly to the spiritual aid of the enslaved Africans. Indeed, it was not until the mid eighteenth-century evangelical revival known as the Great Awakening — which extensively popularized the antinomian concern for opening the way to salvation through the ardent experience of individual conversion (in contrast to the typical lengthy and elaborate instruction required by the established churches) — that some Africans in what is now the United States began to make theirs the consoling and promising messages of Bible-based Christianity. As Albert Raboteau has shown in his classic book on slave religion in the antebellum South, revivalism's emphasis on the individual, "with its intense concentration on inward conversion, fostered an inclusiveness which could border on egalitarianism," and the energized evangelicals, sure "about the capacity of slaves to share the experience of conversion," made the most of this universalizing opening by preaching widely to mixed congregations. But as is too well known today, this "tendency of evangelical religion to level the souls of all...before God" did not conclude with eventual integration.[17] It was always too little, too late, and too threatening.

Even when countered by the evangelical antinomians, who celebrated the religious capacity of the enslaved Africans and strove to return to them a publicly expressible spiritual individualism, for the general population the powerful heresy of ontological corporatism had drawn lines too sharply and indelibly to be even momentarily suspended by the possibility that Africans might also have redeemable souls. The resistance of masters to worshiping alongside slaves, whose coupling of spiritual to civil equality and dreams of liberation they deeply feared, was too great. Overpowering also was the social, economic, and cultural distance between the privileged Christians and the impoverished freedmen and hapless slaves. The few newly formed mixed congregations were so quickly segregated that by 1800 some independent African Baptist and Methodist churches began to appear. But some of the new churches established by Africans were not the result of segregation from previously mixed congregations; instead, they responded to the originally imposed, but then internalized, need for each community to attend separately to their respective spiritual needs.[18] In effect, the second Christian heresy had done its job: as a community, free and enslaved Africans were left on their own, in soul and fate. So to strive for success they would first have to attend to themselves as a separate group.

The creation by Europeans of a Christian heresy — a heresy that made physical differences a defining characteristic of social and religious experience — logically led Africans and their descendants to begin to appropriate for themselves the antiestablishment antinomianism that would permit them to articulate a spirituality and religious organization reflective of their particular conditions. In opposition to the reigning antiuniversalist heresy, evangelical antinomianism worked for the resolution of the struggle between the commitment of the traditional church to individual salvation and to human fellowship in Christ. It did this by putting in the hands of each believer the power to transform him- or herself through a personal conversion, and in the hands of each congregation, the power to define for itself the nature of its collective spirituality. Because of this "spirit of Gospel freedom"[19] — born of antinomianism's strict focus on the power of God's grace to save, independent of a person's behavior or, in the light of the new heresy, his or her civil status — and because of its faith in the interiority of conversion as opposed to a reliance on outward signs, a sacred space began to be conceived in the African American world for spiritual and social creativity. These creativities together could help give a distinct content to the separate universe that slavery and heresy had forced into being.

After the turn of the eighteenth century, Christianity began to spread quickly among city-dwelling freedmen and slaves, but, since the majority of Africans continued to live in rural areas, they remained beyond its influence. The triumph of the North, however, opened the way for widespread evangelization. And given the tragic failure of Reconstruction, after the Civil War Christian African Americans began to turn as never before to the church they had had to build. As Raboteau observes, "In the midst of slavery, religion was for slaves a space of meaning, freedom, and transcendence.... [Later,] as the one institution which freed blacks were allowed to control, the church was the center of social, economic, educational, and political activity. It was also a source of continuity and identity for the black community."[20]

By the twentieth century Christianity, especially evangelical Protestantism, had sunk its roots deep into the fertile spiritual soil of African American communities. Their faithful upholding of the sense of the universal, even as each disillusionment strengthened the temptation to make the church "racial," lent both hope and vision to that part of the nation that began to gear itself up to support a civil rights movement that promised to make integration a reality at last. But, as is widely recognized, this second moment of reconstruction, although hardly to be compared to the first, whose effects after all it sought to reverse, also failed most African Americans. But unlike what had taken place in the past, on this occasion liberalism's shortcomings were forced to the surface. It was an auspicious moment for the emergence of a second illiberal Christian heresy.

In the past, spiritually significant "racial" distinctions had made traditional Christianity impossible for those who believed in them because the basis for the distinctions violated the very core of its orthodoxy. But the heretics were unimaginable as objects of persecution because nonheretical preachers had been both powerless and few, and those excluded by the heretical ideas had been considered by most of the privileged to be ontologically beyond the faith. As Bishop George Berkeley had observed in 1731, following his nearly three-year stay in America, the colonists' "irrational contempt for the Blacks, *as creatures of another species*, who had no right to be instructed or admitted to the sacraments; [has] proved a main obstacle to the conversion of these poor people." But the ancient antinomian heresy smuggled into the United States by evangelism during the Great Awakening had called for inward conversion and universalism, the result of which had been the tendency of evangelical preachers "to de-emphasize the outward status of men, and to cause black and white alike to *feel* personally that Christ had died for them as individuals."[21] In accomplishing this, the ancient heresy — turned evangelical dogma — had helped to undermine for many the new heresy that held that Africans could not be Christianized. One benign (former) heresy, then, was able to cancel or at least redress the negative effects of another.

Affirmative action is that kind of propitious heresy. It is, as many of its opponents claim, illiberal. Rather than supporting the individual in a civil egalitarian manner, it favors a select few chosen on the basis of membership in a group whose physical characteristics have been made legally significant. Because of it, individual rights are indeed often sacrificed to the common good. And to the extent that liberalism, as I argued at the beginning, is rooted in and maintains its legitimacy through Christian beliefs and valuations, affirmative action can also be said to be non-Christian, that is, theologically heretical. At its core this illiberal public policy, by making legally significant the accidental characteristics of its beneficiaries, mimics the heretical thinking of slavers and owners of enslaved Africans. All this I am forced to grant. But as I hope I have shown, a liberating heresy assimilated into the mainstream can indeed help redress the evil consequences of a repressive one, especially when, as in our case, the latter made the former not only possible but necessary. Perhaps the time has indeed come for a third, and possibly final, modern Christian heresy to spread throughout the land, choking off what the second one yielded.

I would prefer that it were otherwise, that physical characteristics could be deracialized and liberalism could be made safe for the impoverished and the estranged. But at the end of the twentieth century it is beginning to appear that social and economic justice, perhaps illiberal demands themselves, cannot come about for the poor through the exercise of unrestrained individual freedom by the privileged, nor through their defense of a now nearly meaningless civil egalitarianism. Maybe an orthodox Christian cannot support affirmative action, but anyone educated in the Western

Christian tradition must demand of him- or herself a thorough understanding of how we came to this sad state before claiming that affirmative action is unfair for being illiberal, or too dangerous for being politically risky. It is not enough to say "we are all children of God" unless something good for all follows from it.

NOTES

1. Michael Wines, "How Affirmative Action Got So Hard to Sell," *New York Times,* 23 July 1995.

2. The following representative examples appeared as I finished this essay: James Brooke, "Colorado Bases College Aid on Need Rather Than Race," *New York Times,* 16 January 1996; Sarah Kershaw, "Regents Decide Not to Change Policy on Bias," *New York Times,* 19 January 1996.

3. See Leroy S. Rouner, ed., *Civil Religion and Political Theology* (Notre Dame, IN, 1986), 2; Stephen L. Carter, *The Culture of Disbelief: How American Law and Politics Trivializes Religious Devotion* (New York, 1993).

4. On this point see Richard John Neuhaus, *The Naked Public Square: Religion and Democracy in America* (Grand Rapids, MI, 1984), and Carter, *Culture of Disbelief.*

5. Charles Taylor, *Multiculturalism and "The Politics of Recognition,"* ed. Amy Gutmann (Princeton, NJ, 1992), 62.

6. Larry A. Siedentop, "Liberalism: The Christian Connection," *Times Literary Supplement,* 24–30 March 1989, 308.

7. The term comes from the Greek *anti,* "against," and *nomos,* "law."

8. Siedentop, "Liberalism," 308.

9. The phrase is Siedentop's, "Liberalism," 308.

10. See Alonso de Sandoval, *Un tratado sobre la esclavitud* (Madrid, 1987), 74. This edition is a translation by Enriqueta Vila Vilar, ed., of Sandoval's *De instauranda Aethiopum salute* printed in Seville in 1627.

11. On the extent to which this phenomenon was unprecedented see, for example, David Brion Davis, *The Problem of Slavery in Western Culture* (Ithaca, NY, 1966), 29–31, 47–49, 61, 101.

12. See, for example, Davis, *Problem of Slavery;* Winthrop D. Jordan, *White over Black: American Attitudes Toward the Negro, 1550–1812* (Chapel Hill, NC, 1968); Orlando Patterson, *Slavery and Social Death: A Comparative Study* (Cambridge, MA, 1982), and Orlando Patterson, *Freedom in the Making of Western Culture* (New York, 1991).

13. See note 11. On the differences between Western perceptions of American natives as opposed to Africans see Davis, *Problem of Slavery,* 10, 167–68,

170–71, 174–77, 181, 186, 192–94, 222, 284.

14. For some of the points raised in this paragraph see Davis, *Problem of Slavery*, 183–85.

15. On the nature of the latter threat as seen by a Jesuit, see Sandoval, *Un tratado*, 142–49.

16. See note 12, esp. Davis, *Problem of Slavery*, and Patterson, *Slavery and Social Death*.

17. Albert J. Raboteau, *Slave Religion: The "Invisible Institution" in the Antebellum South* (New York, 1980), 132–33, 149; on the minimal influence of Christianity on the slaves see *ibid.*, 96–150.

18. *Ibid.*, 137.

19. *Ibid.*, 178.

20. *Ibid.*, 318, 320.

21. George Berkeley, quoted in *ibid.*, 100 (emphasis added); *ibid.*, 148.

An Affirmative View

Judith Butler

The resolutions SP–1 and 2, which were passed by the University
of California Board of Regents in 1995, are restrictive in their
scope and purpose. They make plain that no reference to the
categories of race, gender, or ethnicity is to take place in determining the qualifications of an applicant to the University of California. What does it mean that no reference can take place, and
how are we to understand this restriction on the referential discourse of the admissions process? Certain categories that have,
within recent legal history, described disadvantaged groups must
not be mentioned, or taken into account, as criteria or even in
the discussion of criteria for admission into these institutions of
higher learning. Not only are certain categories to remain un-
mentioned, outside the relevant and decisive discussion, but a
certain kind of silence is being mandated in such contexts. Race
is certainly one of those categories, and this supports the claim
by Angela Harris, a legal scholar at Berkeley's Boalt Law School,
that we are living in a time of "color-blind constitutionalism."[1]
What marks this time rhetorically is precisely the voluminous
talk about race which seeks to make the case that race should not
be a factor in admissions to higher educational institutions nor in
employment decisions. So what we have, then, is the paradoxical
situation in which legal discourse on race intensifies and proliferates precisely in order to make it *unmentionable* in those narrowly defined contexts where it is to be decided who will be
admitted into the institutions where this discussion is taking
place. In other words, the legal discourse on race intensifies and
proliferates precisely in order to make race unmentionable in
those contexts which determine the shape that conversation will

take in future times. In this way, the discourse on the unmention-ability of race may be understood not only to restrict the kind of discourse that will be possible, but, to the extent that this is a discourse that decides the question of who will become part of the community of discourse, produces the relevant parameters of the speaking community.

This is, of course, paradoxical and disturbing for another reason. A common argument against affirmative action is that it provides no educational benefits, and a common argument in favor of affirmative action is that a diversity of ethnic and racial backgrounds and gender balance in the classroom and in the larger educational environment does provide an array of perspectives on topics in public life and that this diversity and balance enhance the project of a democratic conversation — that is, a conversation that has all the tensions and difficulties and promise of talking within and across ethnic and racial lines, the kind of conversation that is part of democratic process itself under conditions where interpretations are invariably at odds, the semantic field of interpretation is not settled, and, in that sense, no unified speech community can be presumed. The argument against affirmative action on these grounds is that the composition of the classroom in no way affects the positions that one takes within the classroom, that *who* gets into the conversation does not affect *how* the conversation takes place or what becomes its focus. The California regents have implicitly decided that it does make a difference, for by making certain categories unmentionable in the course of admissions decisions, they control the question of who will become part of the discussion of race. What appears as "colorblindness" is perhaps a certain enforced blindness to the rhetorical and political consequences of their own decision. For to endeavor to be blind to race is still to be related to race in a mode of blindness. In other words, race does not fall away from view; it becomes produced as the absent object that structures permissible discourse.

The regents' strategy has affinities with the policy on gays in the military which produced a good deal of talk on the airwaves and on television. The point there was to circumscribe a certain kind of speech, namely, of those within the military who might say "I am a homosexual." The price of that speech is to be ex-pelled from the institution of the military unless you can prove that you did not mean it, that you were only that for a day, that you spoke under duress, or that you repent and have now no propensity to act again in that same way. Of course, as the term "homosexual" became unmentionable in the context in which military personnel offer descriptions about themselves, the term became highly mentionable in a regulatory domain in which putatively straight officers decide the context in which the term will operate.

In affirmative action discourse, I would suggest, it is not that terms such as "race," "gender," and "ethnicity" are no longer mentioned, but that a certain discursive power to circumscribe the proper domain of their mentionability is being heightened, and that the power to constitute the meaning of such terms is being monopolized by those who seek to render the words unmentionable in certain contexts. Those words thus become the instrument of a regulatory discourse, one which must state and restate the words as that which is not to be mentioned, and so fortify the place of the words as the possession and instrument of the regulatory power that seeks to render the words unmentionable, and which can only do this by monopolizing the occasions of their mentionability, and thus contradicting itself in that very endeavor.

The assumption of the anti-affirmative action position is that the race or gender or ethnicity of the person in question does not directly relate to his or her qualification and value as a potential member of the academic community in question. In some ways, this view makes sense, for it would be clearly wrong to claim that one might immediately derive something about the potential quality and value of an applicant on the basis of race, gender, or ethnicity alone. Such categories alone do not provide sufficient grounds for any such determination. And as I understand the use of such categories within admissions processes, they have never been treated as exclusive or sufficient grounds for admission. No simple description of a person on the basis of such categories provides an adequate or sufficiently interesting description of that person's potential value in the classroom or in the educational environment more generally. Indeed, one might reasonably question whether such categories are descriptive in their function, whether they can tell us what "standpoint" a particular person might occupy, or whether they can tell us something valuable about the perspectives that a person might have to offer an institution of higher learning.

Any reconceptualization of the defense of affirmative action must make clear the radical incommensurability between the determination of the social category to which a person belongs and the determination of what contribution such a person may make. Clearly, this is not a causal relationship, and any attempt to derive the latter determination from the former in a strictly causal way will and should fail. Any strict derivation would amount to a form of essentialism which presupposes that viewpoints inhere in positionalities, and such a view would override the complex ways in which differing viewpoints remain incommensurable with and irreducible to such categories. Indeed, when progressive forms of identity politics insist on standpoint analyses that assume a structural relation between social positionality and epistemological view, they unwittingly produce the very essentialism that anti-affirmative action forces seek to undo. By resisting the conflation of social position and epistemological view, indeed, by safeguarding the incommensurability of that very relation, a new basis for valuing affirmative action becomes possible: the valuably unpredictable relation between position and perspective is precisely what university environments ought to be in the business of protecting and fostering.

And yet, is that all that can be said about the relationship between race, ethnicity, and gender and the determination of a possible contribution to academic life? Even if such categories do not imply a contribution directly, do they, taken in concert with other considerations, help to form a picture of what a contribution might be? I would argue that such categories can constitute a point of departure for a cultural understanding of a person's background, life experience, aspirations, and perspectives that constitutes a hermeneutic condition for the understanding of that person's past and future trajectory. Hence, the social categories become a condition for the interpretation of that person's value and potential contribution — that is, a condition enabling an observor to locate and narrate the trajectory of that life. But for such categories to constitute hermeneutic conditions for making such a determination is not the same as causally deriving the potential contribution of such a person from the social categories by which they are partially described.

For those of us who, prior to the regents' resolution of July 20, 1995, did not believe that the University of California's commitment to affirmative action could be revoked, the current dismantling of affirmative action criteria in admissions policies has introduced an epistemic crisis into the understanding of the university's political culture. When I came to the Berkeley campus of the University of California in 1993, it seemed to me that I was entering an academic culture schooled in the lessons of affirmative action and that the institution and the culture of affirmative action were indissociable from one another. In other words, it was impossible to think of Berkeley except as an academic culture formed in part through policies of affirmative action. The regents' resolution inaugurated a sense of institutional dislocation, a sense of not knowing where I was, and a need to reclaim some sense of my political and cultural bearings.

As some of my minority undergraduates filed in to register their opinion on the matter of affirmative action, however, I realized that another discourse was filtered through this one, displacing the affirmative action debate onto one that concerns precisely the culture that they understand affirmative action to have produced, one based on the politics of identity and, in particular, practices of exclusionary identity politics. "Wait!" I wanted to yell, hoping still to separate the issues, but for some of these students, the issue had already congealed into the following form: only as freshmen, they told me, did students from various cultural and racial backgrounds hang out together in and out of class, but sometime during the sophomore year, the pressure to acquire and affiliate with an identity category became insurmountable. Sometimes this demand to affiliate took specifically political forms, but for the most part it was exercised in less overt ways. One student suggested that the campus culture made ethnic identities mandatory. What disoriented me most was that these students were fans of Jesse Jackson, positioned at the left margin of liberalism — or even to the left of liberalism — and sought a different sense of multicultural community than the one they saw encoded in, and produced by, affirmative action policy. The kind of multiculturalism to which they aspired would not be reducible to the stringing together of various forms of separatist identity politics.

How is it that affirmative action became, for these students, identified with exclusionary identity positions? And is there a way of reading their response that gives some insight into the cultural disposition of the regents and their supporters? The students' reasoning seems to go like this: affirmative action appears to be a way of *marking* students by "race, religion, sex, color, ethnicity, or national origin." By marking them in this way, students are reduced to the mark, and the mark comes to stand for the reason they are at Berkeley, producing, as it were, a self-conscious class of tokens. Some students complain about being imprisoned by this mark, resenting the reduction it signifies, while others take it on as a sign of pride and accomplishment, which enhances the cultural visibility of minority communities on campus, in extracurricular as well as curricular activities.

The student discussion that came to my attention was not about whether affirmative action remains necessary, whether it is yet to accomplish the goal of realizing substantial equality through admissions procedures, or whether it helps to produce a community of faculty and students who represent the diversity of the population at large. Indeed, this discussion was not about affirmative action at all. Rather, it seemed that the debate centered on the way that policy has been culturally articulated, the way it tacitly structures the ways in which identities are formed, recognized, legitimated, and delegitimated within the academic community.

Whether affirmative action remains necessary and how it has been articulated are, I believe, two separate and separable issues, and their contemporary conflation is responsible for some of the confusion that is propagated under the rubric of "affirmative action debates." Some critics of the culture of identity politics have, rightly or wrongly, attributed responsibility for their present quandaries to the indirect consequences of affirmative action policies. But is it clear that the policy has produced a culture of exclusionary identity politics? Has the policy, perhaps, come to stand for such a culture, one that has its roots in a more complex genealogy?

I am not certain how best to answer this question, but I do think that some common presumptions about how identity categories work condition the debates on both sets of issues, and that a critical examination of those presumptions is necessary to come to grips with the political aims at work in the overall debate. One reading of the regents' proposal suggests that affirmative action has become an occasion to question the relation between minority status and identity, and the relevance of each of these terms to the assessment of merit and achievement. The policy is held responsible for producing and sustaining racial, ethnic, and sexual divisions, rather than a possible remedy for the differential access that minorities and women have had to the resources of the University of California. The policy's language mandates that certain categories *not* be used as criteria for admission or "admissions in exception," thus targeting any reference to such categories and also implying that any such reference amounts to the practice of exceptionalism. The proposal not only prohibits reference to such categories but also actively imagines a set of deliberations in which such categories would no longer be criterial in any way. The policy imagines the obliteration of such categories in the thinking of admissibility, and so bids admissions committees to begin to imagine the community of students as no longer marked by such categories.

In the argument that some of my students offer, affirmative action has effectively produced a culture in which the identities of students are *totalized* by their minority status. According to the presumption at work in the regents' resolution, there is no room for reference to any of these categories as criteria in admissions. What does the very reference admit into the process of admissions that threatens the fairness of the deliberation? Why is it that these categories are now to become wholly unmentionable? If they are mentioned, does this not mean that they become, for that reason, the supervenient factor at work in any deliberation? If they are mentioned, indeed, if they become mentionable, do they immediately threaten to overwhelm all other considerations? To deem the categories unmentionable in the discussion of criteria, as the policy does, is to assume that their mentionability contaminates legitimate criteria. If the categories become mentionable, will they operate unilaterally and as sufficient grounds not only to determine why a given student is admitted, but to constitute the continuing condition of the student's eligibility and legitimacy in the eyes of the university and its culture? The proposed obliteration of the categories is offered as a way to remove the stigma of minority status and to take away a set of blinders in the admissions process, permitting, ostensibly, an illumination of the "merit" and "achievement" of the student under consideration.

The regents' presumption about how affirmative action works, however, is that the student, admitted through reference to such categories, becomes nothing other than the mark of his or her minority status or, at least, acquires his or her legitimacy as a student through recourse to such categories. The policy to revoke affirmative action guidelines thus emerges as a liberation from this stigma, opposing the reduction of the person to his or her minority status, where that minority status is taken to be the primary legitimating ground for admission to the university. The student is thus ostensibly illuminated as a person with variable merits, none of which are to be interpreted in light of his or her minority status, cultural or national background, sex, color, religion, ethnicity, or race.

A number of uncritically accepted presumptions are at work in the argument whose schematic form I have provided above. First, why is it that reference to such categories in the deliberation on admissibility is taken to be a *reduction* of the student under deliberation to the mark of his or her minority status? To make reference to such categories may be one way of establishing the necessary background for an understanding of what the candidate has accomplished. Such a reference helps to contextualize the constraints and opportunities that have formed a student's learning environment, operating to delimit not merely the "cultural trappings" that the candidate may or may not have had to overcome (a view that continues to see minority status exclusively as a liability to be overcome, an injury requiring compensation), but also the cultural contribution the candidate stands to make to the community at large. To acknowledge the ways in which a minority status works *to frame* such issues is not the same as reducing the candidate in question to his or her minority marking. Does affirmative action require that such categories be understood simply and directly as "criteria," or are they, rather, frameworks for the interpretation of criteria? If "minority status" is considered as a mark, a factor, an attribute, a static quality of a person, then the categories do work to reify a set of social dynamics and historical formations, relevant contexts, not only reducing, say, the category of race to the status of an attribute, but also leaving the way open for the reduction of the individual to his or her minority status.

Although one might argue that such a category forms but one

factor among many, it would be better to cease thinking of such a status as a "factor" altogether. Minority status is better understood as a framework for the interpretation and determination of what constitutes achievement, a horizon within which the meaning of achievement can be understood or, for the first time, becomes understandable. Indeed, it very well may be that "achievement" and "merit" become illuminated — that is, rendered visible and interpretable — *only* within a framework that acknowledges the cultural specificity of the meanings of "accomplishment." In this sense, the reference to minority status is not a blinder in the way of determining merit and achievement, but, rather, an epistemic condition for the recognition of achievement and merit, indeed, for an understanding of the various forms that merit and achievement take.

To understand minority status this way, however, is to construe it neither as that which totalizes identity (whereby a person is nothing but this mark of minority status) nor as a totalization that must be overcome through a prohibition on any reference to it (the rendering unspeakable of such terms within the proposed scenario of admissions deliberations). In either case, the categories denoting minority status remain empty, formal, and fixed, understood through the language of the "factor." Even if we understand such categories to be one among many that enter into the constitution of a student's profile, the language of the factor still presumes that minority status might be contained and exhaustively represented in a quantifiable form. Although the language of the "factor" implies that this status will be but one factor among others and, hence, only partially constitutive of the individual's profile, the language nevertheless performs a totalization of the status, suggesting its containment and representability as a statistical unit or discrete attribute. As a "factor," minority status is entered into the quantifiable language of the equation, and the qualitative dimension of minority status becomes eclipsed through that reduction. With that eclipse, minority status is no longer understood as a background, a framework of interpretation, but becomes reduced to a quantifiable item to be tallied along with others, although not one to be read or interpreted as part of the cultural fabric of a life. This "qualitative" dimension, the questions of interpretation that minority status poses to the deliberation process, is precisely what the language of ontology and quantification cannot capture. And this is where the positions for and against the totalizing views of identity fail to question the presumption of totalization — compounded by the operative presumption of quantification — that conditions them both.

In effect, my argument is that minority status ought to be construed neither as a quantifiable factor nor as that which must remain unspeakable within admissions policy. The perspectives on a life that such categories permit are foreclosed both by their unmentionability and their calculability (indeed, both constitute forms erasing this epistemic perspective). What is most relevant about minority status for the determination of merit and achievement cannot be "calculated" according to a quantifiable method. The quantification of minorities not only abstracts from the qualitative considerations of background, history, environment, opportunity, and cultural forms of expression and ideals, but also freezes the status of "minority" in an ahistorical vacuum, subjecting it to a logic of calculability that destroys the very referent it seeks to represent. Minority categories are neither partial nor exhaustive *attributes* of a person, and reference to such categories does not in themselves furnish knowledge about what a person is and what it is a person has done or will do. As markers, they are points of departure for an interpretation, ways of locating accomplishment culturally, specifying the terms by which it can best be understood. When they are taken to represent the person, they work in the service of muting the vital question of how best to interpret this person's efforts, according to which set of frameworks, through a preemptive ontological move: this is what this person is.

A further justification for the inclusion of reference to such categories in the interpretation of criteria has to do with the kind of academic community an admissions procedure seeks to produce. In contrast to the claim that certain underrepresented groups require compensation for past discriminatory practices, the justification for affirmative action offered here insists that discrimination is to be opposed as part of any present or future educational practice. Discrimination does not take place only when it is consciously intended; discrimination is aided and abetted when admissions procedures fail to take account of the importance of cultural, sexual, and racial diversity in the building of an academic community, the democratization of the university, and the enhancement of intellectual exchange and the production of knowledge. Here the question is not how best to compensate for past wrongs. Rather, the questions are how best to build the kind of academic community that reflects the diversity of the community that the university seeks to represent, a diversity that gives concrete cultural meaning to the ideals of democracy that the university seeks to embody and to foster; how best to produce the university as a public site of cultural exchange, one in which the practice of equality is brought to bear on intellectual work, not only in terms of representing the kinds of people who have traditionally been excluded from such work, but also in accepting the challenge to revise traditional assumptions about how knowledge is circulated, produced, and received when it is practiced by communities no longer formed through discriminatory practice. This is, in my opinion, an affirmative view of affirmative action.

This affirmative view, however, seems nowhere in sight in the regents' deliberations or in the policy resolution passed in July 1995. It seems clear that the justification of affirmative action that the regents oppose is one that is based on the demand for remedy and compensation; other kinds of justification are not considered. The notion that a group has suffered historically and therefore deserves admission as a way of compensating for past discrimination is but one way of arguing in favor of affirmative action. If discrimination persists as a present fact, is it necessary to construe affirmative action as compensation for *past* wrongs? That approach is clearly open to all kinds of questions.[2] Alternatively, affirmative action might be based on the principle that a full and adequate description of merit and achievement is often not possible without recourse to the minority status of the candidate, and that minority status does not provide the legitimating ground for eligibility for admission, even though its consideration may be essential for the determination of eligibility.

Oddly, the regents appear to be ambivalently committed to the remedy-based justification of affirmative action. This seems clear from a reading of section four of the resolution, which sets out what kinds of adverse social circumstances might well be rectified through special considerations and replaces considerations of minority status with considerations of economic disadvantage and "unwholesome" family and neighborhood environments. Here it is clear that the regents do consider remedial actions as the proper business of admissions. The regents explicitly approve the admissibility of some considerations of environmental constraints in the determination of a candidate's eligibility for admission, but only on the condition that the candidate has evinced the moral courage or "character" necessary to overcome such hindrances. There the regents remark that "consideration shall be given to individuals who, despite having suffered disadvantage economically or in terms of their social environment (such as an abusive or otherwise dysfunctional home or a neighborhood of unwholesome or antisocial influences), have nevertheless demonstrated sufficient character and determination in overcoming obstacles to warrant confidence that the applicant can pursue a course of study to successful completion, provided that any student admitted under this section must be academically eligible for admission."

Contrary to what one might expect, the resolution does accept the notion that reference to nonacademic factors, such as adverse circumstances, might very well come into consideration in determining the eligibility of a given applicant. Where one might expect a rigorous distinction between academic and nonacademic criteria, the regents offer instead a preferred and acceptable list of nonacademic considerations in admissions: economic disadvantage (a category that resonates with "class" but is also clearly distinguished from it, characterizing contingent and local economic environments and, hence, having none of the systemic or institutionalized status usually associated with class) and abusive and dysfunctional families and neighborhoods. In both sets of criteria, the problem of discrimination is localized, apparently stripped of its racial, ethnic, and sexual dimensions and of any reference to the broader national context of its operation or the systemic ways by which it proceeds.

In a ghostly yet telling way, the very rhetoric of the section mimes one conventional form that the rationale for affirmative action takes. The section isolates a set of suffering applicants, but it also provides a moral and pedagogical imperative as well: only those who overcome their social suffering through manifest heroism ought to be rewarded for their efforts. The unstated text appears to be that, under the former policy, those who failed to overcome their social suffering through manifest heroism were improperly rewarded by the university, gaining admission for no other reason than that their minority status was construed as an adverse circumstance. In section four, what contributes to the determination of a candidate's eligibility is not merely *that* a student has suffered in a dysfunctional family or antisocial environment (left unexplained, but presumed, in this formulation), but that a student has evinced evidence of moral "character" and the capacity to "overcome obstacles" as well. The regents thus seek to reward the efforts of those candidates who show evidence of such moral characteristics, suggesting that the candidate will show similar fortitude in overcoming whatever obstacles stand in the way of completing a course of study. After having established this capacity to overcome obstacles to the task of completing an education, the section ends by taking distance from the connection it has just established, noting that these are not "academic" criteria, but that they may be justifiably added to a consideration of academic criteria in the determination of eligibility.

The rhetorical recirculation of a rationale for affirmative action in this section is an effort both to defeat affirmative action and to rewrite the social narrative of suffering and remedy that the regents understand to be supporting its claims. According to this logic, affirmative action rewards those who have suffered on the presumption that their minority status is both sign and proof of such suffering. The new policy, however, not only identifies a new class of sufferers (ones who presumably have *not* been recognized by affirmative action policy and, hence, have been the victims of affirmative action), but offers a new set of moral criteria for the dispensation of "special consideration." Significantly, while not all justifications for affirmative action require a commitment to "special consideration" (the term itself arises mainly in the context of anti–affirmative action rhetoric), the section above *does* subscribe both to an account of social victimization *localized* within families and neighborhoods and to a *characterological* and *moral* solution to this narrative of suffering, rather than to a political, institutional, or social response. Greater, apparently, than any injustice caused by contemporary practices of discrimination are the kinds of sufferings that putatively follow from the erosion of the family's moral health. In what that moral health consists remains unclear, but the elliptical reference to a putatively common understanding of what constitute "unwholesome" and "antisocial" influences nevertheless supports this rather consequential claim. The decline of "neighborhoods" appears to be, in part, an unavowed reference to who is moving in, who is moving out: in other words, to the racial composition of the area, and that phrase, taken in tandem with the reference to "unwholesome" families, also sustains strong metonymic links to discourses on drugs, single and unmarried mothers, wayward fathers, lesbian and gay families, divorce, incest, and child abuse. In effect, the policy does not oppose a view of discrimination as victimization, but redescribes the field of relevant social injustice such that the "breakdown" of families and the "decline" of neighborhoods are what truly victimize promising young students. Evidence of having come to terms with these forms of adversity is worthy of special consideration in admissions in a way that references to discriminatory practices linked to sex (pointedly, not "gender") or minority status are not. Certain forms of narratively established victimization are admissible into the consideration of eligibility, but they will be ones that make no explicit mention of race, sex, ethnicity, or national origin; they will be ones that relocate the social causes of suffering in economic disadvantage, the family, and the neighborhood, each of which might be understood to euphemize issues of class, sexuality, gender, and race. In other words, the policy prohibits the mentionability of such categories, but the categories it does mention — neighborhood and family — are dense sites for the displacement of racial anxiety and sexual fears attending to the erosion of sexually normative kinship arrangements. Thus the policy prohibits the mentioning of such categories, but their unmentionability structures the categories that now become mentionable and mandatory: the categories that are authorized and require mention for special consideration in admissions are precisely those that mention — and consolidate — problematic notions of race and sex *precisely without mentioning them*.

The analysis of the institutional operation of discrimination that once supported the rationale for affirmative action is countered with a morally sanctified individualism. This anti-institutional politics mirrors the contemporary turn against welfare in favor of workfare, the "Newt effect" in academe. The drama of the heroic individual is reaffirmed as the proper replacement for affirmative action policies, where the latter are understood as remedial actions. The institution is under no obligation to give special consideration to those who have suffered discrimination; on the contrary, the institution will now reward those who have overcome their adverse circumstances with the resources of individual "character." Thus, the institution seeks to reward those who expect no compensation from the institution for their suffering. The institution, under the guise of applauding the individual character and fortitude required to overcome adversity without institutional assistance, thus extends its institutional power (and paternalism) by offering that very reward. The institution thus signals that those who will receive special consideration will be those who describe their suffering as the result of economic disadvantage, unwholesome family, and declining neighborhoods, thus recirculating the tropes that within public discourse defend racial and sexual normativity, but doing so in a way that never explicitly mentions those terms. What will warrant special consideration are those narratives that follow the sequence in which victimization at the hands of local environments is overcome through individual moral tenacity. In many ways, this is a battle over which discourse of recent history will prevail: those who agree to restrict the political account of their suffering to economic, familial, and neighborhood reasons, who make no reference to minority status, and produce a story of individual overcoming — rather than one of institutional or political transformation — will provide the new historiographical norm for those whose narratives warrant institutional compassion.

One may well speculate that section four will produce a stream of confessional admissions statements from savvy high school seniors, regaling the committee with stories of family abuse and heroic survival. The regents not only make clear which narratives will "sell," but also mandate a certain production of individual autobiography in ways that localize every victimization and individualize every solution. Has this kind of narrative taken the place of the discourse of discrimination, or does the narrative of abuse, victimization, and individual solutions constitute the contemporary devolution of antidiscrimination discourse (mirroring the turn to "self-esteem" and abuse narrative that predominates within certain circles of diluted political leftism)? Has the account of discrimination become reduced to an account of abuse that is construed as the consequence of racially inflected and sexually non-normative notions of family and neighborhood? To what extent has an institutional analysis of the differential effects of discrimination against women and minorities become less compelling than an account of victimization that indirectly targets racial and sexual minorities, as well as women, for the apparently "unwholesome" state of domestic life?

It is unclear to me whether this shift is a displacement of a discourse on discrimination by an abuse narrative populated with victims of bad families and heroic individual survivors, or whether there is some eerie way that abuse narratives are the individualist cooptation and domestication of the narrative of discrimination, narratives that have emerged from antidiscrimination efforts and that now work powerfully to thwart their progress.

The lapses in the language of the policy, however, present some ambiguity that might be exploited in further clarifications: "The University of California shall not use race, religion, sex, color, ethnicity, or national origin as criteria for admission to the university or to any program of study." If the policy simply means that none of these categories will suffice as exclusive criteria, then the problem would not be insurmountable. But the language does not restrict the scope of its applicability in that way. If such categories are not to be used as criteria, then it still remains an open question whether an affirmative action policy might not be developed in which such categories work as points of departure for the determination and interpretation of criteria but are not, strictly speaking, criteria in themselves. Moreover, if part of the mission of the university is to offer a nondiscriminatory environment, to enhance the diversity of its faculty and student body, to give cultural meaning to democratic ideals, and to continue the dynamic relation between the university and the communities that it serves, then what a candidate for admission has to contribute to the realization of that mission simply could not be assessed without reference to those distinguishing circumstances. Such a reference need not operate as a criterion in a narrow sense, but could very well operate to enable an interpretation that establishes the likelihood of such a contribution.

If, as seems clear, minority categories are historically formed and continuously in the process of historical formation, then there is no easy recourse to such categories as fixed points of descriptive reference. When we ontologize such categories, we cease to understand them historically and substitute a language of "what one is" for a more complex account of the nexus of cultural location, differential access, social legacy, and community norms that come to form that person's situation and the cultural framework for his or her education. Strictly speaking, we make a mistake if we think that in referring to someone's minority status that we *describe* a person through that reference; at best, the mark of identity works as an abbreviation for a more complex description; we forget the substitution of identity for description when we act as if the reference to identity is itself descriptive. In referring to a minority status within the process of admissions, we mark one point of departure for a relevant description of that person. The relevance of that description depends on a culturally and historically nuanced understanding of the cultural background within which a better illumination of merit and achievement becomes possible. And this understanding is achieved by educators precisely through a cultural engagement with the kinds of issues explored in the kind of scholarship pursued in the various fields of minority studies on Berkeley's campus. Indeed, the future for affirmative action may reside precisely in learning how best to bring to bear on admissions practices the complex and compelling academic work on racial formation, gender construction, the production and transformation of religious, ethnic, and class categories, that, paradoxically, happens few places with greater distinction than it does at Berkeley.

But this brings me back to the question of whether who is in on the conversation makes a difference in what is said in the conversation. The anti–affirmative action efforts, I would suggest, take place at both levels; they not only seek to place restrictions on who will become part of the public conversation on such issues, but they do that knowing that the outcomes will differ depending on who is speaking.

I suppose it seems a bit odd to think of affirmative action as a free speech issue, but consider that the people who will be able to speak, and speak efficaciously on matters of race, ethnicity, and gender — indeed, of class as well — will be precisely those who have been admitted to the institutions that cultivate students to become speakers of public discourse. In a sense, public discourse itself is being allocated along gendered, racial, and ethnic lines by such anti–affirmative action policies, shoring up the ideals of individualism that have supported the privileged classes, indeed, the ideals of individualism that have successfully cloaked the class-status of those advantages.

This does not mean that one can predict the intellectual position that a person of color will hold by virtue of the fact that such a person is of color. We know that that is not true, and no refinement of standpoint epistemology will make it so. Indeed, it is precisely the unpredictability of that relation — between categories that mark the social positionality of an individual and the views that they come to hold — that is what is most interesting and, often, most provocative in the classroom. Educational institutions should not second-guess what form that relation will take. Indeed, an educational institution under contemporary conditions of multicultural democracy is obligated to produce and preserve an environment in which the very meaning and implications of such categories alter over time in ways that cannot be prefigured or contained in advance. After all, education ought to be a place in which one rethinks the conditions of one's own emergence, in which self-reflection on those conditions produces views that cannot be fully known or predicted in advance, and where the very meaning of such social categories are rearticulated. This is part of what makes anti-essentialist thinking vital, and it is precisely this process that is foreclosed by the assumption that the racial and ethnic and gendered lives of applicants can be severed from the discussion of the value of the intellectual trajectory they seek to take. That position is surely as false as the one that claims that the value of that intellectual trajectory can be reduced to those social markings or can be predicted on the basis of those categories. Although the foes of affirmative action appear to think that they will produce a population of neutral persons whose opinions spring from reason alone and whose accomplishments are derived from moral ardor, it seems clear that they will restrict the conversation in such a way that we will find it increasingly difficult to know the history and future of these contested social categories. If these categories have no place in the discussion of an applicant, if they have no bearing on educational life within democracy, then one might well be wary of other sorts of arguments that have emerged in the wake of these — to wit, that there is no educational benefit in women's studies, African American studies, Chicano studies, Asian studies, Native American studies. The stakes of the affirmative action debate will become clearer once we recognize how crucial it is to find a way to think about the relation between matters of identity and ways of knowing that savors rather then closes down that gap. My hope is that that relation remains an importantly open one, that we revert neither to reductionist formulations of identity politics nor to the false neutrality of persons. Although social categories do not fix our identities, they are that without which we cannot begin to know and reknow ourselves: that tension is precisely what animates the intellectual issues that emerge from minority lives. It should be one of the tasks of educational institutions to keep that tension alive.

NOTES

1. Angela Harris, *What Are We Talking About When We Talk About Race?*, manuscript.

2. How is it decided when a past wrong has achieved present compensation? Why is it that present members of a minority group are to be compensated for injuries done against past members? Why not simply accept as valid the urgent necessity to cease the discrimination against such members, reorienting the aim of the policy toward the elimination of present and future discriminatory conduct?

Empowerment Hazards:

Affirmative Action,

Recovery Psychology,

and Identity Politics

Michel Feher

Eager to outdo his conservative rivals, California's Governor Pete Wilson launched his short-lived campaign for the Republican nomination for president with an attack on affirmative action. On 1 June 1995, he issued an executive order urging the University of California and other state institutions to "end preferential treatment and to promote individual opportunity based on merit." Complying with the governor's request, the University of California Board of Regents met on 20 July and decided that, as of January 1997, "race, religion, sex, color, ethnicity, or national origin" would not be used "as a criterion for admission to the University or to any program of study."[1]

While the political motivation of its authors is clear, one of the most remarkable features of the board's policy is that it does not merely repeal affirmative action. Certainly, according to the new rules, the university is obliged to disregard the race, gender, and ethnicity of all its applicants. Yet, if we read the document issued after the board's meeting, it appears that, contrary to the governor's executive order, individual merit and academic achievement will not be the only criteria for admission to the University of California. Claiming that they are still involved in "academic 'outreach,'" the regents want to introduce a different type of preferential treatment based on a new set of criteria.[2] In their own words, they want to give special consideration to candidates who have "suffered disadvantage economically or in terms of their social environment (such as an abusive or otherwise dys-functional home or a neighborhood of unwholesome or antisocial influences)."[3]

Should we understand that the board's decision aims at insti-tuting a revised form of affirmative action, whereby preferential treatment will be based on low income and underprivileged social environment rather than on race, ethnicity, and gender? Coming from the appointees of a Republican governor, such an emphasis on class difference seems rather incongruous. Today more than ever, conservative rhetoric vehemently rejects the concepts of class struggle and class interest as both inappropriate and divisive notions. Moreover, Republican politicians never fail to accuse their Democratic opponents of preaching class warfare whenever the latter dare to object to fiscal or financial measures favoring the richest segments of the population. It is therefore hard to imagine that a former contender for the GOP nomina-tion would condemn affirmative action programs on the ground that they are not properly designed to challenge the continued subordination of the lower classes.

In order to dispel this perplexing first impression of a conser-vative policy that is not only both colorblind and gender-blind but also committed to the "war against poverty," it is important to look carefully at the language used by the regents. On the one hand, the special consideration given to applicants who "have suffered disadvantage economically" is meant to show that, while transcending "special interests" and refusing quotas, the Univer-sity of California still cares about the *truly* needy and assumes that the latter are not necessarily women or minorities. On the other hand, words like "*abusive* or otherwise *dysfunctional* homes" belong not to a class-conscious discourse, whether socialist or liberal, but to the vocabulary of popular psychology, in particular that of the so-called recovery movement. Born in the brochures of Alcoholics Anonymous and developed by the "incest — and other child abuse — survival therapists," this type of language in-forms a large variety of "support groups," whose members share a relatively consistent view of the human condition.

According to recovery psychologists, trauma, especially child-hood trauma, is the defining experience of postmodern subjec-tivity, at least in the United States. Usually inflicted by an "abusive or otherwise dysfunctional family," or by an "unwholesome environment," this founding trauma is the result of actual harmful experiences — such as molestation, harassment, humiliation — though it reveals itself only through the symptoms induced by its denial. Indeed, recovery psychologists contend that most people work particularly hard at repressing their traumatizing experiences and then pay the price for the success of their endeavor. Their state of "denial" is most often expressed by depressive tendencies and disabling addictions — to alcohol, drugs, sex, or other dependent people — and it afflicts them with what appears to be the main problem of contemporary men and women, namely, a low self-esteem. Therefore, recovery psychologists see their therapy as a form of empowerment. They seek to bolster their patients' self-esteem by helping them retrieve the original abuse that caused their post-traumatic condition. In order to find the "courage to heal," that is, the courage to face the pain and overcome the shame inherent in their denial, patients of recovery therapists are invited to join a "support group" composed of people suffering from the same addiction and/or the same kind of traumatic experience. By sharing their feelings and their painful memories with such an empathetic group, recovering patients can rebuild their self-worth: with the help of their newfound peers they come to acknowledge that they were indeed victimized, but only to realize that they are not powerless victims anymore. Precisely because they have had the courage to address and reassess their pasts, they now come to feel that they belong to a proud community of "survivors," whose empathy and respect will enable them to take their lives into their own hands.[4]

During the 1980s, these descriptions of trauma, denial, and lack of self-esteem, as well as the healing process envisioned by recovery therapists, went beyond the realm of popular psychology and made their way into the political arena. This can be explained by the fact that recovery psychology combines individual therapy with collective empowerment. While their purpose is to bring a traumatized and henceforth dependent person toward a state of self-reliance, recovery therapists seek to restore the individual autonomy of their patients by giving them a sense of community: more precisely, their method consists in turning a secret and disabling wound into a badge of collective pride through the production of a shared and uplifting narrative of survival.

In the political realm, this approach was first co-opted by certain strands of feminist and minority legal scholarship: especially by the proponents of antipornography legislation and hate speech regulation.[5] According to these reformers, pornographic images — defined as misogynist performances — as well as racist, sexist, or homophobic slurs are offensive not only to the persons who happen to be exposed to them. They are also, and even primarily, instrumental in perpetuating the subordination of women and minorities because the traumatizing abuse they inflict has the effect of disempowering the people they victimize. Such images and speech thus constitute a violation of the Fourteenth Amendment of the Constitution, which is meant to protect the right of citizens to equal treatment. Conversely, advocates of antipornography legislation and hate speech regulation claim that the symptoms revealing the trauma experienced by a woman or by a minority member upon hearing certain words or seeing certain images — namely, depression, self-abusive behavior, and low self-esteem — tend to prove that these words or images are indeed sexist, racist, or homophobic aggressions. Moreover, these legal scholars contend that the condemnation of pornographers in a court of law and the implementation of speech codes in schools and workplaces constitute an important form of empowerment for the victims of pornography and hate speech. In their view, such sanctions offer both reparation to the plaintiffs' sense of self and public recognition of the cultural identity associated with their gender, race, ethnicity, or sexual orientation.

Although championed by influential feminists and minority activists, this particular blend of identity politics and victims' rights rhetoric remains highly controversial, both in the women's movement and among the proponents of a multiculturalist agenda. Indeed, many voices on the left are at the same time wary of the ethical content and worried about the political implications of a discourse that derives collective rights from the experience of pain, that equates the acknowledgment of a culture with a process of healing, and that assigns a therapeutic mission to legal and political reform.[6] All the same, it is remarkable to see that the jargon of recovery psychology is now embraced by a Board of Regents intent on implementing the agenda of a conservative governor.

While we should be careful not to overinterpret the regents' new policy, the fact remains that their phraseology offers a good illustration of a recent and dramatic shift in conservative rhetoric. Until as recently as the early 1990s, the Right was very keen to stigmatize what it called the "victim talk" of its opponents, that is, the self-fashioning of certain groups as society's helpless victims. Primarily associated with the grievances of women and minorities, such a discourse was denounced by its conservative critics as a blatant betrayal of the famously self-reliant American ethos. However, since Bill Clinton's election in 1992, many conservative ideologues have seemed less interested in condemning "victim talk" than in co-opting it. Indeed, rather than simply rejecting the posture of the victim as unworthy of self-respecting Americans, the resurgent populist Right tends to consider the victim's status as an enviable position, both in terms of obtaining sympathy and entitlements and of securing public attention. Right-wing leaders thus endeavor to claim the "benefits" of victimization for their own constituencies. Hence the ever growing lament of the "angry white man," who complains that his self-esteem is the target of multiple attacks: among the most damaging of which are "reverse discrimination" (affirmative action), "politically correct" thought police, gun control, immigration, and, last but not least, federal taxes. The last named is accused of financing welfare and other social programs whose beneficiaries are precisely those who already profit from reverse discrimination.

As a result of recovery psychology's influence over identity politics, the status of "deserving" victim can be granted to anyone who *feels* that his or her pain is caused by a traumatizing abuse, provided that this feeling elicits enough empathy and support. Both recovery therapists and the advocates of race and gender consciousness who use their vocabulary contend that each group whose collective identity is informed by a similar traumatic experience, as well as by a shared commitment to turn pain into pride, is entitled to full authority when it comes to defining the harm done to its members. In other words, the damaging effect of an abuse can be fully appreciated only by the people who have suffered from it. Such privilege granted to subjective experience has at least two implications: on the one hand, it means that women and minorities are best qualified to define what is harmful to them; on the other, it makes it impossible to establish an objective hierarchy among different plights. Consequently, victims of racism and, say, of a smoking parent have an equal opportunity to advance their identity politics.

As far as strategy is concerned, the public recognition of someone's victimhood, which is instrumental to his or her "cultural healing," largely depends on the "empowering" capacity of his or her "support group": that is, on the empathy and the solidarity of its members and on their visibility and their lobbying power. Based on these criteria, it is easy to see how the competition for the most deserving victim of American society will play itself out. This competition is open to the entire range of self-styled communities generated by the recovery movement, including the conservative groups who adopt their rhetoric. Consequently, Robert Bly's men's movement, the so-called Promise Keepers, and their more recent and political extension known as the "angry white men" are bound to fare quite well. From radio talk show hosts to the Speaker of the House, the spokespeople for these reactionary constituencies certainly have the capacity — in terms of audience, financial means, and media access — to put their predicament at the top of the country's agenda, and thus to forward the "empowerment" of their people by enabling them to carry guns, pay low taxes, and see the end of reverse discrimination.

In short, the populist Right has recently discovered that, thanks to its new psychological framework, identity politics is not necessarily a threat to conservative goals and constituencies. On the contrary, if the latter manage to organize themselves as effective "support groups," they can turn community empowerment into an open and competitive market where their cause has a good chance of prevailing. Hence the University of California's new policy, which clearly seeks to open up such a market. Indeed, according to the regents' approach to academic outreach, new types of victimized communities can lay claim to the special consideration of the admissions office: while black youths from Oakland or South Central Los Angeles still qualify — albeit because of economic disadvantage and therefore on a par with poor white "victims" of pre- and post-Reagan "big government" — they are now joined by children of white upper-middle-class parents with an addiction to alcohol — because they come from a dysfunctional home — and even by lower-middle-class children of white separatists unfairly persecuted by federal agents — because government's harassment definitely creates an unwholesome environment.

Beyond the issue of affirmative action, the co-optation of identity politics by the populist Right presents the Left with three major problems. First, as we have seen, conservative constituencies are well suited for a "culture war" in which different communities fight for their mutually exclusive empowerment. While the advocates of a multiculturalist society seek to empower their respective communities by celebrating their culture of resistance against the white patriarchal order, the spokespeople of the new populist Right endeavor instead to bolster the self-esteem of the white middle class by enticing its members to reclaim their allegedly threatened heritage. Thus, conservative leaders proudly hail Christian family values, the American work ethic, and gun-carrying resistance to state bureaucracy as the unique patrimony of their "people." But they also present their constituency as the real victims of the federal government and its protégés — that is, women and minorities. In this respect, the tears shed by Republican senators at the Ruby Ridge hearings — in line with their "humane" and sympathetic attitude toward the Oklahoma City terrorists — are but a chilling foretaste of what the proponents of a white conservative identity politics can and will do for the people they seek to represent.

The second problem facing the Left, whether liberal or multiculturalist, stems from the success encountered by right-wing identity politics: that is, from the fact that a populist mixture of reactionary ideology and antiestablishment posturing is undeniably "empowering," especially when the empowerment of a community is equated with the self-esteem of its members. Consequently, right-wing populism tends to become contagious: more precisely, it induces a reciprocal co-optation, this time by the feminist proponents of a women's culture and by the advocates of nationalism among minority organizations. Hence, in particular, the rising influence of the Nation of Islam and the success of the Million Man March, whose law, order, self-help, and family values program demonstrates the remarkably empowering capacity of a conservative nationalist agenda, even among subordinated communities. The endorsement of the march by the declining Rainbow Coalition, as well as the very discreet reservations expressed by black feminists, further suggest that when the political scene is dominated by the issue of collective representation, reactionary demagogues are given a clear advantage and a disquieting legitimacy. For if the strengthening of a group identity is the sole political stake, the rhetoric of the "besieged fortress" often prevails: in other words, a call to traditional values and cultural homogeneity, accompanied by a strict policing of the community's mores and a paranoid suspicion of other groups, prove to be the easiest way to create a sense of national or communitarian unity.[7]

Finally, the growing success of a conservative approach to community empowerment weakens the Left even further by pushing its liberal wing toward the Right. Threatened by the progress of identity politics among feminists and minority activists, many liberals are tempted to use pretexts such as the local alliances of antipornography feminists with the Christian Coalition on the one hand, and the very similar social and moral values defended by Louis Farrakhan and Newt Gingrich on the other, in order to condemn indiscriminately all the proponents of a community empowerment agenda. Weary of their bitter debates with the other wing of the Left, that is, with the advocates of a gender- and color-conscious multiculturalism, gender- and colorblind liberals are all too eager to expose the pitfalls of community empowerment for its own sake, especially when the promotion of collective self-esteem takes as dubious a route as the acquittal of O. J. Simpson. Similarly, liberals take advantage of the Right's intention to repeal affirmative action, in order to criticize equally opponents and supporters of preferential treatment when the latter do not support it for "liberal" reasons.

Faithful to the spirit of Lyndon Johnson's speech founding affirmative action back in 1965, liberals condone affirmative action programs as both a temporary compensation for past discrimination and a shortcut to a fully integrated society. In their view, "positive" discrimination aims at creating a truly colorblind and gender-blind society by remedying the underrepresentation of women and certain minorities in universities and other positions of power. Thus, from a liberal point of view, diversity is not an end in itself: it is a means for granting equal opportunity to every American citizen regardless of his or her race, gender, and ethnicity. By contrast, the proponents of identity politics see affirmative action as a necessary tool for the promotion of a racially and culturally diverse society. According to them, affirmative action is not meant to pave the way for a fair "meritocracy." Rather than a temporary compensation leading to equal opportunity, affirmative action should be treated as a permanent commitment to actual diversity. In their eyes, a truly multicultural society should not be blind to race, gender, and ethnicity: on the contrary, these must remain pertinent criteria for admitting a student and hiring an employee, alongside individual merit and professional achievement.[8] After many years of discreet criticism, liberals have recently become more vocal in condemning the communitarianist contention that affirmative action is about acknowledging and promoting cultural diversity rather than securing equal access to higher education or upward mobility. Indeed, some of them do not hesitate to use the emergent white male identity politics as a welcome pretext for dismissing equally the self-styled victims of "reverse discrimination" and their multiculturalist foes.

Claiming to represent the democratic golden mean between two sectarian excesses, self-righteous liberals cannot help but position themselves in what Colin Powell has called the "sensible center." In turn, multiculturalist activists interpret such a move as a confirmation of their long-standing suspicion that liberal integrationism is merely a gentle version of mainstream conservatism. Consequently, the prospects for a revamped civil rights coalition seem, at least for now, particularly grim.

But the same psychological vocabulary that has proved so detrimental to the survival of an already strained leftist coalition enables us to end on a note of hope. In spite of the increasing tensions between the two wings of the American Left, there is still reason to believe that the psychological cost of parting will be too high. For it is hard to imagine that both the liberals who let themselves stray toward the "sensible center" and the progressive multiculturalists who contribute to the legitimacy of authoritarian populists can do so without losing some of their self-esteem.

NOTES

1. Regents of the University of California, *SP–1: Adoption of Resolution: Policy Ensuring Equal Treatment — Admissions*, § 2.

2. *Ibid.*, § 1.

3. *Ibid.*, § 4.

4. The Recovery Movement ranges from popular self-help books expanding the AA doctrine, such as Melody Beattie's *Codependent No More* (New York,

1987), and John Bradshaw's *Homecoming: Reclaiming and Championing Your Inner Child* (New York, 1990), to "incest survival" and other "repressed memory" literature, such as Ellen Bass and Laura Davis, *The Courage to Heal: A Guide for Women Survivors of Sexual Abuse* (New York, 1988), and Judith Lewis Herman, *Trauma and Recovery* (New York, 1992). For a harsh critique of abuse survival therapy, see Carol Tavris, "Beware the Incest-Survivor Machine," *New York Times Book Review*, 3 January 1993, and Frederick Crews, "The Revenge of the Repressed," *New York Review of Books*, 17 November 1994. For a critique of the Recovery Movement, see Wendy Kaminer, *I'm Dysfunctional, You're Dysfunctional: The Recovery Movement and Other Self-Help Fashions* (New York, 1992).

5. See, in particular, Catharine MacKinnon, *Only Words* (Cambridge, MA, 1993), and Mari J. Matsuda et al., *Words That Wound: Critical Race Theory, Assaultive Speech, and the First Amendment* (New York, 1993).

6. See Henry Louis Gates Jr., "War of Words: Critical Race Theory and the First Amendment," in Henry Louis Gates Jr. et al., *Speaking of Race, Speaking of Sex* (New York, 1994), 20–58, and Martha Minow, "Surviving Victim Talk," *UCLA Law Review* 40, no. 1411 (1993): 1410–45.

7. For a critique of identity politics' tendency to elicit a policing of identity, see Judith Butler, *Bodies That Matter: On the Discursive Limits of "Sex"* (New York, 1993), 117–19.

8. On the contrast between liberal and multiculturalist approaches to affirmative action, see Gary Peller, "Race Consciousness," in Dan Danielsen and Karen Engle, eds., *After Identity* (New York, 1995), 67–83.

The Regents on Race

and Diversity:

Representations and Reflections

Marianne Constable

> Believing California's diversity to be an asset, we adopt
> this statement: Because individual members of all of Cali-
> fornia's diverse races have the intelligence and capacity to
> succeed at the University of California, this policy will
> achieve a UC population that reflects this state's diversity
> through the preparation and empowerment of all students
> in this state to succeed rather than through a system of
> artificial preferences.[1]

This clumsy sentence from section 9 of the University of California (UC) Board of Regents' 1995 Resolution SP-1 entitled "Policy Ensuring Equal Treatment — Admissions" serves as a symptom
of its times. It reveals — to those with ears behind their ears, as
Friedrich Nietzsche put it — difficulties in contemporary conceptions of identity that reach beyond the issue of the admissions
policy of any particular university. By closely examining the sentence — its context, representations, and implications — this essay
shows how the regents' ambiguous statement on diversity echoes
the troublesome state of current thought in the United States
about race and membership.

Section 9 appears at the end of a resolution to abolish racial
preferences in UC admissions and contains the resolution's
only direct reference to diversity. The resolution now serves as
a focal point for debate about affirmative action, although no
explicit mention of affirmative action occurs in the document.
Instead, the preamble of the resolution invokes the governor's

executive order to "end preferential treatment and to promote individual opportunity based on merit" and asserts the regents' belief that

> it is in the best interest of the University to take relevant actions to develop and support programs which will have the effect of increasing the eligibility rate of groups which are "underrepresented" in the University's pool of applicants as compared to their percentages in California's graduating high school classes and to which reference is made in Section 4.

The preamble's only "group" reference is to the groups of "underrepresented" applicants whose identity it defers to section 4.

Following the preamble, the resolution does four things. First, it requires establishment of a task force "to develop proposals for new directions and increased funding for the Board of Regents to increase the eligibility rate of those currently identified in Section 4" (section 1).[2] Second, it abolishes "race, religion, sex, color, ethnicity, or national origin" as criteria in UC admissions and "admissions-in-exception" (sections 2 and 3). Third, it requires the president and academic senate "to develop supplemental [admissions] criteria" for the regents' consideration:

> In developing such criteria, which shall provide reasonable assurances that the applicant will successfully complete his or her course of study, consideration shall be given to individuals who, despite having suffered disadvantage economically or in terms of their social environment (such as an abusive or otherwise dysfunctional home or a neighborhood of unwholesome or antisocial influences), have nonetheless demonstrated sufficient character and determination in overcoming obstacles to warrant confidence that the applicant can pursue a course of study to successful completion, provided that any student admitted under this section must be academically eligible for admission. (Section 4)

According to section 4, then, individuals who have suffered disadvantage economically or in terms of social environment yet have overcome obstacles, and who, according to the preamble, tend not to fulfill UC's admissions requirements, constitute the so-called underrepresented groups in UC's pool of applicants whose eligibility rates, and presumably application and admission rates, the resolution would increase.[3] Finally, section 5 requires that 50 to 75 percent of a campus's entering class be admitted "solely on the basis of academic achievement."[4]

In this context, the language of section 9 is revealing. For after abolishing it as a criterion for UC admission (sections 2 and 3), the resolution singles "race" out from among the banned admissions criteria and suggests its importance to "a UC population" properly reflective of "this state's diversity."[5] The section's concern with "all of California's diverse races" gestures toward inclusiveness: all races' individual members have "the intelligence and capacity to succeed at the University of California." The colon following the introductory declaration of faith in "diversity" associates such inclusiveness with diversity. Even if the resolution's policies alone will not prepare and empower "all students in this state" (as the passage on its face seems to declare), the passage suggests that its policies will contribute to achieving a racially inclusive UC population reflective of the state's diversity.

Section 9 thus asserts the compatibility of its policy for admitting to UC (or at least "prepar[ing] and empower[ing]...to succeed") economically or socially disadvantaged individuals, with inclusion of members of all races in the UC population, and with reflection of the state's "diversity." Such a claim demands attention if only because targeting disadvantaged individuals, including racial-group members, and reflecting diversity are not the same even if they should happen to coincide. To begin with, the resolution's commitment to "individual opportunity based on merit" produces a reliance on "economic" and "social" factors to identify a target group of individuals, the racial identity of whom is an empirical matter on which the resolution offers no light. More to the point for the purpose of this essay, the "'underrepresented' groups" with which the resolution concerns itself are sets of "individuals who, despite having suffered disadvantage economically or in terms of their social environment... have nonetheless demonstrated sufficient character and determination in overcoming obstacles to warrant confidence" in their success at UC. The resolution's "groups" are thus aggregates of "individuals" to whom certain economic and social characteristics (disadvantages that have been overcome) attach. These individuals as such share no membership. They neither belong to some collectivity nor hold something — beliefs or practices, say — in common. They can thus be contrasted to another kind of group in which membership comes from a quality or aspect of experience shared by the whole. Group identity that comes from the attribution of characteristics to individuals (such as economic hardship, dysfunctional homes, or even "character" and "determination") is conceptually distinct from the group identity that comes from shared membership. Further, while *differentiation* pertains to characteristics attaching to *each individual* of a group, *discrimination* against group *members* pertains to qualities common to (or perceived as common to) the group *as a whole*.

In maintaining that "individual members of all of California's diverse races have the intelligence and capacity to succeed" at UC, the combination of "individual" with "members" suggests some ambivalence on the regents' part as to the character of racial group identity. Nevertheless, the resolution requires UC admissions to differentiate between individuals, considering their academic achievement, their intelligence and capacity to succeed, and their economic and social environments, rather than looking to their membership or to possible discrimination against groups.

In keeping with the resolution's commitment to the individual as locus of concern, section 9 condemns as "artificial preference" the privileging of group membership over individual characteristics; it rejects as artifice the discrimination carried out by the former system in that system's effort to combat discrimination. Section 9 intimates that its own preferences, by contrast, are natural or, rather, that it has none. Comparing the resolution's policy of "preparation and empowerment of all students in this state to succeed" to "a system of artificial preferences," section 9 implies that its achievements involve no "system": the diverse population it claims to produce seems to result from an inclusiveness that requires no preference or selection at all. Like natural selection, such natural nonpreference ostensibly needs no process or system for it to "reflect" natural diversity or the variety within the state.

The resolution's invocation of "diversity," like its reference to racial-group identity, is profoundly ambiguous, though. If diversity is taken to mean mere variety, then diversity is more likely within categories that have a low correlation to standards of admission. Thus when intelligence and capacity to succeed serve as standards, characteristics that correlate closely to intelligence and capacity to succeed are likely to be overrepresented in the resulting population. Conversely, greater variety will occur among characteristics from categories randomly related to, or equally distributed among, levels of intelligence and capacity to succeed. The regents' declaration of belief in diversity as "an asset" in section 9 suggests a meaning of diversity that is different from mere variety, however. It suggests that the presence or inclusion of particular groups, whether or not their selection would be randomly correlated to standards of admission, may be desirable.

In the context of section 9, then, there are three possibilities regarding the diversity of the categories that sections 2 and 3 eliminate from consideration in UC admission. The categories may be understood to be naturally diverse insofar as they are randomly correlated to admissions standards; nonrandomly correlated yet desirable for the sake of diversity; or nonrandomly correlated and of insufficient independent value to warrant including in admissions standards. Section 9 shows that the resolution is ambiguous as to which possibility it means to embrace and the ambiguity is most pronounced vis-à-vis race. When section 9 contrasts its policy to "a system of artificial preferences," it suggests the first possibility: that the selected population will be naturally diverse. When section 9 proclaims a belief in diversity as an "asset," it suggests the second possibility: that the presence of particular differences within the selected population is desirable although not necessarily natural. When section 9 fails to mention categories other than race, it suggests of section 2 and 3 categories — unlike the affirmative section 4 categories — that they are of insufficient independent value to warrant considering in admissions standards. When section 9 mentions "race," these ambiguities surface.

Consider first the nonrace categories of sections 2 and 3. On the one hand, "sex" (if separated from gender and sexual orientation) and "color" (as skin tone alone) could be taken to point to individual physical attributes that might be considered contingently related to an individual's "academic achievement" (the standard, once UC eligibility has been established, that section 5 adopts for most of the entering class). On the other hand, "religion," "ethnicity," and "national origin" seem to refer to memberships shared or held in common by a group. As such, they (like more cultural understandings of "sex" and "color") are arguably less randomly correlated to academic achievement than merely physical attributes. If diversity understood as variety is connected to a physical, more random set of categories, diversity understood as asset links to so-called cultural categories of differences that may even extend to the very definitions of achievement and success held by group members whose beliefs, practices, experiences, and/or traditions vary. When differences are purely random (in relation to the standard of selection), that is, the achievement of diversity is natural, although possibly trivial. When differences are not random, the depiction of diversity as "asset" suggests the desirability of particular differences to the quality of the overall population.[6]

Since section 9 concerns diversity, its appeal to "race" — the only category it invokes — is significant. "Race" in this context represents all categories — unnamed though they may be — about which diversity is an issue. At the same time, the selection of race to represent other categories confirms its uniqueness as category and as name. Recall that throughout the text up to section 9, the resolution posits the primacy of the individual over the group member. In discussion of UC eligibility, of academic achievement, of the "character" and "determination" that are demonstrated through "overcoming obstacles" in places such as "home" and "neighborhoods" that are "abusive" or "dysfunctional" or that have "unwholesome" or "antisocial" influences, no mention is made of group membership. In section 9, however, reference to the "individual members" of all of California's "diverse races" raises — however ambivalently — the specter of group membership. The emergence in section 9 of "race" as a "membership" category renders problematic the exclusive privileging of individual identity throughout the rest of the resolution. Given the history of race in the United States and in the West, it is perhaps not surprising that "race" comes to name what is elsewhere denied: both membership and discrimination. While the description of underrepresented groups gleaned from section 4 suggests that the underrepresentation — and overrepresentation — of *membership* groups is not an issue, the reinsertion of race in section 9 after its ostensible abolition in sections 2 and

3 suggests that membership — and discrimination — of all sorts cannot be set aside or eliminated as easily as the rest of the resolution would have it.

The statement in section 9 that the resolution's policy will bring about diversity thus grounds itself awkwardly in the regents' belief that diversity is an asset: "Believing California's diversity to be an asset, we adopt this statement:... this policy will achieve a UC policy that reflects this state's diversity." The policy described up to section 9 has little to do with diversity and much to do with individual qualification. Section 9 thus articulates a hope for diversity rather than a goal of diversity. Allusion to "diverse races" makes the hope concrete. "Race" does more than point to the familiar paradox of using a category to call for its own elimination as category, as would have been the case had the regents stopped with section 8. "Race" in section 9 names, in and for the United States at the end of the twentieth century, the impossibility of forgetting about group membership and discrimination — even as the rest of the resolution seeks to do so.

NOTES

The author thanks Jeremy Elkins and Robert Post for their helpful comments.

1. Regents of the University of California, *SP-1: Adoption of Resolution: Policy Ensuring Equal Treatment — Admissions*, 20 July 1995, § 9.

2. The task force report, dated 7 December 1995, was not available for consultation at the time of writing.

3. "UC eligibility" currently means attaining a certain grade point average in high school, having taken a number of required courses, and scoring at a particular level on required Scholastic Achievement Tests. Section 1 refers to eligibility rates; section 4 to admissions criteria. Section 9's "preparation and empowerment" seems to refer to eligibility and admission.

4. Sections 6 through 8 contain no major changes to the current system: sections 6 and 7 assert that section 2 shall not prohibit action necessary to maintain federal or state funds nor interfere with the university's practices relating to remedies for discrimination; section 8 requires the president to report to the regents on implementation of the resolution's provisions.

5. To be sure, section 9 does not assert but only implies the significance of race. It mentions "California's diverse races," without calling "diversity" "racial diversity" as such. Indeed, the passage shies away from the term "race" even where its usage seems warranted. Thus the section speaks of "all students"

where "(some) students of all races" or at least "students of diverse sorts" would be not only more accurate but also more to the point of the section.

6. Because assets generally have exchange value and can be turned into something productive, they are potentially enriching. Similarly, while cultural differences may not be random and naturally diverse in a given university population, they are nevertheless valuable for purposes of exchange; like properly managed assets, they are enriching.

Warhol Paints History,

or Race in America

Anne M. Wagner

It may seem inappropriate, given my title, to start with a photograph that puts us in Paris in 1964, at the Galerie Ileana Sonnabend (figure 1). Andy Warhol had his first European solo exhibition there, a show he wanted to call "Death in America," though it actually opened under a tamer rubric, bearing only the artist's name.[1] The Sonnabend exhibition was proof that, only two years after his notorious debut as an "artist" (that show lined up soup can paintings on a shelf, just like soup cans), Warhol had made his name. And he had left his beginnings with Campbell's cans far behind. Even the most glancing description of the paintings shown in Paris — suicides, electric chairs, fatal car crashes, portraits of two women who lost their lives to tainted cans of tuna fish (unlikely saints, they seem literally to fade away, along with the instruments of their martyrdom) — explains why such an ambitious and morbid title was the first to come to Warhol's mind. There was only one image where death was not directly pictured, a version of *Race Riot* of 1963; yet it took pride of place in the installation. *Race Riot* will have the same status in this essay, and even supplies its subtitle: "Race in America." As in Paris, death is not far away.

Warhol produced at least thirteen canvases on this subject, though only three on the wall-sized scale of the one shown at Sonnabend; the group's existence is the reason I offer the blunt assertion: Andy Warhol was a history painter. This is not a notion with much currency, past or present; nor have Warhol's *Race Riots* been studied before. Yet in this essay I claim that these pictures constitute a special — and specially recalcitrant — category within Warhol's work. Its difference from his other main mode of representation is above all a matter of race.

Figure 1. Installation photograph of *Andy Warhol*, exhibition at the Galerie Ileana Sonnabend, Paris, 1964. Photo: Harry Shunk.

This is my main proposition. Making it stick involves first defining Warhol as a painter in general, the better then to spell out the implications of his foray into the particular genre called history. My argument proceeds from the conviction that our understandings of Warhol's painting and of history painting, and even our grasp on the notion of history, all have something to gain from the result. But above all there is something to be learned about the ways the two key terms work together: about what history painting has been, in the late twentieth century, and how it makes meaning from, or gives meaning to, contemporary events. Some of those meanings, where Warhol was concerned, involve race in America. Like much of the recent American past — the 1960s in particular — their implications live on in the present, in ways I mean to show.

Let me be the first to admit that the odds seem stacked against me: problems and objections crop up right from the start. There is an issue about definitions, for example. How satisfactory is it to call Warhol a *painter*, let alone a history painter? We can label him an artist, certainly, or even better, a conceptual artist; we can term him a performer and discuss him as a filmmaker. Those identities are by now securely ratified by critical interpretations and professional awards and mass-cultural notoriety and a Warhol museum sited back in Pittsburgh, the artist's home town. Such labels sit easily on an individual whose career aimed to rewrite artistry as pure mechanics, and who made this intention patently clear from the moment he first attracted critical attention. When Warhol first explained his painting to an interviewer, in November 1963, he famously declared: "The reason I'm painting this way is that I want to be a machine, and I feel that whatever I do and do machine-like is what I want to do."[2] In keeping with this purpose, Warhol's techniques are a compendium of ways to circumvent the need to paint, from the projector he used to trace comic books and newspapers and advertisements, to the silk screen, where "painting" simply meant sliding a squeegee up and down and back and forth and side to side, and accepting any accidents of inking or registration that were the result.[3] But even this description may be too personal, may make Warhol seem too active in the process, may mistakenly evoke a notion too close to painterly practice. Note, therefore, that though he was sometimes photographed working, he was not necessarily the one to man the squeegee, certainly not the one to make the silk screen, nor the one to design the image from which the screen was cut. "This way," he said, "I don't have to work on my images at all."[4] In keeping with this practice, Warhol used images from elsewhere, raided tabloids and magazines and wire services and supermarket shelves; like a squatter he staked his claim to studio publicity photographs and mug shots and the strips of snapshots churned out by photo booths — this is how the nearly parodic narcissism of a serial portrait such as *Ethel Scull 36 Times* of 1963 came to be. He recycled his silk screens with appropriate disinterest in unique images and doubled, sometimes tripled, the square footage and price of his screened canvases by joining to them empty monochromes.[5] Is it any wonder he called his studio The Factory, or that photographers recorded its stacked-up contents as they would any warehouse packed with goods?

Is this painting? To pose this question is not quite the same as asking: Is this art? The difference lies in the fact that Warhol's work — or these strategies and techniques of "mechanization" I am describing as his work — was easily assimilable to the notions of art-as-concept, art-as-decision, art-as-event, art-as-behavior so epochally ratified by Marcel Duchamp and so decisively renovated in the early 1960s, both in Europe and the United States. Hence Warhol's prompt emergence for his contemporaries as a questioner of traditional definitions,[6] as "one of the principal didactic artists of all time," whose main lesson was how to negate "the uniqueness of the art object, and even its claim to originality."[7] How better to support this claim than through recourse to Duchamp himself? Warhol's commentators made sure to cite Papa Duchamp's opinion on Warhol's signature work: "If a man takes fifty Campbell Soup cans and puts them on a canvas, it is not the retinal image which concerns us. What interests us is the concept that wants to put fifty Campbell Soup cans on a canvas."[8] To cite Duchamp on Warhol in 1965 was a way of signaling what interested the 1960s about Warhol: the possibility of assimilating his art to the emerging conceptual paradigm — of emphasizing its interest, not as picture, but as idea.

For some writers, of course, Warhol's lesson had (and still has) a somewhat wider scope; his appropriationist tricks were not merely ideas — they were ideas about the contemporary world. By these lights his art takes its cue straight from modernity, though whether by posing as its clone or its critic seemed — may still seem — harder to say: did his work expose, or merely echo, the numbing repetitiveness of the commodity? The idea of Warhol's art as critique lagged slightly behind the notion of it as concept; its emergence seems, in retrospect, to have been contingent on the politicization of art and criticism in the aftermath of 1968. The Warhol machine was then retooled, regeared to take a different cultural and critical course. The new direction is clearly indicated in a 1971 essay by Gregory Battcock, a minor man of letters and art world weathervane.[9] Battcock's opinion is emphatic: "Warhol's greatest contribution to art is not to be found in the paintings themselves but rather in the fact that through his paintings he exposed the shoddy mechanics of both contemporary art and society.... He has revealed the hypocrisy of the social system and the absurdity of its culture."[10]

The main problem about putting these questions to the issue of the tone and posture of Warhol's art is not that the questions are not interesting. It is that they are not answerable in any very reliable way. The arguments boil down to claim versus counterclaim — the impassioned *yes* versus the vehement *no*. Does Warhol's art expose or reflect the culture it images? Both answers have been given, yet it has been the speaker's own beliefs and critical protocols that count the most in either case. And no matter which side is argued, in the first wave of Warhol literature one encounters few suggestions that his work functions in anything like a traditional way: as paintings, in other words, or as "retinal images," to cite Duchamp once again. One meets with few claims that the forms his pictures take shape or inflect their subjects and the viewer's understanding. Like Battcock, critics read past or through "the paintings themselves," without really asking how they look or how viewers respond to them — if, that is, the retinal has really been left aside. These omissions were necessary for Warhol to play his assigned role — they were needed if it was to be claimed, to cite Battcock still further, that "Warhol correctly foresaw the end of painting and became its executioner."[11] I want to argue, *pace* Battcock, that Warhol executed paintings, rather than acted as painting's executioner.

Against the uniformity of this critical backdrop (remember that I am describing the criticism of the 1960s and early 1970s above all), opinions to contrary stand out like sore thumbs. Yet they did exist: in demonstration of that claim, I want to cite the late Henry Geldzahler, who, from his base as a curator at the Metropolitan Museum, was one of the most influential forces in the art world of his day; he made the rounds of studios and galleries, and of course was to be spotted, microphone in hand, discoursing at a symposium on pop art convened at New York's Museum of Modern Art in 1963. The panelists spent the day trying to answer a question they found troublesome: they were discussing whether pop art is really art at all. By the following year Geldzahler had made up his mind. The answer, in the case of Warhol, was yes:

> Warhol's paintings sometime[s] strike us as not being art at all, as not being enough, as not being sufficiently different from life, from our ordinary experience. The artistry with which they are made is concealed and reveals itself slowly and the brash and brazen image, all we can see at first, becomes, in time, a painting, something we can assimilate into our lives and experience.[12]

Although Geldzahler's was an isolated opinion, I think it is an important one. It is important to my argument because it is the response of someone who does more than supply expectations to Warhol's work. Instead he seems to have looked at it and aims to speak of a process of viewing and its result, a transformation of image to painting. As Geldzahler describes it, that process involves distinct stages, each marked by changes in the status of the image. At first the image is too familiar, too close to ordinary experience for the viewer to see the difference — in other words, to allow a secure enough distinction from the experience of the everyday. Familiarity is the dominant characteristic of a Warhol canvas: it is "all we can see at first," and it initiates a purely visual experience of the work. To become a painting, Geldzahler claims, the image must come to seem *less* familiar. This happens as we look. Only in looking — in a paradoxical process — when it seems less visually present and obvious, does it become a painting; only then, when it can be understood as more than merely familiar, can the picture's artistry be seen, can it begin to mean something for its viewers' "lives and experience."

Geldzahler's definition of painting — of Warhol's painting in particular — crops up in this context because it is useful in under-

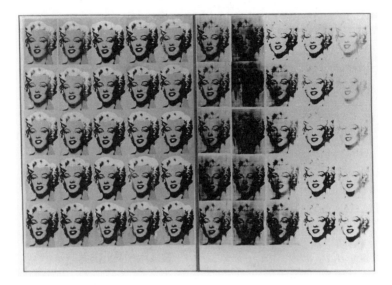

Figure 2. Andy Warhol, *Marilyn Diptych*, 1962. Silk-screen ink on synthetic polymer paint on canvas. Tate Gallery, London. Photo: Tate Gallery, London / Art Resource.

standing how his pictures might fit that category — the category "painting" — rather better than they do that of "conceptual art." The point is essential to my purpose — important enough for me to want to show straightaway how its terms might apply to a particular Warhol canvas. If familiarity is the key, what could be more familiar than Warhol's image of Marilyn Monroe — the *Diptych* he famously generated within weeks of her suicide in August 1962 (figure 2). And what could be more brazen in its pursuit of just that "familiarity" effect? It is produced not just by Warhol's makeover of a studio portrait (a publicity still shot by Gene Kornman in 1953) into a silk screen inked and re-inked to look like a particularly fast and low-cost printing job; and not just by his careful choice of a photograph taken some ten years before Marilyn's death: his source shows Monroe in her screen idol heyday, as the representation the woman was to become.[13] The effect of familiarity also results from this painting's chief technical procedure; it revels in its own redundancy, insisting with each repetition that the viewer has *surely* gotten the point.

There's no question about it: one image equals the next, or at least differs from it meaninglessly; repetition prompts indifference and licenses us to turn away. It is only in refusing that permission, in resisting redundancy, that we are able to speculate about such differences and effects as do emerge:[14] perhaps, *faute de mieux*, we start to try to make sense of the contrast between color and black and white, for example, and to see it as a matter of medium, or to register the quasi-filmic succession of the image frame (filmic because changes are so very imperceptible); we note the way the image both blackens and fades, conjuring presence and absence through opposite means. The apparent integrity of Marilyn's glamorous visage — its parted lips and arched brows and beauty mark — becomes a mask that even familiarity cannot keep from fragmentation and decay. In its very exhaustion, the image is remade as its visual opposite. It is as if Warhol, in insisting so utterly on a single image as a singular meaning, is back-handedly courting a kind of referential plenitude.

It might be possible to claim this picture, and others like it — Warhol's *Blue Liz as Cleopatra*, for example, or his series of *Suicides* — as history painting by virtue of their registration of the glamour and redundancy and immanent violence of American life under late capitalism. These paintings declare their dependence on particular circumstances of time and place: indeed, their reliance on them is complete. Yet they do not describe or analyze those circumstances so much as adopt the moment's underlying protocols as their own visual terms and rules. The meanings of these works — if they have meanings — are not the particular events and individuals they illustrate — this car crash, that movie star, this can of soup. Instead they refer outside themselves to a particular set of conditions, which, however real, *cannot* be illustrated as a totality. They refer, that is, to the system — the "image world" — of commodification and desire that gives them currency, and invoke that system as a set of generalities. We might say that they convey their meanings allegorically, producing themselves as "phantom proxies" of a larger whole.[15] Marilyn "means" the entertainment industry the way a mirror in a seventeenth-century Dutch painting "means" vanity: the equation seems sufficient, even satisfying, though this is only the case by convention, by a kind of tacit agreement or assumption. That these pictures can so refer is dependent of course on the initial choice of image; be it brazen or blatant, it must also possess the kind of content that can make it representative of a wider category — and conversely lack those contents that would stand in the way of such reference. The appropriated image must be both resonant enough — and empty enough — to allow the process of allegorizing to occur.

Warhol's work from 1962 onward demonstrates his utter commitment to this way of painting. Repetition and silk screen had come to stay, and their apparent simplicity almost hypnotically wills us to forget how deliberately these effects were achieved: it takes poking at the edges of Warhol's early production to understand that his brand of deadpan took some finding. We need to look, for example, at his early drawings and paintings of soup cans with the labels torn and sullied, or stuffed with dollar bills, to see that his most familiar models once were shown in different postures, even assigned a kind of attitude. There is plenty of metaphorical pathos in evidence in those drawings, and not much metonymic cool. Likewise we should look at other 1962 paintings — *Before and After*, for example, and the *Do It Yourself* series — to see with how much glee and irony Warhol bore down on regularity and dumb repetition as his paintings' central tropes.

I think it is certain that when Warhol painted his *Race Riots*, sometime early in the summer of 1963, he borrowed the requisite images with these requirements in mind, with the intention, that is, of giving them his signature treatment (plate 1). Silk screen and squeegee stood ready to transpose three news photographs into a handful of paintings in red and mustard and mauve. We can only conclude that the chosen photographs seemed to Warhol to possess the necessary resonance — had allegorical potential — although given our own distance from this moment thirty-three years ago, it cannot come amiss to spell out why.

The reasons are somewhat more various than they might seem. For a start, *any* picture of black protest was in 1963 emphatically topical, given that black activism had reached new urgency and visibility under the John F. Kennedy administration and the leadership of the Reverend Martin Luther King Jr. Remember that since the late 1950s King had been advocating "direct action," his term for the strategy of peaceful demonstration in the name of civil rights — demonstrations that brought his own repeated arrests, as well as those of thousands of other blacks. Both demonstrations and arrests were meant to be visible: when King was booked in 1958, at Montgomery, Alabama, under the eyes of his wife, Coretta Scott King, the camera of Charles Moore was present and so, by extension, were the nation's eyes. In the charged spring of 1963 — the centennial year of Negro emancipation — King had focused the attention and resources of the Southern Christian Leadership Conference on the integration of another Alabama city — Birmingham — a city that despite its wishful self-advertising (its gateway declared it "The Magic City") had the appalling distinction of being, in King's blunt phrase, "the most segregated city in America."[16] To say Birmingham was segregated is to say it was racist: under the leadership of Commissioner of Public Safety, Bull Connor, a policy of discrimination and exclusion held sway; the city was notably resistant to protesters' insistence on their rights to the most basic civic services — to eat, for example, at public lunch counters, to use public restrooms, to swim in public pools, to play on public playgrounds. Connor's intransigence made Birmingham ideal for a demonstration: action could count on reaction; King was prepared both to risk and to milk the response. He welcomed photographic coverage of the demonstrations, and when he was again imprisoned in the course of these efforts, in April 1963, he wrote his celebrated "Letter from Birmingham Jail" — a document, among other things, of his tireless ability to use the controversy his actions aimed to provoke.

But Warhol's subject was not just generally topical; the specific images he chose for his *Race Riots* were also familiar. They were lifted from *Life*, that mainstay of American photojournalism and prime source for white middle-class impressions of the week's *actualités*. *Life*, it is said, was at the time the "single most important organ of the media, reaching more than half of the adult population."[17] The three screens Warhol used in the *Race Riots* came from the *Life* exclusive "They Fight a Fire That Won't Go Out," a photo essay by the same Charles Moore, a civil rights veteran as dedicated as he was skilled (figures 3, 4, and 5).[18] Though he was part of a press corps that flocked to the city — other photographers are often visible in his pictures — Moore is the one who seems to have been most in the thick of things: he was there when the dogs were called out and there when the high-pressure fire hoses were leveled at the protesters and there again when they rallied and regrouped on nearby church steps in the course of one long and turbulent weekend. It is symptomatic of both the media's presence, on the one hand, and Moore's own tenacity, on the other, that he got himself photographed by an unidentified member of the press corps at work making one of the same pictures Warhol was soon to use.[19]

Yet looking at Moore's photographs and Warhol's silk-screened paintings — matching originals with copies, then back again — questions emerge concerning Warhol's chosen source. The images may have been familiar, but are they quite empty enough? The question is relevant because one main requisite of Warhol's tested painterly strategy — that sensation of attention sapped or exhausted in confrontation with a repeated visual form — no longer prevails in quite the same way. Though now suffused with color, the photographs survive within Warhol's paintings: a bit grittier, more like newsprint, they still seem pretty much intact. The more we look at both originals and copies, the clearer it becomes why Moore was the photographer *Life* used for an exclusive, and why he then defended his authorship (the photographer eventually sued Warhol for unauthorized use of his work).[20] These pho-

Figures 3, 4, and 5. Charles Moore, Birmingham police using police dogs against black demonstrators in Birmingham, photographs from "They Fight a Fire That Won't Go Out," *Life*, 17 May 1963. © 1979 Charles Moore / Black Star.

tographs have protagonists and action and drama. The same set of characters — dogs and officers, onlookers and victim — groups and regroups before Moore's lens. Looking through the sequence it is obvious that Moore meant a narrative to unfold. The story is that of the young black man with the hat, who wheels around in surprise and annoyance as his trousers are ripped from his leg. Then, in the second image, he strains to get away. At first the attack is isolated, but the ensuing photograph — the third — shows that his vulnerability seems to have been communicated to other officers and beasts, who are quick to join the fray. His first attackers then back off, as if content to let the others finish the job. Under supervision, that is: the lead dog surely has some fight left in him — he is ready to take on Moore.

One way to confirm the drama and narrativity of Moore's photographs is to compare them with the images that circulated in the daily press. Of these, an Associated Press wire photo of another confrontation between a young black man, a dog, and his policeman handler was by far the most widespread.[21] Unlike Moore's work, the photograph is notably stable; it freezes black and white together, with the lunging dog to link the two. Yet out of their formal equation comes not similarity but a pointed rhetorical difference; this may be one reason that the picture's various captions — "A city police dog lunges at a negro youth," or more simply "With police dog" — override the presence of *three* protagonists within the image and provide the policeman a protective invisibility.

These four photographs are only the tip of the iceberg: a whole variety of images of the Birmingham actions circulated in the public realm; they included many others taken by Moore himself. His *Life* essay, as I say, showed protesters drenched by hoses, rallying, praying, and being carried off to jail. All these pictures take sides and tell stories and use words to tie down meanings that images alone could not convey. Take the caption that accompanies a photo of a wet and worried young black man: "Face of Hatred. Glaring sullenly at firemen who just soaked him with hose jet, Negro expresses Birmingham's long-standing racial bitterness."[22] These same firemen, we have already learned from the *Life* essay, are the ones who "fight a fire that won't go out." Put these two images together — in fact they were printed only pages apart — and that fire takes on a face and a meaning: what burns, we are meant to understand, is the "hatred" and "bitterness" of the young and virile black male.

With so many images in circulation, with their rhetorical charge at maximum, the issue of Warhol's choice of images takes on special urgency. Why this particular sequence of a black man harried in fresh and repeated attacks, rather than some other image of the day? Why not Moore's photographs of women praying or being taken bodily into custody? — these too were published in *Life*. Or what of the photographs of children under arrest, or the bodies of teenagers being pounded into buildings by the relentless jet of high-pressure spray? These last might well have been seen as particularly characteristic of the Birmingham protests, since thousands of children actually did take to the streets to be arrested. These were the children for whom black parents acted, and who acted themselves: they were the ones who integrated the schools, those little girls in pigtails that photographers recorded crossing the tracks on their way to the classroom, the same little girls that painters even more pointedly commemorated — my example is Norman Rockwell's brilliant and passionate canvas, *The Problem We All Live With*, painted for *Look* in January 1964 (figure 6). The main questions concerning Warhol's *Race Riots* are not so much *how* he chose his imagery — ultimately there is no sure way of telling — but *what* he chose and *why*, for in these questions, in the implications of those choices, lie his works' connections to history.

Warhol's *Race Riots*, I submit, paint history from two specifiable points of view. First, he paints as a liberal, and this political stance helps explain the fact that he is actually working in such a surprisingly traditional way. We need to make a distinction between the signature "look" of the *Race Riot* pictures — the silk screens, the appropriation, and the like — and the nature of their chosen photographic frames. The frames he uses bear comparison to Salon painting, in full historical flight. They have singular protagonists, actions and reactions, onlookers and actors, all caught equally in the ongoing swirl of events. The sequence narrates. It is charged with before and after. We are nearly back with the "significant moment" so dear to Jacques-Louis David and his school. Warhol's interest in such effects accounts likewise for his decision to screen more than one image into a picture: remember how rare it is for him to do this. Apart from a few portraits of living sitters that use sequential snapshots — think back to Ethel Scull primping in the photo booth — the *Race Riots* and his portraits of Jacqueline Kennedy in her tragic transition from First Lady to widowhood are the major examples in his work. In interrupting his standard staccato with such variation and phrasing, I think Warhol is taken over by a special, unaccustomed purpose: to return narrative and temporality to his work and thus to locate his work's narrative within the temporal world. Hence the care exerted, in *Red Race Riot*, for example, to use three screens in strict narrative sequence, with repetitions for emphasis: a mini–morality play. One frame alone would have reeked of untidy happenstance, the apparently accidental freezing that is the news photo's stock in trade. As it is, an image that started out as chance ends up as drama — to repeat, a mini–morality play. And when the final screen is cut and partly repeated (along the upper right-hand edge) the effect is emphatic, not disruptive; the repetition does not break the overall narrative flow. On the contrary, the story starts up again, to finish on just the same note.

In the case of the *Race Riots*, this decision to return to narrative is bolstered by other moves, and mere repetition is suspended in other ways. For example, in a group of *Little Race Riots*, four smaller pictures that make use of a single screen (the one I have called the second in the sequence), redundancy is countered by color: the screens are pointedly tinted red, white, and blue, those eminently nationalist hues (plate 2). Yet that's not quite right: they are really colored red, red, white, and blue. The two reds are different through different admixtures of blue and yellow, though only a stickler for precise description — preferably one attuned to the stress the artist so consistently places on repetition — will notice this false redundancy.

What does this difference amount to? I think the chain of colors connotes the flag and blood. The thought sends me back to the context in which Warhol spoke of his coming show in Paris and death in America:

> We went to see *Dr. No* at Forty-second Street. It's a fantastic movie, so cool. We walked outside and somebody threw a cherry bomb right in front of us, in this big crowd. And there was blood, I saw blood on people and all over. I felt like I was bleeding all over. I saw in the paper last week that there are more people throwing them —

Figure 6. Norman Rockwell, *The Problem We All Live With*, 1964. Oil on canvas. Norman Rockwell Museum, Stockbridge, MA. Photo: © 1964 Norman Rockwell Family Trust.

Plate 1. Andy Warhol, *Red Race Riot*, 1963. Synthetic polymer paint and silk-screen ink on canvas. Andy Warhol Foundation, New York. Photo: © 1996 Andy Warhol Foundation, Inc. / ARS, New York.

Plate 2. Andy Warhol, *Little Race Riot*, 1963. Silk-screen ink on synthetic polymer paint on canvas. Present location unknown. Photo: Courtesy of the estate of Robert Mapplethorpe, © 1996 Andy Warhol Foundation Inc. / ARS, New York.

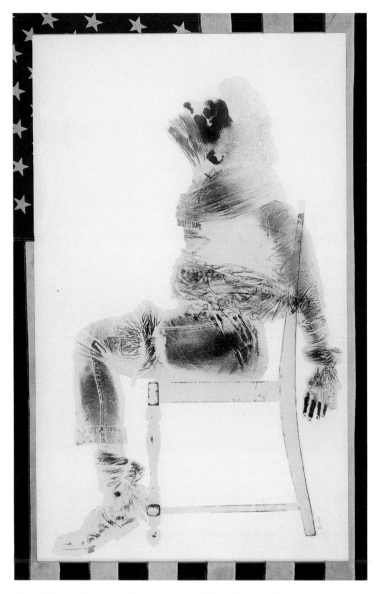

Plate 3. David Hammons, *Injustice Case*, 1970, Mixed media print. Los Angeles County Museum of Art, Museum Purchase with Museum Associate Acquisitions Fund. Photo: © 1996 Museum Associates, Los Angeles County Museum of Art. All Rights Reserved.

it's just part of the scene — and hurting people. My show in Paris is going to be called "Death in America." I'll show the electric chair pictures and the dogs in Birmingham and car wrecks and some suicide pictures.[23]

"I felt like I was bleeding all over." Thus empathizing, Warhol arrives at "Death in America": at fatal accidents and suicides and executions, and, yes, the dogs in Birmingham. Thus empathizing, Warhol seems to lose sight of distinctions among perpetrators and victims and causes — about the agents and objects of history. Yet these are the same distinctions that, as painted, his *Race Riots* try hard to supply. I think they do so unconsciously, more or less despite themselves. They do so because there is never any confusion, in representation, about the matter of race in America. The dramatic narrative and personae preexist Warhol and outlast him. He paints within them: they both contain and override his empathy.

To speak of the unconscious of Warhol's paintings is to specify further their point of view. Warhol is representing the drama of race, yet in so doing works with and within that drama's structuring assumptions. Those assumptions, like Warhol's pictures, endlessly — repetitively, redundantly — dramatize the encounter between black and white as a conflict between black and white men. The white man has the dog and the stick and the belly; we don't need Danny Lyon's 1963 photograph of defiant state troopers in Clarksdale, Mississippi, to understand his characteristically phallic stance (figure 7). Nor do we need Lyon's photograph of the Maryland arrest of a black man to grasp that the stripping of the black male body emasculates: unmanned, it is the obscene gesture's counterpart (figure 8). Let me state the obvious: in both images masculinity is racialized. What is striking about Lyon's photographs is how directly they confirm and echo the meanings of Warhol's paintings, and of the imagery he used for them. The same point could be made again and again; on it hinges a history of black and white men both lived and represented as masculine antagonism. What is the history of race in America? Or better stated, what is the *image* of race in America? Whether heroic or abject (or both), it is the physical confrontation of men. It is the mutilated body of the fourteen-year-old Emmet Till, a Chicago boy murdered in 1955 while on vacation

Figure 7. Danny Lyon, Policeman, Clarksdale, Mississippi, 1963. Photograph.
© Danny Lyon, Magnum Photos.

Figure 8. Danny Lyon, Arrest in Cambridge, Maryland, 1964. Photograph.
© Danny Lyon, Magnum Photos.

in Mississippi for allegedly having whistled at a white woman: his mother insisted that an unretouched photograph be published in *Jet* for "all the world" to see. It is the 1991 beating of Rodney King by four Los Angeles police officers; the beating as captured on video has now become the image repeated in a painting by Danny Tisdale, just as Birmingham was repeated in the *Race Riots*. It is the declaration of the sanitation workers who in 1968 marched in Memphis, each one bearing a placard with the same emphatic statement: "I am a man," they each insisted, because the manhood of black laborers was not functionally obvious to the powers they addressed.[24] It is the Million Man March, when in October 1995 hundreds of thousands of African American men descended on Washington from all over the country for much the same purpose: to announce and reclaim their identities and responsibilities as men (though this time class allegiances seem to have been left at home).[25] What is striking about this series of events and images is not just its content; it is its tragic recursiveness.

When Warhol spoke of painting "the dogs in Birmingham" — when he painted *Race Riot*, in other words — he declared through his words' omissions his historical parti pris. What is omitted? Exactly what is present in each picture. White male master, black male victim: the standard drama of race. Though these characters are his paintings' actors, they are also its givens, its unconscious, you might say. They take over the painted image, somewhat against its will. By this I mean to point to the way that in *Race Riot* the mode of allegory (Warhol's tested way of painting) is undermined. The rhetoric of sameness, of rote and standard repetition, can no longer be made to apply. Pictorial structure makes a semblance of these effects but recasts them in the language of nation and history.

This is not only because Warhol was waylaid by his loyalties as a liberal — by his need to "feel" and "identify" — but also because race is a different kind of historical object than the "commodity" or "celebrity" or "mass production." It cannot be allegorized. The mirror may be vanity, Marilyn Hollywood, but what are black and white men? They emerge as scripted narrative, no matter what Warhol tries. (Perhaps he called his picture *Race Riot*, rather than *Protest*, or *Demonstration*, or *State Violence*, in tacit acknowledgment that this would be the case.) Their bodies are present as violence and power: this is the essence of the story they have to tell.

These same narratives are likewise the assumption of the African American historical experience, so much so that paintings by black male artists done in the wake of Warhol — David Hammons's *Injustice Case* of 1970, say, or Philip Lindsay Mason's *Manchild in the Promised Land*, painted the year before — also seem to internalize the plot (plate 3, figure 9). No, not internalize, so much as embody: both analogize the black experience using bodily metaphors. Both understand, to paraphrase Fred Orton, that metaphor is founded on a proposed analogy between the literal subject — black experience in the American promised land — and a subject substituted for it, the black male body — the kid with the target T-shirt; the bound and gagged black male.[26] But the metaphor goes even further. When black is embodied as victim, he is the object of an oppressive or lethal gaze; for white to be embodied as viewer is to be the aggressor too.

While I think that Warhol's canvases likewise imagine white viewers, I am less confident that he grasped the complexity of his imagery and its central metaphor.[27] He did know that photography was central and why this was the case. Photography not only communicated the image of racism, it gave racism historic form. (It seems that even after painting the *Race Riots* Warhol was still drawn to the paradigm: figure 10 reproduces another photograph of police and protester that entered his clipping file in the summer of 1963.) The sheer ordinariness of the photographic image comes through as gray grain and loss of detail: visual saturation is once again the rule. But we've seen that the rule was not merely stretched; it was broken: the resulting pictures don't quite operate as savvy staccato repetition or translate into a quick fix on the "information metonym." Warhol could not resist retelling race's story; could not freeze or stop its narrative. The result is images caught between modes of representation: stranded somewhere between allegory and history. They have actors and drama and even a moral purpose, yet the drama stays disconnected from any wider explanatory framework — anything as namable as "mass culture" or "the commodity." Their only context and framework is racism; yet they are its image, not its proxy. And they are more haunting than any phantom could ever be. Warhol was caught in the circuitry — the circularity — of racism, more or less despite

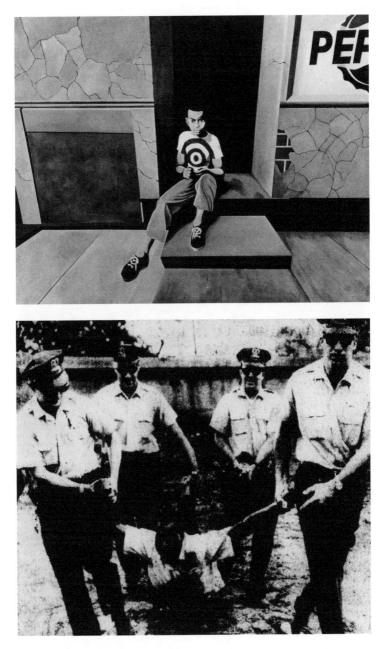

Figure 9. Philip Lindsay Mason, *Manchild in the Promised Land*, 1969. Oil on canvas. Present location unknown. Reproduced from Robert Doty, *Contemporary Black Artists in America* (New York, 1971).

Figure 10. Associated Press, Bound for police van, *New York Times*, 13 August 1963. Photograph. Photo: Library Services, University of California at Berkeley.

Figure 11. "Rethinking the Dream," *Newsweek*, 26 June 1995. Photographs by Charles Moore and Lou Dematteis.

himself. He was right: this is death in America, and it isn't history. Can anyone fail to notice that the subjects absent from his pictures — women and children and labor — are exactly those that are absent from our current social policy, even while our culture feeds itself on the endless spectacle of conflict between black and white men?

That is why, thirty years later, this image of black protest still cannot be laid to rest. It is much too useful: it has too much mythic clout. Note that the climactic photograph in Moore's sequence has recently turned up again in the national media — in *Newsweek*, to be precise (figure 11).[28] There it helped to give an image (and a justification) to the waning of affirmative action — or, as it is euphemistically, parodically, termed, the current "rethinking" of "the Dream." I say *helped*, because the photograph was given a partner, rather than made to work alone. It was printed face-to-face with a picture captioned "California 1995: Defending preference programs for minorities in Sacramento." The second image — in full color this time — shows a cluster of people, mostly black and white women and children, gathered behind an upraised sign: "No Retreat! Stand Up For Affirmative Action." The words are vehement, but the moment chosen by the 1995 photograph construes this action less as a contained dramatic encounter than as an insistent, even querulous confrontation with the magazine's readers (no other object is in sight). The contrast is a matter of bodies and formats as well as an issue of address: the tense diagonals of Moore's photo (the angular weave of nightsticks and leashes and dogs and legs and white lines on the road) and its disjunctive scale (look back at the way the black victim is dwarfed by the looming cop) are replaced by well-dressed, well-fed people standing in solid self-possession, oblivious to the light rain. Their placard has been professionally printed; like its bearers, it seems to issue its commands from an established position; given its sheer visual stability, the photo too takes its subjects' part quite formally, dwelling on how comfortably, how easily, they claim entitlement.

Of course such photographic confrontations are meant to be open to many readings, and it would be wrong to tie this one down too firmly. But partly, I am sure, it is meant to put into images an argument dear to current opponents of affirmative action, regardless of niceties of political (neoconservative/neoliberal) stripe. Once upon a time, says the black-and-white photo, there was the Civil Rights movement — a heroic struggle for basic human dignity. Look what has happened to that heroism, says the full-page color update: it has turned into nothing more than the assertive self-interest of racially advantaged individuals trying to hold onto their perks. Once again Charles Moore's photograph is called on for a job of ideological work, conjuring women and children off the stage of the "historic" civil rights struggle, so that they can reappear as a 1990s "special interest group" angling to keep "preference programs" intact. For *Newsweek* readers to approve of civil rights, it seems, they must be the rights of the absolutely victimized. If you are not a victim, your interests must be "special." The problem with that label, of course, is its political implications: "special interests" nowadays ends up naming almost any concerted or collective minority effort to escape from the victim's role. In a male-dominated discourse of "victims" and "aggressors," moreover, any loosening of these new political strictures seems desperately hard to secure. Nor will we be able to attend to the social threats against women and children, whatever their color, until the nightsticks have been put away. Only then will the version of history inscribed in Warhol's paintings have passed out of currency.

NOTES

It is a pleasure to acknowledge the contribution of Beth Dungan to this paper; her work as my research assistant was accomplished with great intelligence and efficiency. I am grateful for support from the Committee on Teaching, University of California at Berkeley, which made the assistantship possible, and to Dean's Research Funding for illustrations and permissions. Thanks also to Sabine Kriebel for her help in gathering photographs and to Richard Meyer for alerting me to the presence in the Warhol Archive of the photograph here reproduced as figure 10.

1. Andy Warhol declares this intention to name the show "Death in America" in an interview with G.R. Swenson. See Swenson's "What Is Pop Art?" *Art News*, vol. 63, no. 7 (November 1963): 60. The catalog of the Sonnabend exhibition prints brief comments by Jean-Jacques Lebel, Alain Jouffroy, and John Ashbery. Of the three, only Lebel speaks directly to the *Race Riot* Warhol had put on view; he makes it evident that its narrative was perfectly clear: "L'assaut des manifestants anti-segrégationnistes par la chiennerie des state-troopers

dont nous suivons le déroulement réel à travers quatre phases: le chien policier approche, il mord, il arrache le bas du pantalon d'un manifestant, celui-ci s'éloigne.... le tout [he means the whole list of subjects he has just described] dans un rose de Times Square, un blanc de laboratoire de pharmacie, un bleu d'acier et un noir de sang caillé, un noir de supplice." Galerie Ileana Sonnabend, *Warhol* (Paris, 1964), unpaginated. My thanks to Sarah Kennel for tracking down the catalog at the Centre Beaubourg, Paris.

2. Warhol, as quoted in Swenson, "What Is Pop Art?," 26.

3. To cite one of his studio assistants, Nathan Gluck: "Andy has *always* said over and over, 'It's too much trouble to paint.' And that's one of the reasons he silk-screened." See Patrick S. Smith, *Warhol: Conversations with the Artist* (Ann Arbor, 1988), 60.

4. As quoted in Frayda Feldman and Jörg Schellmann, *Andy Warhol Prints: A Catalogue Raisonné* (New York and Munich, 1985), 14. They are quoting a remark from Andy Warhol et al., eds., *Andy Warhol* (Stockholm, 1968), unpaginated.

5. For two different accounts of the meaning of Warhol's monochromes, see Benjamin H.D. Buchloh, "Andy Warhol's One-Dimensional Art: 1956–1966," and Marco Livingstone, "Do It Yourself: Notes on Warhol's Techniques," in K. McShine, ed., *Andy Warhol: A Retrospective* (New York, 1989), 46–48, 72.

6. Irving Sandler, "The New Cool-Art," *Art in America,* vol. 53, no. 1 (February 1965): 100.

7. Barbara Rose, "The Value of Didactic Art," *Artforum,* vol. 15, no. 9 (April 1967): 32, 35.

8. Marcel Duchamp, as quoted by Samuel Adams Green, *Andy Warhol* (Philadelphia, 1965), unpaginated.

9. For a brief account of Gregory Battcock's art world activities see my "Reading *Minimal Art*," in Gregory Battcock, ed., *Minimal Art: A Critical Anthology* (Berkeley, 1995).

10. Gregory Battcock, "'an art your mother could like,'" *Art and Artists* 5 (February 1971): 12.

11. *Ibid.*

12. Henry Geldzahler, "Andy Warhol," *Art International,* vol. 8, no. 3 (April 1964): 35.

13. Livingstone, "Do It Yourself," has identified and printed the still Warhol used, complete with his cropping marks.

14. In his "Saturday Disaster: Trace and Reference in Early Warhol," Thomas Crow has offered a suggestive reading of the *Marilyn* pictures; he sees their tone as mournful valedictory. See *Art in America* (May 1987): 129–36.

15. The term comes from Samuel Taylor Coleridge's scathing definition of

allegory, advanced in his *Lay Sermons* of 1816. See *Samuel Taylor Coleridge*, ed. H. J. Jackson (Oxford, 1985), 661.

16. Martin Luther King Jr., *Why We Can't Wait* (New York, 1963), 50. King's characterization is borne out by other studies of Birmingham, which also make clear the poverty of the city's working-class blacks. See in particular David J. Garrow, ed., *Birmingham, Alabama, 1956–1963: The Black Struggle for Civil Rights* (Brooklyn, 1989); also James A. Colaiaco, "The American Dream Unfulfilled: Martin Luther King, Jr. and the 'Letter from Birmingham Jail,'" *Phylon*, vol. 45, no. 1 (Spring 1984): 1–18.

17. Steven Kasher, *Appeal to This Age: Photography of the Civil Rights Movement, 1954–1968* (New York, 1995), unpaginated.

18. Charles Moore, "They Fight a Fire That Won't Go Out," *Life*, 17 May 1963. Many of Moore's civil rights photographs have been collected in Michael S. Durham, *Powerful Days: The Civil Rights Photography of Charles Moore* (New York, 1991).

19. The photograph was first published in the *Birmingham News* and is reproduced in David R. Goldfield, *Black, White, and Southern: Race Relations and Southern Culture, 1940 to the Present* (Baton Rouge, 1990), 173. I am grateful to Steven Kasher for this reference. It seems to me likely, given the often noted resistance in Birmingham to integration, that the appearance of this particular photo in the paper was meant to signal the presence of "foreign" journalists as interlopers in city affairs.

20. For an account of the dispute between Warhol and Moore, see Gay Morris, "When Artists Use Photographs," *Art News*, vol. 80, no. 1 (January 1981): 104–5.

21. This picture appeared in *Time*, 10 May 1963; *Newsweek*, 13 May 1963; and in newspapers the week before, on Saturday, 4 May 1963. These include the *Los Angeles Times, New York Times*, and *San Francisco Chronicle*. I wager it appeared in many more.

22. Moore, "They Fight a Fire," 32.

23. Warhol, as quoted in Swenson, "What Is Pop Art?" 26, 60.

24. Reproductions of the *Jet* photograph of the body of Emmet Till, Danny Tisdale's painting, and the 1968 Memphis workers' march are all included in Thelma Golden, *Black Male: Representations of Masculinity in Contemporary American Art* (New York, 1994).

25. Both *Time*, 30 October 1995; and *Newsweek*, 30 October 1995, ran Les Stone's photo of Ben White, both arms raised in an exultant salute, as one image of the March. In this photograph, as in the 1968 image, a printed message is visible: it may be worth noting how much the message has changed. In 1995, White's T-shirt read: "Million Man March Led by Minister Louis Farrakhan."

26. Fred Orton, *Figuring Jasper Johns* (London, 1994), passim.

27. One justification for this supposition lies in the presumed audiences for *Life*, as well as for contemporary high art. Note too that *Ebony*, a monthly that modeled its format on *Life*, while addressing a black audience, made no mention of any events in Birmingham in spring 1963. It was a lifestyle magazine imaging black success and upward mobility: racial demonstrations were definitely out of place.

28. Evan Thomas and Bob Cohn with Vern E. Smith, "Rethinking the Dream," *Newsweek*, 26 June 1995, 18–21.

Camouflaging Race

and Gender

Barbara T. Christian

University of California Regents voted last night to kill affir-
mative action in admissions, hiring, and contracting after
a marathon meeting that erupted into an angry, raucous
protest causing regents to find another room in which to cast
their historic vote.
— *San Francisco Chronicle*, 21 July 1995 (emphasis added)

For as long as I can remember, my daughter has been interested in the law, possibly because my father, uncle, brother, and cousin are impressive lawyers with an intense appreciation for the law. In high school she took courses in law in which she earned A's, and in her junior year she auditioned for and got on the mock trial team. She did really well on the team; partly because of her efforts her team made it to the finals in the state's competition. It was for her the most educational and social event of her high school experience.

Juniors on the mock trial team who audition in their senior year usually make the team again. My daughter had done very well in her junior year, so she auditioned again for the senior year and expected to get on the team. Surprisingly, of all the seniors, including a few black men, she did not make the team. She was devastated. A usually composed young woman who did extremely well in school, she collapsed in tears and was barely able to function.

Since her rejection from the team had been so unexpected, I went to her high school to find out how to explain this to her. Had she been terrible in her second audition? I'd been to most parent/teacher meetings. Yet it took me four days to find the teacher/mentor of the mock trial team despite the tens of messages I left him and the fact that I went to her high school on three successive days. I shudder to think of parents who would not have the time to pursue the matter or the confidence to question their child's teacher about the reasons for her "failure." When I did find my daughter's teacher, he told me that she had been very good on the team, but as a black girl, she spoke "too well" for the roles they needed on the present team. They needed blacks to play witnesses, blacks who sounded like "inner-city girls."

This was not the first time my daughter had been expected in school to "be" the stereotypical black girl, in other words, a gum-cracking, slurred-speaking, sassy girl — the image, unfortunately, even teachers often have of who black girls are supposed to be. My daughter had found herself during her years in high school to be the *only* black girl in calculus, and so on. But this was the ultimate blow for her. She'd loved the mock trial team, had devoted hours and hours to it, fitting it into her homework, giving up social time to succeed at it. She was devastated. And here it was again — as she said to me, "If you're black, you can't win for losing."

I begin this reflection on affirmative action debates within the University of California system with this incident because so often the opponents of such policies insist that the issue of race is dead — that poverty rather than race is the real issue — that we should give special "preference" *only* to the poor. Remarkably within this construct, no one says the issue of gender equity is dead; its significance to affirmative action debates is typically sidelined, though, despite the fact that there are people of color who are also female. While I'd like a thorough restructuring of this country's characterizations and treatment of the poor *it* produces, I find this shift in rhetoric disingenuous in that so many of the people who use the argument that the issue of race is dead also insist that there is no such thing as "class" in America.

Nonetheless, as an intellectual, as a black woman, and as a feminist, I have tried to answer the question, Why should race and gender, or precisely race/gender, be taken into account? Doesn't the foregrounding of race privilege middle-class people who just happen to be black? Why is gender a hidden, though powerful, construct in the anti-affirmative action arsenal?

Although in this essay I do not wish to focus on the long-standing debates among blacks about whether race or class is the primary root of our oppression, some history may be useful. I was born in the Caribbean, in a society like the United States that is saturated with racism, but unlike it in that blacks are in the majority. Certainly that majority status is one of the reasons the Caribbean has produced so many scholars who have focused on class oppression as primary. As descendants of European colonialism, and as inhabitants of societies where people of the same race were often managers of their own people for the colonists, Caribbean scholars tend to foreground *class* as the basis for our analysis of racism. Scholars such as C.L.R. James and Walter Rodney have emphasized how class oppression is at the root of poor people's condition around the world as well as in the Caribbean. Still, when you come to *this man's country* ("this man's country" is a phrase that Caribbeans have used for the United States since the 1920s), Caribbeans discover that class analysis of their oppression is undermined by *this man's country*'s discourse on race. Especially after studies of difference emerged in the 1980s, scholars all know that there are different forms of racism and that there is a form of racism that is specifically American in its contours.[1]

Debates among blacks as to the relationship between class and race have not until recently included the centrality of gender to knowledge production. During the 1970s and 1980s, a much-fought-for realization among many scholars became increasingly important in public discourse, that there was more than *the woman question* that the traditional Left had proposed; rather, gender was central to the critical choices human beings could make.

The affirmative action debates have tended to foreground race as the central issue of controversy. Yet I tend to agree with Gloria Steinem that the anxieties caused by affirmative action policies may be more about gender than about race, since people of color have made but small increases in their numbers, whether one counts students, faculty, or contracting agencies. Rather, it is white women who appear to have forged ahead, who present more of a threat. That appearance of success may in fact be short-lived. In the 1990s, there has been a steady attack not only on welfare mothers but also on professional women. For example, on 8 January 1996, the *New York Times* reports: "Equal Opportunity Recedes for Most Female Lawyers." It is a report that relates to my daughter — I clipped it out for her — though most people would think of this report as having to do only with white women. While nearly half of the students in the nation's law schools are women, "women have been disproportionately hurt by the recent shrinking of law firms after a rapid expansion in the 1980s."[2] As Steinem mentioned in a 1995 talk in the City Arts and Lectures series in San Francisco, the issue of race (including the perception that immigrants of color are taking over America) might well be a camouflage for the issue of gender, since race in this country is such a trigger point. Rather than being rewarded for their accomplishments, black women are sometimes punished precisely because they are *successful* black women.

My theoretical and literary writings on the intersections of race, class, and gender did not prepare me for this country's assault on black girls. I submit to you the case of my daughter, the daughter of a UC professor, an excellent student who went on to major in sociology at UC Santa Cruz, graduated with highest honors in her major, and is presently at Georgetown Law School — clearly a middle-class black. She was dealt the major blow of her high school career not because she was poor but precisely because she was a successful black middle-class student who spoke "too well," in other words, who did not exhibit the signs of blackness that are equated with black poverty and the inner city. That experience was so pivotal for my daughter that her personal statement in applications to law school began with her remembrance of the mock trial incident and the strategies she'd used to turn it into a strong determination to pursue her dreams of becoming a lawyer.

And yet I wonder how many other young middle-class black women have experienced some variation of this experience and how many have decided like my daughter that "if you're black you can't win for losing." And if you're a woman, you've somehow got to overachieve. Why, in any case, should they have to overcome this emotional trauma? "Merit, merit," I had preached to my daughter. And here it was. Merit turned into disadvantage because she did not fit the stereotype of what so many conceive of as being a black woman in this society. Lord knows what such a characterization might mean for those inner-city black women who do "speak well."

I think of the scholar Thomas Sowell's insistence that Caribbean Americans constitute a model minority: immigrants who work hard, go to school, and ignore the racial nibblings at our soul that are alive in American society.[3] In that context, my Afro–Caribbean American daughter's *mock* trial experience could be interpreted as the peak of model minorityness. Ironically, she was born in the United States. My brother was not. A partner in a major law firm, one of few such blacks, my brother has accomplished remarkable achievements, though his are not as remarkable as those of my father, who clawed his way up through a plantation system to become a lawyer at a time when class background in the Caribbean was central to mobility. Yet even though my brother's way was easier, the psychological battering of racism in the United States has turned him into an angry black man. My father, who remained in the Caribbean, cannot fathom the depths of his son's anger at the "glass ceiling" he's repeatedly bumped his head against. The primacy of racism in the United States has been for my brother, as well as for so many other model minority Caribbean Americans, the initiation into the "American Way." My brother's point of view is a tribute to the tremendous impact of the psychological battering of racism — by racism I mean not just lynchings or beatings but also the assault on the spirit.

In that regard, I think of myself here at UC Berkeley as a person who feels, despite her accomplishments, alienated from the culture of this university. What do my black and colored students feel if I still feel strange and often unappreciated, despite my accomplishments at *this* university? One of my Caribbean American colleagues, Opal Palmer Adisa, writes in one of her pieces that "racism drains [her] energy leaving [her] feeling psychically weak and wasted so that it takes a concerted effort to will [her]self to continue to move, to smile at [her] children, to not detonate from anger."[4] The UC regents meeting might have been angry and rancorous; my life, for more than a night, has been too often fired by the emotion of anger. It is this effect of racism that whites who talk about poverty as the only disease we face refuse to acknowledge. It is not only poverty that explains the inner cities. It is this nibbling at the spirit, this wasting of the soul. Those of us who sustain these war injuries, what Alice Walker calls "warrior marks," understand only too well that the interpretation of any issue in this society is based on one's position and stance.[5]

I hold a relatively unique position at this university. I am one of a handful of black women who are full professors in the University of California system (we could comfortably sit around a lunch table), a position I reached partly because of the "liberal" atmosphere of the 1970s. Although I received a Ph.D. with high honors from Columbia University, I am well aware that the few black women academics that preceded me were restricted to appointments in the historically sexist black universities and that they had very limited access to historically racist and sexist white universities until the 1970s, when a few, and I mean a very few, of us gained entrance into what was considered to be *the* American academy. And unlike most actors in the affirmative action debate, I have been a part of the process of affirmative action at UC Berkeley, for I have been a faculty participant on the Special Admissions Committee, possibly the most time-consuming committee service I have ever done for the university (and one that minorities are typically expected to perform — in a sense, part of our affirmative action benefits). My participation in the Special Admissions Committee, as well as my position as one of the few full professors in the system who is a black woman, has informed the theoretical bases of my work. That is, at the center of my work is the notion that it is the intersections of differences rather than one single difference that is always at work.

I was appalled at how misinformed the discussants at the regents meeting were about *how* the UC system actually admits students. So many claimed that standards had declined as a result of affirmative action. Yet in the last twelve years, eligibility standards have been raised five times; in fact, standards are higher than ever before in UC's history. There are three tiers of admission to the University. The first 50 percent of students are admitted based on grade point averages and SAT scores, as well as on special talents. The next 45 percent are the top students (defined by grade point averages; test scores; and assessments of essays, activities, and awards) from categories of students defined by UC diversity criteria. Such criteria include socioeconomic disadvantage, ethnic underrepresentation, geographic origin, athletic recruitment, age, special talent, and disability. Also considered are applicants whose academic index scores narrowly missed the requirements for the first tier. The remaining 5 percent are admitted based on a particularly intensive, qualitative, case-by-case evaluation by a Special Admissions Committee. Students considered in this tier are from the diversity categories defined above who have not been admitted in the first two tiers but who demonstrate a high probability of achieving success at Berkeley. For example, there are exceptional music students who do not do well in math but who will, without question, succeed at Berkeley.

The affirmative action debate has focused especially on race, sometimes on gender. Legislators, even some UC faculty, seem to believe that race and gender are the only factors taken into consideration in special admissions. In fact, there are many factors the committee considers: gender; race; region; and special situations such as disabilities, special talents, special hardship situations, and the challenges faced by returning students.

The Special Admissions Committee consists of faculty members, students, and administrators, each of whom reads and critiques each student's application. In other words, there is a discussion of each individual student's possibilities, the problems the student has faced, and how that student has dealt with those problems. We look at students' personal statements, their records, their SATs and grade points, comments from their teachers, as well as notes taken by administrators of the students' interviews. We carefully consider the case of, for example, a Chicana whose family is opposed to her going to college, even to the extent of restricting the hours she can go to the library, who yet manages to achieve a 3.4 grade point average; or a white working-class man from a rural area in Northern California, whose family wants him to work rather than go to college, but who has, against tremendous odds, achieved a 3.5. We do not simply admit students when there are special situations that affect their performance. We may consider whether the student would benefit more by going first to community college or to special bridge programs. But the committee is aware that maturity, persistence, and intellectual focus are factors as important for educational growth as grade point averages and SAT scores, as many studies of successful college students have shown.

The idea of difference as an energizing force was proposed by the poet and theorist Audre Lorde, whose thoughts filtered into universities as well as society at large through the work of scholar-activists like myself, who stormed the intellectual barricades during the 1970s.[6] It was as a result of policies like affirmative action that the monolithic intellectual community of that time was allowed access to our thoughts. White middle-class students (the public's image of *the* college student) have benefited, perhaps even more than students of color or disabled students, from the diversity of *bodies* and *minds* in the classroom. Through it they have come to know the America they are living in, the world they are living in. Contrary to my colleague Todd Gitlin's most recent study on multiculturalism, which tends to be very critical of cultural balkanization, I think that the separativeness of groups of students at Berkeley is in fact the seed of their ultimately understanding one another. Students are more honest, I often think, than faculty are. They know you've got to really get to know yourself, your "group," and then struggle to know others, not just their bodies, but their histories, points of view — what I call cosmologies — if you are to really know yourself and others. They know that change has to be honest if it is to be lasting. Often "adult" faculty want a ready-made solution based on their desires for a better world, without being willing to work out power relations, racial and ethnic relations, gender relations. Often adults want a pretty picture of integration.

The classes at Berkeley, at least my classes, are like a United Nations, filled with students from a multitude of backgrounds — Bangladeshi, West African, Canadian, East Asian, Latin American, European — who are Americans. Scholars and students of color have generated entire new areas of inquiry on, for example, diasporas, sexualities, borders, and languages. The young people I teach (including young white men) are engaging each other in a conversation that is inclusive of ethnicities and cultures world-wide, the kind of conversation we need if we are to save this planet. Not only are these young people concerned with issues of race, ethnicity, gender, sexual preference; they also confront other major issues of our time, such as the environmental devastation of the planet and the intense injustices brought about by political waste.

I am not an affirmative action beneficiary per se. Yet I am, in the sense that the work I did on such African American women as Audre Lorde, Alice Walker, and Toni Morrison would not have been heard if it had not been for affirmative action policies. I do not apologize for the atmosphere created by affirmative action. American universities and society at large have gained much from what African American women writers and scholars have written during the last thirty years. In fact, we have produced a golden age of writing — one that this country has yet to acknowledge despite Toni Morrison's winning of the Nobel Prize. The University of California system has produced the very best scholars of American literature, and by that I mean *American* literature, precisely because a few like me were allowed into its halls. But what a price we have paid. More than it was worth, I sometimes think, since, in this anti–affirmative action atmosphere, we continue to be called on to defend our right to inclusion. And yet all I hear from the media is that white men are upset.

I too am upset. The July regents' decision marks people like myself, faculty hired in good faith by the university, as people who somehow do not make the grade. I really resent this effect of the regents' decision, perhaps even more than its effects on students. Faculty members like myself have introduced into this university vital intellectual issues of our society to which white students, as much as any other group, are responding. Faculty of color have, against great odds, constructed an alternative canon that has made it possible for such writers as Frances Harper, the most famous African American woman writer and thinker of the nineteenth century, as well as such twentieth-century writers as Toni Morrison, Ishmael Reed, and Alice Walker, to be taken seriously.

I take the regents' insult against faculty personally because I risked my entire academic career to do the work that I have done. We (and by *we*, I mean the few African American scholars admitted into the historically white universities in the early 1970s) have launched an industry that has invigorated academic departments and disciplines throughout the entire university. We get very little in return for our labors. In a published essay, "Diminishing Returns: Can Black Feminism(s) Survive the Academy," I explore the apparent contradiction that, while there has been a tremendous surge of interest in African American literatures and studies, the number of black Ph.D.s has declined.[7] I am concerned that the message of the regents' decision, especially to African American graduate students, who now account for only 4.4 percent of our total graduate student population, is that they are not wanted at UC, an embarrassing situation that I have had to contend with when I have spoken, since the decision, at universities in Europe as well as in this country.

Academics of color have not just performed a civil service. We have extended the landscapes of American and British literatures (to include, for example, Irish and South Asian traditions within the United States and Britain). We are forging ahead to transform the concept of American literatures as including the literature of South America, possibly the richest in the world today. And we are transcending the borders of disciplines to produce interdisciplinary studies.

Academics of color are being used as scapegoats for California's problems because the state is unwilling to face the real issue underlying the affirmative action debate. The real issue is that the state is not using its vast resources to create what some of my colleagues, in an open letter to the UC regents printed in the *New York Times*, call "the need for a robust, healthy educational environment."[8] This state's governing bodies have been criminal in their refusal to provide resources for our educational system and in their propagandizing against the very educational systems they are weakening through budgetary legislation and "symbolic actions" such as the regents' decision on 20 July.

In its political process, this state is destroying one of the world's greatest public universities, even as private institutions such as Stanford are broadcasting their support for affirmative action. The regents have made UC a laughingstock among universities even as they, like many of the state's governing bodies, are overtly using fears about race, and covertly those about gender, as a camouflage for their actions. The university may never again be able to recuperate what already has been lost and what will surely be lost as a result of the 20 July decision — unless it is rescinded as soon as possible.

Finally, the question — the *real* question — is not about that decision, but about whether the system will abandon its responsibility to the educational process and allow its role in the affirmative action debate to camouflage the political machinations of the supporters of the California Civil Rights Initiative.

NOTES

1. For example, see Henry Louis Gates Jr., ed., *"Race," Writing, and Difference* (Chicago, 1986).

2. "Equal Opportunity Recedes for Most Female Lawyers," *New York Times*, 8 January 1996, A10.

3. Thomas Sowell, *Civil Rights: Rhetoric or Reality* (New York, 1984).

4. Opal Palmer Adisa, "For the Love of My Children," *Oakland Voices Quarterly Community* 1 (Fall 1995): 13.

5. Alice Walker and Pratibha Parmar, *Warrior Marks: Female Genital Mutilation and the Sexual Blinding of Women* (New York, 1993).

6. Audre Lorde, *Sister Outsider* (Trumansburg, NY, 1984).

7. Barbara T. Christian, "Diminishing Returns: Can Black Feminism(s) Survive the Academy," in David Goldberg, ed., *Multiculturalism: A Cultural Reader* (London, 1995), 168–79.

8. The Hispanic Coalition on Higher Education, "An Open Letter to the Regents of the University of California," *New York Times*, 20 July 1995, A11.

Diversity of What?

Miranda Oshige McGowan

Many colleges and universities practice some form of affirmative action based on race or ethnicity in their admissions process. They often justify affirmative action on the grounds that it promotes educational "diversity," somewhat loosely defined as a multiplicity of ideas, experiences, and viewpoints in the classroom and on the campus as a whole. A diverse student body and faculty is often said to be desirable for two main reasons. Schools hope that having a student body and faculty that hold many different viewpoints and approach issues from different perspectives will promote learning and lead to the production of greater knowledge for all. Seeing their mission as one of socializing their students and helping them to grow into good citizens, many schools also believe that if people from different backgrounds, who hold different values, can learn to communicate and respect differing points of view, both in and out of the classroom, they will be better prepared to deal with the challenges of living in a pluralistic and multicultural democracy.

A racially and ethnically diverse student body is generally thought to be necessary for the accomplishment of these goals. No one can deny the power and importance of racial and ethnic categories. These categories are not arbitrary; instead, they reflect powerful social and historical forces. Like it or not, the racial and, to a lesser extent, ethnic categories with which a person identifies, or which others ascribe to a person, make an enormous difference in the way a person lives her life. People from different races and ethnicities are therefore reasonably presumed to have different experiences and thus to have developed different perspectives and viewpoints.[1] Affirmative action is one way

to ensure that people from different cultural backgrounds, especially people whom the school identifies as belonging to certain
racial or ethnic groups, are represented on campus.[2]

My purpose in this article is not to question the importance of
these categories. Rather, my purpose is to probe their salience to
the educational mission of diversity. Although race and ethnicity
are concepts with considerable power, one can argue that they
fail to capture adequately the actual social diversity of various
groups. Such categories thus may fail to promote the goal of
diversity of many schools' affirmative action programs.

Although there are other justifications for affirmative action,
such as the need to make reparation for past discrimination or
the desire to prevent historically disadvantaged groups from
remaining disadvantaged, schools most often publicly embrace
the goal of creating a diverse student body and faculty because
diversity relates directly to their educational mission. Affirmative
action programs premised on diversity are less vulnerable to legal
challenge because the Supreme Court has deemed the promotion
of diversity on university campuses a compelling state interest;
schools may thus take race explicitly into account when making
admissions decisions.[3] In contrast, affirmative action programs
designed as reparation for the harm done by past discrimination
are vulnerable to constitutional challenge if a particular school
has not itself practiced racial discrimination in the past.[4] Affirmative action programs founded on notions of distributive justice
that hope to promote the future success of members of specific
racial groups are even more constitutionally vulnerable; the state
interest of undoing the consequences of past societal discrimination (as opposed to state-enforced discrimination) in order
to insure the future success of a group has been held to be too
amorphous an interest to justify taking race into account when
making admissions decisions.[5]

My discussion of the structure of many schools' affirmative
action programs begins with the premise that race and ethnicity
are socially constructed concepts. There is nothing immutable
about the definition or content of racial categories. Although
people from different "races" share certain gross morphological
similarities, there is no gene or cluster of genes that determine
race.[6] Whatever physical or genetic differences exist are inconsequential to our daily lives and to public policy. Their only im-

portance is that which we attribute to them. "Race" is thus a conclusion we come to — a category that represents decisions and biases influenced by many different factors. Because race is socially constructed, we can disagree about the proper way to draw racial lines.

Much the same can be said about ethnicity. Indeed, the difference between race and ethnicity is sometimes unclear and contested.[7] Ethnic categories can be seen as divisions among groupings of people within a given "race," generally based more on cultural similarities among people than on perceived physical differences between the group and others.[8] But because ethnicity is related to culture, it is, if anything, a more elusive concept than race. Culture is not an inherited characteristic; it is a practice or group of practices. As such, it too is constructed and, in theory at least, mutable.

The United States Census, for example, has a racial classification for Asians and an ethnic classification for Hispanics. Both categories define people according to their own or their ancestors' geographic origins. But the contours of these categories are subject to debate, as is the question whether these groupings are "racial" or "ethnic" in any meaningful sense at all. Some definitions of the racial category Asian, for example, include persons of Pakistani or Indian descent, while other definitions do not.[9] Some include persons of Pacific Islander descent, while others consider Pacific Islanders racially distinct.[10] Recently, the term Latino has begun to replace the term Hispanic. As the terms have evolved, the definition of the category has also changed. People from Spain can be Hispanic, but they are generally not considered Latinos, who are persons of Central and South American descent. That people can disagree over who is Asian or Latino (or Hispanic) underlines the social constructedness of race and ethnicity and the blurred line between the two concepts. Professor David Hollinger's observation that the category *Latino* has come to be a category with racelike overtones further emphasizes the constructedness of race. As Hollinger points out, until relatively recently (perhaps twenty years ago) people within this category were generally considered racially "white." But *Latino* is increasingly referred to more and more as a race. In fact, the National Council of La Raza has asked the census to reclassify *Hispanic* as a race rather than as an ethnicity for the next census.[11]

Because there is no biological definition of race or ethnicity, these concepts must be socially defined. In defining them for the purposes of administering affirmative action in admissions processes, schools must face at least three distinct issues. First, they must decide which individuals belong to which races and ethnicities. For example, is a person Asian American, African American, or something else if her mother is Asian American and her father is African American? Is a person Mexican American or white if her father is Mexican American and her mother is Irish? At what point does she become one race or another, and will the school take into consideration the way she defines herself racially or the way that others define her? Do some groups assimilate more easily than others into racial or ethnic categories not normally included in diversity-based affirmative action programs? Is there a principled basis for a school to conclude, for instance, that a child of one white and one Asian parent is "white," while a child of one white and one African American parent is African American?

Second, schools must determine whether racial or ethnic groups are internally uniform with respect to their contributions to diversity. If a school decides that *Latino* is an ethnic category, and that being a Latino will contribute to diversity, it will ask whether there are a sufficient number of Latinos on campus, but it will not necessarily consider whether there are any Salvadoran, Cuban, or Mexican Americans who attend the school. Even if all of the Latino students happen to be of just one national origin, that school might not notice or care if it is only concerned with making sure that the Latino experience is represented on campus.

Finally, in deciding this question, schools must decide whether they will look to a group's conception of itself or to dominant social conceptions of racial and ethnic groups. These are often different, and this difference forces us to choose between an individual's definition of himself and others' definitions of him. That choice is a critical one for schools seeking to increase diversity. For example, if an individual of Filipino heritage identifies most closely with other Filipino Americans but feels little affinity with Japanese or Chinese Americans, is that person "Asian" in a way that contributes to a school's goal of promoting diversity?

This analysis exposes a subtle but fundamental problem. As affirmative action programs have expanded to include groups other than African Americans, it has become quite difficult to construct coherent definitions of different racial and ethnic groups and their memberships.[12] This problem arises because many members of the groups schools include in (or, conversely, exclude from) their affirmative action programs do not primarily define themselves in racial, or even in ethnic, terms. Instead, culture, national origin, religion, or how recently they immigrated to the United States may be more important to the self-conception of many individuals than their race or ethnicity. Similarly, rather than identifying with others of the same race or ethnicity, some people identify and form communities with people of the same national origin, who speak the same language,[13] or who face the same problems they do as recent immigrants.

The lack of symmetry between the definition of groups within schools' affirmative action programs and the self-definition of persons within these groups is in tension with the goal of these programs to promote diversity of ideas and viewpoints through group preferences. This lack of symmetry undercuts the assumption that racial and ethnic identity play pivotal roles in defining how the members of these groups perceive and experience the world; it means that race and ethnicity may be less important than other characteristics not taken into account when deciding who should benefit from affirmative action. By choosing race or ethnicity as the proxy for diverse viewpoints and perspectives, schools may fail to consider the factors that members of these groups see as defining themselves and distinguishing themselves from other groups, which they presumably would bring to bear in campus life.

This failure subordinates the individual and group self-conception to the conceptions held by policy makers and administrators, which are likely to reflect dominant social constructions. Such programs, in other words, may fall victim to the same lack of understanding they are supposed to promote. Schools cannot expect to increase the variety of perspectives and experiences on campus without taking seriously the ways in which people actually identify themselves and identify with others. Taking a cue from critical race theorists, schools that seek to promote diversity should look to the actual experiences, history, and cultures of people when they define the groups they wish to include in their affirmative action programs.[14] In doing so, schools should value the actual experience of these groups rather than express dominant social conceptions. Admittedly, any assertion that members of a particular group see themselves in a certain way will necessarily fail to capture the complexity of opinions and experiences among individuals. Thus, any definition of group membership will be subject to the attack I level here against the definition of racial and ethnic groups: all categories are incorrect at some level and for some people. Yet an attempt to see how individuals and groups define themselves and what factors are important in forming a group identity will have at least a comparative advantage over group definitions arrived at with reference only to the dominant social understanding of race and ethnicity.

The racial category *Asian* provides an example of how such categories can undermine the goal of diversity. As touched on earlier, people categorized racially as Asian often do not view themselves as such, nor do they necessarily feel a sense of identity or kinship with others categorized as Asian. Instead, many Asian Americans define themselves primarily in terms of national origin and feel an affinity with others of the same national origin. Often Asian Americans feel they share common interests and goals with people of the same national origin but not with people with different national ancestry.[15] Filipino Americans, for example, often feel that Japanese and Chinese American interests and goals differ from their own and that aligning with Japanese and Chinese Americans would undercut the progress of Filipino Americans.[16] Other cleavages between different national origin groups can be traced back to age-old historical conflicts like those between Japanese and Koreans. Linguistic, cultural, and religious differences also make a unified Asian American identity difficult.[17]

Complex Asian immigration patterns complicate issues of racial identity further. For example, 63 percent of Chinese Americans are foreign born,[18] as are more than 75 percent of Filipinos.[19] In contrast, only 28 percent of Japanese Americans are foreign born.[20] Many foreign-born Asians see themselves as Chinese, Cambodian, or Filipino, not as "Chinese American," "Cambodian American," or "Filipino American," and they have little in common with, and thus feel little affinity toward, their American-born counterparts.[21] Linguistic and cultural differences have made for little commonality of experience on which common identity might be forged.

A multilayered diversity of experience, culture, and identity thus exists within the racial group *Asian American*. This diversity makes itself apparent in political affiliations and attitudes on social issues.[22] An immigrant who fled communist Vietnam may have a different opinion on American military support for anticommunist factions than would a third-generation Japanese American; a wealthy Taiwanese American businessperson may have no interest in providing low-income housing in China-town.[23] It can be argued that the category *Asian American* makes little sense in light of historic animosities, linguistic differences, cultural distinctions, and diverse experiences as immigrants.[24] Professor Bill Ong Hing notes that "the diversity of Asian America" calls into question the very notion of a unified racial identity.[25] Individuals from some Asian national origin groups may share little more than "similar racial features in a predominately white society"[26] and the experience of discrimination because they are "Asian."

This is not to say that the racial category *Asian American* is meaningless to all who fall into it. Some people do see themselves as Asian. For example, American-born Chinese and Japanese Americans whose ancestors immigrated to the United States decades ago often do identify themselves as Asian American.[27] This raises a different problem, however. American-born Japanese, Chinese, and Korean Americans are the Asian Americans most likely to attend college without the help of affirmative action.[28] Schools that are attuned only to the absolute numbers of Asians in attendance may find that, while many Japanese, Chinese, and Korean Americans are present, other groups, such as Filipinos, Southeast Asians, and Pacific Islanders are nearly absent. Moreover, American-born Japanese, Chinese, and Korean Americans may have little in common with these other Asian groups.

The idea that different Asian nationalities identify with one another implies that one group can in some situations represent the interests of another. This idea is likely correct in many circumstances. But Professor Hing is rightly troubled by the idea "that Japanese and Chinese Americans... are viewed by others as spokespersons for Vietnamese or Asian Indians" because too often that has meant "a de facto incorporation or loss of identity for other Asian Americans. Japanese and/or Chinese American experiences cannot duplicate the Vietnamese refugee, Asian Indian, Korean, or Pacific Islander immigrant experience."[29]

Persons who fall into the racial or ethnic category *Latino*, or *Hispanic*, similarly tend not to identify themselves primarily as Latinos or Hispanics. For example, in a recent study 82 percent of American-born Cubans, 55 percent of Mexican Americans, and 49 percent of Puerto Ricans identified themselves as racially white, while very few of the Cubans, and less than half of the Mexican Americans and Puerto Ricans surveyed, identified themselves as racially Latino.[30] Although this result may be to some degree problematic because many consider *Latino* an ethnicity, not a race, it nonetheless underscores the lack of resonance *Latino* has for many persons who might fit into that category.[31] Equally troubling for diversity programs that seek to increase the number of "Latinos" on campus is the fact that persons from the different national origins included in the group *Latino* also report feeling little cultural affiliation with one another. Cuban Americans, Mexican Americans, and Puerto Ricans say they feel closer to whites than to any of the other Latino national origin groups.[32] These groups also report that they have little contact with people from other nationalities, which may account for some of the lack of Latino identity.[33]

To complicate matters further, one cannot make meaningful generalizations about the socioeconomic status of the groups *Latinos* or *Asians*. To say that Asians are a model minority is to ignore that the category contains wide disparities in wealth and education, many of which track national origin divisions and recentness of immigration.[34] For example, Laotians, Hmong, and Cambodians have poverty rates far above the national average, while Japanese, Chinese, Koreans, and Filipinos have poverty rates far below the national average.[35] Furthermore, even though the Filipino poverty rate is very low, school-age Filipino Americans are far less likely to attend college or professional school than are Japanese, Chinese, and Korean Americans.[36]

Similarly, on average Cuban Americans tend to be far better educated than either Puerto Ricans or Mexican Americans.[37] Cubans are also on average less likely to live in poverty than Mexican Americans, Puerto Ricans, or Central or South Americans.[38] Some schools, including Stanford, have noticed this fact and have chosen to include Mexican Americans but not Cubans in their diversity programs.[39] Oddly, though, schools tend not to make the same differentiations within the race of Asians.

Moreover, all of these groups have very different experiences as immigrants. Indeed, national origin communicates little about the immigrant experience because there have been waves of immigration from a single country. For example, descendants of nineteenth-century Chinese immigrants have a vastly different history from those who immigrated in the 1960s and from those now immigrating. Third-generation Chinese Americans bring different experiences and perspectives to the university than those of recent Chinese immigrants. The experience of Latino immigrants also varies greatly for different national origin groups. Many Cuban immigrants are, or are the descendants of, political refugees who fled communist Cuba, while most Mexican immigrants have come to the United States because of poor economic conditions at home. Some Mexican Americans are not the descendants of immigrants at all; their ancestors were already living in the Southwest when it was annexed by the United States. Many Puerto Ricans have come to the United States with the intention of returning home, and many do. (As United States citizens, Puerto Ricans are not even technically immigrants.) Because these groups have each had such different immigration experiences, their contribution to a school's diversity will also be very different.

The foregoing suggests that categorization by race or ethnicity fails to capture the complexity of social experience of many groups and their members. Diversity programs that use race or ethnicity as proxies for diversity of social experience and social affiliation may thus fail to capture accurately the perceptions and experiences of the groups they seek to include. As a result, real diversity may suffer. Thus, when deciding whom to admit through affirmative action, schools should pay closer attention to the ways in which individuals and groups define themselves rather than defaulting to the socially dominant understanding of who belongs to what race or ethnicity. Instead of having students "check the box" for a given racial or ethnic category, schools could ask more open-ended questions, perhaps asking applicants to explain how they define themselves racially, ethnically, or otherwise. Giving students a limited range of racial or ethnic categories to choose from presupposes strong affiliations even when in actuality they may be weak. From the responses to these questions, schools could devise categories that more accurately reflect different groups' and individuals' conceptions of identity and affiliation.

If the use of race and ethnicity as proxies for diversity of thought and experience is not an effective means of promoting such diversity, then the idea of affirmative action based on race or ethnicity may be undermined, at least insofar as it is meant to achieve diversity. At the very least, this insight requires us to change our conclusions about how to define the groups that we think must be included to achieve diversity. Such altered definitions may in turn affect our conclusions as to which groups ought to benefit from affirmative action. If we resist giving up affirmative action based on race or ethnicity as a method to increase diversity on campus, it may not be because we fear that schools will become less diverse in the ideas and attitudes represented on campus; we may instead resist because we are motivated by goals other than diversity, such as reparations or distributive justice. Although race and ethnicity may not accurately reflect the self-perception of many groups, these categories are socially salient because throughout our history people have been given better or worse treatment based on their perceived race or ethnicity. Racial and ethnic categories may not serve the educational mission of diversity very well, but they may do a better job of serving the goals of reparations and distributive justice. Schools may feel constrained, however, to limit their stated objectives to diversity and to conceal genuine redistributional or reparationist objectives because of *Bakke*, which allows schools to take race explicitly into account to promote educational diversity, but greatly limits their ability to do so for the purposes of reparations or distributive justice. Complete candor may be too risky.

Putting *Bakke* to the side for analytic purposes, however, a school can tailor an affirmative action program to fulfill its true goals only if it is clear about the nature of these goals. Different objectives will lead to different conclusions about which groups should be included in an affirmative action program and how these groups should be defined. If a school is motivated by distributional goals, race-based programs work well for some groups but less well for others.[40] For example, a school could defensibly grant affirmative action preferences to African Americans on the theory that affirmative action would help improve the socioeconomic status and political power of African Americans as a group. The long history of discrimination against African Americans and the importance of race to the social identity of African Americans make race a fairly useful category for analysis and for achieving the goals of distributive justice and reparations.[41]

It would be much more difficult, however, to make an analogous argument with regard to Latinos. Because Latino panethnic identity is relatively weak compared to other kinds of affiliations, granting affirmative action to racially or ethnically Latino students would likely not serve a school's distributional or reparations goals. A program more sensitive to differences among Latino nationalities and the complexities of Latino group affiliation would probably serve these goals better.

The point is that in the last analysis schools should be sensitive to the actual group identities and social affiliations of students and applicants, whatever the purpose of an affirmative action program, whether it be to promote diversity, or to grant reparations, or to promote distributive justice. If schools rely only on dominant social understandings of race and ethnicity, their affirmative action programs will be handicapped.

NOTES

I wish to thank Paul Brest, David McGowan, Robert Post, and Betsy Röben for helpful and incisive comments and suggestions.

1. See Paul Brest and Miranda Oshige, "Affirmative Action for Whom?" *Stanford Law Review* 47 (1995): 855, 860–61, 862–63.

2. Stanford University's affirmative action program is fairly typical of university affirmative action programs. Stanford aims to admit a "class characterized by diversity in terms of academic interests, artistic and athletic accomplishments, leadership qualities, and ethnic and social backgrounds." Stanford gives special admissions consideration to African Americans, Native Americans, and Mexican Americans. (Gerhard Casper, "President Casper's Statement on Affirmative Action," reprinted in *Stanford Observer*, Fall 1995, 22.) Stanford's inclusion of Mexican Americans rather than all members of the race (or ethnicity) of Latinos is interesting because it is an example of a school granting affirmative action based on a person's national origin rather than race. Interestingly, though, Stanford excludes all Asian Americans from its affirmative action program even though not all Asian national origin groups are well-represented on university campuses. See text accompanying notes 28–29.

3. *Regents of University of California v. Bakke*, 438 US 265, 312 (1978) (Powell, J.). Schools, however, may only consider race a "plus factor" and cannot have different sets of admissions criteria for persons of different races. *Ibid.*, 317.

4. *Ibid.*, 307.

5. *Ibid.*, 310.

6. L. Luca Cavalli-Sforza, Paolo Menozzi, and Alberto Piazza, *The History and Geography of Human Genes* (Princeton, 1994).

7. David A. Hollinger, *Postethnic America: Beyond Multiculturalism* (New York, 1995), 33.

8. *Ibid.*, 36.

9. Professor Bill Ong Hing, for example, includes Asian Indians in his study of Asian Americans because they share with other Asians a common experience of being defined by others as "Asian." He recognizes, however, that some might take issue with his doing so because the "unique racial features" of Asian Indians "supposedly set them apart from Chinese, Japanese, and Vietnamese" and because they have a distinctive culture. Bill Ong Hing, *Making and Remaking Asian America Through Immigration Policy, 1850–1990* (Stanford, 1993), 14.

10. The United States Census seems to consider Asians and Pacific Islanders one racial group. One of its collections of statistical data on socioeconomic status is entitled "Asians and Pacific Islanders in the United States." See also Paul Ong, ed., *The State of Asian Pacific America: Economic Diversity, Issues, and Policies* (Los Angeles, 1994).

11. Hollinger, *Postethnic America*, 31–33.

12. I should be clear that my discussion of the weakness of racial and ethnic identity probably does not apply, for the most part, to African Americans. The research Paul Brest and I have done indicates that schools rightly assume that the racial category *African American* is quite important to the social identity of the people generally considered to be African American: nearly all people identified by others as being African American also identify themselves as African American. Christopher Jencks, *Rethinking Social Policy: Race, Poverty, and the Underclass* (Cambridge, MA, 1993), 29. Furthermore, this category appears to have a great deal of meaning for most African Americans. For example, many successful middle- and upper-class African Americans feel that they have a responsibility to help other African Americans and to give to that community. Lois Benjamin, *The Black Elite: Facing the Color Line in the Twilight of the Twentieth Century* (Chicago, 1991), 13. Of course other bases for social identity, such as language or national origin, have historically been denied to African Americans, except for recent immigrants, because of slavery.

13. Ian F. Haney Lopez, "The Social Construction of Race: Some Observations on Illusion, Fabrication, and Choice," *Harvard Civil Rights-Civil Liberties Law Review* 29 (1994): 1, 9 n.34.

14. See Mari J. Matsuda, "Looking to the Bottom: Critical Legal Studies and Reparations," *Harvard Civil Rights-Civil Liberties Law Review* 22 (1987): 323, 325.

15. Brest and Oshige, "Affirmative Action," 895–96.

16. Yen Le Espiritu, *Asian American Panethnicity: Bridging Institutions and Identities* (Philadelphia, 1992), 104.

17. Hing, *Making and Remaking*, 172.

18. Ronald Takaki, *Strangers from a Different Shore: A History of Asian Americans* (Boston, 1989), 421.

19. *Ibid.*, 432.

20. *Ibid.*, 421.

21. Hing, *Making and Remaking*, 178.

22. *Ibid.*, 172.

23. *Ibid.*

24. *Ibid.*, 173.

25. *Ibid.*, 171.

26. *Ibid.*, 175.

27. Espiritu, *Panethnicity*, 29.

28. See L. Ling-chi Wang, "Trends in Admissions for Asian Americans in Colleges and Universities: Higher Education Policy," in *The State of Asian Pacific America: Policy Issues to the Year 2020* (Los Angeles, 1993), 49, 55.

29. Hing, *Making and Remaking*, 177.

30. Rodolfo O. de la Garza et al., *Latino Voices: Mexican, Puerto Rican, and Cuban Perspectives on American Politics* (Boulder, CO, 1992), 23.

31. It may also reflect the advantage identifying as white has rather than any sense of cultural affiliation as white. Haney Lopez, "Social Construction," 28.

32. De la Garza et al., *Latino Voices*, 66–67.

33. *Ibid.*, 67–68.

34. See Brest and Oshige, "Affirmative Action," 892–93.

35. Bureau of the Census, *Asians and Pacific Islanders in the United States, 1990* (Washington, D.C., 1993), 5, table 5.

36. Espiritu, *Panethnicity*, 107.

37. Bureau of the Census, *Persons of Hispanic Origin in the United States, 1990* (Washington, D.C., 1993), 81–83, table 3.

38. *Ibid.*, 157–59, 163, 174, table 5.

39. Stanford Law School also includes Puerto Ricans in addition to Mexi-

can Americans in its diversity program, but not Cubans. Brest and Oshige, "Affirmative Action," 855.

40. For a much more extensive exploration of the importance of group identity and affiliation to the success of affirmative action programs intended to promote distributive justice or provide reparations for past discrimination, see generally ibid., esp. section 3.

41. *Ibid.*, 877–80.

Unrepresented

Rachel F. Moran

In the face of growing racial and ethnic controversy, California has become the first state to take serious steps to eliminate preferential programs for particular minority groups. My central question in this essay is, why has the affirmative action debate been framed in black-white terms, especially in a state like California, where Latinos represent the single largest racial or ethnic minority — one that is rapidly expanding? I argue that Latinos have been unrepresented in the controversy because their identity and entitlements have been undercut by two competing policy models: civil rights and immigration. I demonstrate how Latinos' immigration status has eroded their claims for civil rights protection and how fears stemming from their special treatment under civil rights law have undermined their demands for inclusion as immigrants. I conclude by describing the challenges that Latinos face in merging these models in ways that mutually reinforce the definition of their unique identity and history, rather than mutually destroy their life chances.

The Affirmative Action Debate in California Higher Education

The nationwide debate over affirmative action is lively, but in California, the controversy has become particularly intense. On 20 July 1995, the regents of the University of California voted to prohibit the use of "race, religion, sex, color, ethnicity, or national origin" in admissions, hiring, and contracting at the university's nine campuses.[1] In adopting the resolutions, the regents disregarded the opposition of the president of the university, the Council of Chancellors, the Academic Council, and the Student

Association. Despite calls by faculty, students, and staff to reconsider the abolition of affirmative action policies, the regents to date have steadfastly refused to revisit the issues.[2]

Although the regents' resolutions eliminate racial, ethnic, and gender preferences in admissions, hiring, and contracting, the new policy explicitly embraces outreach programs to increase the pool of qualified candidates from underrepresented groups. Even with aggressive outreach initiatives, however, it seems likely that the numbers of black and Latino students at the University of California will decline; moreover, the drop will be particularly striking at the most competitive campuses: Berkeley and Los Angeles. The regents' resolution on admissions provides that admissions policies may take into account economic and social disadvantage, and as a result, some have argued that the resolution will not seriously undermine racial and ethnic diversity at the university.[3] Projections for enrollment based on grade point average, standardized test scores, and income indicate, however, that blacks and Latinos would still suffer a significant drop in numbers at the campuses even if socioeconomic status were considered; in fact, the primary beneficiaries of an income-based approach appear to be Asian Americans, whose grades and test scores are higher than those of other racial and ethnic groups when socioeconomic status is held constant.[4]

Measuring social disadvantage by other means, furthermore, remains an untested strategy. The university so far has provided only general guidance on how to implement this portion of the regents' policy.[5] Campus efforts to evaluate social disadvantage are complicated by concern that the use of some factors, such as distinctive linguistic or cultural background, could be challenged on the ground that they are illicit proxies for race and ethnicity.

The flurry of activity in response to the regents' resolutions will seem modest in comparison to the adjustments in statewide operations that will be required if the California Civil Rights Initiative is placed on the November 1996 ballot and passes.[6] Under the initiative, all institutions of higher education in California, including the California State University system, its community colleges, as well as the University of California, will be covered. Because the state universities and community colleges serve a large number of black and Latino students, these students' access to higher education in California will be restricted by the initiative.

Moreover, outreach programs that receive state funds will be prevented from remaining racially or ethnically specific and, arguably, an individual would even have the right to sue under the state constitution if a university program used proxies that allegedly tracked race or ethnicity too closely. The initiative thus would sweep far more broadly and deeply than do the regents' resolutions.

The Unrepresented: The Absence of Latinos from the Affirmative Action Debate

Most of the coverage of these changes in California's affirmative action policy has been framed in black-white terms. For instance, when I am contacted by reporters, they typically ask whether the time to rectify past discrimination against blacks is over and whether affirmative action programs now engender more unfairness than they eliminate. Media representatives often highlight the dangers of reverse discrimination by questioning preferential treatment for the black bourgeoisie, wondering why the son of a black surgeon or black banker should get special consideration. Latinos are nearly completely omitted from the discussion. This oversight is particularly baffling in California, where Latinos will constitute 36 percent of public high school graduates by the year 2000; this percentage is second only to whites at 41 percent and represents six times the number of blacks at 6 percent and slightly over twice the 17 percent of Asian Americans. Moreover, the salience of Latinos is growing nationwide: by 2010, Latinos are projected to become the largest minority group in the United States.[7]

In earlier skirmishes related to the demographic transformation of California, Latinos occupied a prominent place. For example, when Proposition 63, an initiative to make English the state's official language, was placed on the ballot and passed by an overwhelming margin, commentators focused on the Spanish-speaking population and the prevailing sense that Latinos were not assimilating as earlier generations of immigrants had. When Proposition 187 — designed to curtail illegal immigration by cutting off education, health, and social services to the undocumented — was adopted by a wide margin, the dominant images in the press were of Mexicans surreptitiously crossing the border at night or of pregnant Mexican women entering the country so that their American-born offspring could command the privileges of citizenship.

Now Latinos face a new challenge to their sense of belonging in the California polity: the assault on affirmative action threatens to limit their upward mobility as English-speakers legally present in the state. Indeed, the size of the Latino population, its low levels of education and income, and its persistent under-representation in positions of leadership suggest that this group will be seriously affected by a declining commitment to affirmative action in California. Nevertheless, in describing the sequence of recent political events in California, one *Los Angeles Times* article began with and developed this observation by an attorney at the National Association for the Advancement of Colored People: "First the Latinos. Now the blacks. It is getting ugly."[8] This framing of the story suggests that, while earlier efforts to declare English the official language and cut off benefits to undocumented immigrants affected Latinos, the anti–affirmative action movement in California is "getting ugly" by undermining civil rights in a way that would primarily harm blacks. Like blacks, Latinos will be significantly affected by a retrenchment in affirmative action, but they have become "the disappeared" in this public policy debate.

The Paradigmatic Apostrophe: Why Latinos Find No Space in the Affirmative Action Debate

I believe that the presence of Latinos in the affirmative action debate has been elided because the two key models used to define their identity and entitlements have required them to conform to the experiences of other racial and ethnic groups. The mixed message of the civil rights paradigm, which is rooted in the black experience, is that Latinos have been treated similarly to blacks, but in reality they are more like white ethnic immigrants. The second model, the immigration paradigm, undercuts Latinos' claims to identity and entitlement because recent Latino immigrants are alleged to be different from earlier generations of ethnic immigrants. Latinos' shortcomings in assimilating American values have been substantiated, ironically, by invoking the same history of exclusion that they themselves invoke under the civil rights model. Here, the shorthand message is that Latinos should assimilate as white ethnics do, but in reality they will remain isolated and unassimilable as have blacks.

Civil Rights: You're Supposed to Be Black, But You're Really White Immigrants

The civil rights model in the United States is clearly based on the African American experience. Modern civil rights protections arose primarily as a response to the persistence of a caste system rooted in slavery. The civil rights movement aimed to dismantle official segregative practices and to promote equal opportunity without regard to race. Early supporters of civil rights reform learned that individual antidiscrimination principles were insufficient to overcome a lengthy history of segregation and inequality. First, these individualized remedies placed the burden on victims to come forward to demand legal redress; yet, precisely because of their oppressed status, these individuals were often least able to muster the resources to advance their claims. Second, an individual rights model was ill equipped to address those systemic forms of discrimination without clearly identifiable victims. If, for example, an employer failed to recruit broadly and equitably for a job, those who never received word of the opening would be largely unaware of the harm they had suffered.

For these reasons, the federal government adopted proactive programs, like affirmative action, designed as temporary measures to undo the lingering effects of past discrimination. As the federal presence in the civil rights arena grew during the 1960s and 1970s, so did the number of groups (other than African Americans) that asserted an entitlement to special protection. Among those groups was the Latino population, which cited its own history of segregation and discrimination as a justification for inclusion in remedial programs including affirmative action. Eventually, Latinos gained recognition from Congress, the Supreme Court, and civil rights agencies as an ethnic group that should enjoy protections comparable to those available for blacks.[9]

Although Latinos earned formal recognition, informal doubts about the propriety of their inclusion in a civil rights model remained. First, Latinos are not a monolithic racial group: their ancestors may be white, black, or indigenous peoples. Indeed, because the U.S. Census requires respondents to identify themselves as a single race, Latinos often mark "other" and then must be reclassified. To accommodate the ambiguities surrounding Latinos' racial identity, the census identifies them separately as an *ethnic* group.[10]

This shift from a racial to an ethnic categorization calls into question Latinos' entitlements under a civil rights model. African American advocates of civil rights emphasize race as a central feature of disadvantage. Judges and legislators often lament that individuals are judged by the color of their skin rather than the content of their character; the Supreme Court has applied a stringent standard of review, "strict scrutiny," for racial classifications in part because it views race as an immutable characteristic.[11]

These depictions of race emphasize its links to biological expression through phenotype. The only relevant social correlate of race in this model is subordination. Ethnic categories, on the other hand, turn on ancestry but are typically associated with malleable social traits, such as language and culture: one can learn a new language or adopt new cultural practices. Precisely because ethnic classifications appear more mutable than racial ones, policymakers often are tempted to conclude that Latinos can escape the strictures of ethnicity by assimilating to dominant norms but blacks are not similarly able to free themselves from racial prejudice. The perception that many Latinos have arrived in the United States as voluntary immigrants and, like earlier waves of newcomers, should be able to adapt themselves to an American way of life, has only reinforced this view.

The black civil rights movement was rooted in the hardships of slavery. The small numbers of African immigrants from Haiti, Jamaica, and African nations represent such a tiny portion of the African American population that their presence does not significantly dilute blacks' demands for corrective justice.[12] By contrast, Latinos have diverse histories: some are the descendants of Mexicans or Puerto Ricans whose lands were conquered by the United States. Others from Mexico and Central or South America arrived as immigrants, both legal and illegal, searching for a brighter economic future than their home countries could offer. Finally, many Cubans and Central Americans came as refugees seeking asylum from repressive political regimes. Because Latinos reflect such a wide-ranging mix of experiences, policymakers question their treatment as a collective group entitled to rectification of past discrimination. Latinos often find, therefore, that current patterns of segregation and inequality are an insufficient basis for relief because they are not necessarily an artifact of past governmental discrimination.

A good example of the ambivalence about including Latinos in affirmative action programs under a compensatory justice rationale is the recent article by Paul Brest and Miranda Oshige entitled "Affirmative Action for Whom?"[13] In the article, Brest and Oshige identify two broad justifications for affirmative action: (1) diversity in the educational enterprise, and (2) corrective and distributive justice in society at large. The diversity claim focuses on how the pedagogical process is enriched by the exchange of ideas among people from a wide array of backgrounds. According to Brest and Oshige, "What matters to an institution's intellectual mission is not group membership or background as such, but a multiplicity of intellectual perspectives. But it is a fact that people's backgrounds affect the way they perceive and evaluate the world."[14]

The corrective justice rationale "focuses on remedying the present effects of past discrimination."[15] Brest and Oshige concede that the fit between beneficiaries and cost-bearers under affirmative action programs is imperfect. Candidates to whom compensatory relief is not granted are not necessarily wrongdoers, and those who enjoy the benefits of preferential treatment may not have suffered individual injury. The distributive justice rationale focuses on reducing inequality in income and power among individuals; to this end, it is appropriate to consider the group characteristic of race or ethnicity, "to the extent that the success of an individual depends on the success of other members of the groups to which she belongs."[16]

Brest and Oshige describe several mechanisms that enhance affirmative action programs' capacity to advance the corrective and distributive justice goals. They argue that when members of a racial or ethnic group are closely connected with one another, the success of one individual due to affirmative action programs will have a multiplier effect, since others benefit materially from that person's improved access, information, and support. In addition, indirect benefits may accrue to the extent that the successful individual serves as a role model; again, the more strongly that group members identify with each other, the more powerful this effect will be. Finally, group members may benefit if the success of one individual mitigates negative stereotypes held by outsiders; the greater the tendency to label a group and evaluate it collectively, the more helpful the reduction in stereotypes will be to each member.

Using this framework, Brest and Oshige assess the propriety of including various racial and ethnic groups within affirmative action programs. After defining Latinos as "immigrants or the descendants of immigrants from Puerto Rico, Cuba, [Mexico,] and the many countries of Central and South America," the authors find that, while Latinos suffer from persistent and severe disadvantage, "some of the gap in socioeconomic status may be due to the fact that recent immigrants account for a large proportion of the total Latino population."[17] Brest and Oshige also note that "Latinos were typically classified as 'white' by the Jim Crow laws that existed between the end of Reconstruction and the mid-1960s," but were nevertheless subjected to negative stereotypes and systematic discrimination.[18] Brest and Oshige believe, however, that "the extent to which discrimination has contributed to the poverty of Latinos is open to dispute" because "some social scientists attribute much of the wage differential to Latino immigrants' lack of marketable job skills and English literacy."[19]

Brest and Oshige also worry that the internal diversity of the Latino population undercuts the extent to which the success of one member will benefit the larger group. Although some Latinos do identify themselves collectively to combat common problems of discrimination (through organizations such as the National Council of La Raza and the League of United Latin American Citizens), these authors believe that national origin identification remains stronger than a pan-Latino identity. For this reason, Brest and Oshige conclude that the multiplier effect of affirmative action programs is diluted for Latinos. Interestingly, the authors focus heavily on the compensatory and distributive justice rationales and do not argue that the internal diversity of the Latino population enriches their capacity to contribute to the robust exchange of ideas within academic institutions.

Based on the foregoing analysis, the authors ultimately find that the case for a national commitment to affirmative action for Latinos is weaker than for groups such as blacks and Native Americans. Brest and Oshige therefore recommend that the decision to include Latinos should be made by each institution based on its program rationales and regional demography. Where Latinos constitute a large segment of the local population, the authors believe that: "Whatever uncertainties there may be about the causes and long-term intractability of the disadvantaged status of Latinos, the social salience of some groups — for example, Puerto Ricans in the East and Mexican Americans in the West — speaks to the importance of their presence to the educational mission of many law schools."[20]

The Brest and Oshige article aptly illustrates the ways in which Latinos' civil rights claims are undermined by their depiction as an immigrant population. Having cast Latinos as voluntary white ethnic immigrants, the authors easily conclude that they have not suffered the sort of historical injustices that blacks have suffered. No mention is made of the fact that the Puerto Rican and Mexican American populations singled out as intractably disadvantaged were not only immigrants but also the objects of conquest. What is significant about this history is not how many members of each group are the descendants of residents of annexed territories and how many are recent immigrants; rather, what matters is that officials found it necessary to create structures of subordination to subdue the seemingly untrustworthy, alien, and inferior former Mexican and Spanish citizens in their midst.

In recounting the history of Anglos and Mexicans in Texas, for example, David Montejano describes how, in the wake of the Mexican War, settlers who arrived carefully distinguished themselves as "white folks," rather than Mexicans. Settlers often were surprised at Mexicans who asserted their rights. Frederick Law Olmsted reported that one newcomer to Texas during the 1850s expressed astonishment that a Mexican was carrying a revolver. When the settler asserted that Mexicans should not be permitted to bear arms, another Texan replied that there was little to be done because "they think themselves just as good as white men."[21] Settlers, in addition, frequently resented the treaty protections accorded to Mexicans. Over time, this initial relationship of distrust and racialization of Mexicans was perpetuated, and it resulted in pervasive systems of segregation and inequality. As Texas's agricultural economy expanded, Mexican immigrants often provided a source of cheap labor. Native-born Texans of Mexican origin often mediated between these laborers and their white employers, while newly arrived farmers expressed ambivalence about their reliance on Mexican laborers.

Scholars of the period noted the dilemma posed to Southwestern society by the Mexican population. University of Texas Professor William Leonard argued that: "Society in the Southwest cannot easily adapt itself to the handling of a second racial problem.... for Mexican immigrants, there is no congenial social group to welcome them.... They are not Negroes.... They are not accepted as white men, and between the two, the white and the black, there seems to be no midway position."[22] In a similar vein, Texas sociologist Max Handman wrote in 1930 that "American society has no social technique for handling partly colored races. We have a place for the Negro and a place for the white man: the Mexican is not a Negro, and the white man refuses him an equal status."[23] Both men predicted that Mexicans could cause trouble by destabilizing race relations in the state.[24]

Because Brest and Oshige only perfunctorily acknowledge that Latinos have encountered systematic discrimination, the authors dismiss its impact by linking differences in socioeconomic status between Latinos and whites to the former's lack of English proficiency and inadequate job skills, characteristics that should change as immigrants and their progeny assimilate. In reaching this conclusion, the authors fail to address the ways in which pervasive prejudice blocks assimilation and forces newcomers to adapt themselves to existing structures of racial and ethnic inequality.[25] By requiring Latinos to conform to a model of compensatory and distributive justice rooted in the African American experience, Brest and Oshige conclude that Latinos' entitlements to affirmative action protections are ambiguous, clouded by the suspicion that they are really white ethnic immigrants. At no point in the paper do Brest and Oshige examine the ways in which a recent history of immigration reinforces racism and heightens the need for civil rights protections.

Immigration: You're Supposed to Assimilate Like Whites But You'll End Up a Minority Like Blacks

The immigration model is rooted in the white ethnic experience. The traditional recounting of the immigrant experience is arguably a nostalgic exercise that omits the harsher aspects of newcomers' treatment.[26] Whatever the historical inaccuracies,[27] this account holds considerable sway over popular perceptions of current immigrants and the legitimacy of their demands for inclusion in the American polity.

According to the traditional immigration story, immigrants arrive in the United States by invitation only. Immigrants who accept the invitation are expected to make a permanent commitment to their new country; most become citizens through the naturalization process. By undergoing naturalization, immigrants forswear allegiance to their homelands and ally themselves exclusively with the United States. Through this commitment, newcomers can expect to traverse a steady path of upward mobility; whatever sacrifices they make will redound to the benefit of their children and grandchildren.[28]

This story is seriously incomplete, particularly insofar as it omits the instances of racial intolerance that have marred immigration policy. Due to concerns that some newcomers would be incapable of assimilating to an American way of life, the federal government has at various times restricted immigration from particular areas of the world. The Chinese Exclusion Act of 1882, for instance, prohibited Chinese from emigrating to the United States and becoming citizens.[29] In addition, state governments often adopted Americanization programs in public schools to ensure that immigrant populations assimilated to dominant norms and values. These federal and state initiatives punished certain newcomers for their perceived inability to conform to dominant norms.[30]

Latinos have similarly faced doubts about whether they legitimately belong to the American polity, especially since their experience does not jibe with that of earlier white ethnic immigrants. First, the terms of the invitation to come to the United States sometimes have been ambiguous. In contrast to an offer to join the polity on a permanent basis, Latinos have regularly received quite different signals: they have been offered the opportunity to work on a temporary basis with every expectation that they will return to their home countries. Sometimes this approach has been formalized through *bracero* programs. At other times, the approach has been informal; the federal government is lax in policing its borders against illegal immigration so long as low-wage jobs are plentiful in the United States. In either case, these sojourners can be promptly dispatched to their countries of origin through termination of temporary work programs or deportation when labor cycles change.

Second, the close proximity of many Latinos to their homelands has made it more difficult to sever ties to their original language and culture than may have been true for earlier generations of immigrants. The steady influx of new immigrants, the continuing ties with friends and relatives in other countries, and the rise of transnational communities that challenge the neat lines drawn by official borders — all of these contribute to a sense that Latinos are not assimilating on the same terms as earlier generations of immigrants. Indeed, dual loyalties to the home country and the United States are proffered as the reason for low rates of naturalization among Latino immigrants.[31]

Finally, Latino immigrants have found the path to upward mobility for their children and grandchildren rocky and unsure. Although numerous commentators have suggested that Latinos will pursue the same patterns of success as earlier immigrants, others have argued that racial stratification and subordination will impede Latinos' access to educational and economic opportunities. In the field of public health, for instance, recent studies suggest that second- and third-generation Latinos have poorer health than do first-generation Latinos. Analysts have hypothesized that, among other things, blocked acculturation has damaging effects on the progeny of immigrants. In particular, first-generation Latinos compare their standing to that of others in the home country and consider themselves successful; by contrast, their children and grandchildren compare themselves to others in the United States and conclude that they are less successful than their peers. Moreover, second- and third-generation Latinos may doubt that they can overcome systemic prejudice and therefore turn to self-destructive, risk-taking behaviors like drug use and unsafe sex.[32]

Just as Latinos' claims to civil rights protections are undercut by referring to their immigrant status, their status as immigrants is undermined by alluding to their potential claims under a civil rights model. The immigration model requires Latinos to conform to the experience of white ethnics, but they cannot; in fact, Latinos' difficulties stem to a substantial extent from a fear that they are unassimilable because of their distinctive ethnic identity. In brief, Latinos are expected to acculturate as white ethnics do, but at the same time there is a strong suspicion that, like blacks, they will constitute a permanent minority.

A good example of how restrictionist immigration arguments and concerns about affirmative action can intersect appears in Peter Brimelow's recent best-selling book *Alien Nation*.[33] Concerned about rising numbers of Latino immigrants, he points out that "no matter how new, all immigrants from the right 'protected classes' — black, Hispanic, Asian — are eligible for preferential hiring and promotion. They are counted toward government quota requirements that were allegedly imposed on employers to help native-born minority Americans." Based on the availability of these programs, Brimelow believes that Hispanics "are much less encouraged to 'Americanize' than anything seen in the previous Great Wave [of immigration during the late 1800s and early 1900s]" because "they are being issued with a new, artificial 'Hispanic' identity."[34]

Characterizing affirmative action as "government-mandated discrimination against white Americans,"[35] Brimelow decries the decision to treat "Hispanics" as a homogeneous protected class. He contends that their favored treatment is "a result of ethnic lobbying in Washington" rather than of a genuine claim to compensatory justice. Moreover, their illegitimate political demands and rising numbers threaten opportunities for whites. Citing the prospects of his white son, Brimelow argues that "the sheer size of the so-called 'protected classes' that are now politically favored, such as Hispanics, will be a matter of vital importance as long as he lives. And their size is basically determined by immigration."[36]

Brimelow concludes that the confluence of race-conscious civil rights policy and liberal immigration threatens American traditions: "Race is destiny in American politics. Its importance has only been intensified by the supposedly color-blind civil rights legislation of the 1960s — which paradoxically has turned out to mean elaborate race-conscious affirmative action programs. Any change in the racial balance must obviously be fraught with consequences for the survival and success of the American nation."[37] Having questioned the legitimacy of Latinos' civil rights claims, Brimelow in turn argues that these claims undercut the authenticity of Latinos' expressed desire to immigrate to the United States. He says that Americans should be asking themselves, "if the 'protected classes' are so oppressed in the United States that they must be rescued by this unprecedented government intervention, how can it be right to allow any more members of the 'protected classes' to immigrate into this oppression?"[38] In stark form, Brimelow's arguments demonstrate that not only have civil rights entitlements been called into question because of the immigrant status of Latinos, but their petitions to immigrate have been portrayed as dangerous because of their status as beneficiaries under civil rights law.

The Latino Challenge

Because Latinos are asked to conform to a black experience under the civil rights model and a white experience under the immigration model, they never succeed in fully establishing the legitimacy of their claims under either approach. The first step that Latinos must take to avoid being whipsawed by civil rights and immigration models is to establish the ways in which each paradigm accentuates the need for a heightened commitment to fairness and equity under the other. Under the civil rights model, it is essential that Latinos demonstrate that the recent influx of immigrants increases, rather than diminishes, the likelihood of discriminatory treatment. The growing visibility of Latino immigrant populations may reinforce stereotypical beliefs that Latinos are foreign and unwilling to assimilate. These stereotypes in turn are rooted in those historical practices that degraded Latinos out of fear that they would be less trustworthy Americans than other groups.

Under the immigration model, it is key that Latino advocates demonstrate that the failure to regularize the inevitable flow of cheap labor across a semipermeable border creates vulnerable populations trapped in poverty and ignorance. As the Supreme Court wrote in *Plyler v. Doe*:

> Sheer incapability or lax enforcement of the laws barring entry into this country, coupled with the failure to establish an effective bar to employment of undocumented aliens, has resulted in the creation of a substantial "shadow population" of illegal immigrants — numbering in the millions — within our borders. This situation raises the specter of a permanent caste of undocumented resident aliens, encouraged by some to remain here as a source of cheap labor, but nevertheless denied the benefits that our society makes available to citizens and lawful residents. The existence of such an underclass presents most difficult problems for a nation that prides itself on adherence to principles of equality under law.[39]

Recent proposals to eliminate benefits not only for undocumented persons but also for permanent resident aliens aggravate the dangers of creating hierarchical tiers of belonging and entitlement in a society committed to civil rights for all.[40] The destruction of the dignity and humanity of one segment of the population cannot easily be confined; tolerating the creation of a permanent underclass and then of a class of semilegitimate resident aliens makes it all too easy to retreat wholesale from a general commitment to equal treatment. Latinos must make clear that intelligent and humane immigration policy is integrally related to preserving the civil rights of all Americans.

Although I think that it is critical in the short run to contest the application of the civil rights and immigration models to Latinos, in the long run I hope that the Latino experience will challenge scholars and policymakers to reconsider the conventional parameters of each paradigm. The civil rights model is rooted in a black-white experience, but with the growth of Latino and Asian populations, this bilateral approach to race relations must be reconsidered. As was true in the 1930s, Latinos today do not fit either a black or a white typology, but instead of forcing them into a procrustean bed, it may be useful to analyze how this black-white vision has blinkered America's understanding of race. Perhaps race has been cast in excessively biological terms, when its correlation to social characteristics, such as religion, language, and culture, is critical; race may be wrongly treated as monolithic when race mixing has been a long-standing, if largely undiscussed, feature of American life. As Latinos gain prominence, their experience may facilitate a thorough reexamination of America's outmoded conceptualization of race.[41]

Similarly, the Latino experience could alert us to the limitations of traditional accounts of immigration. The rise of transnational communities may be the first harbinger of the global economy's impact on personal and national identity. As labor and capital flow across international borders, traditional boundaries may be less effective in marking and preserving an American way of life. Although the rise of immigrant populations is the most immediate and concrete evidence of these changes, the restructuring of the United States economy may have other serious long-term implications for traditional conceptions of American customs and values. As capital is exported abroad to draw on cheap labor supplies, Americans confront a growing inequality of opportunity between the highly skilled on the one hand and the semiskilled or unskilled on the other. Many Americans now find that, instead of high-wage manufacturing jobs with benefits, they must settle for part-time work without benefits or security of employment in the service sector.

At some point, this rise in economic inequality may threaten the predicates of political equality so critical to the democratic process. The well-to-do will increasingly require that the political process insulate them from the discomfort and dangers associated with a class of unfortunates with little hope for personal advancement. By demonstrating how global flows of labor and capital affect a range of domestic traditions, scholarship on Latinos may alert the United States to the perils of failing to place immigration policy in the context of larger international economic imperatives. At a minimum, this work is likely to demonstrate that cracking down on immigration is by no means a complete answer to the larger challenges facing this country — now part of an international community with a range of political, social, and economic traditions.[42]

The transformation of popular thinking about civil rights and immigration is a tall order for Latinos. To accomplish this goal, government officials, foundations, think tanks, and universities must support scholarly work on the burgeoning Latino population. Generating a substantial body of research on this group is a first step, but these findings then must reach policymakers and the media in accessible forms. To facilitate this dissemination, at least some Latinos must assume the role of public intellectuals, providing commentary for newspapers, magazines, and television. Only in this manner can the conventional wisdom about Latinos be challenged. To maximize the impact of these commentators, Latinos should organize media watchdogs to ensure fairness, accuracy, and balance in the coverage of Latino concerns.[43]

Latinos need to show how the civil rights and immigration models interact in forming their identity and forging their life chances. Ultimately, though, the greatest contribution that Latinos may make is to alert Americans to the ways in which each paradigm has become obsolete. Latinos may not fit the models because the models just don't fit the complications of a multiracial, multiethnic, multicultural, multilingual America.

NOTES

1. Regents of the University of California, *SP–1: Policy Ensuring Equal Treatment — Admissions*, 20 July 1995; Regents of the University of California, *SP–2: Policy Ensuring Equal Treatment — Employment and Contracting*, 20 July 1995.

2. Edward Epstein, "Faculty Opposes Gutting Affirmative Action at UC; They Want Share in Decision-Making," *San Francisco Chronicle*, 21 October 1995, A13.

3. Regents, *SP–1* , §4.

4. Gale Holland and Maria Goodavage, "California's Asian Students Face Quandary," *USA Today*, 23 August 1995, A1; Howard Witt, "At University of California, A New Set of Rules; With Affirmative Action Out, Racial Mix Could Change," *Chicago Tribune*, 30 July 1995, 13; B. Drummond Ayres, "Affirmative Action's End? Now, It's Not That Simple," *New York Times*, 24 July 1995, A1.

5. Pamela Burdman, "UC Officials Roll Out Plans on Preferences," *San Francisco Chronicle*, 14 December 1995, A19. When the president of the University of California asked for additional time to implement the resolution on student admissions, he met with a stinging rebuke from the regents. "University's Leaders Are Torn by Affirmative-Action Ban," *New York Times*, 28 January 1996, A1; Pamela Burdman, "Regents Let UC Chief Off Hook: Conciliatory Letters Appease Critics," *San Francisco Chronicle*, 30 January 1996, A1.

6. Gayle M. B. Hanson, "Color-Blind Initiative Makes Foes See Red," *Washington Times*, 20 February 1995, 6.

7. Jorge Chapa and Richard R. Valencia, "Latino Population Growth, Demographic Characteristics, and Educational Stagnation: An Examination of Recent Trends," *Hispanic Journal of Behavioral Science* 15 (1993): 165, 167; Bureau of the Census, *Current Population Reports: Population Projections for States, by Age, Sex, Race, and Hispanic Origin: 1993 to 2020*, prepared by the Population Division, Bureau of the Census (Washington, D.C., 1994), 21; Bureau of the Census, *Current Population Reports: Population Projections of the United States by Age, Sex, Race, and Hispanic Origin: 1993 to 2050*, prepared by the Population Division, Bureau of the Census (Washington, D.C., 1993), xxii; Jean Suhr Ludwig and Judy Kowarsky, "Eligibility of California's 1990 High School Graduates for Admission to the State's Public Universities," in ed. Aida Hurtado and Eugene Garcia, *The Educational Achievement of Latinos: Barriers and Successes* (Santa Cruz, CA, 1994), 259, 263.

8. Cathleen Decker, "Affirmative Action: Why Battle Erupted," *Los Angeles Times*, 19 February 1995, A1.

9. See, e.g., *Keyes v. School District No. 1*, 413 U.S. 189, 197–98 (1973) (not-

ing that Latinos, like blacks, had suffered a history of discrimination and were entitled to special protection); *Hernandez v. Texas*, 347 U.S. 475, 478–80 (1954). For a general discussion of how civil rights statutes have been expanded to cover a range of minority groups, including Latinos, and the problems this expansion has posed, see Deborah Ramirez, "Multicultural Empowerment: It's Not Just Black and White Anymore," *Stanford Law Review* 47 (1995): 957.

10. Office of Management and Budget, "Race and Ethnic Standards for Federal Statistics and Administrative Reporting, Directive no. 15," *Federal Register* 43, no. 19 (1978): 260, 269; House Committee on Post Office and Civil Service, Subcommittee on Census, Statistics, and Postal Personnel, *Review of Federal Measurements of Race and Ethnicity*, 103d Cong., 1st Sess., 14 April 1993, 50 (remarks of Reynolds Farley, research scientist, Population Studies Center, University of Michigan).

11. See, e.g., *McLaughlin v. Florida*, 379 U.S. 184 (1964) (establishing strict scrutiny for racial classifications); *Frontiero v. Richardson*, 411 U.S. 677 (1973) (plurality opinion; explaining relevance of immutability to heightened scrutiny under equal protection law).

12. However, African Americans themselves are well aware of these differences, which often lead to hostility between native-born and immigrant blacks. See Sam Fulwood III, "U.S. Blacks: A Divided Experience," *Los Angeles Times*, 25 November 1995, A1.

13. Paul Brest and Miranda Oshige, "Affirmative Action for Whom?" *Stanford Law Review* 47 (1995): 855.

14. *Ibid.*, 863.

15. *Ibid.*, 867.

16. *Ibid.*

17. *Ibid.*, 883–84, 886.

18. *Ibid.*, 888.

19. *Ibid.* The debate over the costs of immigration, particularly illegal immigration, and the contributions immigrants make remains a heated one. See, e.g., James Bornemeier, "Study Plays Down Cost of Immigrants; It Says Natives Get More Welfare," *San Francisco Chronicle*, 11 December 1995, A4.

20. Brest and Oshige, "Affirmative Action," 890.

21. Frederick Law Olmsted, *A Journey Through Texas; or, a Saddle-Trip on the Southwestern Frontier* (1857), quoted in David Montejano, *Anglos and Mexicans in the Making of Texas, 1836–1986* (Austin, Tex., 1987), 29.

22. William Leonard, "Where Both Bullets and Ballots Are Dangerous," *Survey*, 28 October 1916, 86–87, quoted in Montejano, *Anglos and Mexicans*, 181.

23. Max S. Handman, "Economic Reasons for the Coming of the Mexican

Immigrant," *American Journal of Sociology* 35 (1930): 601, 609–10, quoted in Montejano, *Anglos and Mexicans*, 158.

24. Montejano, *Anglos and Mexicans*, 181.

25. For a discussion of the potential dangers of blocked assimilation, see Jorge Chapa, "The Question of Mexican-American Assimilation: Socioeconomic Parity or Underclass Formation?" *Public Affairs Comment* 35 (1988): 1, 6.

26. Kevin R. Johnson, "Los Olvidados: Images of the Immigrant, Political Power of Noncitizens, and Immigration Law Enforcement," *Brigham Young University Law Review* (1993): 1139, 1150. See, generally, Nathan Glazer and Daniel P. Moynihan, *Beyond the Melting Pot: The Negroes, Puerto Ricans, Jews, Italians, and Irish of New York City* (Cambridge, MA, 1970); Pastora S. J. Cafferty et al., *The Dilemma of American Immigration: Beyond the Golden Door* (New Brunswick, NJ, 1983).

27. Assimilation was not a straightforward proposition for earlier generations of immigrants. According to David Hollinger, of those immigrants who came to the United States during the great migration of 1880 to 1924, about one-third returned to their country of origin. David A. Hollinger, *Postethnic America: Beyond Multiculturalism* (New York, 1995).

28. See Milton M. Gordon, *Assimilation in American Life: The Role of Race, Religion, and National Origins* (New York, 1964), 107–8.

29. *Chae Chan Ping v. United States* (The Chinese Exclusion Case), 130 U.S. 581, 595 (1889).

30. See, generally, Heinz Kloss, *The American Bilingual Tradition* (Rowley, MA, 1977), 45, 46–47, 52–53, 60–61, 67–74; Shirley Brice Heath, "English in Our Language Heritage," in Charles A. Ferguson and Shirley Brice, eds., *Language in the USA* (New York, 1981), 14–17.

31. See Johnson, "Los Olvidados," 1223 (the naturalization rate for Latinos was less than half the average for all immigrants); see also Sam Dillon, "Mexico Woos U.S. Mexicans, Proposing Dual Nationality," *New York Times*, 10 December 1995, A10.

32. See Elizabeth Hervey Stephen et al., "Health of the Foreign-Born Population: United States, 1989–90," *Advance Data* 74 (1994): 1, 4; Paul D. Sorlie et al., "Mortality by Hispanic Status in the United States," *Journal of the American Medical Association* 70 (1993): 2464, 2468; Jacqueline M. Golding and M. Audrey Burnam, "Immigration, Stress, and Depressive Symptoms in a Mexican-American Community," *Journal of Nervous and Mental Disease* 178 (1990): 161, 169.

33. Peter Brimelow, *Alien Nation: Common Sense About America's Immigration Disaster* (New York, 1995).

34. *Ibid.*, 218.

35. *Ibid.*

36. *Ibid.*, 11.

37. *Ibid.*, 264.

38. *Ibid.*, 263–64.

39. *Plyler v. Doe* 457 U.S. 202, 218–19 (1982). The insularity of this class of persons would be further entrenched by proposals to deny citizenship to children born to undocumented persons residing in the United States. See Neil A. Lewis, "Bill Seeks to End Citizenship as Birthright for Everyone," *New York Times*, 14 December 1995, A20.

40. See Robert Pear, "The Nation; Deciding Who Gets What in America," *New York Times*, 27 November 1994, A5.

41. There is evidence that these developments are already unfolding. See Luis Angel Toro, "'A People Distinct from Others': Race and Identity in Federal Indian Law and the Hispanic Classification in OMB Directive No. 15," *Texas Tech Law Review* 26 (1995): 1219, 1221–22. See generally Ian Haney-Lopez, "The Social Construction of Race," *Harvard Civil Rights–Civil Liberties Law Review* 29 (1994): 1.

42. For preliminary scholarship on how a global economy will affect social and political as well as economic conditions in the United States, see M. Patricia Fernandez Kelly, "Underclass and Immigrant Women as Economic Actors: Rethinking Citizenship in a Changing Global Economy," *American University Journal of International Law and Policy* 9 (1993): 151; Michael S. Knoll, "Perchance to Dream: The Global Economy and the American Dream," *Southern California Law Review* 66 (1993): 1599.

43. Latinos are seriously underrepresented in the media, accounting for only 2 percent of all prime-time television roles, although they currently make up 10 percent of the nation's population. Blacks, by contrast, play 18 percent of all roles, even though they represent 13 percent of the population. Mark A. Perigard, "Alien Nation: How Well Does Prime-Time TV Match the Makeup of Society?" *Boston Herald*, 5 November 1995, 1. See also Valerie Menard, "The Latino Angle; Latino Community Journalists," *Hispanic* 8 (September 1995): 14; Mary Anne Perez, "Community News: East: Eastside; Media Watchdog Committee Formed," *Los Angeles Times*, 12 February 1995, 9.

Situating Asian Americans in the Political Discourse on Affirmative Action

Michael Omi and Dana Y. Takagi

The hegemonic "black/white" paradigm of race relations has fundamentally shaped how we think about, engage, and politically mobilize around racial issues. Historical narratives of racialized minorities in the United States are cast in the shadows of the black/white encounter. Contemporary conflicts between a number of different racial/ethnic groups are understood in relationship to this bipolar model, which the media then utilizes as a master frame to present such conflicts. During the Los Angeles "riots" of 1992, for example, various racial subjects were identified (for example, Koreans, Guatemalans), but the popular interpretation of the civil disorder was fundamentally shaped by the hegemonic paradigm.

This prevailing bipolar model of race significantly obscures the complex patterns of race over time. Tomás Almaguer, in his study of race in nineteenth-century California, breaks from the dominant mode of biracial theorizing by illustrating how Native Americans, Mexicans, Chinese, and Japanese are racialized and positioned in relation to one another by the dominant Anglo elite.[1] His discussion draws attention to how the Asian American historical experience is essential to a full comprehension of racial dynamics in the West.

We want to suggest that a more complex and nuanced understanding of the affirmative action debate needs to be attentive to how distinct political positions socially construct and represent Asian Americans. Our intent is to locate Asian Americans within the political discourse on affirmative action, a move that would serve to deepen a critical analysis of the black/white paradigm, and, in doing so, reveal some intriguing aspects about racial politics in the current period.

Gary Y. Okihiro, in a collection of essays on Asian American history and culture, asks: "Is yellow black or white?"[2] His discussion of this question highlights how Asian Americans have historically been located somewhere between black and white. Depending on the period in question, Asian Americans have been seen as racially "black"[3] or as a group "outwhiting the whites."[4]

The question of how to situate Asian Americans on a spectrum — close to African Americans at one end or closer to whites on the other — helps to critically define the distinctive political positions on affirmative action. Both the Right and the Left of the political spectrum implicate, in varying degrees, Asian Americans in the ongoing debate. Unlike "black" and "white" as racial categories, there is a greater fluidity to "Asian American" that can be manipulated in particular ways to suit particular positions. It may not matter whether specific claims about Asian Americans are empirically correct or not. In fact, much of what both the Left and the Right claim about Asian Americans is contestable. Thus, the "truth" of the claims is immaterial. What matters are the kinds of rhetorical constructions, and their emotional impacts, that the Right and the Left deploy.

Right Political Discourse and Asian American Victims

In January 1996, Governor Pete Wilson upheld his support for the July 1995 decision by the University of California (UC) Regents to eliminate race as a consideration for admissions, hiring, and contracting. It was the "right decision," he argued, one premised on the principles of equal opportunity: "Racial preferences are by definition racial discrimination. They were wrong 30 years ago when they discriminated against African-Americans. And they're wrong today, when they discriminate against *Asian* or Caucasian Americans" (emphasis ours).[5] Wilson's strategic assignment of Asian Americans to the white side of the battle lines is noteworthy. The UC Regents' questioning of affirmative action was precipitated by a complaint lodged by Jerry and Ellen Cook, a white San Diego couple who began examining statistical information on the five medical schools in the UC system when their son was denied admission to the UC San Diego Medical School. The Cooks claimed that at UC Davis, for example, Chicanos were offered admission at five times the rate of whites and *nineteen times* the rate of Japanese Americans.[6] The signal was clear. "Preferential policies" victimized Asian Americans as much as, perhaps more than, whites.

Deploying this particular social construction serves an important political purpose. By raising the issue of Asian American victimization, the Right could deflect the charge levied against them by their critics that their opposition to affirmative action represents merely a thinly veiled attempt to preserve white skin privilege. At work here is a specific *rearticulation* of the issue of affirmative action.[7]

This rearticulation has several interesting effects that creatively engage the existing field of racial meanings. One effect, as we suggested above, is to disrupt the understanding of the racial issue as an expression of white/nonwhite difference and conflict. The Right evokes Asian Americans to demonstrate that another nonwhite, racialized minority is being hurt by such policies. This representation of Asian Americans as disadvantaged by affirmative action plays into popular constructions of Asian Americans as "friends" of whites and "foes" of African Americans. The specter of black/Asian American conflict, evident in numerous cinematic portrayals of ghetto life,[8] is elevated to a national level of policy debate.

The historical experience of Asian Americans becomes a particularly convenient narrative to exploit. Asian Americans are presented as a group that has been subject to extreme forms of racial discrimination in the past (including immigration exclusion, the denial of naturalization rights, and, in the case of Japanese Americans, incarceration). Despite these obstacles, they have become a "model minority," not by means of state assistance, but through their own hard work and efforts. This narrative questions the efficacy of state intervention to change patterns of racial inequality, and feeds into the reductionist accounts that claim that a group's "culture" is the key to their mobility and success.[9]

The Right also takes pains to note that Asian Americans are not active discriminators in the present. There is, so it seems, no "yellow skin privilege." Given the weight of the past and their location in the present, it is truly unfair, the Right argues, that

Asian Americans must now confront a new and pernicious form of discrimination under the guise of equality. Dinesh D'Souza makes this clear: "One can hardly maintain that preferential policies strictly serve the goals of social justice. Take the case of Asian Americans: Members of this minority group have experienced both *de facto* and *de jure* discrimination, and they have played no part in any of the historical crimes that affirmative action was designed to remedy. In fairness, why should the burden of preferential policies be placed on historically innocent parties?"[10]

In June 1995, Governor Wilson stated that "it is not just the 'angry white males' who think the time has come for change." He went on to describe his conversation with a Vietnamese senior at prestigious Lowell High School in San Francisco. The young woman was "deeply troubled" that Vietnamese students were admitted with lower scores than Chinese students.[11] Many of the Right's principal themes are condensed in this example. The "troubled" Vietnamese student bears more than a passing resemblance to that African American student evoked by numerous conservative political commentators, the student whose self-esteem and sense of worth is shaken by the belief that she or he is an affirmative action case. The example also reveals that the Right's construction of Asian Americans as the victims of affirmative action does not necessarily rely on treating the group as undifferentiated and monolithic. The Right's argument is nuanced and attentive to the diversity among Asian Americans and the different political claims that can potentially surface.

The Right's representation of Asian Americans with respect to affirmative action is full of irony. We read it as the strategic use of race to deflect the issue of race. The Right has rearticulated the racial meanings embedded in the affirmative action debates by representing Asian Americans as an "innocent" group wronged by racial preferences. Race has been rendered more complex, but in so doing, attention has been distracted from the hegemonic position of whites on the playing field. Such an ideological sleight of hand allows racial privilege to be sidelined while an agenda based on individual merit, social justice, and the creation of a "colorblind" society is promoted.

Left Political Discourse and Asian American Invisibility

On 18 January 1996, student advocates for affirmative action staged a dramatic and emotional protest inside the UC Board of Regents meeting in San Francisco. During a brief public comment session on SP-1 and SP-2, approximately fifty students applied whiteface and pasted stickers reading "Reclaim Our Education" over their mouths.[12] Their "white" faces, they explained, represented the increasing whiteness of the University of California, and the corresponding lack of racial diversity that would result when the resolutions took effect. The mouth stickers were worn to underscore the students' lack of voice in UC policy. The visual symbols deployed by the students were a stunning display of what many progressives believe is the future of UC without affirmative action.[13]

Outside the meeting, some four hundred students from across the nine-campus system supported the (mostly but not always) silent protesters inside with a loud and enthusiastic rally. The student protesters were galvanized by chants of "no University without diversity" and "UC diversity, we see hypocrisy." Somewhat predictably, the gaggle of TV news cameras and reporters organized their feature stories and news coverage by juxtaposing images of painted faces and silent protest inside the meeting with those of noisy demonstrators outside the meeting. The imagery and representations of the January meeting, resonant with past debate and demonstrations about affirmative action at UC, prompt us to think about how Asian Americans are positioned in pro-affirmative action and Left discourses on racial preferences.

If Asian Americans assume the status of newfound victims of discrimination in Right narratives, they occupy a kind of racial pariah position in Left and progressive accounts of affirmative action. Left discursive practices have been organized in two ways, both problematic. In the first, Asian Americans are simply left out of the affirmative action debate. Part of this is attributable to the hegemonic, bipolar model of race relations we emphasized earlier. Many pro–affirmative action statements from major organizations, for instance, focus entirely on black/white inequalities, with nary a whisper about Asian Americans. Their absence from the debate can also be accounted for in the argument that historically Asian Americans have not been the beneficiaries of racial preferences. Hence, the debate about SP-1 and

SP–2 does not concern Asian Americans per se. Perhaps another explanation for the deletion of Asian Americans from Left discourses concerns the numerical size of the Asian American population. At 3 percent of the national population in 1990, Asians are arguably a tiny minority — and hence expendable in the "big" picture of race relations. Yet another explanation might be that many progressives worry that Asian Americans, because they see themselves benefiting from the end of affirmative action, are likely to oppose racial preferences. Hence, the less said about Asian Americans, the better.

A second discursive practice, and one that we believe is more prevalent than the first, includes Asian Americans as relatively unproblematic partners in a wider coalition politics. The chant "no University without diversity" is suggestive of a broad phalanx of diverse constituencies, including Asian Americans. Here, while we are sympathetic to the politics of a "united front" of opposition to SP–1 and SP–2, we remain concerned that such a politics presumes that Asian American interests are similar enough to other interests to make the coalition claims viable and rhetorically persuasive. In our view, the assumption that Asian Americans share a similar social location to, for example, African Americans in the affirmative action debate, is wrong. Rather, it is precisely the difference between these groups that has played an important part of the mobilization of the Right. While the Right has capitalized on Asian American achievement in higher education, the Left has weakly insisted on the "shared interests" model of politics.

Interrogating the concept of "shared interests" among people of color raises a host of questions, including that of the nature of racism in the United States. We tend to think of racism as hostility directed against those of a different skin color believed to be "inferior" — in terms of class and status, in intellectual ability, or in cultural orientation. This hostility is coupled with structural forms of discrimination — in the job market, in politics, in residential patterns — and negative cultural representations. Clearly African Americans are subject to this type of racism.

Asian Americans, however, are subject to a different form of racism. They are often the objects of *resentment* by other groups who perceive that they do "too well," that they secure wealth and other material resources and social advantages unfairly. This resentment has resulted historically in political disenfranchisement and exclusionary laws in the late nineteenth to early twentieth century, and in "English-only" initiatives and more stringent curbs on immigration and foreign capital investment today.

The status of Asian Americans in higher education and projections regarding their increased growth renders the "shared interest" model of coalition politics quite problematic. In the midst of debate about UC admissions policy in July 1995, the University's Office of the President projected that Asian Americans would be the only nonwhite group to benefit from passage of SP–1 and SP–2. The estimate that Asian enrollment would increase by 20 percent, while other racial minority enrollments would decline, presented an interesting dilemma for Left and pro–affirmative action activists. While some groups would support racial preferences on the grounds of self-interest in admissions, Asian Americans would presumably support preferences on the basis of altruistic sentiments about the needs of, and rights owed to, other racial minorities.

We wish to emphasize our agreement with the students in whiteface that declining diversity is an inevitable consequence of SP–1 and SP–2. But we also wish to open up a nagging question about the racial narrative conveyed by the dramatic student protest: will the university become primarily *white*? How will the discursive politics about preferences shift and change if, as the projections suggest, the university becomes increasingly *Asian American*?

Black, White, or "Other"?
Both the Right and the Left are vying for custody of the political "interests" of Asian Americans. For the Right, the Asian American "model minority" figures as the Allan Bakke replacement for the 1990s assault on affirmative action. On the other hand, Left and progressive forces hope that Asian Americans will broaden the political coalition of pro–affirmative action and pro-diversity forces and thereby expand the unified front of opposition to the right. One side pits Asian Americans against whites, the other pits Asian Americans against racial minorities. From there, the discussion descends into quibbles over whether Asian Americans are more like African Americans or, alternatively, more like whites in the politics of race in the United States. In our view,

neither the Left nor the Right has custodial rights to the experiences of Asian Americans. Attempts on both sides to meld Asian America into a vision of "whiteness" or "racial diversity" will always be problematic given the unique racial formation of Asian Americans.

Asian American educational achievement, for example, threatens to subvert both Right and Left versions of preferential policies. Members of the Right, including Regent Ward Connerly and Governor Pete Wilson, have argued for the substitution of class preferences for race in UC admissions. Parts of the Left as well have hinged the viability of affirmative action on class, with the assumption that underrepresented racial minorities would continue to be given preference through class variables. But the use of class preferences will present a clear *racial* advantage for Asian American applicants to all UC campuses. If socioeconomic status is used as an admissions criterion instead of race, UC officials predict that Asian American enrollment will *increase* by 15 to 25 percent while African American enrollment will drop 40 to 50 percent, Latino enrollment will fall 5 to 15 percent, and white enrollment will stay about the same.[14]

The class-based initiatives presented above serve as one example of the tendency to delete race from both sides of the rhetorical divide about affirmative action. For the Right, opposition to affirmative action is premised on ideas of individual merit and the advancement of a colorblind society, and any hints of "color consciousness" are suspiciously viewed as forms of racial discrimination. For part of the Left, there is a tendency to keep the Pandora's box of race closed to avoid the messy racial issues that threaten to emerge from it. The UC faculty challenge to the regents' decision, for example, emphasizes threats to faculty governance and the intrusion of partisan politics into the academy, rather than the desirability of racial preferences.

What is missing from the conversations about affirmative action — on the Left *and* the Right — is an explicit discussion of the nature of race and racism in the United States today. Both the Right and Left have wrestled with how to situate Asian Americans in affirmative action debates and how to frame particular strategic representations of them. Their attempts reveal the complexity of race in the current period when the bipolar model of race relations has revealed an increasing inability to comprehend the patterns of conflict and accommodation that now occur between, and among, many different racialized groups. Race in the United States can no longer, if it ever could, be adequately understood by narrowly assessing the relative situations of whites and blacks.

We need a new framework that is attentive to a complex understanding of racial location and interest, one that does not essentialize race but interrogates how groups are constructed and represented, one that understands that social policies — regarding immigration, welfare, crime, as well as affirmative action — have a differential impact on different groups and the way they are defined. This framework will be crucial to an understanding of politics in a period when the traditional discourse of civil rights is being rearticulated by the Right in ways that preserve the structure of racial privilege. A post–civil rights perspective will have to grapple with the increased visibility of Asian Americans and how they are implicated in a range of racial issues. Asian Americans can no longer be cast in the shadows of black/white relations. Yet observers continue to do just that. Andrew Hacker, for example, needs to talk extensively about Asian Americans in order to examine race-based admissions policies in higher education.[15] Unfortunately his analysis does not lead him to consider that the United States, in this area as well as in many others, may be more than "two nations," black and white.

Asian Americans as a group are, we think, a crucial barometer of the contemporary racial climate. It will indeed be interesting to see how the issue of affirmative action is recast by both the Right and the Left if, as a consequence of SP–1 and SP–2, the student bodies of the two UC flagship campuses — Berkeley and Los Angeles — become overwhelmingly Asian.

NOTES

1. Tomás Almaguer, *Racial Fault Lines: The Historical Origins of White Supremacy in California* (Berkeley, 1994).

2. Gary Y. Okihiro, *Margins and Mainstreams: Asians in American History and Culture* (Seattle, 1994), chap. 2.

3. Dan Cauldwell, "The Negroization of the Chinese Stereotype in California," *Southern California Historical Quarterly* 1 (June 1971).

4. "Success Story: Outwhiting the Whites," *Newsweek*, 21 June 1971.

5. Pete Wilson, "Why Racial Preferences Must End," *San Francisco Chronicle*, 18 January 1996, A21.

6. Richard Bernstein, "Moves Under Way in California to Overturn Higher Education's Affirmative Action Policy," *New York Times*, 25 January 1995, B8.

7. By rearticulation we mean "the process of redefinition of political interests and identities through a process of recombination of familiar ideas and values in hitherto unrecognized ways." Michael Omi and Howard Winant, *Racial Formation in the United States: From the 1960s to the 1990s*, 2d ed. (New York, 1994), 163 n.8.

8. A particularly explosive example is the Allen Hughes and Albert Hughes film *Menace II Society* (1993).

9. This position is best articulated by Thomas Sowell in his numerous publications. For the most current example, see his *Race and Culture: A World View* (New York, 1994).

10. Dinesh D'Souza, "The Failure of the 'Cruel Compassion,' " the *Chronicle of Higher Education*, 15 September 1995, B1.

11. Yumi Wilson, "Wilson Explains His Affirmative Action Plans," *San Francisco Chronicle*, 1 June 1995, A16.

12. SP-1 and SP-2 are the two UC Regents resolutions passed on 20 July 1995 that ban the use of race and gender preferences in, respectively, admissions and employment practices at the University of California. The text of SP-1 is reprinted as an appendix to this book on page 397.

13. Indeed, this imagery of the meeting was carried by all the major newspapers the following day — the *New York Times*, the *San Francisco Examiner*, the *San Francisco Chronicle* — and depicted in television reports as well.

14. "Affirmative-Action Aftermath," The *Chronicle of Higher Education*, 4 August 1995, A18.

15. Andrew Hacker, *Two Nations: Black and White, Separate, Hostile, Unequal* (New York, 1992), chap. 8, esp. 9–10. Hacker justifies his bipolar framework by suggesting that over time Asian Americans may be absorbed into a new expansive definition of what "white" is.

California's Collision

of Race and Class

Richard Walker

California is a frankensteinian laboratory of modern hopes and failures. It has provided fertile ground for fast-track capitalist development and experiments in liberal democracy, while at the same time allowing for the mingling of many diverse peoples. But the state has also displayed the antinomies of economic crisis, class hatred, racism, and political reaction. California has repeatedly set the agenda for the United States as a whole, for better or worse, and has set the tone again in the 1990s for a paroxysm of immigrant bashing and black-white racial antagonism. Today's Californians face the profound task of integrating a plethora of non-European peoples into what is still overwhelmingly a white man's republic, and their success or failure will mark this nation's history well into the next century. Alas, the prospects are dimmed by inauspicious circumstances of economic restructuring, class division, political recidivism, and recrudescent racism and classism. If Californians fail at this task, the desperately needed renewal of class and race relations, politics and government, work and economy will be put off yet again, and the United States will remain a staggering, increasingly monstrous presence on the world's stage.

We, the People: Race and Class Recomposition
California has been a state of immigrants since the Spanish conquest in the late eighteenth century. It has never known a decade when the number of newly arriving people did not exceed the number of those born within the state.[1] Since the extermination of the indigenous people, the vast majority of Californians have been of European origin. Nevertheless, Asians and Mexicans have

been a constant presence, and people of African origin finally arrived in large numbers in the 1940s for wartime work. Race in California and the West has never been a simple black-and-white issue.

California became whiter in the mid–twentieth century, thanks to the exclusionary immigration quotas of 1924 and the interwar breakup of the European world system. The gradual return to economic globalism, capitalist penetration of the Third World, and loosening of immigration restrictions in 1965 have returned California to something nearer its appearance in the last century. But the geography of new arrivals has tilted sharply away from Europe and the eastern United States and toward the Pacific Basin, in line with the shift of the center of gravity of world capitalism away from the Atlantic. In the last two decades, California (especially Los Angeles) displaced New York as the chief receiving area for immigrants (35 percent of immigrants to the United States arrived in California in the 1980s versus 14 percent in New York). Some 400,000 migrants per year poured in during the last decade (versus 300,000 births), and the state's population surged past 30 million by 1990, up 12 million from the previous twenty years. Fewer than 50 percent of current inhabitants were born in-state.

This influx has transfigured the face of California. Nonwhites will become the majority in the next century. Latinos rose sharply in number during the 1980s (by 70 percent), Asians more precipitously (by 127 percent). By 1990, whites had fallen to roughly 57 percent of the populace, while Latinos jumped to 26 percent and Asians nearly 10 percent (Africans holding at about 7 percent and indigenous people at one percent). The number of foreign-born residents went up by 80 percent. An economic earthquake moved two and a half million Mexicans northward, where they joined a half million Filipinos, a quarter million Salvadorans, Vietnamese, Koreans, and Chinese and over one hundred thousand Guatemalans, Canadians, Britons, and Iranis. The central cities have undergone the most dramatic recomposition. In 1970, Los Angeles was 75 percent white, by 1990 it was only 38 percent white. San Francisco went from 75 to 43 percent white in the same period.

Racial recomposition of California went hand-in-hand with class recomposition. The working class of the 1990s is composed overwhelmingly of Latinos (mostly Mexicans, Salvadorans, and Nicaraguans) and East and Southeast Asians (mostly Filipinos, Vietnamese, and Chinese), who serve in disproportionate numbers as manual workers. Overall, 79 percent of men of Mexican origin were in blue-collar jobs in 1980 versus 55 percent of Anglo men in such jobs. Because of labor market segmentation, immigrants are largely confined to specific occupational "niches."[2] Mexicans dominate Southern California manufacturing; Salvadorans stock the furniture industry and gardening crews; Guatemalan and Salvadoran women are the principal group of domestics; Chinese and Thai women fill the garment sweatshops north and south; Little Vietnam supplies the electronics belt of Orange County; Silicon Valley electronics feeds off men and women of many origins; Chinese, Central Americans, and Filipinos labor in the restaurants and tourist hotels of San Francisco; and agribusiness in the interior valleys makes hay on the backs of Mexicans, both mestizos and Mixtecans.

Contrary to popular images of hordes of unskilled peasants jumping border fences, today's immigrants include a healthy measure of the highly skilled who are competitive for technical, professional, and managerial jobs, as well as many well-capitalized business owners and entrepreneurs. The numbers of the skilled are particularly large among East Asians, South Asians, and Middle Easterners. Fields such as medicine, engineering, and computing have become immigrant niches for Iranis, Chinese, Filipinos, and Indians.[3] Less visible are the many Canadians and Europeans in electronics, banking, and teaching. These favored immigrants usually arrive already trained, with considerable acculturation to English and American commercialism, and they have permeated the petit bourgeois layers of California society. California has always received an extraordinary bounty from its skilled and well-capitalized migrants and, unlike the rest of the United States, has seldom felt the full impact of mass migrations of the rural poor.[4]

California has always depended on long-distance migration to feed its growth. In fact, the percentage of foreign-born residents was considerably higher a century ago, 39 percent in 1860 and 25 percent in 1900 versus 22 percent in 1990. The recent wave of migration was no larger, nor of longer duration, than the great post–World War II influx and fits closely to a pattern of 15-to-

25-year "long swings" of migration going back a century.[5] The imposing logistics of coping with millions of new people are daunting, to be sure, and require money, ideas, and commitment to rebuilding the state on a new human foundation. But it has been done before. Schools, houses, and infrastructure were built in ample number for the baby boomers of the postwar era of in-migration (including the Walker family). So what has changed? Race, politics, and the economy, to which we now turn.

We, the Laborers: Fuel for the Fires of the White-Hot Economy

California has grown bigger than all but six countries in income and output, with a gross domestic product of $700 billion in 1990 and $900 billion in 1995.[6] It enjoyed a spectacular boom from 1975 to 1990, seemingly immune to the national disease of falling profits, foreign competition, plant closures, and stagnant employment. When the circus was over, the big top fell in with a spectacular crash that triggered widespread panic about the future of the state and left the poor and the dark exposed to the winds of economic destruction and political scapegoating for the debacle.

During the long boom, 5.5 million new jobs were added, employment peaking in 1990 at 14 million. Average income per capita doubled from 1980 to 1990 (18 percent in real income). Well positioned on the eastern flank of the Pacific Rim, California became the national leader in exports to the global market, going from 10 to 20 percent of U.S. foreign trade, and the biggest recipient of direct foreign investment.[7] Southern California manufacturing employment peaked in 1988 at more than 1.25 million jobs, making Los Angeles the biggest industrial center in the United States (twice the size of second-place Chicago), while the Bay Area doubled its employment and Silicon Valley (Santa Clara county) became the densest manufacturing site in the country.[8]

California took over as the principal engine of U.S. economic growth and its high-tech sectors were trumpeted as the model for a nation losing its knack in manufacturing. On one side was electronics, where Silicon Valley was hailed as the world center of the new computer-information age and emblem of American innovation and entrepreneurship at its best. On the other side was mighty aerospace, the American trump card for beating back the Soviets and economic decline; as defense spending shot up to $300 billion, California's share of prime contracts peaked at 23 percent. A new generation of "smart war machines" was ushered in, and Orange County avionics became the biggest electronic cluster on earth, while the Bay Area received huge contracts for satellites, guidance systems, and "Star Wars" lasers.[9]

Then there was finance capital: at the beginning of the 1980s California was home to the world's largest bank (Bank of America) and credit card company (VISA), the country's biggest savings and loans (led by impresario Charles Keating), and the nerve center of the junk bond market (presided over by Michael Milken). New branches of foreign banks sprang up like mushrooms and loans were easy to come by. As regulations fell, fast-buck operators shuffled a deck of dubious assets, backed by the wizardry of Wall Street. Inflated by fire-sale finance, construction ballooned to $40 billion in 1989 (five times the previous peak in 1973).[10] Excess piled upon excess, and the California economy became white-hot.

Economic growth through the 1970s and 1980s was fed by the influx of almost 5 million new people from around the world. Not only were California jobs plentiful, they paid well—better than jobs in the rest of the United States and an order of magnitude higher than in Mexico or China. During the recent boom, incomes were one-sixth above the national average.[11] California's wage and income advantage has not disappeared despite the arrival of millions of new workers, however. California has enjoyed a virtuous circle of investment, employment, and spending in a highly diversified economy, and its skilled labor and ample capital have sustained a high rate of innovation that keeps California products in demand far and wide.[12]

The crisis of 1990–94 slammed the high-flying California economy harder than anything since the Great Depression. The state was forced into collective downsizing in the wake of a decade of overaccumulation of factories, workers, securities, real estate, and executive fat. Wealth shrank, thanks chiefly to real estate values shriveling by 25 to 30 percent. After leading the country in new business formation, California's failure rate soared, with 20 percent of the nation's bankruptcies in 1991–92. Construction came grinding to a halt almost everywhere in the state, with housing starts hitting the lowest point since World War II.

Southern California was the worst hit. The post–cold war military cutbacks cost the state some 250,000 of 400,000 jobs in defense. Greater Los Angeles accounted for over a quarter of all job losses in the country in 1990–93, losing one-quarter to one-third of its manufacturing workforce.[13] The south hit the financial skids as paper empires sank without a trace; Milken, Keating, and other con men went to jail; bank lending stagnated; venture capital plummeted; and Japanese investment dried up (from $3 billion per year in 1990 to $16 *million* in 1994). Then Los Angeles watched helplessly as a revived Bank of America bought out Security Pacific Bank.[14] The Bay Area was less devastated but still lost 120,000 jobs from 1990 to 1993.

Workers bore the brunt of the catastrophe. Gross job loss amounted to almost 1.5 million (10 percent) from 1990 to 1992: 900,000 in wholesale and retail trade, 200,000 in manufacturing, 150,000 in construction, 70,000 in agriculture. Net job growth was negative from 1991 through 1993, with unemployment edging toward 10 percent by 1993 and remaining at 8 percent in 1995 — two points higher than the national average. Not surprisingly, immigrants stopped coming. In-migration plunged after 1990, out-migration increased, and net migration hit zero in 1992–93 as the recession bottomed out. This did not stop immigrants from taking the blame for "glutting" labor markets, even though layoffs of locals and migrants alike were the real culprits, and unemployment rates rose equally for all racial and ethnic groups.[15]

California sits on the cusp of an epochal change in the geography of capitalism in which its place is no longer secure. It has seen such economic sea changes before, and survived them through a combination of new technologies, political initiatives, and cultural change. This time, one cannot be sure.[16] An uptick in the business cycle is restoring some of the bloom to the Golden State, with strengths in electronics, entertainment, and exports to East Asia. But long-run industrial leadership may be passing irreversibly across the Pacific. No region (or nation) is ever immune to the inevitable downswings of accumulation and shifts in the fortunes of places.[17] The economic insecurity — for the bourgeoisie as well as the working class — adds to the uncertainties and conflicts of social recomposition and racial change.

A Nation Divided: The Growing Class Schism

Even as the economy was roaring ahead, a yawning chasm between the classes was opening up that marked the United States as the most divided of all wealthy countries. California led the pack along with the rest of the sunbelt states. Those who owned capital did spectacularly well. California's jet stream of fast-track entrepreneurs and rentier families more than doubled in the 1980s to over 340,000 millionaires (one in a hundred people!), and its richest families — Hearsts, Packards, Waltons, Gettys, Haases, Bechtels — disproportionately filled the top ranks of America's *haute bourgeoisie*.[18] Michael Milken earned the highest personal salary in history, while Richard Riordan, now Mayor of Los Angeles, made $100 million through leveraged buyouts. In the Bay Area the number of million-dollar executive paychecks jumped from five to fifty-four.[19] The professional and managerial class prospered: average income for the top fifth of families rose by 15 percent to $107,000, and the Bay Area, spiritual center of the yuppie lifestyle, remained the richest metropolitan area in the country and the most expensive to live in.

Meanwhile, the working class lost ground. The real income of the middle 20 percent remained flat through the decade (and declined by 10 percent in the costly Bay Area). For the lower 40 percent the bottom fell out.[20] Wages stagnated in full-time jobs, while temporary and part-time work increased. Working people kept their income up by sending more family members out to work, holding two or three jobs, and working more overtime.[21] Chronically high unemployment averaged 7.5 percent over the twenty-year period beginning in the 1970s. A staggering gap opened up between total state income and total wages (including salaried professionals) — a crude measure of total surplus value — which expanded from $155 billion to $330 billion over the decade. This helps explain where all the millionaires came from.

While wages for all workers ebbed, nonwhites fared worse across the board. Latino workers earned 70 percent of what white workers earned, on average. The per capita income of Latinos was 45 percent that of whites because Latinos tend to have larger families. Blacks and Asians did somewhat better, but not much, with per capita incomes 61 percent and 72 percent that of whites, respectively. Unemployment rates have been consistently higher for nonwhites than they are for whites. Immigrant labor has provided the upper classes of California with a new mother lode of economic surplus. The excess profits gained by hiring Latino wage-workers, for example, instead of better-paid white workers was about $85 billion in 1990. All the same, the widening class schism also shows up *within* every race or nationality — European, African, Asian, or Latino — muddying a simple race-class alignment.[22]

Throughout the mean-spirited 1980s, new battalions were added to the armies of the poor. The poverty rate stood at 12.5 percent in 1990, even before the recession sent it skyward to 18.2 percent. This rate put California into the top ten poor states (just behind Arkansas) in this most impoverished of rich nations. South Central Los Angeles has a higher poverty rate now than at the time of the Watts Rebellion, and outside the coastal-urban belt higher unemployment, insecurity, and dependence on social services are permanent features. Saddest of all is California's astronomical rate of poverty among children — over 25 percent (33 percent for children under the age of six).[23]

In short, at the same time that the racial composition of California has changed so dramatically and the economy has gone into free fall, class contradictions have sharpened. Working-class comfort and security have declined in tandem with a massive engorgement of the rich. Anxiety over unemployment, bad wages, poverty, job competition, housing, and health care is rife. All this would be true regardless of the numbers of immigrants and their racial and ethnic composition, because the erosion of working-class incomes and welfare has been taking place throughout the country and, indeed, the world.[24] But Governor Pete Wilson and the Right have used immigration as a scapegoat for the sorry state of the working class. Are they worried, perhaps, that because the working-class and nonwhite peoples now overlap to such a great degree, the combination of class and race resentments could put fire in their bellies? Better to divide the white- and the dark-skinned, the newly arrived and the long resident, than to face their unified protests against an economic miracle gone sour.

At the same time that the economic divide among the people has been widening, an even more egregious political gulf has opened up between the governing and the governed. This begins with the erosion of electoral representation. The voting public remains over 80 percent white, while the populace is only 56 percent white. The median age of the electorate is fifty, and two-thirds earn more than $40,000, while the median income over-all is only $16,400. People of Asian, African, and Latino origin represent 47 percent of the total population, 43 percent of all adults, 30 percent of the citizens eligible to vote, 24 percent of the registered voters, and only 17 percent of the actual voters in 1992. One-third of Latinos, for instance, are ineligible to vote by reason of youth, one-third by lack of citizenship, and of the remaining third only one in three is registered and one in six actually casts his or her ballot: in short, a total of only about one-thirteenth of the Latino population participates in electoral poli-tics. Anglos constituted 37 percent of Los Angeles's residents in 1992, and 12 percent of public school enrollment, but 70 percent of the active electorate; in contrast, Latinos made up 41 percent of the residents and 65 percent of the schoolchildren, but only 8 percent of the electorate in June 1992.[25]

The current political wisdom is that the crisis of California government stems from gridlock in Sacramento and antigovern-ment sentiment among the voters.[26] But the chief problem is a glaring lack of political legitimacy in a polity claiming to be a democratic republic, thanks to the disenfranchisement of the new majority of color. The electorate is an aging white elite dis-inclined to tax itself to pay for government spending on the needs of workers, people of color, and young people. The inter-ests of the mass of these working people for jobs, public educa-tion, or health care are not expressed by elected officials, who are overwhelmingly white and well-to-do. The political logic of the Republican Party's attack on immigrants, cutbacks to cities, and neglect of public schools is thus clear on simple electoral grounds. But neither vote counting nor personal enrichment suf-fices to account for the virulence of the ideological and political assault on the poor, the foreign, and the dark, to which we now turn.

They, the Criminals: The Political Attack on the Poor and the Alien

Faced with economic restructuring and social recomposition, the higher circles of California business and politics have little on offer. In place of industrial policy, educational programs, or strategies for political renewal, we get a reactionary agenda of lower taxes, police patrols, and reduced social expenditures. The basic trope in the ideological armory of the state's elite is the threat posed to the law-abiding citizen by the criminal, the poor, the foreign, and the dark-skinned. Covered up very nicely in the process is any reckoning of the sins of the white male burghers who dominate California's economy and polity.

The Criminalization of the Poor and Dark

California — particularly Los Angeles — has led the national wave of hysteria over crime and the criminal justice system in America over the last thirty years.[27] The Nixon administration unleashed the War on Crime in the face of mass social unrest and urban revolts, above all the Watts Rebellion. Large doses of federal money pumped into state and local governments inflated the legions of police, gave them new armaments, put more bite into criminal penalties, and built hundreds of prisons. All this was radically intensified under the banner of Ronald Reagan's War on Drugs, when Los Angeles's gang wars were engraved on public consciousness and Northern California marijuana fields came under aerial assault.[28] The recent wave of anticrime hysteria was topped off by the $30 billion federal Crime Bill passed in 1994, spurred by events such as the 1992 revolt in Los Angeles and the 1994 kidnapping-murder of the Bay Area's Polly Klaas (the Lindbergh baby of our time).[29]

Since the early 1980s, prison construction has been California's main form of infrastructural investment, with over $5 billion in nineteen new facilities. The 1994 Three Strikes initiative will require an estimated fifteen to twenty new prisons, costing another $20 billion. Vacaville (near Sacramento) is now home to the world's largest prison. The number of people incarcerated has increased from 23,000 in 1980 to 125,000 today (200,000 if one includes local jails and youth camps), and California jails more young black men than does South Africa. Although the salary of prison guards averages $47,000 per year, equal to the pay of a full professor in a state college, the state ranks among the worst in prison brutality (a federal court recently ruled that Pelican Bay, the state's "model" high-security prison, violates constitutional protections against inhumane torments).

While crime and violence are endemic to the United States,

the specter haunting the white and the elite is out of all proportion to the danger. People are arrested and incarcerated in larger
and larger numbers (the highest rates in the world), even though
crime rates have been level since 1970. Crime is still blamed
on lack of deterrence, despite the ineffectiveness of all the new
cops and hardware. The newest bugaboo is the repeat offender,
who can now be locked up for life after three felonies. Affluent
people lock themselves away in gated communities even though
most crime is perpetrated on the poor, and most violence is
wrought within the family. Crime has been radically racialized,
so that people of color are incarcerated at six times the rate of
whites. Even so, because whites are a larger percentage of the
total population, "angry white men" are the largest group com-
mitting crimes of violence; yet they are treated as victims (nine
out of ten murders are *intra*racial).[30]

The attack on the poor is of equally long standing, beginning
with Richard Nixon's dismantling of the War on Poverty and
Great Society housing programs. But it was Reagan who launched
the most virulent campaign to punish welfare mothers, subsi-
dized renters, and free-lunching schoolchildren. Not surprisingly,
social assistance cutbacks threw millions more into poverty and
hundreds of thousands onto the streets without shelter.[31] California's economic decline, stumbling working class, and sagging
safety net continue the Reaganauts' evil work. Statewide AFDC
(Aid for Families with Dependent Children) cases rose 40 percent from 1988 to 1993, even though benefits had fallen 20 percent
in real terms since 1973. While poverty has gone back to depression levels, general assistance has been cut to the nub by counties
all over the state in the name of budget balancing. Wilson's
Proposition 165 to punish welfare mothers was barely defeated
in 1992 — only to reappear as federal policy from the Newt Gingrich Congress. Riverside is now the site of the country's most
notorious experiment in forcing welfare recipients to take jobs,
regardless of the consequences for them, their children, or the
job market. Homelessness catapulted into public view as the
Reagan era hit home, but as time wore on pity turned to disgust.
Los Angeles police unleashed street sweeps to rid downtown of
thousands of vagrants in the late 1980s, and in 1992 San Francisco elected as mayor an ex–police chief who used his "Matrix
Plan" to arrest anyone sleeping in public places.[32] Draconian

antipanhandling laws have been passed in every town from San Diego to Berkeley.

The Anti-Immigrant and
Anti-Affirmative Action Campaigns

Now it is immigrants' turn to bear the brunt of reactionary venom. The Save Our State initiative of 1994, Proposition 187, sought to deprive undocumented immigrants of their rights to public schooling, health care, and welfare. It required school districts and service providers to verify the legal status of students and applicants and report to state officials and the INS (Immigration and Naturalization Service). Proposition 187 made a great deal of the "illegal" acts of some immigrants but was struck down by the courts as unconstitutional. Proposition 187 was the political brainchild of Californians Alan Nelson and Harold Ezell, former commissioners of the INS. Nelson became the chief Sacramento lobbyist for FAIR (Federation for American Immigration Reform), writing anti-immigrant bills for conservative legislators. A national organization, FAIR made its name in the English-only movement, teaming up with former California Senator S.I. Hiyakawa in 1984 and receiving $1 million from the white-supremacist Pioneer Fund. The campaign for 187 was organized by an ad hoc group out of Orange County called Save Our State, drawing on the same people, from Sacramento to Simi Valley, who had fought against busing and had engineered the tax revolt of 1978.[33] Proposition 187 would have gone nowhere, however, if Governor Wilson had not needed an issue to revive his popularity ratings for the 1994 gubernatorial election, lacking any other plausible ideas for solving California's problems. Equally galling was the haste with which Democratic senators Dianne Feinstein and Barbara Boxer jumped on the anti-immigrant bandwagon.

Nativism and opportunism overlay a base of economics. What pushed the anti-immigrant agitation to center stage was the state's permanent budget crisis, caused by a combination of recession and the tax revolt begun by Proposition 13 in 1978.[34] New people need schools, health care, and other government services that a bankrupt state cannot provide. In Pete Wilson's impeccable class calculus, well-to-do white people are the valued taxpayers, while poor immigrants and mothers are nothing but a fiscal burden. In fact, the great majority of recent immigrants to California are not poor and make little use of health and welfare services (the only large groups to do so are *political* refugees invited in by the U.S. government, principally Laotians, Cambodians, and Russians).[35] Overall, immigrants cost less in government services than they pay in taxes. Even Wilson admits that the problem for California is that the tax revenue goes to the federal government while the expenses are paid by the state.[36]

The recession recruited many people to the argument that immigrants take jobs away from "real" Americans.[37] No doubt there is competition, but labor market segmentation channels immigrants into certain employment niches and not others: some sectors, such as garments, that bloat up with sweatshops full of dirt-cheap immigrant labor, would not have expanded at all with more expensive resident labor. Competition for jobs has also increased because more people now work two or more jobs, more women and youth now participate in the labor force, and the number of unemployed workers in all categories remains high. But the crucial determinant is the preference of employers for cheaper and less militant workers. This sometimes shows up in the preference for immigrant labor, but it represents a broad-based strategy against labor in general through the use of temporary workers, part-timers, and subcontractors, as well as through age discrimination, antiunion actions, and the like. In the absence of immigrants, would white and black workers born in the United States have fared better? Not likely. After the mass layoffs of unionized manufacturing workers in the early 1980s, blacks remained unemployed in large numbers right through the height of California's economic boom; they were systematically uninvited to the industrial banquets in Orange County and Silicon Valley.[38] Meanwhile, unemployed white workers had the option of taking jobs in Las Vegas and other locations around the western United States that were booming from the spillover of branch plants and back offices from California.

The fear of immigrants has been driven by the widespread notion that masses of impoverished Third World people are washing onto our affluent shores. But immigrants go where the jobs are, not to regions with poor job opportunities. Migrants are drawn overwhelmingly more by labor demand than they are pushed out of their home countries by poverty, as the close correspondence of business cycles and migration cycles shows. California has drawn very selectively from the worldwide pool of potential migrants and only a small proportion of the world's people have wanted to immigrate here.[39] Employers fish in seas of potential labor. In-migrants tend to be funneled directly into job opportunities. Employers, in fact, regularly recruit in foreign countries — directly, indirectly by leaving it to ethnic labor contractors, or informally by word of mouth. Word passes along immigrant social networks that are remarkably effective in funneling immigrants from specific locales in the sending countries to specific workplaces and neighborhoods in the United States. Once employers begin to hire pioneer immigrants, they set in motion "chains of migration" that keep the labor market well stocked.[40] They may reel workers in for a very long time before the chain of migration breaks.

The central trope in the Proposition 187 movement was the campaign against *illegals*. Again and again one heard the cry, "But they're breaking the law," putting immigration on a par with theft and violence. The civil rights movement and particularly the Civil Rights Acts of 1964 and 1968 had, of course, previously rendered a whole host of restrictions on citizenship, marriage, and voting illegal, and the Immigration Reform Act of 1965 overturned the draconian National Origins Act of 1924. After a generation of relatively open immigration, three restrictive laws were passed by Congress in quick succession: the Refugee Act of 1980, the Immigration Reform and Control Act (ICRA) of 1986, and the Immigration Act of 1990. The ICRA defined illegal aliens as people living in the United States without official government sanction, and it imposed fines against employers that have not been enforced. White people's hypocrisy was everywhere in evidence, as those who regularly hired immigrants to mow their lawns, clean house, and tend their children suddenly raised a hue and cry over illegal aliens (typically, senatorial candidates Michael Huffington and Feinstein were both shown to have hired undocumented immigrants as domestics and to have failed to pay the legally required social security taxes for them).

Most "illegal aliens" — including large numbers of Europeans and Canadians — do not, in fact, sneak across the border but enter legally and overstay their visas. Consider the hundreds of thousands of Mexicanos who move in a continuous circuit back and forth across the border: with family and friends on both sides, they return to home villages frequently for holidays, births, and funerals — or permanently after building a nest egg for marriage, investment, or retirement. Half of those crossing the border into the United States "illegally" already have jobs here to which they are returning. This binationalism is utterly obscure to most whites, as typified by Wilson's remonstrance to President Ernesto Zedillo to "butt out of California's business" for expressing concern over Proposition 187.[41]

Affirmative action has been a target of conservative agitation in California for many years. In 1978 Alan Bakke won the precedent-setting case against the University of California at Davis medical school for "reverse discrimination" against white males. Reagan took up the counteroffensive when he entered the White House, putting the Civil Rights Commission in the hands of Clarence Thomas and his ilk. But affirmative action had, meanwhile, become deeply institutionalized in this state, from local government contracting to University of California admissions policies. Recession and the rightward trajectory of Governor Pete Wilson opened the doors for a renewed campaign against it. This trajectory responded to the fears of job competition among the professional and unionized strata of the labor force in much the same way that immigrant bashing spoke for the unemployed common worker, including African Americans. But once again political ideology and opportunism had the upper hand. Hard on the heels of Proposition 187 came a proposal for a new ballot measure in 1996, cleverly titled the California Civil Rights Initiative (CCRI) by two academics with links to Reed Irvine and Dinesh D'Souza's moribund Accuracy in Academia campaign against political correctness in the classroom. Wilson seized on polls showing CCRI to be a winner and hoped that taking on affirmative action would propel him to the presidency. Wilson's henchman on the Board of Regents, Ward Connerly (a businessman whose success was leveraged by state contracts set aside for minority businesses), led the charge to remove affirmative action from the university system, over the protests of the president of the university and the chancellors of all nine of its campuses, in a nationally showcased decision in mid-1995.

Us and Them: The Politics of Race and Reaction

California has often embodied the best of the American jugger-naut. It has been a place where millions of enterprising people have been able to work for a good pay, exploit the abundance of nature, buy a little property, exercise their imagination, cast their ballots, and maybe even make the leap into the ranks of the bour-geoisie. Impressive opportunity, political openness, and equality were available by comparison with most of the world and with most of capitalist America. Yet California's American identity was hammered out in the mid–nineteenth century at the height of the formation of the racialist ideology of what Alexander Saxton and David Roedinger have called "the White Republic."[42] So California was not only "the one successful revolution of 1848" for the cosmopolitan mix of petit bourgeois argonauts, but equally the triumph of Anglo-Saxon Manifest Destiny on the shore of the Pacific.[43] For the next century, white Americans dominated the body politic. But after World War II the sun began setting on their golden century, as citizenry, law, and ideology underwent epochal shifts due to migration, civil rights struggles, and the disruption of racial triumphalism. Of late, we see Cali-fornia's reactionaries conjuring up the ghost of the White Re-public in hopes of recovering a lost sense of unity among the privileged and unprivileged among the pre-immigration popu-lace. But will the genie perform its magic this time round, in a period not of economic and racial triumphalism but of sustained threat to the old order?

In California's blood-stained racial history, the list of horrors unleashed in the name of commercial conquest and the civilizing mission of the white race is long. The native peoples were mur-dered and enslaved, the Californios divested of their property, African Americans denied the rights of citizenship, the Chinese lynched and driven into ghettos, the Japanese denied land as their enterprise proved threatening, Mexicans deported en masse when labor surpluses appeared in the Great Depression, and Japanese Americans thrown into concentration camps in the Second World War. This is the tragic face of a land in which for-tune smiled on so many, one hidden so well that most whites have lost the memory of their own selection as the children of America's Israel.[44]

California has an equally ignoble history of invidious racial ideology to inspire and justify its practices. One has only to read Richard Henry Dana on the Californios or John Muir on the Basque sheepherders or James Phelan, William Randolph Hearst, and Michael DeYoung on the Yellow Peril at the turn of the century. By the 1920s, Lewis Terman of Stanford, codeveloper of the IQ test, was calling Mexicans "uneducable," and practical eugenicists were sterilizing more "defectives" in mental hospitals and prisons in California than anywhere else in the United States.[45] In the 1960s and 1970s, William Shockley of semiconductor fame and Arthur Jensen of UC Berkeley were the foremost exponents of African genetic inferiority. Today, biologists Paul Ehrlich of Stanford and Garrett Hardin of UC Santa Barbara provide scientific cover for FAIR, peddling fear of inundation by the "fast-breeding races" of the Third World.

Despite the panorama of racism, however, the record is not of a piece. The White Republic of Euro-Americans was constituted from the encounter with subjugated peoples, but in California and the West it was forged in the crucible of a multiple encounter that included Latinos and Asians, as well as Native Americans and Africans. The right to feast at California's petit bourgeois banquet depended heavily on appearance and place of origin, with different races having radically different points of entry into the class structure.[46] White supremacism, unleashed with its full fury against the Indians, was modulated in other cases by ambiguity and conflict: the resistence and partial legitimacy of the Californio elite, who were themselves substantially of European origin and commercialized; the nineteenth-century legal struggles of African Americans and Chinese Americans, as in the successful invocation of the Fourteenth Amendment in *Yick Wo v. Hopkins* (1886); the protests of the Japanese government and Japanese American evasions of the Alien Land Law of 1913; the changing view of the embattled Chinese, who were converted to "honorary Caucasians" in the 1940s.[47] To this mix must be added the purifications of the Anglo-Saxons by means of racialization and class hatred visited on certain "whites," from the vigilante hangings of Australians and Irish in the 1850s to the hysteria over Okies and hobo armies in the 1930s.[48]

In the end, California was often less racist than the rest of the United States, allowing many Africans, Chinese, Japanese, Filipinos, and Mexicans to live and work in peace. That degree of freedom was created by countervailing power, as well as a counterpoint of cosmopolitan tolerance. It can be found in Ross Browne's polemics against the slaughter of the Indians and John Rollin Ridge's heroic rendition of the outlaw Joaquin Murieta; in the ironies of Mark Twain and Ambrose Bierce; in Helen Hunt Jackson's and Charles Lummis's romances with "America's mediterranean"; in Mary Austin's and the Berkeley anthropologists' embrace of the indigenous Californians; and in Carey McWilliams's brilliant denunciations of racism. And it shows up in a thousand humble achievements of multiracial settlement and work.[49]

But the turn of the wheel came during the civil rights era, with beginnings in the 1930s and World War II. The 1930s brought collaboration between the Black Sleeping Car Porters and the middle-class NAACP (National Association for the Advancement of Colored People), as well as between white and black reformers, as evidenced in the fight for the first African American schoolteacher in Berkeley. The Longshoremen's Union that emerged from the General Strike of 1934 was racially integrated, as were the farmworkers' unions of the 1930s. Blacks won legal suits against all-white unions in the wartime shipyards and won the right to integrated public housing. The first school desegregation order came in the California case of *Mendez v. Westminster* (1946), which was enforced by Governor Earl Warren. Victories against miscegenation and naturalization restrictions were won in the courts in the late 1940s. The black leadership finally won employment and housing victories with the statewide Fair Employment Practices Act in 1959 and the Fair Housing Act of 1963. The Black Power movement turned up the heat; Oakland's Black Panthers were the most symbolically charged players in the political theater of a rebellious time. The efforts of Asian and Latino activists added further impetus to battles for Third World colleges and ethnic studies programs. In the 1980s, California universities finally opened their doors to large numbers of nonwhite undergraduates, and Stanford and UC Berkeley became the first colleges to institute non-Eurocentric academic requirements.[50] By 1980, Oakland had become the most integrated city of significant size in the United States, and a remarkable diaspora of middle-class people of various races into former bastions of white exclusion was well under way.

We must therefore be careful not to lay the blame for the present recrudescence of nativism and white supremacy simply on a universal white racism, as if the high tide of Anglo-Saxonism had never receded and as if class and economy played no role in how people are dominated and denigrated. Class and politics must be foregrounded in the study of racial formation. To do this, the dialectic of class and race must first be taken seriously. It is not enough to insert races in a class structure and declare race the central stratifying variable. The scramble for class power and privilege has lent particular force to the suppression of contending "races," and the denigration of those at the bottom of the class system has gone hand in hand with racial character assassination. Not by accident were Africans equated with slaves, Mexicans with hacienda peonage, and Chinese with "coolie labor":[51] Euro-American burghers equated working-class poverty, manual labor, and scruffy appearance with darkness, inferiority, and difference, which fit comfortably with the standard racist tropes.[52] So it is not surprising that white immigrants and workers traded one kind of racialization to escape another in buying into the White Republic. The antiracist literature has been a valuable counterweight to naive Marxist class analysis, but the danger is that the industrialists, financiers, petit bourgeoisie, plantation owners, and merchants disappear.[53] The white working class, for all its racism, has never been in a position to dictate the terms of racial conquest and class encounter. One must therefore keep a sharp eye on the upper classes and their purposes: the commercial and slave interests behind the war with Mexico, the merchant base of the anti-Irish Vigilantes, the petit bourgeois character of the Forty-Niners, the opportunism of Leland Stanford and the railroad magnates in the use and disposal of Chinese labor, the hysteria of imperialist-minded newspaper moguls against the Japanese, the upper-class disdain for defections among the eugenicists, the competitive threat presented by Japanese farmers, the agribusiness role in expelling increasingly militant Mexicans, the Los Angeles Times' instigation of the Zoot Suit riots, and so on.[54]

Second, politics must be taken seriously as a force for change.[55] The White Republic, Manifest Destiny, Chinese Exclusion, Yellow Peril, and the rest were all politically inspired initiatives that became part of the racial structure of the United States by virtue of their political success. Conversely, the liberal opening of the civil rights era was a political achievement against a background of Nazi Germany's racial holocaust, economic prosperity for most of the United States, and the country's imperial role as bulwark against communism and nationalist revolution. So, too, is the reactionary race and class offensive of the last twenty years a political phenomenon in which California has played a leading role. This has not been a working-class movement but an elite war of position. It has had its minions among the everyday folk, the Christians and faith-healers of the market, but it has been led, funded, and imagined by the powerful, and the evidence of their backing and benefit is overwhelming.[56] Despite the right-wing chorus of racial disharmony, the majority of white people in California have welcomed immigrants as fellow workers, neighbors, and members of the commonwealth. It has been political opportunism and mass disenfranchisement, more than popular sentiment from below, that has turned Proposition 187 into a winner and threatens affirmative action programs.

Conclusion

Every epoch is a mortal thing that eventually sickens. It may give way to rebirth of the social order or to perpetual senility — even to barbarity and calamity.[57] California's extraordinary record of expansion left the state with a massive set of strains on its economy, government, and social cohesion. The hasty termination of the social experimentation and political revolt of the 1960s, however, left Californians unable to see their way clear to reconvert the war industries; integrate racially; reconstruct rotting cities; reconfigure corporations; salvage public education; or spend public monies for recovery, employment, and universal health care. The failure of imagination rests partly on bourgeois ideological reflexes, but behind such a failure lies a political impasse born of the right-wing hold on the public agenda. If we are not to mourn the passing of the late, great Golden State, there must be change at the top caused by energy and anger from below.

Can the forces of social reclamation rise again? Promising challenges to the white establishment are now coming from the many hyphenated Americans of post–Anglo California: for example, Mexican Americans are struggling over redistricting in Los Angeles County, Chinese Americans for the first time hold a majority on Monterey Park's city council, and the state's first

Filipino American public official has been elected in Daly City. Proposition 187's threat to the foreign-born has induced hundreds of thousands to seek citizenship in the last year; ironically, Pete Wilson may have written off precisely these potential votes in order to win the 1994 election. When Wilson's presidential campaign petered out, it lent hope that California's anti-immigrant and anti–affirmative action viruses would not spread. Aspiring minority burghers are being politicized by racial attacks, as demonstrated by the formation of the well-heeled Coalition for Immigrant and Refugee Rights. Significantly, tens of thousands of Latino high-schoolers with little political experience turned out against 187, and their march of over one hundred thousand may be the largest demonstration ever held in Los Angeles.[58] Fortunately for California, the racial divide here remains a complex escarpment, not simply a Grand Canyon of black-white incomprehension and mistrust. Nonetheless, the immigrant and antiracist awakening of the 1990s has a long way to go if it is to overcome the political legacy and economic somnolence of the Anglo bourgeoisie.

NOTES

Many thanks to Jeff Lustig and Jorgé Lizárraga for their input to related papers on which this draws.

1. Margaret Gordon, *Employment Expansion and Population Growth* (Berkeley, 1954); and Richard Walker and Jorgé Lizárraga, "California in Flux: Immigration, Economic Growth, and Working Class Welfare," in Anibal Yanez and Lionel Maldonado, eds., *Immigration: The Panic, the Promise* (forthcoming).

2. Half of every major immigrant group in Los Angeles worked in such niches in 1990. Of eighty-three large manufacturing industries counted in the 1990 census, fifty-three were Mexican employment niches. A *niche* is defined as ethnic concentration 50 percent greater than the proportion of that group in the whole working population. Figures from Roger Waldinger and Mehdi Bozorgmehr, eds., *Ethnic Los Angeles* (forthcoming). On labor market segmentation in general, see Alice Amsden, ed., *The Economics of Women and Work* (New York, 1980); Michael Reich, *Racial Inequality* (Princeton, 1981); David Gordon, Richard Edwards, and Michael Reich, *Segmented Work, Divided Workers* (New York, 1982); William Dickens and Kevin Lang, "The Reemergence of Segmented Labor Market Theory," *American Economic Review* 78 (1988): 129–34.

3. See Waldinger and Bozorgmehr, *Ethnic Los Angeles*, and Ivan Light and Edna Bonacich, *Immigrant Entrepreneurs: Koreans in Los Angeles, 1965–1982* (Berkeley, 1988).

4. Waldinger and Bozorgmehr, *Ethnic Los Angeles*, ask, "When else do we find a parallel in American ethnic history?" but seem unaware that the answer is "In California, especially San Francisco." See, e.g., William Issel and Robert Cherny, *San Francisco: 1865–1930* (Berkeley, 1986), chap. 3. Also see Gordon, *Employment Expansion*, 13–17.

5. Gordon, *Employment Expansion*, chap. 6; Walker and Lizárraga, "California in Flux." On transatlantic migration of the last century, see Brinley Thomas, *Migration and Economic Growth* (Cambridge, 1974).

6. On the economic history of California, see Richard Walker, "Another Round of Globalization in San Francisco," *Urban Geography* 17, no. 1 (1996): 60–94.

7. Employment and trade data from State of California. Also see H. Poniachek, *Direct Foreign Investment in the United States* (Lexington, MA, 1988).

8. For overviews of Los Angeles and San Francisco at the end of the 1980s, see Mike Davis, *City of Quartz* (London, 1990); Edward Soja, *Post-Modern Geographies* (London, 1989); and Richard Walker and the Bay Area Study Group, "The Playground of U.S. Capitalism? The political economy of the San Francisco Bay Area in the 1980s," in Mike Davis et al., eds., *Fire in the Hearth* (London, 1990), 3–82.

9. On California's role in the defense buildup, see Ann Markusen et al., *The Rise of the Gunbelt* (New York, 1991). On the electronic and aerospace technopoles, see Annalee Saxenian, *Regional Advantage* (Cambridge, MA, 1994); Allen Scott, *New Industrial Spaces* (London, 1988); Allen Scott, *Technopolis* (Los Angeles, 1993). Other key sectors are entertainment, agribusiness, garments, metal- and woodworking, machining, medicine and biotech, trade and transport, utilities, and construction.

10. On the financial bubble, see Martin Mayer, *The Greatest-Ever Bank Robbery* (New York, 1990); Michael Lewis, *Liar's Poker* (New York, 1989); Steven Pizzo, Mary Fricker, and Paul Muolo, *Inside Job: The Looting of America's Savings and Loans* (San Francisco, 1989); Moira Johnston, *Roller Coaster* (New York, 1990); Michael Robinson, *Overdrawn: The Bailout of American Savings* (New York, 1990). Construction figures from the State of California, presented in Walker and Lizárraga, "California in Flux."

11. For migration, employment, and wage data, see Walker and Lizárraga, "California in Flux," and Gordon, *Employment Expansion*.

12. The plunder of natural wealth, from gold and silver to oil and lumber, has also played a considerable role. See again Walker, "Another Round"; Scott,

Technopolis; Saxenian, *Regional Advantage*; and Harvey Molotch, "Los Angeles as Product: How Design Works in a Regional Economy," in Allen Scott and Edward Soja, eds., *The City: Los Angeles and Urban Theory at the End of the Twentieth Century* (forthcoming).

13. On job shrinkage in Southern California, see Allen Scott, "The New Southern California Economy: Pathways to Industrial Resurgence," *Economic Development Quarterly* (forthcoming): table 1; and Mike Davis, "Who Killed LA? Part I: A Political Autopsy," *New Left Review* 197 (1993): 3–28, and "Part II: The Verdict Is Given," *New Left Review* 199 (1993): 29–54.

14. On the financial debacle, see references in note 10.

15. Unemployment figures from the California Employment Development Department, cited in the *San Francisco Examiner*, 4 November 1992, C1; and the *New York Times*, 19 December 1995, C22. On discouraged immigrants see "Illegal Immigrants Sour on California," *San Francisco Examiner*, 9 January 1994, B3; and "Huge California Exodus as Economy Plunged," *San Francisco Chronicle*, 2 September 1993, A1 (600,000 people left California for the rest of the United States, June 1992–93, while only 450,000 people went the other way). For annual figures on migration and unemployment by race, see Walker and Lizárraga, "California in Flux."

16. For a budding recognition of the task facing California, see Council on California Competitiveness, *California's Future and Jobs* (Sacramento, 1992); and Stephen Levy and R. Arnold, *The Outlook for the California Economy* (Palo Alto, CA, 1992).

17. For a general statement of this idea, see Michael Storper and Richard Walker, *The Capitalist Imperative* (Oxford, 1989). For a recent appraisal of California's improving fortunes, see B.D. Ayres, "California's Economy Shows Signs of Regaining Its Glitter," *New York Times*, 19 December 1995, A1, C22.

18. While only 11 percent of U.S. adults lived in California in 1990, the same year 17 percent of all U.S. millionaires (IRS estimates reported in the *San Francisco Examiner*, 21 August 1990) and 20 percent of the *Forbes* 400 richest Americans resided in the state.

19. *San Francisco Chronicle*, "Annual Report on Executive Compensation," 23 May 1994, B1. The United States has the highest average salaries of CEOs and the lowest productivity gains since 1980 of any country in the world. Andrew Shapiro, "We're Number One," *Nation*, 27 April 1992, 552.

20. California ranked thirteenth among the states in worsening inequality in the 1980s. Figures by quintiles from a study by the Center on Budget and Policy Priorities, Washington, D.C., reported in the *San Francisco Examiner*, 22 August 1994, A6.

21. On the declining fortunes of the American working class as a whole,

see Bennett Harrison and Barry Bluestone, *The Great U-Turn* (New York, 1988); Kevin Phillips, *The Politics of Rich and Poor* (New York, 1990); Juliet Schor, *The Overworked American* (New York, 1991).

22. See the various studies in Waldinger and Bozorgmehr, *Ethnic Los Angeles*.

23. In the San Joaquin Valley, heart of agribusiness, county poverty rates are all over 20 percent and public assistance rates are around 30 percent. Child poverty figures from a study by Victor Fuchs and Diane Reklis of Stanford, reported in the *San Francisco Chronicle*, 3 January 1992, A1; see also the excellent periodic reports by groups such as Children Now, Children's Advocacy Institute, and California Tomorrow.

24. Phillips, *Politics of Rich and Poor*; Schor, *Overworked American*; Barry Bluestone, "The Inequality Express," *American Prospect* 20 (Winter 1994): 80–91.

25. Figures from the *San Francisco Chronicle*, 22 September 1994, A4, and from Leo Estrada, paper presented at the conference "A State Divided," Sacramento, 16 November 1994.

26. For a sharp commentary on "California's Elected Anarchy" see Peter Schrag, *Harper's*, November 1994, 50–57. Schrag, however, stresses "perfectionism" as the cause of the problem, and neglects the systematic rightward swing in politics and the class and race power behind it. For a longer analysis of the political and governmental imbroglio of California, see Richard Walker, "California Rages Against the Dying of the Light," *New Left Review* 209 (1995): 42–74.

27. Thanks to Tony Platt, California State University–Sacramento, in a personal communication with the author, for the basic facts on the war on crime.

28. For a telling portrait of the War on Drugs, see Davis, *City of Quartz*. On marijuana, see Ray Raphael, *Cash Crop: An American Dream* (Mendocino, CA, 1985).

29. Had it not been for the Polly Klaas tragedy, the Three Strikes initiative would not have passed the California legislature or been included in the national crime bill. Its three biggest backers, by far, were Michael Huffington, the California Correctional Peace Officers, and the National Rifle Association.

30. Figures from Tony Platt, in a personal communication with the author, and from Doug Henwood, *Left Business Observer*, no. 62 (7 March 1994): 3.

31. Fred Block et al., *The Mean Season: The Attack on the Welfare State* (New York, 1987); Herb Gans, *The War Against the Poor: The Underclass and Anti-poverty Policy* (New York, 1995).

32. On homelessness in Los Angeles, see Jennifer Wolch and Michael Dear, *Malign Neglect* (San Francisco, 1993); and on Matrix, see Scott Winokur,

"Frank Jordan's War on the Homeless," *San Francisco Examiner Magazine*, 6 November 1994, 14–30; and *San Francisco Chronicle*, 13 December 1993, A1.

33. *San Francisco Examiner*, 12 December 1993, A10; Mike Davis, "California Über Alles," *Red Pepper* (January 1995): 30–31; Elizabeth Kadetsky, "Bashing Illegals in California," *Nation*, 17 October 1994, 416–22.

34. On the budget crisis, see Walker, "California Rages"; Jeff Lustig and Dick Walker, "No Way Out: Immigrants and the New California," (Berkeley, 1995); Lenny Goldberg, *Taxation with Representation* (Sacramento, 1991).

35. The vast majority of immigrants to California are in fact not poor, according to William Frey, University of Michigan Population Studies Center, reported in the *San Francisco Chronicle*, 10 December 1993, A1. A host of contending studies exist on immigrants' use of welfare benefits, each one resting on different definitions of immigrant households and types of benefits. None shows markedly higher welfare payments to immigrants compared to families born in the United States (some show lower payments), especially when adjusted for poverty rates, family size, and age. The best overview is Michael Fix and Jeffrey S. Passel, *Immigration and Immigrants: Setting the Record Straight* (Washington, D.C., 1994).

36. The Urban Institute estimates the revenue gap for undocumented immigrants (as many as one million in California) at $1.8 billion versus Governor Wilson's estimate of $2.5 billion, most of which is for schooling. By comparison, the fifty thousand gunshot wounds suffered each year cost the state roughly the same amount in medical fees as undocumented workers' children cost to educate (about $1.1 billion). Calculation on gun violence costs by the California Research Bureau, reported in the *San Francisco Chronicle*, 22 October 1994.

37. *Los Angeles Times* exit polls showed that 187's main backers were Republicans, men, whites, and older people (income was not a good indicator, however, and the positions of blacks and Asians were midway between those of white and Latino voters).

38. On black unemployment in South Central Los Angeles, see Mike Davis, "The LA Inferno," *Socialist Review* 92 (1992): 57–80; and on Orange County, see Scott, *New Industrial Spaces*, and Scott, *Technopolis*.

39. The classic argument for the priority of labor demand over supply conditions is Michael Piore, *Birds of Passage* (New York, 1979).

40. On networks and immigration as a social process, see Douglas Massey et al., *Return to Aztlan* (Berkeley, 1987).

41. On the migratory circuits of Mexicans, see *ibid*. On recent binational politics, see Jésus Martinez Saldaña, "At the Periphery of Democracy" (Ph.D. diss., University of California at Berkeley, 1993).

42. Alexander Saxton, *The Rise and Fall of the White Republic* (London, 1991); and David Roedinger, *The Wages of Whiteness* (London, 1991).

43. Reginald Horsman, *Race and Manifest Destiny* (Cambridge, MA, 1982); and Gray Brechin, *Imperial San Francisco* (forthcoming). California was a combination of commercial empire and racial conquest, as both Horsman and Brechin make clear.

44. On California's legacy of racism, see, e.g., Sucheng Chan, *Asian Americans* (Boston, 1991); Rodolfo Acuña, *Occupied America* (New York, 1988); Roger Daniels, *The Politics of Prejudice* (Berkeley, 1977); Albert Camarillo, *Chicanos in California* (San Francisco, 1984); Albert Hurtado, *Indian Survival on the California Frontier* (New Haven, 1988); Douglas Daniels, *Pioneer Urbanites: A Social and Cultural History of Black San Francisco* (Philadelphia, 1980); Rudolph Lapp, *Afro-Americans in California* (San Francisco, 1987).

45. See again Brechin, *Imperial San Francisco*; and Gray Brechin, "Conserving the Race: Natural Aristocracies, Eugenics, and the U.S. Conservation Movement," *Antipode* 28, no. 4 (1996): 229–45.

46. Tomás Almaguer, *Racial Fault Lines* (Berkeley, 1994). Almaguer follows a long line of Chicano scholars and new Western historians in arguing for the distinctiveness of the Western regional experience, which is less determined by black-white relations than by relations between several different cultures. Horsman goes even farther in arguing that white supremacy in the whole United States was influenced decisively by the war with Mexico and the westward conquest.

47. For examples of struggle against white domination, see again the sources in note 43, as well as Almaguer, *Racial Fault Lines*.

48. See, e.g., Robert Senkewicz, *Vigilantes in Gold Rush San Francisco* (Palo Alto, CA, 1985); Robert Burchell, *The San Francisco Irish, 1848–1880* (Berkeley, 1980); James Gregory, *American Exodus* (New York, 1991).

49. Despite the efforts of black scholars such as Douglas Daniels to undercut the smug cant of cosmopolitan tolerance in San Francisco, a realistic picture still allows that things were often much better there than elsewhere in the United States. See especially Larry Crouchett, Lonnie Bunch, and Martha Winnacker, *Visions Toward Tomorrow: The History of the East Bay Afro-American Community, 1852–1977* (Oakland, CA, 1989). See, e.g., J. Ross Browne, *The Indians of California* (San Francisco, 1856); John Rollin Ridge, *The Life and Adventures of Joaquin Murieta, the Celebrated California Bandit* (San Francisco, 1854); Helen Hunt Jackson, *A Century of Dishonor: A Sketch of the United States Government's Dealings with Some of the Indian Tribes* (Boston, 1888); and the many works of Carey McWilliams (see note 54).

50. Of course, multiculturalism is itself a problematic slogan that refers

principally to integration for the upper classes. See Katharyne Mitchell, "Multiculturalism, or the United Colors of Capitalism," *Antipode* 25 (1993): 263–94.

51. For a nuanced treatment of the pivotal role of slavery in white racism in the United States, see Audrey Smedley, *Race in North America* (Boulder, CO, 1993).

52. See Etienne Balibar's essays in Etienne Balibar and Immanuel Wallerstein, *Race, Nation, Class* (London, 1991); and Robert Miles, *Racism After "Race Relations"* (London, 1993). Conversely, Anglo-Saxon and Republican ideologies were well established before they became racialized. Horsman, *Race and Manifest Destiny*, chaps. 1 and 2; Smedley, *Race in North America.*

53. See, e.g., Alexander Saxton, *The Indispensible Enemy: Labor and the Anti-Chinese Movement in California* (Berkeley, 1971); Michael Kazin, *Barons of Labor* (Urbana, IL, 1987); Daniels, *Pioneer Urbanites*; and, more generally, Michael Omi and Howard Winant, *Racial Formation in the United States* (New York, 1986).

54. One would do well to start from the superlative work of Carey McWilliams, such as *Factories in the Fields* (Boston, 1939); *Ill Fares the Land* (Boston, 1942); *North from Mexico* (New York, 1961); and *Prejudice: Japanese Americans, Symbol of Racial Intolerance* (Boston, 1944).

55. Martin Carnoy, *Faded Dreams: The Politics and Economics of Race in America* (New York, 1994).

56. See again references at note 21 and note 31. On the new Right's class and race agenda, see, besides Carnoy, *Faded Dreams*; Mike Davis, *Prisoners of the American Dream* (London, 1986); Fred Block et al., *The Mean Season*; James Ridgeway, *Blood in the Face* (New York, 1990); David Roedinger, "The Racial Crisis of American Liberalism," *New Left Review* 196 (1992): 114–19; Cornel West, *Race Matters* (Boston, 1993); Kevin Phillips, *Boiling Point* (New York, 1993); Howard Winant, *Racial Conditions* (Minneapolis, 1994); Stephen Steinberg, *Turning Back* (Boston, 1995).

57. For the longer view, see Perry Anderson, "The Figures of Descent," *New Left Review* 161 (1987): 20–77.

58. Elizabeth Kadetsky, "School's Out," *Nation*, 21 November 1994, 601.

Casuistry

Cass R. Sunstein

Is affirmative action a desirable social practice? My principal claim in this essay is that there is no sensible answer to that question. Affirmative action is best evaluated by close reference to details and consequences, not by blanket rule. It is easy to imagine race-conscious programs that serve important social goals. It is also easy to imagine race-conscious programs that disserve their intended beneficiaries and in any case compromise values that people do and should accept. It is easy, too, to imagine ambiguous intermediate cases.

These points — a defense of *casuistry* in the context of affirmative action — argue strongly against California Proposition 209 and the process that produced it. They bear as well on the general question of government by referendum.

I seek to support this argument partly with reference to the practices of the Supreme Court. The Court has heard a large number of affirmative action cases, but it has taken no general stand on the legitimacy of affirmative action policies. Instead it has proceeded in a narrow, case-specific fashion. In doing so, the Court can be understood to have signaled the general importance and difficulty of the underlying issues, and also to have "modeled" how democratic participants might deal with those issues. The major defect in the debate over the California initiative is that it involved broad and abstract judgments that only modestly illuminated the issues at hand; the major defect in the initiative itself is that it is far too rule-bound, too obtuse, to make sense.

More specifically, I start with the suggestion that the issue of affirmative action should be settled democratically, not judicially.

Certainly the Supreme Court should not invalidate most race-conscious remedial programs. But until recently, there has been little or no sustained democratic deliberation on that issue. The citizenry's ambivalence about — or hostility toward — affirmative action has been expressed mostly privately and not in public arenas. The enormous diversity of affirmative action programs, not to mention the separable justifications for and variable efficacy of such programs, has not received much public attention. Some such programs work well, while some do not; and public judgments about their content and value have rarely been reflected in program design. In these circumstances the Supreme Court's apparently odd behavior in the affirmative action context might be defended as performing a valuable catalytic function. The Court's willingness to hear a number of affirmative action cases, and its complex, rule-free, highly casuistical opinions, have had the salutary consequence of helping to stimulate public processes and of directing the citizenry toward open discussion of underlying questions of policy and principle. In these ways the Court's route has been far preferable to the most obvious alternatives: validation or invalidation of most affirmative action programs pursuant to clear doctrinal categories.

But there is a catch. In the context of Proposition 209, serious doubts might be raised about judicial efforts to stimulate democratic processes. It is far from clear that current public processes are sufficiently deliberative, especially in the area of race. A referendum on race-related issues is too likely to be crude, insufficiently connected with the particulars of the issues that it covers. Certainly this is the case with California Proposition 209. This point raises difficult problems for any defense of the Court's attempted catalytic function; it suggests the importance of efforts to improve democratic processes by replacing accusations and sound bites with closer engagement with the problems at hand. Representative politics has crucial structural advantages over public referenda in this regard, in part because casuistry, understood as a word of praise and charitably conceived, is so unlikely to take place in the context of a referendum.

Social Norms and Public Debate

Let us begin by attempting to see how the Supreme Court might until very recently have understood the affirmative action problem. Notice first that people often think one thing but say another, because social pressures and social norms affect what can be said in public.[1] For example, in most circles in contemporary America, there is a strong social stigma against anti-Semitic statements; people who think anti-Semitic things are unlikely to make such statements on television or in a public debate. In many groups in which religious convictions are both deep and widespread, people cannot confess their uncertainty about whether God exists; they may attend church regularly despite their doubts. In other places, people cannot acknowledge that they are deeply religious; in such places social norms punish public declarations of religious convictions. The general point is simple: social norms drive a wedge between public statements and private beliefs, hopes, and convictions.

"Political correctness" is no isolated phenomenon limited to left-leaning intellectuals. It is a pervasive fact of social life. It appears whenever prevailing norms discourage people from taking issue with a widely held social belief. Those interested in democratic politics should notice the omnipresent role of *public constraints on public statements*.

Is the existence of such constraints something to be lamented? No simple answer would make sense. Sometimes social norms have a healthy "laundering effect," by imposing sanctions on vicious or invidious judgments. The existence of social sanctions can make people embarrassed about those judgments and eventually make them recede or even disappear. If hypocrisy is the tribute vice pays to virtue, then social norms should identify both vice and virtue as such and enable citizens to tell which is which. Hypocrisy can therefore have valuable social uses. It has a civilizing effect.[2] It can produce justice by making unjust behavior seem vicious or otherwise unacceptable.

On the other hand, social norms of the kind I am discussing can cause damage in two different ways. First, they may prevent people from offering arguments that are productive, reasonable, or even right. If prevailing norms are invidious or rooted in confusion, they may even perpetuate invidious or confused practices. Consider the many areas in the world in which social norms strongly discourage advocacy of sex equality; many women who indicate their belief in equality run enormous risks. Second, social norms may discourage the expression of doubt, even when doubt exists and when debate is (partly for that very reason) desirable. In that way prevailing norms can damage processes of public deliberation. Even if prevailing norms are not invidious on their merits — even if they reflect clear thinking or hard-won wisdom — their effects can be pernicious when they impair public deliberation. In a well-functioning democracy, facts and options are clarified through doubt, and people have a sense of what their fellow citizens think.

Of course this is a complex matter. Not everything can be discussed at once; at any time many things must be taken for granted. Some things are properly taken as so obvious that they "go without saying." But in many areas it is safe to say that democratic processes would be better if public debate focused on what really concerns people.

From the standpoint of both law and democratic theory, a great deal needs to be done on this important topic. We do not know the extent to which private judgments are not expressed publicly, even when they are quite widespread, and when the reason for silence is that social norms impose sanctions on those judgments. What we do know is that in the context of race, social norms can make public discussion less candid than it would otherwise be, not least in the context of affirmative action. There are contexts in which those who approve of affirmative action are punished, via social norms, for saying so; there are contexts in which those who disapprove of affirmative action are punished, via social norms, for saying so. And the effects of social norms, in this area, have changed dramatically over time. These points are highly relevant to the debate over California Proposition 209 and also to the role of the Supreme Court in American government.

The Supreme Court as Catalyst

What is the relationship between the Supreme Court and democratic judgments? It seems obvious to say that when the Supreme Court faces a constitutional attack on a law, it has three basic options: it may uphold the law, invalidate the law, or refuse to address the issue, by denying certiorari or by taking advantage of one or another strategy of avoidance.

A detailed literature discusses the third and least obvious of these options.[3] On a familiar view, the Court should often permit issues to "percolate" in lower courts and among the citizenry as a whole, thus allowing many forms of legal and political discussion and debate, while avoiding premature judicial foreclosure of hard questions. The Court might take this route for practical reasons or for reasons of high principle. Perhaps a firm judicial resolution would be poorly received by the community. Surely this point bears on possible judicial foreclosure of affirmative action programs in, say, 1972. Perhaps a judicial resolution would disserve the very cause that the Court is seeking to promote. This point has been vigorously urged in the context of abortion, where, it is said, an early judicial decision helped undermine the movement for sex equality.[4] Certainly judicial decisions (like all other decisions) can have unintended social consequences, and this practical point argues in favor of judicial caution. The Court might also avoid premature foreclosure because of its own humility about aspects of the underlying issue. This may be because of the complexity of issues of consequences: the Court might lack relevant information and for that way seek to see how a certain practice works out in reality. Or the Court might believe that certain issues are difficult from the standpoint of legally relevant morality and that in principle, it is important to ensure that there is a good deal of public deliberation before the Court acts.

These are important possibilities, and, as we will see, they bear a great deal on the issues raised by affirmative action. But the Court, in fact, has a fourth option: it can issue a highly casuistical decision, one that resolves little beyond the single case, but that operates as a *catalyst* or a *model* for public discussion. By assuming jurisdiction, by offering a ruling, but by issuing a ruling that is case-specific and along crucial dimensions not authoritative, it can call public attention to a problem without foreclosing public judgment.

There is, of course, a debate within the Court about the virtues of case-by-case particularism.[5] Defenders of particularism often speak of the need to proceed cautiously in the midst of ignorance about issues not before the Court. But particularism also has a democratic function, and this is so in two different ways. Judicial particularists can promote democratic virtues of participation and responsiveness by ensuring that options are not foreclosed by rulings involving previous litigants who have somewhat distinct complaints. The practice of judicial particularism thus allows each plaintiff to have an independent day in court, invoking the distinctive features of his case. In the context of affirmative action, this is an important point, since all affirmative action programs are not the same. But there is a separate point. Particularists can also allow democratic processes to continue to debate issues, secure in the knowledge that courts have not attempted to have a final say. In this respect, case-specific judgments operate as a kind of "remand" to the public for further proceedings, at least in the sense that they do not foreclose those proceedings and may even spur them through the visibility of court decisions.

The Affirmative Action Muddle

It is easy to be skeptical about the Supreme Court's affirmative action cases. What is especially notable about those cases is that they do not lay down clear and general rules. From the standpoint of the rule of law, the cases are truly a mess. This was so from the very start. In its very first case, dealing with university admissions, the Court was badly divided and could not produce a majority opinion.[6] Of course the often-criticized "rule" of the *Bakke* case was that universities may use race "as a factor" but may not create quotas. This rule has played a crucial role in American society, American education, and American debate; but it represented the views of Justice Powell alone, and that rule was explicitly rejected by the eight other participating justices.

This was not an auspicious beginning for those seeking clear rules. The problem was compounded by the Court's second affirmative action case, *Fullilove v. Klutznick*.[7] In that case no majority spoke for the Court; no standard of review was set for affirmative action cases; and, by the plurality's own admission, the plurality's decision was highly dependent on the facts of the particular case. In another case, with slightly different facts, the outcome might be different. Remarkably, during the next nine years the Court's decisions, based on no clear standard of review, seemed to turn not on rules but on a wide variety of factors, which produced surprising decisions in particular cases. Among the Court's considerations were: whether official findings of past discrimination had been made; whether the relevant program was rigid or flexible[8]; whether it operated as a quota; whether it had been issued by Congress, by another politically accountable body, by a court, or by some other institution[9]; whether innocent victims were injured, and, if so, whether they were injured in a severe way[10]; and more.[11]

Because so many factors were in play, the outcome of a given case was difficult to predict in advance. Notably, affirmative action cases received a good deal of public attention. But the constitutional contours of affirmative action programs remained obscure.

It was not until 1989 that the Court finally settled on a standard of review. In *City of Richmond v. Croson*, the Court held that affirmative action programs would be subject to "strict scrutiny," at least if they had not been enacted by the federal government.[12] And in that case, the Court did make some movement in the direction of a more ambitious understanding of the relevant constitutional principles. But even while doing so, and even while announcing a standard of review, the Court did so in such a way as to leave the law exceptionally obscure, and to call into question the constitutional status of the affirmative action decisions that preceded *Croson*. Despite appearances, *Croson* did not reject the Court's casuistical approach to affirmative action. And when the Court finally announced in *Adarand* that the same standard of review applied to the nation as to the states, it went out of its way to make clear that that standard would not lead to automatic invalidation, that outcomes would turn on particular facts, and hence that we could not foresee certain results in future cases.[13] The lower court's decision in the *Hopwood* case, which required a clear rule of colorblindness, is not supported by Supreme Court precedent and is indeed an astonishing act of judicial hubris.[14] It would be extremely surprising if the Supreme Court were to agree with the lower court if the issue were squarely presented.

It is tempting but far too simple to say that the Court is becoming less hospitable to affirmative action because of its members' shifting moral judgments or because of its vulnerability to political pressure. To be sure, it is possible to detect some movement, within the Court's doctrine, against affirmative action on constitutional grounds and in favor of a somewhat less casuistical presumption in favor of colorblindness. But this is only a matter of degree. The basic picture, involving rule-free, case-specific decisions, has stayed remarkably constant across time. There is still — many years and many Supreme Court cases after *Bakke* — a high degree of uncertainty about the law governing affirmative action. The public reaction to *Adarand* shows that there remains a great deal of doubt about the constitutional question. Now, as before, the validity of an affirmative action program depends very much on the particular case.

What has the Court achieved with all this? Perhaps the Court has succeeded in invalidating the most indefensible affirmative actions plan and in upholding the most legitimate. This would certainly be the optimist's view. But if we step back a bit, we might reach two broader conclusions. First, the Court has helped keep the nation's eye on the affirmative action issue — on the questions of policy and principle that lie behind the debate — while at the same time failing to preempt processes of public discussion and debate. The Court has done this above all because it has heard a large number of cases but proceeded in a highly particularistic manner. Second, the Court has suggested, in a quite public way, that the legitimacy of affirmative action programs is best understood as a matter of particulars rather than in gross. The Court's own particularism might be seen as providing a model for how responsible citizens should approach the topic.

Affirmative Action and Public Debate

The Constitutional Attack on Affirmative Action
It seems reasonable to think that the question of affirmative action should be settled democratically, not judicially. Despite frequent protestations to the contrary, the Constitution contains no clear textual ban on affirmative action. In fact, the textual arguments are laughably inadequate, and it is worth stressing the point, since the debate over California Proposition 209 was rooted in related confusions. To be sure, the Constitution calls for "equal" protection of the laws; but on the validity of affirmative action, this point is uninformative. The term "equal" cannot possibly mean "the same," if "the same" is intended to suggest a ban on all classification. By their very nature, laws classify. Even the law of equal protection classifies, by treating different people and different groups differently. Thus it is no offense to the equal protection clause if courts scrutinize sex-based classifications more skeptically than they scrutinize age-based classifications — even though this difference does not treat people "the same." The question is what the word "equal" requires in this context. Dictionaries are unhelpful here. Because the notion of equality is

empty without some substantive understandings, the only way to make progress is to go beyond the term itself; we must look outside of the text to come to an understanding of the Constitution's equality principle.

Nor is it helpful to say that the Constitution speaks of "any person" rather than of groups. The Supreme Court, together with many others engaged in debate over affirmative action, appears to think that the reference to "any person" means that the clause speaks of individuals rather than of groups and that this point counts against affirmative action. That claim contains some truth, but it is misleading. To be sure, "any person" may complain that a classification is constitutionally unacceptable. But on what grounds can "any person" seek special judicial assistance? Under the equal protection clause, *all claims of unconstitutional discrimination are necessarily based on complaints about treatment that singles out a characteristic shared by a group*. A glance at the cases — or at any imaginable set of cases — shows that anyone who complains of unconstitutional discrimination is necessarily complaining about the government's use, for purposes of classification, of some characteristic that is shared by some number of group members. The serious question is whether the government's use of that shared characteristic is disfavored from the constitutional point of view. There is no serious question about whether the characteristics about which "any person" may complain are shared characteristics; of course they are. In this sense, claims of unconstitutional discrimination are always group-based claims, even if they are made by "any person."

For example, suppose that Jones has been denied a government job. As a "person," she has a right to make a complaint under the equal protection clause. But everything depends on the characteristic on which government has based its decision to deny her the job. For Jones to claim heightened scrutiny under the equal protection clause, she has to say something about the classification that the government has used, and she must say that that classification treats her, *as a member of a certain group*, in a "suspect" way. Thus she has a claim to careful scrutiny of laws disadvantaging her if those laws classify on the basis of gender. But if she invokes another characteristic, she has no such claim. The same plaintiff Jones has no right to heightened judicial scrutiny if those laws classify on the basis of age. She is thus entitled to a degree of scrutiny corresponding to the basis of the classification of which she complains.

In short: All legal classifications involve "groups." The issue is whether heightened scrutiny is appropriate for the particular classification that government has used. The fact that the Constitution refers to "any person" is utterly uninformative on the question whether any particular foundation for classification should or does meet the standard for heightened judicial scrutiny. The Court's use of the constitutional text as a justification for heightened scrutiny is a version of bad formalism — the pretense that the legal text resolves the question when the judgment must actually be based on other grounds.

If the text of the Constitution does not ban affirmative action, what of the history? It might be tempting to say that the lesson of the Civil War is that all racial classifications are unacceptable. But history shows no such understanding on the part of those who ratified the Fourteenth Amendment. On the contrary, the history tends to suggest that affirmative action policies were regarded as legitimate. The authors of the Fourteenth Amendment enacted a number of race-specific programs for African Americans.[15] There was substantial debate about whether such programs were legitimate, and the people who controlled the national legislature after the Civil War concluded that they were. There is no evidence in the ratification debates that all race-conscious programs were deemed impermissible.[16]

Of course history need not be decisive. Perhaps a moral argument justifies the Court in reading the text at a certain level of generality and abstraction. But there is no clear moral argument requiring courts to treat affirmative action policies with great skepticism. Many critics of affirmative action claim that the moral argument lay at the heart of the work of Martin Luther King Jr. and others in the civil rights movements of the 1960s; but this is an historical error. Asked in 1965 whether he thought it "fair to request a multibillion-dollar program of preferential treatment for the Negro, or for any other minority group," King flatly replied: "I do indeed."[17] In 1963 King wrote: "It is impossible to create a formula for the future which does not take into account that our society has been doing something special against the Negro for hundreds of years. How then can he be absorbed into the mainstream of American life if we do not do something special for him now, in order to balance the equation and equip him to compete on an equal basis?"[18] In fact King's 1963 book, *Why We Can't Wait*, criticized the idea that once blacks had been granted simple equality before the law, no further action should be taken. "On the surface," he wrote, "this appears reasonable, but it is not realistic. For it is obvious that if a man is entered at the starting line of a race three hundred years after another man, the first would have to perform some impossible feat in order to catch up with his fellow runner."[19]

Certainly the views of Martin Luther King Jr. need not be decisive. Perhaps a moral principle of colorblindness deserves constitutional recognition; certainly this is so if it is the only intelligible principle behind the constitutional concern for racial equality. But we can identify an alternative moral principle, one that has been responsible for most of the movement for racial equality in America, both during the Civil War and thereafter. In the area of race, the principal target of the Civil War amendments was the system of racial caste, a system that turned the highly visible and morally irrelevant characteristics of race into a basis for second-class citizenship.[20] The Fourteenth Amendment is best conceived as opposing that caste system.[21] And if this is the best conception of the fourteenth amendment—an *anticaste principle*—there is nothing fundamentally illegitimate about affirmative action programs. Such programs are designed to overcome the castelike features of existing practice. This does not mean that they are a good idea. Perhaps they do not have any remedial effect. Perhaps they are bad on grounds of policy and should be rejected in democratic and administrative arenas. But that possibility does not make them objectionable on constitutional grounds.

In fact, the Supreme Court has yet to provide a clear explanation of the principle that requires affirmative action programs to be treated so skeptically. Most of its argument depends on a false claim of symmetry: If discrimination against blacks is presumptively forbidden, how can discrimination against whites be presumptively legitimate? This question is anything but rhetorical. It is no better than the question: If sex-based discrimination is presumed illegitimate, how can the same not be true for age-based discrimination? The anticaste principle helps provide an answer to both questions, and that answer suggests that different forms of discrimination must be treated distinctly. To be sure, the Court has referred to a set of legitimate concerns about affirmative action policies: the social divisiveness of affirmative action, the ordinary moral irrelevance of race, the fact that race is not chosen voluntarily, and the possibility that affirmative action programs will stigmatize their intended beneficiaries. But none of these points supports a convincing *constitutional* complaint about affirmative action. Many things that government does are divisive, and they are not unconstitutional for that reason. Many characteristics that are morally irrelevant, and that are not voluntarily chosen, are used by government as classifying devices (consider height, strength, and intelligence). Affirmative action programs may well stigmatize their intended beneficiaries. But the same is plausibly true for programs that benefit children of alumni or people from underrepresented regions, and those programs are not, because of their stigmatizing effects, unconstitutional under the Fourteenth Amendment.

Do these remarks have implications for the practice of casuistry? It would be possible to conclude, from these remarks, that the Court should understand the Constitution's equality principle in terms of an anticaste principle and that it should therefore uphold all or almost all affirmative action programs. This approach would not be casuistical; it would generate a rulelike judgment in favor of such programs, and that judgment would rest on a theoretically ambitious claim about the appropriate nature of equality in a constitutional democracy. And I do not think that an approach of this kind would be indefensible. Perhaps the Court would have done best to make clear that there is no constitutional problem with affirmative action programs (whatever we might think of them as a matter of policy). If the Court has good reason for confidence in a theoretically ambitious approach that produces rulelike judgments, the Court generally issues rulelike judgments. But the Court has not done this, partly because of the justices' general caution about theoretical ambition and enthusiasm for theoretical modesty, allowing diverse people to converge on low-level judgments. Without endorsing casuistry over an anticaste principle if the latter were a serious constitutional possibility, let us now attempt a sympathetic exploration of the Court's more modest, case-specific approach.

Democratic Debate and Affirmative Action

Nothing that I have said thus far suggests that affirmative action programs are a good idea. The range of such programs is very wide, and to make a judgment on them it is important to have a sense of their variety and their consequences. Such programs include relatively uncontroversial efforts to increase the pool of applicants by ensuring that the candidates are racially diverse; these efforts are certainly race-conscious, but at the stage of recruitment rather than actual appointment. A public university may, for example, seek to recruit students from high schools containing large numbers of African Americans. A recruitment effort of this kind may well be race-based, but it is hard to see why such efforts are objectionable. Affirmative action programs include approaches that treat race as one factor among many others. We can certainly imagine a program in which race operates as a kind of tiebreaker when two applicants are in all other respects deemed equally qualified. Perhaps a police department located in a largely African American community would choose this approach; perhaps its decision to do so would have good or even indispensable consequences. Perhaps a university, attentive to a range of relevant variables, would do the same thing. But many affirmative action programs include rigid quota systems as well. Thus, affirmative action programs taken as a whole include programs that give a minor boost to otherwise highly qualified candidates as well as programs that allow people entry into programs for which they are ill suited.

From these examples we should conclude that evaluation of such programs should depend partly on their content, their goals, and their consequences. A great deal of information is necessary to make judgments of that sort. It is necessary, for example, to know about the experiences and the performances of the intended beneficiaries. Undoubtedly, these will vary across programs. In any case, the term "affirmative action programs" is far too imprecise to allow for sensible global evaluations. Basic principle will take us only so far. This is the casuist's basic plea. Above all, we need to know how such programs are operating in the real world. It is undoubtedly the case that many affirmative action programs work successfully and are perceived as doing so. And, undoubtedly, this cannot be said for many such programs, which operate as interest-group transfers or invitations for abuse.

It is striking but true that until very recently, the nation had yet to have a sustained discussion about the legitimacy and variety of affirmative action programs and about possible alternatives to them. When Congress adopted the Civil Rights Act of 1964, discrimination against African Americans was, of course, the central focus of the debate. Affirmative action programs were in an embryonic state and did not receive much if any consideration. The first important affirmative action program was in fact instituted by executive order. The proliferation of such programs at national, state, and local levels has proceeded without sustained attention to the underlying issues of principle and policy. This is quite disturbing whatever one thinks about the legitimacy of affirmative action.

Indeed, the alleged public backlash against affirmative action may be attributable in part to the perception that the relevant programs had not (until recently) been debated and defended publicly. It is not at all true to say, as many do, that affirmative action programs are a creation of federal courts; many such programs have their origins in private decisions or in decisions of politically accountable bodies. But the widespread perception that affirmative action programs are court-generated is illuminating insofar as it suggests a belief that such programs have not been ratified publicly.

The Court as Catalyst and Model

We are now in a position to discuss the possible catalytic role of the Supreme Court vis-à-vis the affirmative action debate. Suppose it is agreed that the issue of affirmative action should be decided democratically rather than judicially, but suppose, too, that institutions have been operating in such a way as to ensure that any public decisions are taken in an unaccountable way and are not really a product of democratic judgments. Further suppose that while an anticaste principle has considerable force as a reading of the Fourteenth Amendment, it calls for a degree of theoretical ambition, taking a contentious stand on a fundamental issue of democratic theory, which rightly makes mere judges uncomfortable. In these circumstances, the Supreme Court's meandering, casuistical, rule-free path may well be a salutary way of signaling the existence of large questions of policy and principle, at least with constitutional dimensions, when those questions would otherwise have received far less attention than they deserve. Hence the participants in Supreme Court cases involving affirmative action have become familiar "characters" in the national debate, helping to frame discussion: Bakke, Weber, Johnson, minority construction contractors, and others.

The point is especially important in a context in which social norms may well be having an adverse effect on open public discussion. Suppose that a policy persists not because people are in favor of it, but because social norms prevent people from voicing their complaints publicly. Suppose, too, that these complaints are widespread. If this is so, there is a democratic problem that requires attention. At least as a general rule, something should be done to ensure that the issue receives public consideration. There are many possibilities by way of remedy. Private actors can help. We might describe as "norm entrepreneurs" those people who try to activate private beliefs and judgments in favor of a shift in existing social norms.[22] And private norm entrepreneurs have been playing an active role, in California and elsewhere, for and against affirmative action. But official institutions can play a role as well. In particular, the Supreme Court can signal the existence of hard questions of political morality and public policy, by taking cases, drawing public attention to the underlying questions, and refusing to issue authoritative pronouncements. And if we examine the Court's practice in the area of affirmative action, we see that the Court has operated in precisely this way. It has helped keep the affirmative action issue in the public domain without foreclosing public deliberation.

I do not claim that the Court has been self-conscious about this. But some of the justices have undoubtedly been aware of the difficulty and variousness of the affirmative action problem and have chosen a casuistical approach for this reason. Hence an interest in ideas of this sort has affected the Court's deliberations. Nor do I claim that the current public interest in affirmative action, in California and elsewhere, owes its origin to Supreme Court decisions. There are undoubtedly a wide range of factors that could be said to have played a catalytic role. I contend only that the Court's decisions have been among the factors that have kept affirmative action in the public eye and helped focus the public on issues of principle and policy. To the extent that those effects have been salutary, it argues for other meandering paths in the future, perhaps in the area of discrimination on the basis of sexual orientation, where a degree of casuistry also makes a good deal of sense.

Affirmative Action, Deliberative Government, and the Referendum

The suggestion that the Court has helped catalyze, and attempted to help model, public debate should not by any means be taken as a claim that, with respect to affirmative action, the democratic process has been or is now working well. With "norm cascades" — and with respect to affirmative action, we appear to be in the midst of one — there is a serious risk that outcomes will be based on sensationalistic anecdotes, factual errors, misperceptions, accusations of various sorts, or, worst of all, simple racism and hatred. Thus in Congress, as in California, affirmative action has been debated in an unnecessarily accusatory and broad-gauged way; there has been far too little focus on the crucial questions of detail and consequence. Undoubtedly objections to affirmative action programs are often well-motivated; it would be ludicrous to think that such objections are *necessarily* rooted in racial prejudice. But appeals to racism, usually tacit, are a large part of the debate, and they make it harder to focus on the legitimate questions raised by various sides. Indeed, some people might think that affirmative action is an unpromising area for public deliberation precisely because of the likelihood that crude judgments or even racist motivations will be at work, and the correspondingly small probability that casuistical approaches, defensible in the way I have suggested, will prevail.

These risks are heightened in the context of a referendum, which bypasses ordinary filters of political representation and hence poses special dangers.[23] National attention has been focused on California Proposition 209, and, as we saw, the debate over that proposal was far from deliberative. In many ways it was a bizarre parody of constitutional aspirations, involving advertising campaigns, gross hyperbole, and manipulations of various sorts. The American system is, of course, one of representative rather than direct democracy, partly because of a judgment that political deliberation can be best promoted through a representative system.[24]

In the context of affirmative action in particular, there is an evident danger, realized in California, that referendum outcomes will not be based on a careful assessment of facts and values, but instead on crude "we-they" thinking. When the Supreme Court struck down Amendment 2 in Colorado as a form of illegitimate discrimination on the basis of sexual orientation, the Court did not explicitly refer to problems with popular referenda; but its (narrow, highly casuistical) decision may well have been animated by an understanding that "we-they" stereotypes — in the Court's phrase, unacceptable "animus" — were at work.[25] This is a risk whenever the public debates a controversial issue in the referendum setting; it is a special danger in the context of race. It is not my purpose here to evaluate that risk in a comprehensive way. But if a catalytic role from the Court serves to intensify poorly functioning majoritarian processes and does not succeed in showing that casuistry is appropriate in certain places, that role may be nothing to celebrate. Both exercises of statesmanship and institutional correctives — displacing and discouraging the referendum process with more insulated bodies — may be in order. Hence it is appropriate to assemble politically insulated groups to attempt to compile information about the actual effects of affirmative action programs.

This, then, is an important lesson that has emerged from recent events: public referenda on issues of this kind are unlikely to work well, in part because the underlying issues of content, context, and consequence will probably be displaced by anecdote and accusation. Here there lies a large lesson about the virtues of representative institutions. Now that Proposition 209 has been approved, however, it is unclear if any institution — including the Supreme Court itself — can do a great deal to make things better. Some people have suggested that the Court might review the outcomes of referenda with an unusually high degree of skepticism.[26] There is some sense in this suggestion. An approach of this kind finds structural support in the Constitution, which is rooted in faith in representation, and in the Constitution's most fundamental underlying concerns. It is plausible to say that the Court should be mildly more receptive to a constitutional challenge when legislation has been enacted via referendum. But no provision of the Constitution specifically authorizes judges to regard the outcomes of referenda as less legitimate than the outcomes of representative processes, and in any case it is not, under current law, easy to see how someone might challenge a ban on affirmative action on constitutional grounds simply because it emerged from a referendum.

On the other hand, there is a genuine constitutional difficulty with California Proposition 209. To be sure, the Court's decision involving Colorado Amendment 2 is no precedent for invalidating Proposition 209, since the former case depended on a judgment that it was "irrational" to deprive homosexuals of "protection of the laws"; the same cannot be said about Proposition 209. But the constitutional ban on affirmative action at the state level does have something in common with other measures, invalidated by the Supreme Court, that take racial issues outside of ordinary political processes and impose a special burden on civil rights groups seeking remedies for race-related harms.[27] Thus the Court has invalidated a city charter amendment forbidding fair housing legislation; it has also said that a state may not adopt a statewide initiative barring localities from requiring students to attend schools other than those nearest or next nearest their place of residence. In both cases, the measure "uses the racial nature of an issue to define the governmental decision-making structure, and thus imposes substantial and unique burdens on racial minorities." In both cases, the invalidated law prevented measures that "inure primarily to the benefit of the minority." Thus "when the political process or the decision-making mechanism used to address racially conscious legislation — and only such legislation — is singled out for peculiar and disadvantageous treatment, the governmental action plainly rests on distinctions based on race." Hence the Court will be suspicious of any allocation of power "that places unusual burdens on the ability of racial groups to enact legislation specifically designed to overcome the 'special condition' of prejudice."

These precedents are quite complex, but the foregoing passages show that they do raise serious doubts about the California initiative insofar as that measure creates unusual barriers to ordinary political processes involving affirmative action. Hence it is far from impossible to imagine the Court invalidating the California initiative, possibly with a tacit understanding of the risks of the referendum process. Proposition 209 does erect unusual barriers, constitutional in form, to race-conscious measures designed to overcome "the 'special condition' of prejudice." The best prediction is that the Court is unlikely to strike down Proposition 209. But it would be an intriguing irony if the Court, committed to a casuistical path with respect to affirmative action, were to strike down a referendum knowing that it contained a ban that prevented the kind of careful analysis of particulars that has stood behind the Court's own decisions. And the Court's decisions in this area are themselves casuistical in character; they depend on no clear principle but rather a vague understanding that efforts to take racial issues out of the political process (in a way that harms members of minority groups) may not be justifiable in racially neutral terms.

Conclusion

In this essay I have suggested that the Supreme Court sometimes issues highly casuistical rulings that do not settle a great deal but operate as a kind of "remand" to the public, alerting people to the existence of complex issues of principle and policy. In the affirmative action context, the Court (whether intentionally or not) has done precisely this. The Court has emphasized the content of particular programs, their stated goals, and the link between those goals and the affirmative measures undertaken. In sharp contrast to California Proposition 209, the Court has said little that is authoritative. But it has helped trigger public debate, with, perhaps, an understanding on the part of some of the justices that, until recently, that debate was neither broadly inclusive nor properly deliberative — and it did not honestly reflect people's underlying concerns.

Perhaps decisions based on the anticaste principle would be superior to the casuistical path that the Court has taken. But there is good reason for a degree of casuistry in some areas of constitutional law; casuistry makes special sense in the context of difficult issues on which the nation is sharply divided. And if what I have said here is correct, casuistry is appropriate in many domains other than constitutional law. In the context of affirmative action, much depends on details and consequences. Of course, it is easy to imagine programs that do not promote their intended purposes and harm the very people they are supposed to help. It is also easy to imagine programs that are race-conscious and give a fully defensible, modest boost to people who would perform well and add a great deal to (for example) a school or a police department. In light of the enormous variety of affirmative action programs, the debate over Proposition 209 was a parody of democratic aspirations, above all because it turned so centrally on anecdotes and accusations. This is a pervasive risk for government by referendum. It suggests that representative institutions are far better, because they are much more likely to weigh consequences, explore context, and make the kinds of distinctions that are so crucial to a sensible evaluation of complex concepts such as "race consciousness." The problems with Proposition 209, in short, point to the virtues of casuistry in politics as well as in law.

NOTES

1. The best discussion is Timur Kuran, *Public Truths, Private Lies* (Cambridge, MA, 1995), which includes a section on affirmative action. I do not mean to endorse all of what Kuran says on that score.

2. See Jon Elster, "Strategic Uses of Argument," in *Barriers to Conflict Resolution* (New York, 1995).

3. See Alexander Bickel, *The Least Dangerous Branch* (New Haven, CT, 1965).

4. See Gerald Rosenberg, *The Hollow Hope* (Chicago, 1991).

5. See Kathleen Sullivan, "The Justices of Rules and the Justices of Standards," *Harvard Law Review* 105 (1993): 22; Antonin Scalia, "The Rule of Law is a Law of Rules," *University of Chicago Law Review* 56 (1989): 1175; and Cass R. Sunstein, *Legal Reasoning and Political Conflict* (New York, 1996).

6. *Regents of the University of California v. Bakke*, 438 US 265 (1978).

7. 448 US 448 (1980).

8. *Fullilove v. Klutznick*, 448 US 448 (1980).

9. *Ibid*.

10. *Wygant v. Jackson Board. of Education*, 476 US 267 (1986)

11. See, e.g., *Wygant v. Jackson Board of Education*, 476 US 267 (1986); *Sheet Metal Workers v. EEOC*, 478 US 421 (1986); *U.S. v. Paradise*, 480 US 92 (1987).

12. *City of Richmond v. Croson*, 488 US 469 (1989).

13. *Adarand Constructors v. Pena*, 115 Sup. Ct. 2097 (1995).

14. See *Hopwood v. Texas*, F.3d (1996). See Cass R. Sunstein, "Foreword: Leaving Things Undecided," *Harvard Law Review* 110 (1996): 4.

15. See Eric Schnapper, "Affirmative Action and the Legislative History of the Fourteenth Amendment," *Virginia Law Review* 71 (1985): 753.

16. See Andrew Kull, *The Color-Blind Constitution* (Cambridge, MA,1992).

17. Alex Haley, *The Playboy Interviews* (New York, 1993), 115.

18. Martin Luther King Jr., *Why We Can't Wait* (New York, 1963), 146.

19. Martin Luther King Jr., *Why We Can't Wait,* 147.

20. I draw here from Cass R. Sunstein, "The Anticaste Principle," *Michigan Law Review* 92 (1994): 2410.

21. See *Adarand*, 115 Sup. Ct. (Stevens, J., dissenting), and Sunstein, "The Anticaste Principle," 2410.

22. See Cass R. Sunstein, *Free Markets and Social Justice* (New York, 1997), chap. 2, "Social Norms and Social Roles,".

23. See e.g., James Fishkin, *Democracy and Deliberation* (New Haven, CT, 1994), who presents a deliberative conception of democracy.

24. See *The Federalist Papers*, No. 10; Joseph Bessette, *The Mild Voice of Reason* (Chicago, 1994).

25. *Romer v. Evans*, 116 Sup. Ct. 1620 (1996).

26. See the discussion in Julian Eule, "Judicial Review of Direct Democracy," *Yale Law Journal* 99 (1990), p. 1503.

27. See *Washington v. Seattle School Dist. No.* 1., 458 US 457 (1982); *Hunter v. Erickson*, 393 US 385 (1969). See Cass R. Sunstein, "Public Values, Private Interests, and the Equal Protection Clause," *Supreme Court Review* (1982): 183, for general discussion.

PART TWO

Affirmative Action

and Epistemology

James Robert Brown

It is a great irony that "political correctness" — an expression coined by feminists and other progressives to poke gentle fun at themselves — has become a term of abuse. Speech codes, for example, are often ridiculed as the product of political correctness and dismissed on that very ground. Affirmative action policies are also everywhere under attack and similarly rejected for the flimsiest reasons. When arguments are given at all, they usually appeal to "academic freedom" or "excellence" or "merit," notions that are taken to be as obviously virtuous and unproblematic as political correctness is taken to be obviously silly or pernicious. But it may turn out, on close inspection, that such notions as "academic excellence" require something like affirmative action in hiring for the sake of a much needed diversity.

Let me begin by sketching a view of the growth of knowledge which contrasts with a common earlier view that simply says we take our theories to nature and test them against the evidence. According to this earlier, now largely discarded view, we conjecture a theory T; we draw out some of its consequences that are directly testable; we check to see if these testable consequences are true or false; we accept theories that have only true consequences (as far as we know) and reject any with false ones. Moreover, we also try to systematize the observable realm with our theories, that is, organize and explain diverse phenomena by means of a small number of powerful principles. This simple picture applies to the natural sciences, the social sciences, and indeed (with appropriate minor modifications) to any rational intellectual activity including, say, theology and literary criticism.

The crucial thing to note is that on this account of knowledge a single theory can be evaluated *independently* of all other theories. Our conjectures are confirmed (to some degree) or refuted by the evidence — nature says Yes or nature says No. In consequence, it becomes irrelevant that the person conjecturing the theory may be the worst dogmatist, filled with the most vile prejudices, since the evidence supports or refutes the theory, as the case may be, regardless of the theory's odious origin. (Philosophers know this as the well-entrenched distinction between *discovery* and *justification*.) The upshot is that we needn't worry about the genesis of a theory, since honest testing will reveal its true worth.

This picture of the growth of knowledge has much to commend it. But considerable historical labor over the past several years has led to a quite different outlook. Because of the work of Thomas Kuhn and others, rational theory choice is now seen as *comparative*.[1] No longer do we think that theories can be tested directly by the evidence. Rather, theories, to a significant extent, must be evaluated with respect to their rivals. Given some body of evidence, we can say that T_1 is a better theory than T_2; but we cannot say that T_1 is true (or likely to be true, or approximately true, etc.), except in the case that T_1 is chosen from a more or less exhaustive pool of candidates.

Not only are theories evaluated by means of the evidence relative to their rivals, but what counts as evidence may depend heavily on what rival theories are being considered. Perhaps the best illustration of this is Paul Feyerabend's famous example of Brownian motion.[2]. Early in the nineteenth century, a Scottish botanist, Thomas Brown, noticed a remarkable phenomenon. Tiny bits of pollen moved randomly around in a fluid. Are they alive? What is their source of energy? What is the cause of this bizarre motion?

No one for a moment suggested that classical thermodynamics should explain this, any more than it should explain, say, why snow is white. A rival to classical thermodynamics, the kinetic theory of heat, says that heat is average kinetic energy, the energy of motion of tiny bits of matter. At the turn of the century, Albert Einstein, Jean-Baptiste Perrin, and others offered an explanation of Brownian motion: the relatively large bits of pollen are being knocked around by tiny molecules.

The success of this explanation for the rival kinetic theory put classical thermodynamics on the spot. Suddenly, the phenomenon of Brownian motion was put into classical thermodynamics' domain; and that theory was now obliged to explain it. Failing to do so was a strike against the theory. The moral is simply this: Brownian motion became relevant evidence for classical thermodynamics, *only* because a rival had explained it. Without the rival, Brownian motion would have remained evidentially irrelevant.

I stress that comparative theory evaluation is, or at least can be, a perfectly rational affair. There is no question of people merely choosing on the basis of whim, or personal interest, or theory-based prejudice — though perhaps some do. The evidence forces (or at least inclines) us to a rational, objective choice. But the choice that the available evidence forces us to is the best among the *available* rival theories.

So now we face a big problem: What happens if the set of rival theories is skewed in some systematic way? How do we ensure that the set of rivals is the best possible? This turns out to be a fundamental question in epistemology; and it may have a somewhat political answer.

Consider a rather stunning remark made by the great anthropologist Claude Lévi-Strauss. He described a village as "deserted" when all the adult males had left. I doubt that any female anthropologist in the same circumstances would have said: "The entire village left the next day in about 30 canoes, leaving us alone with the women and the children in the abandoned houses."[3] Really! The "entire" village? "Deserted"? Of course, we are sensitized not to say such things today, but the problem is more than mere offensiveness to women. The passage reveals, I suspect, a certain view about the structure and operation of society and how best to explain it. The implicit principle at work with Lévi-Strauss is something like this: "Look for the underlying social relations among adult males; when you have found those, you have found the key to understanding how a society works." Of course, Lévi-Strauss never put things like that; I doubt that he was even aware of making such a deep assumption. And if a female anthropologist in Lévi-Strauss's day had been in similar circumstances, I doubt that she would have thought of explicitly combating such a view. Of course, the principle might even be true. But I dare say a female anthropologist — even one trained by Lévi-Strauss —

might have conceptualized things a bit differently. Not because she is free of all bias, but because she has *different* biases.

We are all full of biases of which we are more or less unaware. Since we do not know precisely what they are, they cannot be systematically eliminated. But we can do the next best thing: we can organize the pursuit of knowledge so that a great variety of *different* prejudices are at work in the production of theories, then select the best theory from among the rivals. The way to ensure the optimal diversity of rival theories, obviously, is to make sure we have a wide variety of theorizers. Currently, the pool of those who make conjectures is heavily skewed toward white males. Future hiring must change the proportions so that a larger number of females, minorities, and others with different biases are included in the group of theorizers. In short, affirmative action is needed for the sake of improving the growth of knowledge; pluralism for the sake of epistemology.

Now, how does this relate to hiring practices? In a number of ways. The rational status of one's own theory is a function of how well rival theories are doing. So it is incumbent on us all to pay attention to alternative views, to support and develop them as far as reasonably possible. Remember, even the evidence itself (as in the Brownian motion case) is to some extent a function of rival theories.

The view of rational theory choice I sketched is akin to an adversarial one, something that comes naturally to many academics. Let the rival views make their case, we say, then an impartial court will decide which is best. But we all know only too well that an adversarial approach works well only under near ideal conditions. No matter how fair-minded a jury is, an ill-defended accused has little chance against a powerful prosecution, regardless of actual guilt or innocence. The fight must be "fair" for truth to win in the end. But in the present circumstances, it is very difficult, if not impossible, to have a fair fight. When resources, expertise, and tradition heavily favor the reigning outlook, it is an extraordinary struggle for rival views to get a hearing. When a situation is so imbalanced, as our current situation is, it is incumbent on all sides to proceed in a different way.

It is difficult to be open-minded — very difficult indeed. Hobbes poked fun at the notion of "good sense." He could have done the same with "open-minded." We, each of us, might wish to be smarter, richer, healthier, but we each consider ourselves to possess exactly the right amount of open-mindedness. But the truth is we have to work very hard at it, and we have to get others involved in the process. Advancing knowledge is a cooperative venture. As individuals, we cannot do it alone; we need strong rivals in order to put our favorite theories to the test. Our hiring practices can and should play a crucial role in creating the optimal intellectual climate.

Affirmative action is supported by a number of considerations, including pedagogical concerns (e.g., the desirability of role models) and social concerns (e.g., ensuring fairness in hiring that might not otherwise be present). But let us not forget that there is another very good, nonpedagogical, nonsocial reason for wanting affirmative action: epistemology. Knowledge is advanced greatly by it.

NOTES

1. Thomas S. Kuhn, *The Structure of Scientific Revolutions* (Chicago, 1962/1970).

2. Paul K. Feyerabend, "Explanation, Reduction, and Empiricism" (1962), reprinted in *Philosophical Papers*, vol. 1 (Cambridge, UK, 1981).

3. Margrit Eichler and Jeanne Lapoint, *On the Treatment of Sexes in Research* (Ottawa, 1985).

A Liberal Defense

of Affirmative Action

by George M. Fredrickson

The assault on affirmative action in California and elsewhere is the result of widespread misunderstanding of what it means and of the tendency of conservative politicians to exploit that misunderstanding for electoral advantage. Affirmative action was inaugurated under the administrations of both political parties in the late sixties and early seventies as one device among several to promote equal opportunities for minorities and women. If it was ever intended to be a policy of rigid quotas and racial or gender "preferences," the *Bakke* decision prevented it from taking that form. My understanding of the policy is that it does not establish group rights or entitlements but is compatible with the traditional American ideal of individual equality of opportunity. Affirmative action assumes that conscious or unconscious prejudices continue to exist against the admission, hiring, and promotion of minorities and women for educational and employment opportunities that have traditionally been monopolized by white males. It also recognizes that minorities and women are often discouraged from applying for certain kinds of openings because of the expectation that they will not have a fair chance. (The recent and drastic decline in minority applications to law schools in California and Texas can be attributed in part to this discouragement factor.) What affirmative action means to me is (1) that special efforts be made to recruit minorities and women; (2) that standardized tests and other criteria that cannot be demonstrated to predict job or educational performance be disregarded or de-emphasized; and (3) that preference normally be given to qualified minority and female applicants when other criteria are equally fulfilled or when those responsible for hiring or admission are closely divided on the question of which candidate is most qualified or will better meet the needs of the recruiting institution. In many institutions, racial, ethnic, and gender diversity is valuable because of the way it reflects the composition of the larger society that the institution serves. What I have set forth is what might be described as a "liberal" justification for affirmative action, and I believe it is one that can become the majority view of Americans if it is explained clearly and effectively. Affirmative action is an equal opportunity program that takes account of the realities of racism and sexism in this society. As such it deserves the support of those who identify with a liberal or progressive conception of the American Dream.

How Affirmative Action Can (and Cannot) Work Well

Amy Gutmann

That the defense of affirmative action for African Americans ever succeeded in American politics is more remarkable than the current assault on it.[1] Rather than ask for an explanation of the assault, we might wonder why the opposition to affirmative action took this long to be effective. Three reasons seem most salient. First, in the Kennedy-Johnson-Nixon years, the American economy was expanding and each president was publicly backing income and employment policies for white Americans at the same time as they were implementing affirmative action plans for disadvantaged groups. Second, support for affirmative action was greatly strengthened once women became beneficiaries of affirmative action programs. Only recently has it become apparent that women are no longer being preferred by many affirmative action programs, such as minority set-asides and college admissions programs. Third, bringing Native Americans, Latino Americans, and Asian Americans under the umbrella of affirmative action has had precisely the opposite effect of including women. It has increased the perception among whites and excluded ethnic groups that affirmative action is not for people like us. Add to this the widely shared perception that affirmative action is unfair and counterproductive, and you have a politically lethal combination.

Advocates of affirmative action cannot afford to dismiss charges of unfairness and counterproductiveness as mere reflections of group interest. By precisely the same logic, critics of affirmative action can dismiss the defense of affirmative action, thus producing a vicious circle of unfair and unproductive criticism. Public opinion on affirmative action is not neatly divided by group identification. Many citizens change their minds about affirmative action after being exposed to counter-arguments and political leaders who take a moral stand on the issue.[2] Those of us who are inclined to support affirmative action would therefore do well to address the strongest arguments against it and to see whether our inclination survives critical scrutiny. The argument that I want to address here has probably done more to weaken support for affirmative action in recent years than any other because it suggests that affirmative action hurts rather than helps African Americans and because it is increasingly made by African Americans. The argument, which reverses one of the strongest arguments in favor of affirmative action, is that affirmative action increases the negative stereotyping of disadvantaged minorities.

If this argument is correct, then not even African Americans are well served by affirmative action. And if African Americans are not well served by affirmative action, then it is unlikely that any other group will be. On the other hand, if affirmative action programs can be designed in a way that helps break down negative stereotyping, then African Americans can be well served and so can members of other groups to the extent that their opportunities to succeed in higher education and high-status occupations are now seriously blocked by negative stereotyping of their group.

The most compelling version of the argument against affirmative action is made by Glenn Loury, who argues that "the widespread use of preferences can logically be expected to erode the perception of black competence." Loury divides black and white applicants for jobs into three categories: "marginals" are those whose hiring status is altered by affirmative action (either by gaining or losing a job); "successes" are those who would be hired with or without affirmative action; and "failures" are those who would not be hired with or without affirmative action. Programs that give preference to blacks by lowering the hiring threshold for blacks (and raising it for whites) will reduce the market's estimate of both black successes and black failures. By the same logic, the reputations of white successes and failures are increased because white successes had to be especially excellent to be hired and white failures might have been successes had there only not been a preference for blacks. "The inferential logic that leads to this arresting conclusion," Loury notes, "is particularly insidious, in that it can serve to legitimate otherwise indefensible negative stereotypes about blacks."[3]

Affirmative action is insidious if its primary effect is to send the signal that black successes should be failures, while white failures should be successes; and that black failures are especially unmeritorious while white successes are especially meritorious. But is this necessarily the primary effect of affirmative action programs? Affirmative action programs that managed to overcome negative stereotyping, by the values implicit in this critique, would be legitimate, indeed admirable. Finding such affirmative action programs is not an idle fancy. Loury himself defends "developmental" affirmative action, which is color conscious and "presumes a direct concern about racial inequality and involves allocating benefits to people on the basis of race."[4] But developmental affirmative action, unlike affirmative action that reinforces or exacerbates negative stereotyping, aims "to enhance performance [of African Americans], while maintaining common standards of evaluation."

Successful affirmative action programs did not merely accept more women into previously male-dominated positions. They also demonstrated that women could succeed and make important social contributions in those positions (some of which could be made by men and others of which could not). So, too, successful affirmative action programs for African Americans must not only accept African Americans into higher status positions but also demonstrate that African Americans can succeed in those positions and thereby make important social contributions. By the same inferential logic that would lead us to reject "preferential" programs that not only lower barriers to entry but also lower standards of evaluation after entry, we should support affirmative action programs that demonstrate the success of African Americans in high-status positions in which they are underrepresented because of our historical legacy of racial injustice. Certainly the conventional success that African American students now demonstrate at places like Princeton, as well as the distinctive contributions that they can make to creating a more diverse educational environment in a traditionally all-white institution, suggests that affirmative action has the potential for overcoming rather than exacerbating negative stereotyping.

There are practical lessons to be learned from this exercise in inferential logic, only a few of which I can mention here. Affirmative action policies can and must do more than aim to admit larger numbers of African Americans or members of other negatively stereotyped groups; they must also help them succeed academically. Otherwise affirmative action becomes a cruel hoax, as when universities proudly proclaim the admission of ever-larger proportions of minority students who then fail to graduate or to achieve high academic standards. Doing away with color-conscious admissions policies is precisely the wrong lesson to be learned from this abuse of affirmative action, especially in light of the fact that no social movement is afoot to forbid athlete-conscious, alumni-conscious, and geography-conscious admissions policies. The lesson to be learned is that color-conscious admissions policies (like athlete-conscious admissions policies) need to be coupled with educational programs that follow through with the aims of a publicly defensible program of affirmative action. Those aims include educating students for future leadership in an environment that exposes them to a broad range of perspectives and encourages them to learn from as diverse a set of people and perspectives as possible. (These aims reflect a commitment to expanding intellectual horizons as well as to creating what Robert Post calls a "democratic public culture."[6])

University admission is not a prize for past performance but a prediction of future performance, and the prediction is importantly affected by the kind of academic programs that universities offer students. There is no good argument for systematically admitting students who cannot succeed academically, but there are compelling arguments for admitting students from negatively stereotyped social groups and then offering them (along with all other similarly situated students) educational programs that foster academic success rather than failure. When selective universities admit African American and other students from disadvantaged minority groups who have the potential to succeed and then offer them an education that is well-designed to develop their potential, negative stereotyping is more likely than not to diminish over time.

There are two reasons to expect negative stereotyping to diminish in the wake of such affirmative action programs. First, universities will be educating future generations of high-status professionals who are more racially diverse than past and present generations. This will help overcome the negative stereotyping of African Americans that has been built up over three centuries. Second, by creating more socially diverse learning environments where students of different backgrounds learn from each other, and learn to respect each other, universities will be countering the negative stereotyping of the views of African Americans. "How can a college educator convey to students the lesson that 'not all blacks think alike,'" Loury asks, "with too few blacks on campus for this truth to become evident?"[7]

Affirmative action policies that overcome negative stereotyping should be targeted especially to those groups whose members are most burdened by negative stereotyping. African Americans are the paradigm case of such a group, but affirmative action directed toward Latinos and Native Americans can also serve this purpose. Affirmative action that aims to overcome negative stereotyping makes sense only for groups that are negatively stereotyped by virtue of their relatively low representation in selective universities and high-status professions. But there is another way in which this rationale for affirmative action is more inclusive than many others. Once the negatively stereotyped groups are targeted, affirmative action on this rationale does not recommend singling out the least advantaged members of those groups for preference. The purpose of this kind of affirmative action is not to compensate individuals for past discrimination but to send positive signals to all Americans that members of these groups are no less likely to succeed than any others in attaining positions of leadership in our society.

Affirmative action that aims to overcome negative stereotyping does not address the far more troubling problems of poverty, unemployment, and inadequate education that beset the most disadvantaged members of our society, regardless of color (although the most disadvantaged are disproportionately African American, Latino American, and Native American). Instead, it contributes to making the competition for high status positions somewhat fairer.[8] Even if this is not the most urgent of our social problems, it is one worthy of support, especially by those of us who have already succeeded in a seriously skewed competition.

NOTES

1. For an interesting explanation of how the coalition for and against race-based affirmative action developed, see John David Skrentny, *The Ironies of Affirmative Action: Politics, Culture, and Justice in America* (Chicago, 1996).

2. Paul M. Sniderman and Thomas Piazza, *The Scar of Race* (Cambridge, MA, 1993).

3. Glenn Loury, "How to Mend Affirmative Action," *Public Interest* (Spring 1997), 5.

4. *Ibid.*, 9.

5. *Ibid.*, 8–9.

6. See Robert Post, "Introduction: After *Bakke*," in this volume.

7. Loury, "How to Mend Affirmative Action," 5.

8. A far fuller discussion of affirmative action and fairness can be found in Anthony Appiah and Amy Gutmann, *Color Consciousness* (Princeton, NJ, 1996), 108–51.

Affirmative Action

as Culture War

Jennifer Hochschild

An examination of any collection of books on affirmative action over the past twenty-five years shows two phenomena — a huge outpouring of legal and philosophical analyses of its merits and a paucity of empirical studies of its practices and effects. The legal and philosophical analyses range from passionate assertions that quotas are essential to mitigate American racism to equally fervent arguments that any racial or gender-based preference violates core American values of equality of personhood and opportunity. One can even find nuanced intermediate positions that subtly distinguish among recipients, procedures, triggering circumstances, and the like. Without denigrating the energy and creativity of many of these efforts, I believe it is fair to say that the core legal and philosophical arguments were laid out in the first few years of this debate, and, with the exception of the new argument about diversity for its own sake, the succeeding volumes have mostly developed or elaborated on them.

There are, in contrast, huge holes in the literature about how affirmative action works in practice. For example, we know very little about just how people are hired or admitted to universities: When is race (or gender) a tiebreaker? When does minority status still count against the applicant? When are less qualified African Americans or women hired or admitted over more qualified whites, Asians, or men? When does the reverse occur? How could one tell? Do certain kinds of universities or firms consistently treat affirmative action in ways different from those of other kinds of firms or universities?

Another set of questions: What happens after a person is hired or admitted in circumstances where affirmative action is presumed to have played a role? Do African Americans or white women feel stigmatized, inferior, insecure? If so, do they over-compensate by rigidity or timidity or superhuman accomplish-ments? Do they feel any more insecure than, for example, white working-class athletes admitted to bolster Ivy League football teams or than the boss's nephew put in charge of the front office? Alternatively, if they do feel insecure or are stigmatized, are they able to overcome their initial obstacles and succeed at about the same rate as other workers or students? What are the processes by which "affirmative action hires" move toward success or fail-ure? Does the outcome have more to do with internal fortitude, organizational culture, structural opportunities, or other factors? Do some contexts facilitate success, or reify stigma, more than others?

To choose another direction: How many whites or men are told by admissions officers or personnel directors that they would have been admitted or hired were it not for affirmative action pressures? After all, that is an easy and mutually gratifying response from a gatekeeper to an angry or disappointed can-didate — even to many such candidates in a row, so long as each is addressed in the absence of the others. To my knowledge, no one has conducted research to document the ways in which affirma-tive action is presented to nonminorities denied jobs or admis-sion or promotion.

Broader political research would also be useful. Why did affir-mative action surface as a "hot" political issue in 1995, given that white men (and, to a lesser degree, white women) have always disliked strong versions of it? And why didn't corporations, uni-versities, most political candidates, and city governments jump on the anti–affirmative action bandwagon in 1995 or subse-quently? Conversely, Stephen Carter and Edna Bonacich remind us that in the 1960s some on the left saw affirmative action as an individualistic sell-out, encouraging personal mobility of the most energetic and effective actors within a racial or gender group at the expense of structural transformation that would benefit the whole group. What happened to that view? Presi-dent Nixon established the Philadelphia plan intended to bring more blacks into the construction trades, partly to give African Americans a stake in the extant economic system. Why in the past thirty years did support for affirmative action move from being a relatively right-wing position to being a relatively left-wing position?

There has been some excellent empirical research on the subject of affirmative action. Historical research on its formation and growth has demonstrated that federal policy was effective; once federal officials decided to endorse affirmative action and develop an institutional structure to implement and enforce the policy, it happened. Economic research has demonstrated another kind of effectiveness. Affirmative action policies in firms and universities contributed to the creation of a substantial black middle class in the 1970s, did not target only those already well educated or well-off, and have not harmed the productivity of participating firms. Affirmative action was not, however, the most important factor in decreasing the racial wage gap between the 1960s and 1980s. Enforcement of laws against employment discrimination, as well as increasing educational attainment and achievement among African Americans, did more.

Psychological research shows that if people are told that affirmative action influenced their attainment of a position, they devalue the position or their performance — more so if they disapprove of affirmative action to begin with, or if it was described as playing a central role, and less so if they see the apparent authority as racially biased. Co-workers may change their initial judgment that a new black manager is incompetent if he demonstrates that he is not or if they want to help him succeed. Organizational research shows that firms have constructed a wide variety of practices and structures to comply with affirmative action mandates. Forms of affirmative action that comport with the economic goals of a corporation — such as "diversity" for certain firms or in certain markets — have become part of the corporate culture and were thereby eased into ongoing procedures. Many executives and managers strongly support affirmative action as they understand it.

In short, bits of empirical evidence show that affirmative action is much like any other public policy. It has unintended consequences: arguably, it benefits corporate personnel managers and attorneys more than any other single group of people, since it invests them with new tasks to perform, and great influence in the corporate arena. It operates in rather predictable ways: if co-workers help a new black manager, she settles into the job more quickly and effectively than if they try to impede her. Its effects vary: it benefits a few people greatly and some people a little; it harms some people a little and a few people very much. It has probably had less impact than other policies which are much less controversial, such as improved schooling and the reduction of wage discrimination.

None of this is very dramatic or startling, which leaves us with two puzzles. Why are so many people so exercised over a policy that behaves like so many other public policies which do not evoke passionate public debate? And why is the empirical base for understanding the practice and effects of affirmative action so thin — paltry even, when compared with the rich philosophical and legal literature that the issue has elicited?

These puzzles are both resolved by the same answer: political actors find affirmative action an intensely valuable issue over which to debate and therefore have little desire to figure out just how it operates. That is, affirmative action is too valuable as a political weapon in a slightly different war to be blunted by attention to real-life complexities.

Many opponents of affirmative action are less concerned with the policy per se than with a broader assertion that racial (or gender) discrimination no longer exists and that African Americans' continued claims of its persistence are merely whining or self-seeking. At their crudest, opponents are racially hostile. Less crudely, they are unable or unwilling to see structural barriers or institutional advantages that are independent of individual intentions or awareness. The most sophisticated opponents are more concerned about class or individual, rather than racial or gender, barriers, or they hold a principled vision of individual meritocracy which supersedes all caveats or shadings.

Many proponents of affirmative action demonstrate an equal but opposite dynamic. They are less concerned with the policy per se than with a broader assertion that racial (or gender) discrimination is just as virulent as it has always been and that whites' opposition is merely covert racism or inexcusable naiveté. At their crudest, proponents are paranoid or self-seeking. Less crudely, they believe, as one of my students recently put it, that blacks have just as much right to a class structure as whites do, and just as much right to use every tool legally available to reach the top of it. The most sophisticated proponents see affirmative action as a essential means for individual African Americans to overcome persistent racism and attain resources that will help the African American community and the nation as a whole to overcome a shameful past — Du Bois's talented tenth.

Political elites within these opposing groups do not talk to one another and have no electoral or organizational incentive to do so. Legally, they each have a rich set of court cases, laws, and regulations to bolster their claims. Normatively, each group has available to it more philosophical justifications for its position than anyone can possibly read. Historically, each group can point to its preferred victories and defeats. Politically, each group has a core constituency and a wider set of citizens to whom it can turn for occasional support. Organizationally, each group has well-established but complex and constantly renegotiated (thus energy-draining) internal ties of communication, bargaining, and resource extraction leaving little incentive to question its own position or to give serious consideration to the other's. Both groups instead have strong incentives to exaggerate the venality of the opposing view and the purity of their own.

Thus the debate over affirmative action does more to exacerbate the tensions of American race relations than it does to solve the problem of overcoming past and present racial (and gender) discrimination in organizations that serve public purposes.

What, if anything, should be done about this situation? I would encourage, at a minimum, more attention to affirmative action as it is practiced and its actual accomplishments and failures. I urge this for several reasons. First, only research that aims toward dispassionate analysis can provide the intellectual space for people to separate their broad views about American racial practices from their particular judgments about the efficacy of affirmative action as compared to other policy possibilities. Only if there is a cohort of people who can persuasively say, "it works in this regard but not in that one," or "it works better than X but not as well as Y to achieve goal Z," can we as a nation get past the shouting.

Second, the public actually supports more affirmative action (of particular types) than the polarized politics suggests. Although about three-fourths of white Americans consistently agree that "blacks should work their way up ... without any special favors," so do about half of black Americans. Similarly, although 85 percent or more of whites endorse "ability" rather than "preferential treatment" to determine who gets jobs and college slots, so do about two-thirds of blacks. Conversely, fully seven in ten whites (compared with over eight in ten African Americans) favor affirmative action programs "provided there are no rigid quotas." Solid majorities of both races endorse special job training and educational assistance for women and people of color, extra efforts to identify and recruit qualified minorities, redrawing of voting districts to ensure minority representation, and other "soft" forms of affirmative action. One quarter of those who voted for California's referendum banning affirmative action in 1996 would have preferred a "mend it, don't end it" option.

There may be, in short, a majority political constituency for a set of affirmative action policies that could have significant impact, if anyone would do careful comparisons of various alternative practices. There may also be, unfortunately, a majority political constituency for ending all but the weakest forms of affirmative action. There is not, however, a viable majority political constituency for the strongest forms of affirmative action.

But this need not be a disaster. To make my central point again, what paltry empirical evidence there is suggests that the careful location of firms, full employment policies, vigorous pursuit of Title VII antidiscrimination law, improving educational attainment and achievement — all would do more to boost African Americans' employment and wages than affirmative action has done (except in specific sectors, such as police departments and customer relations units).

Thus my final recommendations: Put most of our energy into structural changes in inner-city elementary and secondary schools and urban labor markets; put a little energy into research on and publicity about effective affirmative action policies; declare victory and withdraw from the polarized battles over affirmative action in the political arena.

The Strange Career

of Affirmative Action

David L. Kirp

The cacophonous chorus known as the Left — a chorus in which I frequently sing — is often criticized for mimicking Chicken Little, squandering its credibility by exaggerating the terrible consequences of policy initiatives promoted by the Right. No matter how justified this criticism may sometimes be (consider, for instance, the liberal assault on the Clinton administration's initial welfare reform proposal), such criticism is misplaced with respect to affirmative action. To an extent unanticipated even by the Cassandra crowd, the ending of racial and ethnic preferences in Texas because of the federal court order in *Hopwood*,[1] as well as in California as a result of the Board of Regents' decision, has diminished the black and Latino presence in higher education, most dramatically in those states' law and medical schools.

The symbolic impact of this transformation is almost as startling as are the numbers themselves. Nearly half a century ago, in *Sweatt v. Painter*, the State of Texas was ordered by the United States Supreme Court to admit black students to the University of Texas Law School; the school's preeminence in matters legal meant that black students who could not enroll because of their race had been unconstitutionally denied equal educational opportunity.[2] Now as then, the University of Texas Law School remains the gateway to that state's legal establishment, but for the first time since the epochal *Sweatt* decision, there is not a single African American among the entering class. In effect, ending affirmative action legally accomplished what Jim Crow could not. If we are all multiculturalists now, as the sociologist Nathan Glazer contends,[3] at least in public universities multiculturalism may become more a matter of academic interest, a subject like philosophy or botany, than a demographic fact.

In the face of these swift-rushing developments, the left has been impotent. Hundreds of University of California professors signed a petition that objected, not to the substance of the regents' colorblind policy, but rather to the high-handed way the university's overseers went about adopting that policy. This formulation of the grievance, meant to portray the herd-of-cats faculty as more united than it really is, was too clever by half. Since an autonomous professoriat is even less popular than affirmative action itself, the strategy stirred few outside the academy to indignation. Meanwhile, black and Latino students and their white and Asian allies were quiescent — remarkably so, in a university that not so long ago was synonymous with student activism.[4]

There has been, as well, a rush to the courts in California, in hopes that the judges could undo the political damage. Civil rights groups contemplated challenging Governor Pete Wilson's behind-the-scenes regental vote buying; subsequently, they filed a lawsuit to test the constitutionality of Proposition 209, a 1996 ballot measure that bans affirmative action in state and local government activity. In an earlier judicial era, this approach might have worked; not now, though. The federal appeals court not only rejected the argument that such a proscription amounted to discrimination, it also slapped the wrist of the trial court judge who had taken this claim seriously.

More of the same hostile reaction is to be anticipated from both politicians and judges. The Supreme Court has grown increasingly critical of affirmative action in its various guises.[5] Other states are preparing to emulate California's call to colorblindness. The review of federal affirmative action, ordered by President Clinton in response to well-orchestrated outcries against racism in reverse, has left in place a policy that is a mere shadow of its former self.[6]

Articles and books decrying these happenings regularly appear in venues like this one, which have far more prestige than mass audience appeal.[7] To borrow a lament of the Spanish Civil War republicans, while the Left has all the songs the Right has all the guns.

Changing the Subject

Most astonishing about this recent history is not that affirmative action fell so suddenly from political and legal grace. Rather, it is the fact that affirmative action ever existed as national policy; that it first flowered in the strange garden of Richard Nixon's social policy;[8] and that it endured long after other civil rights initiatives of the time, most notably integration, withered and died.[9]

Affirmative action — in the commonly used, preference-bestowing version of that term[10] — amounts to a substantial redistribution of highly valued goods (jobs, university places, and the like) from the have-mores to the have-lesses. Despite all the elaborate normative justifications that have been offered, such an inherently divisive approach, one that produces clear and identifiable losers as well as winners among the polity, is not a likely way of designing policy for the long haul. Historically, less visible and confrontationist strategies for redistribution, such as Social Security, have been more resistant to subsequent political attack.[11]

Situating race at the center of the preference equation made affirmative action even more vulnerable.[12] Race remains the most fraught of American social issues, "an explosive on the tongues of men," as Bill Bradley called it on the floor of the Senate. The remarkable popularity of The Bell Curve has to do with the fact that, by advancing a scientific-sounding argument for racial inferiority, an idea widely accepted by white Americans, the book provides the intellectual camouflage needed to build a respectable argument against race-based affirmative action.[13] Disadvantage is one thing, as the artless text of the California Regents' resolution banning race-based affirmative action suggests; race is something else entirely. The white middle class, increasingly insecure in the face of major economic shifts,[14] will not readily hand over what it regards as its hard-won prerogatives to African Americans, either out of racial guilt or to accomplish such admirable but abstract goals as boosting diversity or nurturing a public culture.[15]

For more than a generation, the pragmatic rationale for affirmative action — that it is a relatively cheap way to buy racial peace — carried the day, producing something approaching consensus among politicians and business leaders (who themselves did not have to bear the personal costs of the policy). Policy making about racial preferences was then dominated by elites: the familiar triangle of interest groups, bureaucrats, and elected officials, as well as by the judiciary, which struggled to develop a pragmatic and coherent reading of conflicting constitutional claims and produced decisions that appeared to shift with the political winds.[16]

Once affirmative action was effectively politicized by failed presidential aspirant and California Governor Pete Wilson, the pragmatic approach fell out of favor, replaced by a politics of resentment.[17] In the argument over public values, the contention prevailed that preferences were fundamentally unfair, even un-American, among a polity loath to accept structural, rather than individual, explanations for success and failure — a polity that widely embraces Pete Wilson's campaign mantra that "individuals should be rewarded on the basis of merit." During the Proposition 209 campaign, legions of citizens who regarded themselves as innocents victimized by race-based social engineering — who believed as well that minorities were getting something for nothing — found their pocketbooks and consciences in happy harmony.[18] For them, a vote against affirmative action was a no-brainer.

Affirmative action dominates current discussions of race and social policy. The Left fears — not without cause — that unless the tide of reaction can somehow be reversed, the gains of a generation will be dissipated. Blacks and Latinos, deprived of a new cadre of educated leaders, will slip further down the social ladder. Besides, intellectuals of the Left cluster in universities, where incursions against affirmative action have been most acutely felt. From the Left, there are calls to devise new rationales for affirmative action.[19] More promisingly, some universities are formulating their admissions standards to take into account plausible indicia of disadvantage that are not explicitly racial: parents' income and education level, dropout and college matriculation rates from the high school a student has attended, and the like. On another front, there are proposals to forge new alliances with groups, especially in the labor movement, that will predictably suffer under education and employment regimes that claim to be meritocratic.[20]

Meanwhile, matters of racial and ethnic justice that bear even more fundamentally on this perennial American dilemma go almost entirely unaddressed.[21] "Integration" has almost disappeared from the American vocabulary, even as minorities, especially blacks, remain effectively sealed into inner-city ghettos (and old suburbs that, because of white flight, often become new ghettos), obliged to live in inferior (and more costly) housing, to send their children to worse schools, and placed at a geographic disadvantage in the competition for non-dead-end, "Edge City" jobs.[22] Moreover, even as a black middle class has emerged in the last generation, partly because of affirmative action, the most disadvantaged, who are disproportionately black and Hispanic, keep falling further behind in this ever-more-stratified, competitive, and market-driven society.[23]

What do we talk about when we talk about race? Not these things. Perhaps it is time to change the subject.

NOTES

1. *Hopwood v. Texas*, 78 F.3d 932 (1996).

2. *Sweatt v. Painter*, 339 U.S. 629 (1950).

3. Nathan Glazer, *We Are All Multiculturalists Now* (Cambridge, MA, 1997). Compare David Hollinger, *Postethnic America: Beyond Multiculturalism* (New York, 1995).

4. In recent years, the only issue that has evoked notable gestures of student solidarity at the University of California is the demand, on the part of graduate student teachers, that the university recognize their right to bargain collectively.

5. See, e.g., Paul Brest and Miranda Oshige, "Affirmative Action for Whom?" *Stanford Law Review* 47 (1995); David Kirp and Nancy Weston, "The Political Jurisprudence of Affirmative Action," in Ellen Frankel Paul et al., eds., *Equal Opportunity* (New York, 1987), 223–49.

6. Christopher Edley Jr., *Not All Black and White: Affirmative Action and American Values* (New York, 1996).

7. See, e.g., Barbara Bergmann, *In Defense of Affirmative Action* (1996); Susan Sturm and Lani Guinier, "The Future of Affirmative Action: Reclaiming the Innovative Ideal," *California Law Review*, vol. 84 (1996); Neil Rudenstine, "Diversity and Learning: Report to the Board of Overseers of Harvard University" (www.harvard. edu/presidents_office/home.html).

8. Kenneth O'Reilly, *Nixon's Piano: Presidents and Racial Politics from Washington to Clinton* (New York, 1995).

9. Douglas Massey and Nancy Denton, *American Apartheid: Segregation and*

the *Making of the Underclass* (Cambridge, MA, 1993); Christopher Jencks and Paul Peterson, eds., *The Urban Underclass* (Washington, DC, 1991); David Kirp, John Dwyer, and Larry Rosenthal, *Our Town: Race, Housing, and the Soul of Suburbia* (New Brunswick, NJ, 1996).

10. Robert Fullinwider, "Achieving Equal Opportunity," in Robert Fullinwider and Claudia Mills, eds., *The Moral Foundations of Civil Rights* (Lanham, MD, 1995).

11. Theda Skocpol, *Social Policy in the United States: Future Possibilities in Historic Perspective* (Princeton, NJ, 1995); Richard Titmuss, *Commitment to Welfare* (London, 1976).

12. Paul Sniderman and Thomas Piazza, *The Scar of Race* (Cambridge, MA, 1993).

13. Charles Murray and Richard Herrnstein, *The Bell Curve* (New York, 1995).

14. Katherine Newman, *Declining Fortunes: The Withering of the American Dream* (New York, 1993).

15. Robert Post, *Constitutional Domains: Democracy, Community, Management* (Cambridge, MA, 1995), 134–96.

16. Kirp and Weston, "The Political Jurisprudence of Affirmative Action."

17. Robert Frank and Philip Cook, *The Winner-Take-All Society* (New York, 1995).

18. During the Proposition 209 campaign, supporters of affirmative action tried downplaying the race issue, focusing instead on creating opportunities for women. While women were more likely to favor affirmative action than men, this attempt to substitute one wedge issue for another ultimately failed.

19. The philosophical arguments on both sides of the issue were thoroughly aired in the aftermath of the *Bakke* decision. See, e.g., Robert Fullinwider, *The Reverse Discrimination Controversy* (Lanham, MD, 1980).

20. Bergman, *In Defense of Affirmative Action*.

21. At Harvard University, Christopher Edley Jr. and Gary Orfield have launched the Civil Rights Project, which emphasizes these neglected issues of racial and ethnic justice.

22. Gary Orfield and Carol Askhinaze, *The Closing Door: Conservative Policy and Black Opportunity* (Chicago, 1991); Joel Garreau, *Edge City: Life on the New Frontier* (New York, 1991).

23. William Julius Wilson, *The Truly Disadvantaged: The Inner City, the Underclass, and Public Policy* (Chicago, 1987).

Maintaining Diversity at

the University of Texas

David Montejano

At the beginning of the twentieth century, the noted scholar W. E. B. Du Bois predicted that the problem of the century would be that of the "color line." As we approach the end of the twentieth century, it has become increasingly evident that we will carry this problem of color over into the next century as well. This is the case even as a number of politicians, judges, university officials, and others embrace the logic of "color blindness" to reverse the civil rights gains of the 1960s and 1970s. Affirmative action, once seen as a means to redress past wrongs and present-day inequities, is now cast as "reverse discrimination" against whites. This was the reasoning that led the Fifth Circuit Court of Appeals, based in New Orleans, to bar (on March 18, 1996) the University of Texas at Austin from considering race in law school admissions. (Named after the lead plaintiff in the case, this court order became known as the *Hopwood* decision.) Shortly thereafter, the same colorblind reasoning led Texas Attorney General Dan Morales to apply *Hopwood* to the admissions and scholarship procedures of all state universities and colleges. Within the span of a few weeks in March, all affirmative action programs at Texas universities had been banned. For those who recalled the twenty-plus years that the State of Texas had fought court-mandated desegregation, the sudden implementation of a federal court order reeked of opportunism and hypocrisy.[1]

What follows is a brief comment on the significance of *Hopwood*, with an emphasis on an initial strategy developed by a number of concerned academics and legislators. I also outline, in passing, some differences between the affirmative action battles in Texas and California.

Misframing the Debate

One thing is fairly clear: those in favor of affirmative action have lost the current round of the ongoing debate about race. Affirmative action has been pitted against some idealized notion of individual merit. Framed in this way, some Latinos and blacks argue that they want to make it on their own, that they need no special help from affirmative action.[2] Such personal pride, however, leads to a serious misunderstanding of affirmative action policies. Affirmative action was never a question of individual qualifications or abilities; rather, it was a question of rectifying the institutional practices that continually reproduced virtually all-white work forces and all-white student bodies. Such practices were referred to as "institutional racism." Affirmative action, operating at the level of institutions, was intended to commit institutions to cast a wide net in recruitment and admission in order to provide access and opportunity. Once such access was provided, the targeted individuals had to prove their mettle: affirmative action did not take the exams, write the papers, or pass the bar.

This success in misframing the debate on race reflects a profound amnesia. On the one hand, it points to a loss or dismissal of historical memory. This dismissal was quite evident in the *Hopwood* decision of the Fifth Circuit Court, which took no account of the long history of de jure racial exclusion at the University of Texas Law School. The loss of memory was also evident in the idealistic interpretation of Texas Attorney General Dan Morales, who argued that race or skin color should carry no weight in university admissions or financial assistance.[3] One can agree with Morales that this should be the case in an ideal world, but has Texas, with a thick history of segregation and exclusion through the 1970s, reached this idealized utopia? Can one seriously argue that the segregationist legacy in schooling, in the labor market, in business, and in residential patterns no longer carries present effects? That being black or Mexican in Texas is no different than being white? (This is why my Texas history class laughed when I told them the day after the *Hopwood* decision, "Boy, it sure feels great to no longer be a minority." My class understood the irony of my statement.)

There is historical precedent for our present situation. Before the *Brown* decision of 1954 overturned school segregation as unconstitutional, Texas Mexican civil rights lawyers routinely argued that Mexican Americans were Caucasian and therefore not subject to the segregationist policies developed for non-Caucasians. In 1948, in *Delgado v. Bastrop ISD*, the federal courts agreed and ordered Texas educational officials to dismantle the Mexican school system. In response Texas officials merely dropped the use of the word "Mexican" in their listing of schools. Thus while Mexican American students remained segregated in Mexican schools as before, "Mexican schools" no longer officially existed. When civil rights lawyers complained about noncompliance, the officials replied that, since the so-called Mexican schools were Caucasian schools and the Anglo schools were Caucasian schools, there was in effect no segregation.[4]

There is also a sociological amnesia evident in the discussion of affirmative action. Affirmative action policies were meant to redress serious race divisions; they were intended to have a "leveling effect" on a society with obvious race inequalities. Created in response to the civil rights movement of the 1960s and 1970s, affirmative action was an attempt, in the short run, to assure social peace. In the long run, it was seen as a means by which to develop significant "minority" middle class communities. Universities, the institutions that have traditionally facilitated upward mobility, were especially entrusted with this charge. In this sense, affirmative action reflected a political agreement that diversity in the professions, in business circles, and generally in the middle classes was a desirable societal goal. This goal of diversity, established in the *Bakke* decision of 1978, has now explicitly been rejected in the *Hopwood* decision of the Fifth Circuit Court.

The sociological wisdom of the Fifth Circuit Court (and of Attorney General Dan Morales) will be severely tested in the near future, as supposedly "race neutral" criteria decrease the number of blacks and Mexican Americans in university programs. Already one can see the negative impact in the first University of Texas Law School class admitted under the *Hopwood* guidelines. Whereas in 1996 the law school admitted sixty-five blacks, in 1997 it admitted only eleven, and only four have decided to enroll. The 1997 class of 501 students may have the lowest number of African Americans since Heman Sweatt "integrated" the law school in 1950. The number of Mexican Americans admitted has likewise suffered a serious decline, from seventy in 1996 to thirty-four in 1997, with twenty-six deciding to enroll.[5]

University of Texas Law School Admitted

	Total	White	Black	Mexican American	Asian American	Other Minority
1996	1,105	841	65	70	93	36
1997	1,040	865	11	34	105	25

University of Texas Law School Enrolled

	Total	White	Black	Mexican American	Asian American	Other Minority
1996	488	370	31	42	30	15
1997	501	424	4	26	45	7

At the undergraduate level, *Hopwood* has also had a negative impact on minority admissions. African American admits declined from 421 in 1996 to 314 in 1997, a drop of nearly 25 percent. Mexican American admits likewise declined from 1,568 in 1996 to 1,333, a drop of 15 percent. These figures represent the first reductions in minority admissions since 1975, the first year that the university began compiling such statistics.[6]

University of Texas at Austin Freshmen Admitted

	Total	White	Black	Mexican American	Asian American	Other Minority
1996	10,459	6,854	421	1,568	1,553	59
1997	10,651	7,140	314	1,333	1,715	45

In a state where currently 40 percent of the population is either African American or Mexican American, such lack of diversity at the law school and the flagship institution presents a politically explosive issue. But exactly what should be done has not been clear. Or, as one African American legislator, Rep. Sylvester Turner (Dem.–Houston), pointedly asked of Attorney General Morales, "Where do we go from here?" Morales had no answer.[7]

The Ten Percent Plan: A Partial Alternative

A pernicious aspect of the Fifth Circuit Court ruling was its threat to hold any university officials liable for punitive damages if they failed to follow the dictates of the *Hopwood* decision. The president of the University of Texas, Robert Berdahl, who had criticized the *Hopwood* ruling and Attorney General Morales's subsequent interpretation as a prelude to the "resegregation" of the university, was barred from considering alternatives or transition programs.[8] University administrators had no choice but to comply fully and immediately with *Hopwood*. No leadership could be expected from the "tower." For faculty and students involved with ethnic studies programs, the situation was especially untenable. Recruitment and retention programs were being dismantled, scholarships were being redefined, and even the existence of ethnic study programs and centers appeared to be in jeopardy. Fortunately a number of state legislators, many of them university alumni, were also quite concerned about the implications of *Hopwood*.

At the request of State Senator Gonzalo Barrientos (Dem.–Austin), several faculty associated with the Center for Mexican American Studies at the University of Texas, along with colleagues from the University of Houston and the Mexican American Legal Defense and Educational Fund in San Antonio, formed a task group to develop a strategy in response to *Hopwood*.[9] The task group had the responsibility of developing proposals that could be drafted into legislation.

One proposal took direct aim at the historical amnesia discussed above: it called for a joint resolution of the House and Senate acknowledging a history of discrimination against African Americans and Mexican Americans, which in turn would sanction the use of race as one criterion in university admissions and financial assistance. Essentially this legislative resolution would negate the impact of *Hopwood*. With Republicans in control of the Senate, the task group never placed much hope on this proposal and, predictably, the resolution died in legislative committee.

The second proposal did not contest the mandate to employ "race neutral" criteria. Instead it used the fact of segregation and geographic concentration of minorities at the high school level to achieve diversity at the university level. Called the "Ten Percent Plan," this approach called for the automatic admission of the top ten percent of each graduating high school class to the Texas university of their choice. SAT scores were not to be taken into account. Moreover, universities were free to set the automatic admissions threshold at the top 25 percent level. Admissions beyond the automatic threshold level had to consider a number of criteria, including family socioeconomic status, extracurricular activity, first generation college status, and so on. This plan became the bill on which we focused our collective energies.[10]

The numbers generated by a ten percent plan looked promising. Data for 1994, for example, showed that a breakdown of the 13,000 graduating seniors who were in the top ten percent and had taken the SATs yielded the following:

Breakdown of Top Ten Percent Who Took SATs, 1994

Total	Whites	Hispanics	Asians	Blacks
13,000	8,500 (65%)	2,400 (18%)	1,300 (10%)	800 (6%)

Moreover, there were an additional four thousand graduating students in the top 10 percent who, for whatever reason, had not taken the SATs in 1994. Presumably a good fraction of these students were minorities; if so, when added to the above numbers, the automatic admissions pool would likely consist of approximately 20 percent Hispanic and 10 percent black students.[11] One had only to compare these figures with the current percentages at the University of Texas at Austin — 12 percent Hispanic and 4 percent black — to realize that a top ten percent plan might be the best way to maintain a minimum floor for diversity.

A final advantage of the ten percent plan was that it was easy to present and defend rhetorically: it was simple, fair, predictable, and, most importantly, it did not use race-specific criteria. This rhetorical advantage became evident in the various public forums where the ten percent plan was discussed. To those white critics who argued cynically that it would let in "many poor white kids from rural areas," the response was that "they deserve a chance at our flagship universities as well." To those who argued that it would let in too many from "low-performing high schools," the response was that we should remedy that problem at the high school level and that universities in the meantime could adjust to the situation much as they were adjusting to *Hopwood*. To those who argued that SAT scores were critical measures of future success, the response was that they were not as accurate as academic performance measured over several years of high school. And to those who worried about over-inflated admissions, the response was that historically only one-third of the "top ten percent" apply to the University of Texas at Austin and that the plan would create a healthy competition among Texas universities for this academic elite.

Armed with these figures and arguments, the ten percent plan was presented in the Texas House of Representatives by Irma Rangel (Dem.–Kingsville) with support from Hugo Berlanga (Dem.–Corpus Christi). The measure passed by a 77–68 vote divided largely on partisan lines. In the Senate it was carried by Gonzalo Barrientos (Dem.–Austin), Royce West (Dem.–Dallas), and Teel Bivins (Rep.–Amarillo). With the quiet endorsement of Republican Governor George W. Bush, the bill passed the Senate 27-4 with the bipartisan support of Democrats and moderate Republicans. Governor Bush signed the bill on May 20, 1997.

There were a number of other bills introduced to deal with *Hopwood*, but all failed or were effectively gutted. Most notable was legislation filed by Rep. Ron Wilson (Dem.–Houston) that would eliminate special college admissions standards for student athletes. Like the ten percent plan, this bill did not challenge the dismantling of affirmative action directly. Instead it pushed the concept of "race neutral" academic admissions to its logical conclusion — to the elimination of separate standards for athletes. Wilson's position was that if the University of Texas would not admit blacks into law school or other professional schools, then blacks should not play football or basketball for the University. As expected, strong opposition was mounted by officials from the University of Texas and Texas A & M University. Passage of such a bill would destroy the multi-million-dollar football and basketball programs at both institutions. Legislators who supported the *Hopwood* decision but who desired nationally-ranked football were momentarily caught in a rhetorical bind. Resolving the paradox was not difficult: the bill passed after being rendered ineffectual.[12] Wilson's point, nonetheless, had been made (and will not be soon forgotten).

A Contrast with California

It would be instructive to compare the way affirmative action battles have played themselves out in California and Texas. A quick note here will have to suffice.

An obvious point of contrast lies in the role of the political leadership of each state. Unlike in Texas, where affirmative action was struck down by a federal court, in California there was an actual movement spearheaded by Republican Governor Pete Wilson. Concerned in 1993 about reelection, Governor Wilson faced strongly unfavorable ratings because of a depressed economy. With an orchestrated campaign of immigrant bashing and race bashing, Wilson was able to shift the focus of discontent. The campaign was successful and resulted in the passage of Proposition 187 (the anti-immigrant measure) as well as in Wilson's reelection in 1994. The following year, when Wilson launched his short-lived campaign for president, he championed Proposition 209 (the anti–affirmative action measure), which passed in 1996. In sharp contrast, the popular Republican governor of Texas, George W. Bush, presiding over a healthy economy, has publicly warned against the politics of immigrant bashing and Mexico bashing and has come out in support of bilingual education.[13] While silent on the *Hopwood* case, his staff let it be known that he supported the ten percent plan.

The question of leadership, however, goes beyond governors. One has to look at the political substratum and explain why, in comparison to California, there exists a significant Mexican American presence in both houses of the Texas legislature. As recently as 1990, there were only 4 Mexican Americans in the 80-member California Assembly and 3 in the 40-member Senate.[14] In Texas, on the other hand, there has been a sizable number of Mexican American legislators since the 1970s. In the recent 1997 legislative session, for example, 28 of the 150 House seats and 7 of the 31 Senate seats were occupied by Mexican American officeholders. African Americans added another 14 House members and 2 Senators. Such representation, I would argue, reflects local community activism dating back to the civil rights movements of the 1960s and, in many instances, even before that. A deep level of analysis, in other words, would be a historical one. Herein lies the irony: in Texas, Jim Crow segregation created highly organized minority communities that have long understood the dynamics of realpolitik. There has never been any illusion that Texas was a liberal state. In this context, one could say that an affable Governor Bush, wishing to preside over a relatively conflict-free term in office, understood that it would be best to support the damage-control efforts of the minority legislators.[15] Realpolitik had simply led to different outcomes in Texas and California.

The Next Steps

Philosophically and politically the debate over affirmative action will continue unabated into the next century. Without waiting for some conclusive resolution, we have created a law that promises the "talented tenth," to use W. E. B. Du Bois's phrase, admission into the Texas university of their choice. Basically the ten percent plan works because de facto segregation or concentration of African Americans and Mexican Americans at the high school level will assure diversity at the university level.

Everyone involved in the design and passage of the ten percent plan, academics and legislators alike, understands that it is merely a first step in devising a "post-*Hopwood*" strategy. The task group intends to monitor and assess the ten percent plan in order to strengthen its potential for maintaining diversity. The group will continue its efforts for a scholarship fund that would truly empower the ten percent framework. Rhetorically we may employ a sports analogy to insist that universities invest the same energies in recruiting and retaining "intellectual athletes" as it does physical athletes. And there remains a sense of urgency to address the problem of graduate and professional school admissions. The unique collaboration of concerned professors and politicians, a collaboration forged by the *Hopwood* crisis, will continue to offer legislative remedies to deal with this crisis.

NOTES

1. For a discussion, see David Montejano, *Anglos and Mexicans in the Making of Texas, 1836–1986* (Austin, 1987), especially Part Four; also Guadalupe San Miguel Jr., *Let All of Them Take Heed: Mexican Americans and the Campaign for Educational Equality in Texas, 1910–1981* (Austin, 1987).

2. Or as Ward Connerly, the prominent leader of the anti–affirmative action movement in California, put it, "you can travel the freeways of opportu-

nity without special consideration based on the color of your skin." See "Questions of Race Run Deep for Foe of Preferences," *New York Times*, 27 July 1997, 1 and 10–11.

3. A less charitable view would say that Morales was advancing his political ambitions by pandering to the right. See Dan Morales, "Hopwood Opens New Era in Pursuit of Diversity," *Austin American-Statesman*, 7 Feb. 1997; and "Morales Opinion Hardly Settles State's Affirmative Action Debate," *Austin American-Statesman*, 7 Feb. 1997; also "AG's Hopwood Strategy Assailed," *Daily Texan*, 2 May 1996.

4. See Jorge Rangel and Carlos Alcala, "De Jure Segregation of Chicanos in Texas Schools," *Harvard Civil Rights–Civil Liberties Law Review* 7 (March 1972): 307–91.

5. Memorandum from Shelli Soto, assistant dean for admissions, School of Law, University of Texas at Austin, 28 July 1997. Also see "Single Black Enrolled So Far," *Dallas Morning News*, 21 May 1997; "Black Law Student Happy to Avoid Spotlight," *Austin American-Statesman*, 13 July 1997.

6. "UT Austin Offers of Admission to Freshman," *On Campus*, 15 Apr. 1997. Figures at the other flagship institution, Texas A & M University at College Station, reveal a similar marked decline in African American and Mexican American admissions and enrollments. See "UT, Texas A&M See Minority Enrollment Drop," *Austin American-Statesman*, 19 July 1997.

7. "Morales Opinion Hardly Settles State's Affirmative Action Debate," *Austin American-Statesman*, 7 Feb. 1997.

8. "Appeals Court Bars Racial Preference in College Admissions," *Chronicle of Higher Education*, 29 Mar. 1996, A26–A27; also "Segregation Anew," *New York Times*, 1 June 1996, editorial page.

9. The task group consisted of University of Texas professors Ricardo Romo, Jorge Chapa, Gerald Torres, Susan Gonzalez-Baker, David Montejano; University of Texas students Oscar de la Torre and Mariela Olivarez; University of Houston professor Michael Olivas; and MALDEF attorney Al Kaufmann. Legislative aides Steve Kester and Linda Garza represented Senator Gonzalo Barrientos and Representative Irma Rangel, respectively.

10. There were two other proposals as well. One called for endowing the "ten percent plan" with a scholarship fund. Another would have indemnified university officials in the case of *Hopwood*-related lawsuits. The scholarship proposal died for lack of an adequate revenue source in a tax-cutting climate; the indemnification proposal died because it was perceived by Republicans as countermanding the Fifth Circuit Court.

11. Data derived from the SAT Testing Agency by the Texas State Data Center at Texas A & M University. When I first proposed the 10 percent plan at

the "Hispanic Summit on Affirmative Action" in August, 1996, I presented hypothetical figures based on the degree of high school segregation in the state. Assuming that half of the high schools were segregated (and that minorities would not make the top 10 percent in integrated schools), the numbers of blacks and Mexican Americans in the top ten percent were estimated to be 1,250 (7.3 percent) and 2,250 (13.2 percent), respectively. A comparison with the complete data will likely suggest that the degree of segregation of Texas high schools exceeds 50 percent.

12. *Austin American-Statesman*, 3 June 1997.

13. "Immigrants Are Off-Limits, Bush Warns," *Austin American-Statesman*, 14 Aug. 1995; "Texas Avoiding Mistakes Made by California," *Austin American-Statesman*, 14 Sept. 1995; and George W. Bush, "No Cheap Shots at Mexico, Please," *New York Times*, 20 Sept. 1995.

14. The 1996 California elections, perhaps reflecting a Latino backlash to three years of immigrant and Mexico bashing, increased the number of Latino assembly persons to fourteen and the number of Latino senators to four. Cruz Bustamante became the first Latino Assembly speaker in California history. See "Bustamante Begins Historic Speakership," *Los Angeles Times*, 10 Dec. 1996; "Polanco's Efforts Bear Fruit with Latino's Rise in Assembly," *Los Angeles Times*, 26 Dec. 1996.

15. Governor Bush had other priorities, especially a property tax–cutting proposal, to pass through the Democrat-controlled House. Even in the Senate, where Republicans held a 17–14 edge, a bloc of twelve senators could procedurally undermine legislation. Thus the significance of a letter to President Clinton, signed by twelve senators, to "take a stand against the resegregation of Texas public universities" (*Dallas Morning News*, 7 Apr. 1997).

Self-Defeating Identities

Daniel R. Ortiz

In recent years, affirmative action has come under surprising pressure. Long-standing political settlements have come undone: in many places, particularly in California, the ensuing battles have forced a dramatic rollback in governmental preferences. Part of the reason lies, paradoxically, in the success of affirmative action itself. As affirmative action became more generally accepted, it changed the way we thought not only about it, but also about ourselves. These newer conceptions of identity, however, have provided an unsuitable foundation on which to build the political support necessary to sustain affirmative action programs. In part, the recent turnabout in affirmative action represents the self-defeating consequences of the very concepts of identity that affirmative action has itself nurtured.

Although affirmative action has always reflected conflicting rationales, its dominant form of justification has shifted greatly over the last twenty-five years. In the beginning, as *Regents of University of California v. Bakke* illustrates, we thought of affirmative action primarily in liberal, individualistic terms.[1] As Justice Powell's opinion in that case and the leading opinions in subsequent cases made clear, "societal discrimination," no matter how bad, could not serve to justify preferences.[2] Only two goals could sustain affirmative action: attaining diversity and remedying an institution's own past discriminatory behavior — and both justifications sounded in individualist terms.[3] The goal of racial diversity could be pursued only so long as other nonracial differences counted as well; diversity was conceived as reflecting a universal individuality in which there was no single, overwhelming type of difference. The goal of remedying one's own past discrimination resonated even more deeply with traditional liberalism. By requiring a showing of past institutional responsibility, the Court maintained that affirmative action was permissible only as a means to correct *individual* instances of past injustice. The requirement effectively barred public entities from acting to correct past injustices for which they themselves were not responsible.

But *Bakke* and subsequent cases undercut these liberal commitments at the same time they made them. As Robert Post notes in his introduction to this collection, although Justice Powell said in *Bakke* that race could count only as one "plus" among others, he also approved Harvard College's affirmative action plan, which allowed "some attention to numbers"[4] and therefore assumed that every member of a disadvantaged racial category — no matter what that individual's personal experience — was entitled to a racial plus. Thus, although group difference could count as only one difference among many, it was assumed that everyone in the particular group possessed the distinctive characteristics that warranted preferential treatment. The opinion thereby looked two ways at once. While promoting the liberal view that we are all individuals and that people in different groups are at bottom the same, it simultaneously defended the conflicting view that groups do possess critical, defining differences.

The other authorized justification for affirmative action, remedying past individualized discrimination, looked both ways too. Although in subsequent cases the Court clung to Powell's view that past societal discrimination could not justify preferences, the Court never required a showing that the person taking advantage of a preference had ever been personally injured by the institution granting it. The institution had to show only that it had a "strong basis in evidence"[5] that it had acted unlawfully in the past against someone in the preference-taking group, not that it had ever injured the particular person to whom it was awarding the preference. This compromised the overall inquiry in an interesting way. On the preference-giving side, the Court adhered to a "liberal," individualistic approach — it required *some* showing of institutional responsibility — and so avoided criticism that it was working out a theory of group harms. On the preference-taking side, however, the Court acted as if all members of the benefited class had been injured — it required *no* showing of individual injury — and thus allowed preferences to remedy past group harms. Both of the Court's authorized legal justifications, then, stand conflicted between individualist and group notions of identity. While publicly invoking liberal notions of identity, both justifications secretly admit group difference.

We should not be surprised that the Court is so deeply conflicted. Both views of identity have strengths and weaknesses. From the Court's perspective, for instance, the liberal view promises greater political support for its decisions. By grounding affirmative action either in a type of diversity that operates even within the majority group and in individual responsibility for past discrimination, or both, the Court aligns preferences with majoritarian norms and interests while at the same time reducing the practical threat preferences pose to the majority class. Some members of the majority can, after all, take advantage of diversity pluses, while restricting preferences to institutional "bad actors" both reduces the absolute number of preferences and limits them to the cases likely to be perceived as the worst.

The liberal view of identity also promises to help minority groups' claims of justice go down more easily. It allows minorities to argue their claims from within the majority's own belief system. They can avoid challenging the majority's values from outside — always a politically difficult move, and one that may alienate potential supporters. The claim "we are like you," which the liberal notion of identity makes, does not require the majority to revise its own values, merely to extend those values' protection to a wider circle of people whom it recognizes to be like itself. Although expanding the boundaries of the group may threaten the majority, such a strategy is apt to be less threatening than demanding that the majority recognize the values of fundamentally different groups to be as worthy of respect as its own.

The liberal move does, however, pose one great disadvantage for minority groups: although politically efficacious, it may not provide what the minority wants. It may provide the minority what the majority accords itself, but, since the liberal notion of identity denies any important differences between groups, it cannot provide the minority anything else. Thus, to minority groups, liberalism proves something of a bind. It may provide them access to the privileges the majority grants itself, but only at the cost of denying whatever is critically distinctive about themselves. It provides, in short, a greater likelihood of political success, but under someone else's political agenda.

Identity politics seeks to avoid this danger. It insists that the majority recognize and respect the minority's fundamental difference and provides space for the minority to pursue its own aims, not the majority's. Identity politics cannot, however, avoid the disadvantages of liberal identity theory without also giving up its main advantage: greater political efficacity. Unlike liberal identity theory, identity politics gives the minority no means to leverage its claims of justice off the majority's sense of itself. Identity politics largely forecloses arguments internal to the majority's own system of belief. It promotes external claims instead, and therein lies its political difficulty. To the extent identity politics envisions identity groups as sovereign states, intergroup justice becomes a form of international relations, with the danger that majority realpolitik will rule. Identity politics, thus, presents its own bind. Although it may allow minority groups to assert their own, not the majority's, interests, it allows them to assert them less effectively. What identity groups gain in defining their agenda they lose in carrying it out.

As Judith Butler notes in her contribution to this collection, affirmative action has led to a flourishing of (often exclusionary) identity politics.[6] This is no accident. Despite the many liberal justifications originally asserted for it, affirmative action is best and most simply understood as rough justice among different groups. The increasing popularity of diversity as a rationale, moreover, has only reinforced the idea that people in different groups differ fundamentally from one another. But this rhetoric of difference has made affirmative action politically difficult to sustain. The more identity groups come to resemble separate, sovereign states, the more demands for affirmative action come to resemble pleas for voluntary foreign aid. And we all know where such claims lead — at least in this country. In this one respect, then, identity politics has become politically self-defeating. The more it flourishes, the less likely the majority is to recognize others' claims of justice. Affirmative action's very success has to some extent proved its own undoing.

NOTES

1. *Regents of University of California v. Bakke*, 438 U.S. 265 (1978).

2. *Ibid.*, 307–10. Justice Powell rejected "'societal discrimination' [as] an amorphous concept of injury that may be ageless in its reach into the past" (*Ibid.*, 307). Later cases have even rejected past discrimination in narrower areas, such as the construction industry, absent some showing of individual institutional responsibility. See, e.g., *Richmond v. J.A. Croson Co.*, 488 U.S. 469, 498–506 (1989).

3. *Regents v. Bakke*, 307–9, 311–14.

4. *Regents v. Bakke*, 323.

5. *Richmond v. J.A. Croson Co.*, 500.

6. See Judith Butler, "An Affirmative View," in this volume.

Affirmative Action

Frances Fox Piven

It hardly needs saying that the strident attack on affirmative action is a partisan political strategy. Republicans persist in harping on race as a way to rub raw the wounds the Democratic Party has suffered over the past three decades as a result of race conflict.

The Democratic coalition that emerged in the 1930s was, of course, inherently unstable, based as it was on a near-feudal white South and the working class of the big cities of the North. Agricultural modernization set blacks free from southern feudalism. It also forced their migration to the big cities and, in the North, into the electoral system and the Democratic Party. These conditions made possible the rise of black political and economic demands, and of a movement to give those demands force. This was progress for the country, but a disaster for the Democratic Party, which emerged from the turmoil of the 1960s with its white southern base eroding and its white working class constituency in the North deeply alienated by black demands for school and housing integration, for jobs, and for a share of local political patronage and honorifics.

Republicans could hardly have been oblivious to these vulnerabilities. By 1969, the black movement was fading, but race conflict did not subside, partly because Republicans worked to keep it alive. Tutored, if that was indeed necessary, by Kevin Phillips (*The Emerging Republican Majority*, 1969) the Republican leadership worked to fan the antagonisms that the rise of racial politics had generated. Nixon campaign rhetoric pioneered the use of crime and welfare as proxies for blacks, and the Nixon Justice Department pursued school busing orders with a vengeance. The Nixon administration revived a plan to require construction firms with federal contracts to show that their minority hires would be roughly proportional to minorities in the local population. This Philadelphia Plan had originated, to be sure, in the Johnson administration, but it had then been vetoed by the U.S. comptroller general. The Nixon administration revived it and also supported the extension of minority preference hiring to other firms with federal contracts. And, when blacks gained ascendance in the city governments, local governments often followed suit by developing their own affirmative action plans.

Affirmative action policies were, like so much else in life, morally ambiguous. For one thing, and this is what the opponents fasten on, affirmative action substituted group membership for individual merit as a criterion for advancement. No doubt many whites, especially white men, who felt themselves to be directly affected by affirmative action decisions, were deeply resentful. But most people were not directly affected and probably would have ignored the issue. After all, individual merit was never the main basis for success and failure in American life — Harvard's admissions criteria, for example, included alumni set-asides long before they included minority set-asides — and most people knew it. The widespread indignation over affirmative action owes more to the flamboyant use of the issue by Republican politicians seeking to incite indignation over race than it does to popular shock over a new injustice.

Affirmative action policies are morally ambiguous for another reason. The data suggest that they benefit only the better-off and better-educated among blacks. Meanwhile, large numbers of blacks have in recent decades become increasingly impoverished. Nevertheless, the policies did at least help to enlarge the black middle class. It created a numerous group of successful blacks, who are visible participants in American life as consumers, as professionals, as suburbanites. That is new, and in our racially polarized society, it is at least something.

In any case, the Republican warriors campaigning against affirmative action are certainly not proposing alternatives to give the worse-off among blacks a hand up. To the contrary, their agenda of tax cuts and spending cutbacks is at least partly responsible for why the living standards of poorer blacks are declining. Meanwhile, the campaign against affirmative action works to sustain the politics of race hatred that makes these policies possible.

A Personal Perspective

on Affirmative Action

Chang-Lin Tien

These comments are written in the last few months of my chancellorship at Berkeley. Proposition 209 has passed and it is now being challenged in the courts. The regents' decision to abolish affirmative action in admissions and hiring in July 1995 still stands and is in the process of being implemented. For the fall 1998 freshmen class, race and ethnicity will have no bearing whatever on decisions of admission. The result at Berkeley will be a precipitous decline in the number of underrepresented minority students and a campus that will become largely Asian and white.

I have been an outspoken advocate for affirmative action as long as the quality of the institution is not compromised. Berkeley has demonstrated that diversity and excellence go hand-in-hand. In the process of becoming more diverse over the past two decades, the quality of Berkeley and its student body have continuously improved.

I also believe that affirmative action is a necessary tool at this time to undergird the democratic values we cherish. We need to do everything we can as a society to be inclusive and appreciative of the qualities that different races and cultures bring to the whole. Our world is shrinking daily as our contact with other races and cultures increases exponentially. We need to view this as a positive situation and not something to fear.

It is no accident that Berkeley has been front and center in our most recent debate over race. Berkeley is one of the world's great educational institutions. It is an economic engine powering the economy; it is a gateway for the future leaders of our society; and it has always been a beacon of hope for all who wish to better themselves. Berkeley did not shy away from making its position clear that, with regard to admissions, merit cannot be defined solely on the basis of grades and test scores because the playing field for our applicants is not level. Nor can the overall composition of any entering class be determined solely by academic criteria, because it would not necessarily lead to the best educational outcome for the students in that class. Applicants from all races and ethnicities receive some form of preference beyond strictly academic criteria (athletic ability, socioeconomic status, geographical location, disability, etc.). In exit interviews, our graduates cite the diversity of our student body as one of the most positive factors in their overall educational experience.

It may be argued that I have a bias because I am a minority and have benefited from affirmative action. I certainly don't deny that. I would argue, however, that I am an example, in microcosm, of America's racial dilemma. As a refugee immigrant, I was a beneficiary of the openness and opportunity that the United States proffers. I was also an object of ridicule and discrimination. I took advantage of the former, fought against the latter, and became a successful Chinese American. I have been successful for myself and my family, by American standards, but I also believe that my research, my leadership of the Berkeley campus, and my other activities have benefited all of society. Because I have benefited so much from my United States citizenship, I am ever mindful of my responsibility to give back to my country in every way that I possibly can.

I would now like to make some general observations on issues of race and ethnicity. I am not a sociologist by training. What follows are my own reflections and intuitions.

It goes without saying that race is a pervasive theme throughout the history of this country. It is particularly uncomfortable because the manifestations of racism are so at odds with the fundamental values of our country. We are not alone in this regard. The collapse of the Soviet Union permitted the rekindling of the ethnic hatred that had been smoldering for many years. Similar difficulties are found in Bosnia, Africa, China, the Middle East, and elsewhere. Because we are still a relatively young country, and because this country has such wealth, power, and lofty values, there are greater expectations and thus greater collective guilt surrounding questions of race.

Interestingly, in our more recent history, which parallels my own arrival in this country in 1956, I do believe that we have made remarkable progress. As a young man pursuing my master's degree at the University of Louisville in Kentucky in the latter half of the 1950s, not only was I shocked at the overt discrimination directed at African Americans, I was totally confused about where I stood, as an Asian American, in that society. When I came to Berkeley, certain areas of the city excluded Asian Americans from renting or owning homes. And yet today I am the chancellor of the Berkeley campus. As other articles in this publication indicate, there has been progress for all minority groups. In my mind, there has not been sufficient progress to warrant the elimination of the most essential tool in bringing that progress about.

I worry that we as a nation have tired of confronting the race issue. One cannot help but notice the striking parallels between the roughly thirty-year period following the Civil War and the thirty-year period following the passage of the Civil Rights Act of 1965. Following the Civil War and the passage of the Thirteenth and Fourteenth Amendments to the Constitution, there was a momentum to redress the consequences of slavery. It withered, and, by 1896, segregation was institutionalized in *Plessy v. Ferguson*. Has the intent of the Civil Rights Act of 1965 barring discrimination and Executive Order 11246 implementing affirmative action been turned on its head as a result of the passage of Proposition 209? Unless a revolutionary increase in funding for public education occurs in this country — which would go a long way to leveling the playing field — I fear that we may be taking a minor step backward.

This is a minor step because the world has changed so fundamentally since the end of legally sanctioned segregation in the 1960s. Our community is no longer California or this nation, but the world. All of us are struggling, and will continue to struggle for the indefinite future, to appreciate our differences and to come to some accommodation with regard to a more humane and tolerant governance of ourselves.

In California, we have a great opportunity, because of our rapidly changing demographics and our incredible wealth of resources, to lead the world in this regard. I am very confident that we will. I think that Governor Wilson's commitment to reduce class size in the public schools is a major step in the right direction. The corporate world, too, is realizing the need for a diverse workforce because of its impact on the bottom line. And there is much more institutional cooperation — collaboration between universities and lower schools, for example, and business-sector involvement in public education.

One final note on a possible future direction for Berkeley and other universities. Many observers were surprised that there was not more active protest against Proposition 209 and the regents' earlier action ending affirmative action in hiring and admissions. Some observers speculated that students are apathetic and more concerned about job security. They are not willing to take the risks that the 1960s student activists took. I disagree with this analysis. The race issue today is much more complex than it was in the sixties. Then it was a black/white issue. Shocking, hate-filled racial images confronted a rather monolithic culture. Our actions were so at odds with our ideals that large scale protest was a natural outcome.

Today, legitimate questions are raised about why a black surgeon's son should receive preference over a disadvantaged white, Asian, or Chicano applicant. We are confronted with international images of starvation in Rwanda, genocide in Bosnia, continual racial confrontations in South Africa, human rights violations in China. Our young and very bright students are confronted with the same question we all face: Where do we begin to address these worldwide challenges? In this country, at this time, it is clear that old forms of protest are naive and insufficient. What we do need is a better understanding and appreciation of diverse cultures and more creative thinking about a new way to order our world.

It is here that our universities must make more progress. Our past approaches were understandable and appropriate for the times, but they are inadequate for the future that is hurtling toward us at ever greater speed. It will not be possible for the next chancellor to talk about "excellence through diversity" without providing much more clarity on what diversity means, particularly if our student body becomes largely Asian and white. Perhaps it is time to rethink our curriculum and our requirements. For a truly prepared graduate, is education abroad even an option any more? Should we have full-fledged campuses, offering a Berkeley degree, in different countries throughout the world? Can we create large-scale student exchange programs and break out of our old ways of thinking about diversity only in a statewide context?

I thus conclude on a cautious note of optimism. Our world has changed sufficiently that experiencing another "dark age" of race relations in the United States is not likely. And there are considerable resources and the will in California to lead the way in creating a more united nation.

Humility and the
Curse of Injustice

Jeremy Waldron

The first thing to say is that the supporters of the California Civil Rights Initiative (CCRI) and similar campaigns may possibly be right. Perhaps affirmative action is, as they say, unjust and unwise as a matter of social policy. Maybe they are right that in the long run it will make things worse not better. I don't believe this, but I cannot say that anyone who does is a fool or a racist. It is surely a matter of judgment — not just moral judgment, but complex empirical judgment about social dynamics, social mobility, and social morale. Supporting affirmative action is not like opposing slavery, apartheid, or segregation — matters where there was a clear moral imperative. Affirmative action, in its various forms, *is* morally counterintuitive; it *does* seem to involve discrimination on the basis of race or ethnic background; and so one has some sympathy with those who believe that the moral situation would be more satisfactorily straightforward if we were to avoid classifications, quotas, preferences, and weightings on this sort of basis altogether. Certainly those of us who favor affirmative action must balance the benefits we expect these policies to produce against the negative impact that morally counterintuitive policies are likely to have on social morale — by which I mean (among other things) the effect on the moral confidence that ordinary people have in the social and political arrangements of their society. And since even the expected benefits are fraught with ambiguity — experts worry about whether affirmative action targets the worst aspects of inequality, whether it stigmatizes and demoralizes some of its immediate beneficiaries, whether it generates its own forms of corruption and patronage — any judgment in its favor ought to be cautious and hesitant at best.

Supporters of affirmative action therefore do their cause no good by defending it as a matter of fundamental moral principle. The *goals* of affirmative action are matters of fundamental principle: its aim is racial and ethnic equality; it seeks to purge from this country the legacy of violence and expropriation against native peoples, chattel slavery, segregation, and our own nasty little versions of ethnic cleansing. These are noble goals. But their nobility does not make questions about means and strategies any easier. We would do well to cultivate some humility in our decisions about how best to pursue these goals. We may think that they are best pursued by attempting directly to allocate positions of social power and privilege to those we reckon would have achieved them but for the practices and legacies we are trying to eliminate; and so we may try directly to ensure that positions in a police force, say, or places in law school, are allocated on a demographically more representative basis than a colorblind policy could possibly achieve in present circumstances. That does seem like a reasonable and prudent response to what everyone admits is a desperate and difficult situation. But that is how we should defend it against those who in good faith express their doubts about affirmative action: we should defend it as a reasonable and prudent policy and be prepared to listen to and answer the misgivings of those who doubt its fairness or its wisdom. We should not treat their opposition to our policies as though it were opposition to our principles or opposition to our goals. We should not respond as though there were something inevitably racist about caution or hesitation in this area. And we certainly should not denigrate reasonable doubt on a matter of social judgment with labels like "Uncle Tom" or "white backlash."

I have emphasized how complicated, how fraught with doubt and ambiguity, any decent policy in this area is bound to be. This in itself is a matter of general moral importance in relation to the evils we are addressing. Great injustices like those I have mentioned — violence against and expropriation of native peoples, chattel slavery, segregation, official and unofficial racial discrimination — inflict terrible harm on their immediate victims. But they can also lay a curse on a land — a curse that is never easily or ever unambiguously lifted, but lingers on in memory, culture, and the million and one ways in which what has happened to a people in the past infects the capillaries that nourish their future.

The biblical prophets understood that curse as God's judgment on the injustice. They understood that part of what was wrong about one generation's wickedness, oppression, or rebellion against God was that it would blight the future for later generations, even those who were in large part innocent of the original wrongdoing. "Woe betide those who enact unjust laws, depriving the poor of justice, plundering the widow and despoiling the fatherless! What will you do when called to account? To whom will you flee for help, and where will you leave your children?" (Isaiah 10:1–3). The curse of injustice is that it leaves the children, even the great grandchildren, of the original perpetrators in a situation in which there is little that their good intentions can do to redeem the past and lift the curse, except to plead unconditionally for God's mercy.

Now I am not saying that we have to see our current predicament in a biblical light (though it is in part that vision which lent such grandeur to Abraham Lincoln's second inaugural address). We don't need theology or metaphysics to understand the curse or, if you like, the legacy of an injustice such as slavery. We know the sociology. There is, first, what we might call attitudinal hangover — the half-conscious residue of arrogance and contempt on the one hand, fear and mistrust on the other. Secondly, the effects of slavery and segregation are bound to be reflected in social structure and social dynamics long after the institutions themselves have been abandoned. In the United States, slavery and segregation were, for a whole people, forms of *legislated hopelessness* (in the case of slavery, *constitutionalized* hopelessness). They were designed to keep blacks "in their place," to destroy and undermine any attempt by slaves or their descendants to make something of themselves. Think what this does to a people over a few generations in a competitive and radically unequal society, where hope and opportunity are transmitted through family, and where it is normal for a man to work, if not for his own prosperity, then for that of his children and grandchildren. Once the legal barriers are lifted, then some sort of hope may return, some opportunities may blossom, and after a generation or two some success stories may be there for the telling. But it would be idiotic to think that the situation is now as it was before the injustice or as it would have been if the injustice had never been perpetrated. It would be idiotic to think that hope, and the intergenerational connections that nourish hope, could survive such injustice unscathed and reappear magically today to vindicate the good intentions of those whose grandfathers did their best to destroy it.

So far as the affirmative action debate is concerned, the importance of the curse of injustice is that it deprives us of any guarantee that our own good intentions will bear good fruit. It leaves us quite unsure of where we stand and what we can achieve. Defenders of affirmative action recognize this when they say to their opponents, "We are no longer in a position to proceed on the basis of intuitive moral principles, such as colorblind hiring or promotion on the basis of merit alone. Those principles might be fine for a pristine Eden, uncontaminated by the past. But their Pollyannaish application, without regard to the blighted and poisoned ground that we are attempting to cultivate, may well do more harm than good. We have to go back to scratch and develop new policies — perhaps counterintuitive policies — to deal with the mess that our forefathers have left us with." That's what we can say to explain (not explain away) the moral ambiguities of affirmative action policy. But the more thoughtful opponents of affirmative action may also recognize something like this when they respond: "OK, if we can no longer trust our good intentions or the simple moral maxims we were brought up with, if we have to develop new policies from scratch to deal with the legacy of racism, then let us at least pursue those policies in a spirit of humility. Maybe they will work, but maybe they won't. We will not know unless we confront the harm that they undoubtedly do, as well as the benefits that they generate. Whatever may be the appropriate response to the curse of past injustice, it is surely not willful blindness to the detrimental consequences of our attempts to deal with it. And we suspect that that blindness on the part of defenders of affirmative action — that willingness to defend affirmative action as a moral imperative, at all costs, come what may — is in part a consequence of the very self-righteousness that a recognition of the curse of injustice ought to preclude."

Maybe I am overestimating the number of CCRI supporters who are willing to say something like that. But I am certain that the debate about affirmative action would be immeasurably improved if there were more people on both sides who were prepared to proceed in this spirit.

Affirmative Action:

Psychology Meets Sociology

Alan Wolfe

How should supporters of racial justice react when both established institutions such as the University of California and public
opinion (as evidenced by the passage of Proposition 209) repudiate their preferred strategy for achieving racial justice? If they
are contributors to a journal called *Representations*, they first try
to represent and then to interpret what opponents of affirmative action are saying. I find their arguments unpersuasive, less
because of political disagreement than because of methodological
inadequacy. In trying to understand why some people might find
affirmative action inappropriate for the University of California,
more is explained away than is explained. For those convinced
that opposition to affirmative action is in reality opposition to
diversity and therefore a manifestation of racism, almost anything said in defense of such opposition is considered inauthen-
tic. Thus, when white people say, as they often do, that in their
opinion racism and discrimination have receded substantially in
the United States, their views tend to be dismissed as naive and
ill-informed at best or hypocritical and false at worst. Since it is
obvious to affirmative action's defenders that abolition of the
policy will result in far fewer African American and Latino students at the University of California, opposition to affirmative
action is automatically linked to a desire, whether consciously
expressed or not, to return the University to its suspect days as a
predominantly all-white institution. Yet sometimes interpretation calls for consulting those whom we interpret.

I believe that most people who oppose affirmative action are
trying to convey a different message. Comparing the way most
Americans represent their opposition to affirmative action with

the way most academics represent their support, I am struck by the presence of two radically different languages. I will call the language of opposition "psychological" and the language of support "sociological."

Inherent in the conviction of affirmative action's critics is a psychological concern with the importance of motive. Racism, they believe, is wrong because the motives behind it are wrong. From such a point of view, any deliberate effort by any state official to exclude qualified African Americans and Latinos from the University of California would constitute racism and ought not to be permitted. On the other hand, if there are no explicitly racist motives to be found among those who make such decisions, then there is no racism, however much the result of such decisions may appear to produce racially tinged results.

Yes, it is true, many people who think this way believe that the immediate abolition of affirmative action would result in few Latino and African American students attending the university. But the cause, they would maintain, would be different than the cause of segregation thirty or forty years ago. From the standpoint of motive, indeed, the cause would be opposite. For such reductions in the numbers of minority students, in their view, would reflect the fact that too few minority students were motivated enough to improve their grades and test scores to levels sufficient for admission to the university on the same conditions as others. In between the Civil Rights Act of 1964 and our current concern with affirmative action, they would argue, the burden of motive has shifted. Under the Civil Rights Act, institutions and individuals that acted in a racist manner were the exception and required legislative redress. But now, institutions and individuals are under suspicion of acting as racists until they prove otherwise.

There is, of course, much that is problematic in this view, including the fact, quite rightly stressed by affirmative action's defenders, that special exceptions to merit-based rules are made for athletes, the rich and politically connected, and children of alumni. Moreover, it is surely worth emphasizing the fact that high school students struggling with poverty and discrimination might make better college students than those whose grades are better but whose lives are more comfortable. Finally, there is great deal to be said on behalf of the point that merit is illusive in nature: no one knows what makes for success later in life. Still, when supporters of affirmative action defend the policy, all too often they do not respond to the psychological emphasis important to its opponents, but instead substitute a sociological language.

From a sociological perspective, affirmative action, especially in universities, asks to be judged not on the basis of the motives it encourages but on the basis of the results it achieves. Relying on numbers, affirmative action substitutes a preoccupation with group aggregates for a psychological concept of prejudice. Not only is life organized through groups, but the groups that matter most are those of race and gender, in which, as Marianne Constable writes in her essay included in this volume, "membership comes from a quality or aspect of experience shared by the whole." Affirmative action, in Judith Butler's account, presupposes that our culture determines our choices more than our choices shape our culture. The world according to affirmative action's defenders is a macro world ruled by social structures, not a micro world governed by individual agency.

The shift from a psychological to a sociological understanding of the world may be perfectly justifiable, but it has never been accompanied by an effort at legitimation. Indeed, while affirmative action was developing as policy, most Americans still believed we were living under the psychological regime established by *Brown v. Board of Education* and the Civil Rights Act of 1964. Still, I think there is an even larger problem with this substitution of sociological language for psychological language: its quite public application to universities, where psychological principles are expected to govern, compared to the relative lack of attention to the psychological at business corporations, where sociological principles are more appropriate.

Ever since ideas about the organization man flourished in the 1950s, we have known that business corporations, although ostensibly private, are organized internally by Durkheimian principles of solidarity to group norms. Conformity, adjustment, avoidance of conflict — these are the ways of life in big firms. Most people know that strongly driven people operating out of highly individualistic motives do not do well in the modern corporation. Nor, in many cases, is merit all that important. The idea is that you should stay in your career trajectory, never make too much of a fuss, and be patient; eventually your reward will come. Even now, with corporate downsizing and aggressive global competition, going along is still the best way of going up.

Universities, by contrast, are far more likely to be organized by principles of individual psychology than by reference to group norms. Faculty are encouraged to find their individual areas of specialization. They are granted tenure so that they need not follow the dictates of the crowd. Cooperative harmony is rarely the rule in academic departments; charismatic individualism often is. Much the same emphasis on individualism is expected to characterize admissions to the university. Students are asked about their motives for wanting to attend a particular college, and their individual grades and achievements are weighed. Many of them will leave the university to enter the corporate world, but they are also expected to remember their college days as the time when they found themselves. College offers four years in which to be an individual before the demands of society swallow one up. Obviously, large-scale universities take on characteristics shared with large-scale organizations of all kinds, including corporations. But in the public mind, universities are expected to pay attention to the unique, individual character of the people who compose them, in ways that business corporations are not expected to do.

If anything in this account is true, then affirmative action ought to be vigorously practiced in private companies. There the sociological language for justifying affirmative action is already in place. Results matter. Everything is counted by numbers. We all have to get along for the good of the firm. Let the diversity of the market justify the need for diversity within the company. And for all these reasons, affirmative action ought to be downplayed in the university. The sociological justification of affirmative action sharply conflicts with the individualistic psychology of the university's self-image in ways that an earlier language of combating individual prejudice never did.

Many academics are sympathetic to affirmative action. Believers in the idea that you should practice what you preach, they look to apply its principles at the institution closest to hand and are relatively indifferent to the (often quite successful) reliance on affirmative action in corporate suites. As much as one may admire their consistency, however, their efforts to apply affirmative action to the one institution where its application would be most resisted by the general public creates an inevitable conflict with the tax and tuition payers who fund higher education.

Those who believe strongly in affirmative action, and who think that the university is the key institution for putting its principles into effect, have every right to argue their position vigorously. But if they want to keep alive the struggle for racial justice, they ought to do a better job at hearing what those who think differently are saying. As theorists of culture and language, many of the defenders of affirmative action who contributed to this volume would surely argue that we can never understand the Other without empathic efforts to see the world as the Other sees it. Without taking significant steps to apply that same methodological principle to the regents of the University of California and those who voted for Proposition 209, the proponents of affirmative action are likely never to understand exactly what hit them.

Affirmative Action:

A Long-Range Perspective

Howard Zinn

The current onslaught against affirmative action (which has had striking success in California and Texas) may prevail in the short run. But in the long run, affirmative action is here to stay, until, in the even longer run, there is no longer a need for it.

It is here to stay because in the long run, I believe, the case for it is too powerful to ignore, except temporarily. The American people are not devoid of common sense. They can be temporarily aroused out of economic desperation against blacks and women. But they cannot indefinitely deny the clear truth that blacks and women have been shunted back for centuries and deserve some special attention. They may not know the statistics, which are certainly clear (though so manipulable that scholars of repute can say with a straight face that blacks and women no longer need special help). But they know in their hearts that people of color and women have been treated unfairly for a long time.

The argument that affirmative action is "discrimination" cannot be countered by simple denial. Of course, it is discrimination, but it is nonetheless rational and just, for the same reason that various discriminations we make in society are necessary and morally defensible. After World War II we discriminated against civilians, by giving veterans extra points on civil service examinations and free tuition for college. We discriminate on behalf of poor people when we give them, and them alone, food stamps. We discriminate on behalf of manufacturers when we set tariffs against foreign goods, and on behalf of corporations when they get enormous subsidies from the government. All of these might be considered forms of affirmative action, and, once pointed out to people, the similarity is irrefutable.

In other words, I believe that the campaign against affirmative action has to some extent been successful only because the facts have not been presented, the arguments have not been clearly made. Over the long run, the truths should prevail, and Americans will accept them, out of a natural desire for fairness.

Even so, there is still bound to be resentment by white men who, because of affirmative action, lose out on something they want and need. This poisons relations between the races and between the sexes. The only way of overcoming this is to end a situation where people of different colors and different genders must compete for scarce resources.

The most serious battleground is for jobs, and the solution is obvious. No one should be unemployed who wants a job. No one who is qualified for a job should be refused it. There should be enough jobs available for everyone, so that the competition between races and genders is not necessary.

We need to reawaken the goal of full employment, which at various points in recent history has been declared as an objective of this nation and of nations everywhere. In 1944, Franklin D. Roosevelt spoke boldly and eloquently of an "Economic Bill of Rights," which included the right to a job. In 1946, Congress passed the Full Employment Act, which declared the government as an employer of last resort, but had no enforcement mechanism. Also, the U.N. Declaration of Human Rights, signed by the United States as well as other nations, includes the right to work, with adequate wages and working conditions.

Ultimately, that is the solution to the bitter argument over affirmative action. In the meantime, we must do for women and people of color what we have done at different times for many other groups in society—give them a helping hand, to make up for a long history of injustice, and simply to be fair.

APPENDIX

SP-1: Resolution of the University of California Board of Regents Adopting a Policy "Ensuring Equal Treatment" of Admissions, 20 July 1995

Whereas, Governor Pete Wilson, on June 1, 1995, issued Executive Order W-124-95 to "End Preferential Treatment and to Promote Individual Opportunity Based on Merit"; and

Whereas, paragraph seven of that order requests the University of California to "take all necessary action to comply with the intent and the requirements of this executive order"; and

Whereas, in January 1995, the University initiated a review of its policies and practices, the results of which support many of the findings and conclusions of Governor Wilson; and

Whereas, the University of California Board of Regents believes that it is in the best interest of the University to take relevant actions to develop and support programs which will have the effect of increasing the eligibility rate of groups which are "underrepresented" in the University's pool of applicants as compared to their percentages in California's graduating high school classes and to which reference is made in Section 4;

Now, therefore, be it resolved as follows:

SECTION 1. The Chairman of the Board, with the consultation of the President, shall appoint a task force representative of the business community, students, the University, other segments of education, and organizations currently engaged in academic "outreach." The responsibility of this group shall be to develop proposals for new directions and increased funding for the Board of Regents to increase the eligibility rate of those currently identified in Section 4. The final report of this task force shall be presented to the Board of Regents within six months after its creation.

SECTION 2. Effective January 1, 1997, the University of California shall not use race, religion, sex, color, ethnicity, or national origin as criteria for admission to the University or to any program of study.

SECTION 3. Effective January 1, 1997, the University of California shall not use race, religion, sex, color, ethnicity, or national origin as criteria for "admissions in exception" to UC eligibility requirements.

SECTION 4. The President shall confer with the Academic Senate of the University of California to develop supplemental criteria for consideration by the Board of Regents which shall be consistent with Section 2. In developing such criteria, which shall provide reasonable assurances that the applicant will successfully complete his or her course of study, consideration shall be given to individuals who, despite having suffered disadvantage economically or in terms of their social environment (such as an abusive or otherwise dysfunctional home or a neighborhood of unwholesome or antisocial influences), have nonetheless demonstrated sufficient character and determination in overcoming obstacles to warrant confidence that the applicant can pursue a course of study to successful completion, provided that any student admitted under this section must be academically eligible for admission.

SECTION 5. Effective January 1, 1997, not less than fifty (50) percent and not more than seventy-five (75) percent of any entering class on any campus shall be admitted solely on the basis of academic achievement.

SECTION 6. Nothing in Section 2 shall prohibit any action which is strictly necessary to establish or maintain eligibility for any federal or state program, where ineligibility would result in a loss of federal or state funds to the University.

SECTION 7. Nothing in Section 2 shall prohibit the University from taking appropriate action to remedy specific, documented cases of discrimination by the University, provided that such actions are expressly and specifically approved by the Board of Regents or taken pursuant to a final order of a court or administrative agency of competent jurisdiction. Nothing in this section shall interfere with the customary practices of the University with regard to the settlement of claims against the University relating to discrimination.

SECTION 8. The President of the University shall periodically report to the Board of Regents detailing progress to implement the provisions of this resolution.

SECTION 9. Believing California's diversity to be an asset, we adopt this statement: Because individual members of all of California's diverse races have the intelligence and capacity to succeed at the University of California, this policy will achieve a UC population that reflects this state's diversity through the preparation and empowerment of all students in this state to succeed rather than through a system of artificial preferences.

Proposition 209:

Text of Proposed Law

This initiative measure is submitted to the people in accordance with the provisions of Article II, Section 8 of the Constitution.

This initiative measure expressly amends the Constitution by adding a section thereto; therefore, new provisions proposed to be added are in *italic type* to indicate that they are new.

Proposed Amendment to Article I

Section 31 is added to Article I of the California Constitution as follows:

SECTION 31 *(a). The state shall not discriminate against, or grant preferential treatment to, any individual or group on the basis of race, sex, color, ethnicity, or national origin in the operation of public employment, public education, or public contracting.*

(b) This section shall apply only to action taken after the section's effective date.

(c) Nothing in this section shall be interpreted as prohibiting bona fide qualifications based on sex which are reasonably necessary to the normal operation of public employment, public education, or public contracting.

(d) Nothing in this section shall be interpreted as invalidating any court order or consent decree which is in force as of the effective date of this section.

(e) Nothing in this section shall be interpreted as prohibiting action

which must be taken to establish or maintain eligibility for any federal program, where ineligibility would result in loss of federal funds for the state.

(f) For the purposes of this section, "state" shall include, but not necessarily be limited to, the state itself, any city, county, city and country, public university system, including the University of California, community college district, school district, special district, or any other political subdivision or governmental instrumentality of or within the state.

(g) The remedies available for violations of this section shall be the same, regardless of the injured party's race, sex, color, ethnicity, or national origin, as are otherwise available for violations of then-existing California antidiscrimination law.

(h) This section shall be self-executing, if any part or parts of this section are found to be in conflict with federal law or the United States Constitution, the section shall be implemented to the maximum extent that federal law and the United States Constitution shall permit. Any provision held invalid shall be severable from the remaining portions of this section.

AAUP Commission on

Governance and

Affirmative Action Policy

Report
May 29, 1996

This commission was created in November 1995 in response to a request from some faculty in the University of California system concerned about the regents' decision, on July 20, 1995, to end affirmative action in admissions, hiring, and the awarding of contracts. The faculty members who contacted the AAUP were opposed to the substance of the decision, but they were equally disturbed about the process by which the decision had been reached, a process they felt had violated traditions of shared governance in existence at the university since 1920. The AAUP is on record for its support of affirmative action, but its help was sought in this instance primarily on the issue of governance.

For eighty years the AAUP has been engaged in developing standards for sound academic practice, and it has served as the authoritative voice of the academic profession in this regard. Its Statement on Government of Colleges and Universities has, since 1966, articulated the principles on which shared governance rests (Appendix A). These principles stress the importance of mutual understanding among the various components of a university: its governing boards, administrators, faculty, and students. Such understanding requires an awareness of interdependence, a commitment to communication and the exchange of ideas, as well as a commitment to joint action in the interests of solving educational problems. Given its long experience in articulating principles of shared governance and in assessing practices in terms of these principles, the AAUP was in a position to provide a fair-minded account of what had transpired in California.

Following AAUP assessment procedures, the members of this commission read through masses of printed materials and interviewed regents, administrators, faculty representatives, and interested observers on all sides of the controversy. (A list of those interviewed appears in Appendix B.) We concluded that although the regents had the legal authority to take the action they did, principles and longstanding practices of shared governance were nonetheless ignored in the process which culminated in the July 20 decision. The regents violated the spirit, if not the letter, of shared governance. We also concluded that, because shared governance had been breached, the educational impacts of the decision to abolish affirmative action were insufficiently considered. Indeed, the striking fact about the July 20 decision was that it involved no sustained consultation with faculty and administrators about the educational issues at stake.

Our report has three sections. The first deals with shared governance, presenting a narrative of the events leading to the regents' action. The second considers the educational impacts of affirmative action and of the regents' decision to end it. The third offers three recommendations.

I. Shared Governance

The University of California was chartered in 1868 and is one of the few state universities to have been granted constitutional autonomy. The regents were established as the governing body of the university, with the power to delegate authority to administrators and faculty. One of the goals of autonomy was to shield the academy from political intervention because, the founders believed, educational and political goals not only might differ, they also might conflict. Thus, the constitution stated that "The university shall be entirely independent of all political or sectarian influence and kept free therefrom in the appointment of its regents and in the administration of its affairs."

Over the years, the role of the faculty in the management of the University of California has increased, establishing a tradition of what has come to be known as "shared governance." Shared governance involves both the formal delegation of authority on certain educational matters to the faculty Academic Senate and the principled commitment by regents and administrators to consult with faculty on matters of educational policy, and, when there is conflict, to exchange views to ensure that the various opinions are understood prior to action being taken. Shared governance involves a complex system of collaboration, communication, and understanding among faculty, administrators, and regents. The principles of shared governance are recognized in the California legal code, which specifically states that "joint decision-making and consultation between administration and faculty or academic employees is the long-accepted manner of governing institutions of higher learning and is essential to the performance of the educational missions of these institutions."

Faculty participation takes place through the institution of the Academic Senate. All ladder rank and equivalent faculty members at each of the nine campuses of the University of California system are represented on a campus-based senate, whose chairs and committee heads sit on the statewide Academic Council. The chair and vice-chair serve as nonvoting Faculty Representatives to the Board of Regents. In 1920, a standing order of the regents gave the senate the authority to advise the president on budgetary matters, the appointment and promotion of faculty and deans, and educational policy, including curriculum. This standing order recognized that faculty had the unique expertise on these matters that was needed to implement an effective educational system. The senate now oversees the curriculum and sets conditions for admissions and for the awarding of degrees. A special committee of the senate, the Board of Admissions and Relations with Schools (BOARS), determines standards for eligibility (in line with the broad policy set by the legislature and the regents), while campus admission committees and the faculty of professional schools set specific academic qualifications for admissions.

It is widely acknowledged that shared governance has been one of the essential elements in making the University of California the outstanding institution it is today. California is the model on which many other academic institutions base their own governance practices. Faculty members in the University of California system are important participants in the formulation of educational policy and in the articulation and maintenance of high standards of admissions and hiring. They provide information that the regents and administration do not otherwise have about the educational process and about the workings of a complex institution with a mission and ethos different from that of other institutions (such as factories or corporations) of comparable size. Shared governance has served to protect academic freedom and to foster academic excellence, making the University of California system one of the finest in the nation.

Although a clear division of labor assigns ultimate authority for large policy questions to the regents and responsibility for implementing this policy to the administration and faculty, commitment to shared governance has meant exchanges of information and opinion, consultation, reflection, mediation, and compromise. This deliberative, consultative practice has mitigated the inevitable political differences within and among various university constituencies. As a result, it has contributed to an atmosphere of mutual respect and trust.

The events surrounding the regents' decision of July 1995 involved a breakdown in the process of shared governance. Legally, of course, broad policy decisions are the regents' prerogative. But the assertion of such prerogative with very little deliberative consultation and in the face of objections from the president and all the chancellors of the system, from substantial numbers of faculty, and from representatives of the student government, breached principles and traditions of shared governance that had long been observed. The result has been a profound loss of trust on all sides.

The history of the July 20 decision seems to have begun more than a year earlier, with a letter of protest from a white student who had been turned down for medical school admission. Data submitted to support his claim suggested that a differential system of admissions to medical schools was in effect that might be discriminating against whites. Around the same time, a former Faculty Representative to the Board of Regents whose term had ended suggested the need for a review of the effects of affirmative action on different campuses in the system. The regents, some of them declaring hostility to affirmative action, asked for information about procedures for implementation. In the fall of 1994, the president began scheduling a series of presentations for the regents on admissions and affirmative action. There were twelve presentations made to the board, some by faculty and campus administrators. These meetings of the regents were public, involving discussions of the materials at hand. In addition, information related to admissions was distributed by mail between meetings of the board on twenty-three occasions. Eight of the mailings were initiated by President Jack Peltason; the others were in response to regents' requests for information.

The regents' attention to affirmative action took place within a larger political context in the state. A California Civil Rights Initiative (CCRI) was being proposed as a statewide referendum by opponents of affirmative action. President Peltason, with the support of the leadership of the Academic Senate, sought to postpone a decision by the regents on affirmative action until this referendum had been either passed or defeated. His actions, whatever the motivation, were taken as "stonewalling" by some of the regents.

As the regents' review of affirmative action continued in the winter of 1995, some problems were identified. The president called for investigation of them and, where appropriate, instituted corrective measures. His position, and that of the nine chancellors, was that the administration of affirmative action might need to be improved, but the policy itself was educationally sound. No systematic, documented overview of the educational and administrative aspects of affirmative action was offered or undertaken.

The growing sense of pressure led the chair of the Academic Senate to refer the question of affirmative action to its Committee on Affirmative Action. This prompted a series of resolutions passed by the campus divisions of the Academic Senate endorsing affirmative action. Instead of provoking consultation or requests for more information from the regents, these resolutions seem to have hardened the determination of some of them (led by Regent Ward Connerly) to abolish affirmative action. In the spring, President Peltason convinced Regent Connerly to postpone action on what would be a controversial issue until after the legislative budget negotiations had ended. And Regent Connerly agreed.

At the June meeting of the Board of Regents (by which time the budget talks had ended), affirmative action was put on the agenda for July. The resolutions pertaining to affirmative action matters were distributed to the regents only one week before the board meeting. Regent Connerly told the press that an effort to end affirmative action was under way. California Governor Pete Wilson (also a regent), who had made the elimination of affirmative action one of the planks of his presidential campaign, had announced his intention to attend the July meeting. These public pronouncements politicized an already polarized situation and linked the regents' effort to Governor Wilson's presidential campaign. The fact that this issue was being considered in July, when faculty and students were on summer break, also seemed to indicate to many observers that consultation was not on the regents' agenda.

Still, the July meeting involved fourteen hours of public hearings. In the course of these hearings it became clear that, with the exception of a slim majority of the Board of Regents, all of the constituencies of the university — president, chancellors, and substantial numbers of faculty and student representatives — opposed the abolition of affirmative action. Had there been any consideration of the principles of shared governance, this situation would have mandated further discussion and consultation in a setting and time frame more conducive to deliberation. There were seven requests from various regents for a postponement of the decision so that such deliberation could take place. The chair of the Academic Council also asked for a delay. In addition, suggestions for more discussion and consultation came from a number of elected officials, public figures, and invited speakers. But the requests for serious study of the various positions in the controversy were ignored or overruled. This, in our view, constituted a serious breach of the principles and spirit of shared governance.

A thorough and careful systemwide examination of the practices, procedures, and educational impacts of affirmative action was never undertaken jointly by the regents, the administration, and the faculty. Instead, information came in and was considered in a piecemeal fashion. A thorough and sustained examination would have permitted the regents to tap faculty expertise and experience, to gather the kind of information that leads to considered and informed decision-making, and to hear the many opinions that exist about affirmative action on the campuses of the university system. It also would have permitted the formulation and consideration of a range of solutions to problems that had been and would have been identified in the course of such an examination. An examination of this kind is typically undertaken either by existing committees or by a special task force composed of representatives of the regents, the administration, the faculty, and the students. A task force works slowly, amassing and analyzing data and coming up with recommendations, usually after considerable discussion and debate. A task force might well have come to the same conclusion that the regents did in their vote of July 20; it might also have come up with alternative solutions. Whatever the outcome, however, this more deliberate process would have respected the procedures of consultation and engaged debate that historically have characterized shared governance at the University of California.

II. Affirmative Action

Affirmative action has been a policy of the University of California since 1964. In that year the Educational Opportunity Program was established to provide access to the university for promising students from primarily, but not exclusively, minority backgrounds whose economic, social, and educational circumstances otherwise prevented them from attending the university. In 1974, the state legislature effectively endorsed the principles upon which affirmative action at the university would be based: "Each segment of California public higher education shall strive to approximate by 1980 the general ethnic, sexual, and economic composition of the recent high school graduates." In 1988, the legislature reiterated this recommendation for a student body that was broadly representative of the state's demography: "Each segment of California public higher education shall strive to approximate by the year 2000 the general ethnic, gender, economic, and regional composition of recent high school graduates, both in first-year classes and subsequent college and university graduating classes."

There were at least three motives for affirmative action. The first followed from the university's public responsibility to provide higher education, in as inclusive a way as possible, to the citizens of the state. The second followed from a social commitment to rectify discrimination against minorities and women. The third followed from an educational theory, untested in 1964 and now widely subscribed to as the result of thirty years of experiment, that a diverse and heterogeneous campus provided important educational benefits for all students. Not only would students experience a richer, more dynamic intellectual environment, but they would also learn how to negotiate their differences as members of an academic community.

To achieve these broadly representative goals without compromising high academic standards, the university developed a number of criteria for selecting students for admission. The California Master Plan for Higher Education, which was ratified by the legislature, provides that all California residents in the top eighth of the state's graduating high school senior classes are eligible for admission. At most of the campuses of the University of California system, eligible students were simply admitted. At Berkeley and UCLA there was greater competition for entry, and this led to the use of additional criteria for selecting an entering class from the pool of those academically qualified for admission. These criteria assessed merit not only by numerical rankings, but also according to individual talents and achievements. At Berkeley, for example, a certain percentage (roughly 50 percent in the 1970s, at least 40 percent but not more than 60 percent after 1988) were admitted solely on the basis of quantitative measures (such as grade point average, SAT scores, and Achievement Test scores). Another percentage (between 16 and 20 percent in the 1980s) were reviewed on the basis not only of test scores, but also of other criteria including economic background, high school coursework, and the quality of a written essay. Still another segment was considered because of special talents and achievements (including art and athletics), geographic origin, disabilities, and racial and ethnic backgrounds. (In 1988 this segment amounted to about 38 percent of freshmen admitted.) Finally, a very small group, no more than 6 percent at its highest point, was admitted on a Special Action basis. Because of unusual achievements, talents (usually athletic), or experiences of racial and economic disadvantage, the eligibility requirement was waived for this group. The controversy about affirmative action was not just about this small group of Special Action admits; it was about the idea that merit among those already determined to be in the top eighth of high school graduates could be assessed by anything but numerical standards.

This admissions procedure successfully diversified the Berkeley campus (and other campuses in the system) with no compromise in the quality of students admitted and in their performance as undergraduates. In fact, the quality of students, by any measure (quantitative scores, diversity of achievement and experience, retention and graduation rates), increased between 1964 and 1990. A recent investigation by the U.S. Department of Education's Office for Civil Rights found that Berkeley not only was in compliance with the law in its admissions procedures (there were neither quotas nor discrimination), but also that the system offered a good example of how to implement compliance with positive educational consequences.

The method of balancing quantitative and qualitative assessments of students to determine admissions is the typical procedure followed by admissions committees all over the country. The University of California adheres to national practice. The process of admissions aims to be fair and equitable, but it can never he completely objective or neutral. It cannot be for two reasons. First, it must balance comparative assessments of individuals with the collective good of the university (defined as a diverse, heterogeneous community). Second, in order to achieve diversity, measures are used that are not strictly comparable and so cannot establish the absolute superiority of one student over another. Merit is, in any case, not a strictly quantifiable characteristic.

This does not mean, however, that standards have been abandoned in admissions decisions. A great deal of thought has gone into elaborating mixed standards of admissibility to college. The system is based on a belief — confirmed by years of experience and systematic study — that merit and potential cannot be assessed solely on the basis of grades and test scores. (Often — and this has been the case at Berkeley — as many as 5,000 students with 4.0 grade point averages apply, and only 2,500 can be admitted. This means that numerical standards alone cannot be used to make distinctions.) Depending on the size of the university or college, the process is more or less complex, but nowhere are grades and board scores the sole determinants of selection. Typically, admissions committees seek balance with respect to geography, socioeconomic background, race, gender, ethnicity, alumni ties, parental wealth and/or fame, academic interests, extracurricular activities, and so on. This attempt to ensure diversity is tied to an educational philosophy that defines college and university experience, inside and outside the classroom, as broadening and transforming. According to this philosophy, students must be exposed not only to ideas they have not encountered before, but also to new perspectives and people. Such exposure is practical because it prepares students for the ever more global worlds of business and the professions. It also deepens their humanity by giving them the ability to interact with and understand others whose lives and experiences are different from their own.

It is wrong to call this system of selection a system of racial preference, because many considerations go into creating a freshman class. And race is not given priority over these other considerations. Since 1964, race has been only one of the many factors taken into account when admissions committees assess the range of different experiences they want represented on their campuses. Race is only one of the factors taken into account about an individual's characteristics and achievements when he or she is under consideration for admission.

Similarly, it is wrong to describe this system of selection as one which ignores or downplays the achievements of individuals as individuals. The process of selection takes into account the qualities of individuals, and these qualities are affected by socioeconomic status, as well as by cultural background, race, gender, and ethnicity. In a society which regularly takes differences of this kind into account and which treats individuals as members of groups (whether for purposes of negative discrimination, community membership, or political mobilization), it is wrong to say that these differences are of no consequence in the experience of individuals. While they surely do not determine who a person is or what he or she becomes, these experiences are part of what individuals deal with as they make their way in life. So the fact that a talented dancer with an interest in science and a desire to become a doctor is black should be taken into account.

Admissions procedures are complex. They must balance the needs of individuals and those of the academic community, and they must select individuals for admission according to noncomparable standards. As a result, they are always open to criticism and revision. The history of admissions procedures at the University of California, as elsewhere, is a history of change and adjustment in response both to internal and external criticism. Indeed, a remarkable aspect of the California admissions policy is that it has been extremely sensitive to the need for periodic examination and adjustment. Not only did the California Postsecondary Education Commission regularly review the Master Plan for Higher Education in the state, but each of the nine campuses kept records that monitored the impact of admissions decisions on such things as the representation of minorities as well as rates of student achievement and attrition. Internal scrutiny and recommendation for change came from standing committees of the academic senates, from special task forces, and from admissions officers. While such monitoring could not create a perfect system, it managed to identify serious flaws and to make the system responsive to its critics. Two examples illustrate this process. In 1989, a special committee on Asian American admissions to Berkeley recommended changes in 1984 admissions procedures, which were found to have had a disproportionately negative impact on the enrollment of Asian Americans at Berkeley. In 1990, also at Berkeley, where increasing numbers of UC-eligible students sought admission as a first choice, a number of changes were implemented, including a new emphasis on admitting students from economically disadvantaged backgrounds, a limit of 6 percent for Special Action admissions and more careful consideration of their potential for success, and an increase in those admitted solely on the basis of numerical criteria to a minimum of 50 percent of those eligible for the entering class. As these examples indicate, the self-correcting mechanisms have worked well for fine-tuning the admissions process.

While this kind of self-correcting mechanism worked effectively, it could never resolve the tension created by the need to balance judgments of individuals, on the one hand, with the collective goal of diversity, on the other. As long as there was general commitment to maintaining that balance, however, criticism could be addressed through established administrative, legislative, and faculty channels. The political climate of the 1990s changed this situation by calling into question the need ever to consider a collective good at the expense of the presumed "rights" of individuals. Affirmative action was one of the collective principles attacked in the name of individual rights.

In 1995, the regents of the University of California voted by a narrow majority that race, gender, and ethnicity could no longer be a consideration in admissions, hiring, and the awarding of contracts. This rating was justified in terms of fairness to individuals, and, although other criteria (including evidence of strong character in the face of social, economic, and physical disadvantages or dysfunctional family situations) were allowed to be used, they, too, stressed the need to consider individuals only as individuals. (The regents' resolution began by citing Governor Wilson's Executive Order to "End Preferential Treatment and to Promote Individual Opportunity Based on Merit.") When the regents also raised to 75 percent the maximum proportion of students to be admitted solely on the basis of academic achievement, they signaled their intention to give academic assessments priority over supplementary evaluations, thus reducing the complexity of the process of selection and the future makeup of the higher education community. Diversity was redefined in terms of the psychological attributes of individuals rather than of the social composition of the community. Evaluation of merit was reduced to performance on standardized tests. And the aim of the university was now narrowly limited to the education of those qualified according to standardized measures to enter it.

Affirmative action was described as a failed social policy that was, in any case, not part of the mission of the university. The 1995 ruling effectively rejected the idea that the university had a public responsibility to reflect the demography of the state and the belief that it could have a role in reversing social patterns of past and current discrimination. Although the regents' resolution expressed the hope that new admissions policies would be responsive to the diversity of the state's population, statistical projections from a university admissions task force indicate that the regents' ruling will result in an increase in white and Asian students and a decline in African American and Latino students, and that this change will be especially apparent at the UCLA and Berkeley campuses. A report from the University of California in February 1995 indicated a drop in applications from Latino students and a lower-than-anticipated number of applications from African Americans. The regents' new policy is likely to have a racial impact precisely because it refuses to take race into account.

Surprisingly, the educational impact of affirmative action was barely considered by those who supported the regents' decision. And yet some thirty years of experience, in California and nationally, suggest that there have been, on the whole, important educational benefits. First, at least one study has documented increased cultural awareness and greater sensitivity to race on the part of students. Where concerted efforts have been made to address racial tensions, students have a greater sense of their own ability to influence interpersonal dynamics and social interactions. Second, students have acquired familiarity with a range of disparate cultures and styles; they have learned that their perspective is not the only way of understanding a situation. The exposure to ideas and attitudes fundamentally different from one's own is never easy; these encounters can be difficult, even painful. The result, however, has been to prepare those who will be the future leaders of the state and nation to understand the different perspectives of their employees, students, and constituents. Third, the curricular expansions that have accompanied affirmative action and the diversity of faculty hired have given students the knowledge they need to deal with an increasingly global economy and an increasingly interconnected pattern of world affairs. Fourth, universities have provided important experiments in democracy. The diversity of the population has made the negotiation of differences a fact of public life in the university, and this has opened important discussions about tolerance and identity and about the forms of trust and mutual respect required for the creation of democratic communities.

This last point is often overlooked in discussions of the impact of affirmative action. The inevitable problems produced by diversity (hostility among groups, reluctance of individuals to be identified in terms of group membership, the pressure to choose one identity as more dominant than others) have been emphasized to the exclusion of the positive results. And the ongoing discussions among faculty, students, and administrators who have addressed these problems and found innovative solutions for them have been ignored. Thus "identity politics" has been presented as the necessary result of affirmative action when, in fact, there has been a strong critique of such politics from those who support diversity. Within the university, philosophers, historians, anthropologists, and others have developed a critical perspective on identity, enabling students to distinguish between those political pressures (such as an attempt to create an organized response to discrimination) that lead people to make race or gender their primary identities, and psycho-social influences that make individuals distinctive and unique beings. This kind of critical thinking developed in the context of the concrete experiences produced by diversity: the need to balance individuals and communities and to create a community of people who can live together despite their different assumptions and experiences. To the extent that democracy is an active and inclusive process requiring an educated and critical citizenry, affirmative action in the universities has been, and continues to be, an important training ground.

Instead of urging more critical attention to the problems of negotiating difference, instead of recognizing that democracy always requires a delicate balance between individual and collective interests; instead of upgrading the influence of the agencies charged with monitoring the balance in order to correct excesses in one direction or the other, a narrow majority of the regents of the University of California opted to end its thirty-year experiment with affirmative action. We conclude that, in the absence of sustained and careful consideration of the educational impact both of affirmative action and of the decision to end it, the regents' action — though technically legal — was ill-advised.

III. Recommendations

1. The regents, administration, and faculty ought to reaffirm their commitment to the principles and practices of shared governance. We were surprised, in the course of our investigation, to discover that there were regents who had never heard of the concept. Because shared governance is not simply the formal delegation of authority, but also a shared commitment to consultation, communication, and collaboration, it is a difficult practice to uphold. We therefore recommend the provision of regular orientation on the principles and practices of shared governance for new members of the Board of Regents, the administration, and the faculty senate. Such an orientation is vital if the University of California is to preserve a method of governance that has historically trained the leadership of the California system and provided a model for universities in the rest of the nation.

2. Many issues that come before the university are unavoidably political, but in this case the issue was dealt with in a partisan political matter that gives the appearance of promoting the interest of a particular candidate and party. We recommend that

every effort be made to avoid partisan political activity in deliberations about educational policy both in appearance and in fact. No better formulation is provided than the one in the Constitution of the State of California: "The university shall be entirely independent of all political or sectarian influence and kept free therefrom in the appointment of its regents and in the administration of its affairs."

3. The regents should not implement any recision of affirmative action until a thorough review of the educational goals and impact of diversity, and of the educational effects such recision may have, has been conducted by a joint task force of regents, administrators, faculty, and students.

Members of the AAUP Commission on Governance and Affirmative Action Policy

Joan Wallach Scott, Chair

Robert Atwell

Larry Gerber

A. Leon Higginbotham, Jr.

Candace Kant

Ronald Oaxaca

Shirley Yee

James T. Richardson

Marsha Nye Adler

Contributors

The American Association of University professors (AAUP) is a national organization serving college and university faculty members. AAUP is dedicated to the defense of academic freedom and tenure and to the promotion of sound academic standards and process.

James Robert Brown is Professor of Philosophy at the University of Toronto. He is the author of *The Rational and The Social*, *The Laboratory of the Mind*, *Smoke and Mirrors*, *Proofs and Pictures*, and *A Guide to the Science Wars*.

Judith Butler is Professor of Rhetoric and Comparative Literature at the University of California at Berkeley. She is the author of *The Psychic Life of Power: Theories in Subjection* and *Excitable Speech: Contemporary Scenes of Politics*.

Barbara T. Christian is Professor of African American Studies at the University of California at Berkeley. She is the author of the prize-winning study *Black Women Novelists: The Development of a Tradition, 1892–1976*, *Black Feminist Criticism: Perspectives on Black Women Writers*, and many articles and essays. Presently she is the editor of contemporary works for the first *Norton Anthology of African American Literature*.

Marianne Constable is Associate Professor of Rhetoric at the University of California at Berkeley. She is the author of *The Law of the Other: The Mixed Jury and Changing Conceptions of Citizenship, Law, and Knowledge*, and is currently working on a book on silence and speech in American law and politics.

Troy Duster is Professor of Sociology and Director of the Institute for the Study of Social Change at the University of California at Berkeley.

Michel Feher is a founding editor of Zone and Zone Books, New York.

George M. Fredrickson is Robinson Professor of American History at Stanford University, and president of the Organization of American Historians. He is author of *On the History of Racism, Nationalism, and Social Movements.*

Amy Gutmann is the Laurence S. Rockefeller University Professor of Politics at Princeton University.

Jennifer Hochschild is Professor of Politics and Public Affairs at Princeton University, with a joint appointment in the Department of Politics and the Woodrow Wilson School of Public and International Affairs. She is the author of *Facing Up to the American Dream: Race, Class, and the Soul of the Nation, The New American Dilemma: Liberal Democracy and School Desegregation, What's Fair: American Beliefs about Distributive Justice,* and co-author of *Equalities.*

David A. Hollinger is Professor of History at the University of California at Berkeley. His most recent books are *Science, Jews, and Secular Culture: Studies in Mid-Twentieth Century American Intellectual History* and *Postethnic America: Beyond Multiculturalism.*

David L. Kirp is Professor of Public Policy at the Goldman School of Public Policy, University of California at Berkeley. He is the author of *Our Town: Race, Housing, the Soul of Suburbia, Our Town: AIDS and Schoolchildren in America's Communities,* and *Just Schools: The Idea of Racial Equality in American Education.*

J. Jorge Klor de Alva is Class of 1940 Professor of Comparative Ethnic Studies and Anthropology at the University of California at Berkeley. He has recently edited *Tramas de la identidad* and is currently at work on *The Norton Anthology of Mesoamerican Indigenous Literature* and, with Cornel West, *Together Forever Tonite: Black-Latino Relations in the U.S.*

Miranda Oshige McGowan is a law clerk to the Hon. John T. Noonan Jr., United States Circuit Judge for the Ninth Circuit

Court of Appeals. She received her J.D. from Stanford Law School in 1995 and her B.A. from the University of California at Berkeley in 1991.

David Montejano is Associate Professor of History and Sociology and the director of the Center for Mexican-American Studies at the University of Texas at Austin.

Rachel F. Moran is Professor of Law at Boalt Hall School of Law, University of California at Berkeley. She served as Chair of the Chicano/ Latino Policy Project at the Institute for the Study of Social Change from 1993 to 1996. Currently she is working on a book on interracial intimacy and a case study of a lawsuit involving bilingual education and desegregation in the Denver public schools.

Michael Omi is Associate Professor of Asian American Studies at the University of California at Berkeley. He is the co-author (with Howard Winant) of *Racial Formation in the United States.*

Daniel R. Ortiz is the John Allan Love Professor of Law and Elizabeth D. and Richard A. Merrill Research Professor at the University of Virginia Law School.

Francis Fox Piven is on the faculty of the graduate school of the City University of New York. She is co-author (with Richard Cloward) of *Regulating the Poor and Poor People's Movements* and, more recently, *The Breaking of the American Social Compact.*

Robert Post is Alexander F. and May T. Morrison Professor of Law at Boalt Hall School of Law, University of California at Berkeley. He is the author of *Constitutional Domains: Democracy, Community, and Management.*

Michael Rogin is Robson Professor of Political Science at the University of California at Berkeley. He is the author of *Blackface, White Noise: Jewish Immigrants in the Hollywood Melting Pot.*

Reva B. Siegel is Professor of Law at Yale Law School. She has written a variety of articles examining the modernization of racial and gender status law during the nineteenth and twentieth centuries.

Cass R. Sunstein is the Karl N. Llewellyn Distinguished Service Professor of Jurisprudence, University of Chicago, Law School and Department of Political Science.

Dana Y. Takagi is Professor of Sociology at the University of California at Santa Cruz. She is the author of *The Retreat from Race: Asian American Admissions and Racial Politics.*

Chang-Lin Tien holds the professorial title of NEC Distinguished Professor of Engineering, a post he assumed after seven years as the University of California at Berkeley's Chancellor. He was the first Asian American to head a major research university in the United States.

Anne M. Wagner is Professor of Modern Art at the University of California at Berkeley and has written on a variety of topics in nineteenth- and twentieth-century art. She is the author of *Three Artists (Three Women): Modernism and the Art of Hesse, Krasner, and O'Keeffe*. Her current work concerns Barbara Hepworth, Henry Moore, maternity, and Melanie Klein.

Jeremy Waldon is the Maurice and Hilda Friedman Professor of Law at Columbia Law School.

Richard Walker is Professor and Chair of Geography at the University of California at Berkeley and the author of *The Capitalist Imperative* and *The New Social Economy*. He is currently at work on a book on the San Francisco Bay Area.

Alan Wolfe is University Professor and Professor of Sociology and Political Science at Boston University. His latest book is *One Nation, After All*.

Howard Zinn is Professor Emeritus at Boston University and author of *A People's History of the United States* and a memoir entitled *You Can't be Neutral on a Moving Train*.